THE SUICIDE OF MISS XI

THE SUICIDE *of* MISS XI

DEMOCRACY
AND
DISENCHANTMENT
IN THE
CHINESE REPUBLIC

BRYNA GOODMAN

HARVARD UNIVERSITY PRESS

Cambridge, Massachusetts   London, England   2021

First printing

Library of Congress Cataloging-in-Publication Data

Names: Goodman, Bryna, 1955– author.
Title: The suicide of Miss Xi : democracy and disenchantment in the Chinese Republic /
 Bryna Goodman.
Description: Cambridge, Massachusetts : Harvard University Press, 2021. |
 Includes bibliographical references and index.
Identifiers: LCCN 2020050649 | ISBN 9780674248823 (hardcover)
Subjects: LCSH: Xi, Shangzhen. | Democracy—China—Shanghai—History. |
 Sexism—China—Shanghai—History. | Stock exchanges—China—Shanghai—History. |
 Civil rights—China—Shanghai—History. | Shanghai (China)—History. |
 Shanghai (China)—Economic conditions—20th century. | China—History—
 Republic, 1912–1949.
Classification: LCC DS776.6 .G66 2021 | DDC 951/.132041—dc23
LC record available at https://lccn.loc.gov/2020050649

For David and in memory of Fanny,
who was born in the same year as Xi Shangzhen

CONTENTS

THE SUICIDE OF MISS XI

A Scandal in the City

Because neither the law of the country nor the power of the government is clearly defined, remarks the Shunpao, schemes are plotted in the dark and executed in the street. People may be thrown into gaol and their lives imperiled or their character disgraced by so cleverly conceived "frame-ups" that nobody can easily determine upon the charges being genuine or false. Such cases cannot be judged by common sense or ordinary rules. They seem simply unfathomable.

—*North China Daily News*, November 23, 1922

I once knew a young lady who wanted to commit suicide, and, in a rash moment, selected the office of a friend of mine in which to do it. He was away and she was working there. She couldn't think of a better place, so she picked his room. He immediately lost face because the assumption was that, had there been no reason for it, she wouldn't have picked his room and therefore he must have done something which drove her to suicide, and it wrecked the man's life.

—George Sokolsky, 1950, remembering 1922

ON THE EVENING OF September 8, 1922, the body of a twenty-four-year-old female clerk named Xi Shangzhen was found hanging in the office building of the Chinese newspaper, *Journal of Commerce* (*Shangbao*). The building was located in Shanghai's International Settlement, the Anglo-American-dominated enclave that constituted one territorial authority in a city of multiple and fragmented jurisdictions. A graduate of a progressive girls' school, Xi had been the first female employee of the newspaper. Prior to her employment at the newspaper, she taught briefly at her alma mater and at another girls' school in the city. She also wrote essays, poetry, and fiction, but published little in her name.

The clerk's employer was an influential US-educated businessman in his early forties named Tang Jiezhi, the managing director of the *Journal of Commerce*. Prominent in commercial circles, Tang achieved celebrity in the popular nationalist mobilization in Shanghai of the May Fourth Movement of 1919, in which Chinese protested the terms of the Treaty of Versailles, which transferred German concessions in Shandong province to Japan, circumventing Chinese sovereignty. As the movement subsided, Tang redirected his political acumen and expansive social and commercial ties into the establishment of a progressive newspaper. Under his leadership the *Journal* achieved acclaim for its critical political voice and comprehensive economic reporting.

At a moment when the entrance of women into public life was heralded as a sign of a new democratic era for China, the discovery of Xi's corpse near the window of the office she shared with her employer was certainly inauspicious. Contemporary concern for the sexual integration of workplaces—and Tang's reputation for championing social reform, including female employment—ensured that the news reverberated beyond the newspaper office and the social, political, and intellectual circles of both Xi and Tang.

Early reports on the matter revealed that Xi's apparent suicide was also linked to a devastating Chinese stock exchange bubble that had engulfed Shanghai in the previous year. Like many in the city, Xi had invested in the market and suffered substantial losses. In the words of one observer, Xi's mother was "heartbroken, to think of her lively, loveable daughter dying at a young age, as a result of economic oppression."[1] The connection to the recent financial turmoil intensified media attention to the suicide. Indeed, the dynamism of Shanghai newspapers in this moment was itself tied to the financial exuberance of the stock exchanges. Chinese newspapers enjoyed considerable advertising revenue from the sudden rash of stock exchanges that had sprung up in the city, as the cliché had it, "like bamboo shoots after a spring rain." A timely subsidy from the most prominent of these exchanges had in fact enabled the opening of Tang's own *Journal of Commerce* in January 1921, easing financial challenges that had initially appeared insurmountable. Public preoccupation with economic news also stimulated increases in newspaper subscriptions.

The combined electricity (or for some, the corrosive radioactivity) of links between celebrity and finance—and the eroticization of office space that accompanied the new sexual integration—would generate discussion for months in Shanghai's print media, teahouses, offices, and other public venues, activating the pens of Shanghai's literary lights and early members of the Nationalist (Guomindang) and young Communist Parties. The discovery of Xi's corpse also set in motion a surprising chain of events: Tang was arrested, placed on trial for financial fraud, and sentenced to prison. Some would see this as Tang's just dessert and Xi's cosmic revenge on her tormenter. Such commentators hailed Xi as a "new woman" and a martyr to the cause of women's independent livelihoods. Others framed her choice to end her life as a regrettable weakness of character, evidence of women's frailty and unsuitability as self-determining citizens. Whereas some writers who called attention to Xi's recent losses on the stock exchange suggested that she had been foolish in her investments and susceptible to the temptations of the market, others described what happened as a crime of capitalism. Still others, Tang's defenders among them, understood the unfolding events quite differently, as a miscarriage of justice and a silencing of public speech, another nail in the coffin of China's early twentieth-century republic and a betrayal of the principles of popular sovereignty in their formative moment.

THE SUICIDE

The circumstances of Xi Shangzhen's suicide and the events it unleashed are crucial to understanding why and how, for the arbiters of Shanghai society, this suicide so "greatly shook public opinion" that in the course of the "tremendous social furor" that ensued, "not a pen remained dry."[2] Some facts were quickly established. Others were mysterious, hinted at only in rumors, silences, odd behavior, or peculiar choices of words. Further material (some of it possibly manufactured) was unearthed, attested, and contested in investigations undertaken by journalists, public associations, and the Chinese court in the weeks and months that followed.

A preliminary narrative of what happened on the evening of September 8 took shape almost immediately. *Shangbao* employees customarily ate supper together each evening at 5 P.M.[3] When Xi failed to appear, Wang Jipu, an older member of the staff, dropped by her desk. Xi explained that she felt ill and had no appetite. Her pallor and something about her manner worried him. When she brushed off his suggestion that she go home, he left and sent someone to alert her family members.

The unmarried Xi lived with her family on a lane in the old Chinese city, the formerly walled core of the urban conglomeration that comprised modern Shanghai. To get there from the newspaper office, a person needed to walk south through the grid of streets in the International Settlement, traverse the avenues of the French Concession, and navigate the dense maze of alleyways that wound through the old city. Not long after Wang sent his underling on this mission (probably around 6 P.M.), Xi closed the office door, mounted a chair, slipped an electric teakettle cord through a metal ring near the window, placed her head through the loop, and stepped into the air.[4] Xi's poise as she balanced on the chair, grasping with both hands the cord on which she would hang herself, is imaginatively portrayed in a woodblock print that was published shortly after her suicide (Figure 0.1).[5]

Xi's family was eating supper when the messenger arrived. Either because he didn't indicate that the matter was urgent or perhaps because interactions with Xi's office were not out of the ordinary for the family, Xi's sister finished her meal before making her way to the newspaper. When she arrived at the building, not less than an hour later, she found the office door locked, and it was necessary to call for Chen Aliu, the gatekeeper, to fetch a key. Chen opened the door and stood aside, revealing Xi dangling in front of the window frame. Several employees who had gathered in the doorway lifted Xi's body, loosed the cord from around her neck, and gently laid her down. A Dr. Zhang, who was summoned to the scene from St. Luke's (Renji) Hospital, pronounced Xi dead at approximately 8:00 P.M.[6] Tang Jiezhi was not present at the discovery of Xi's body.

Although his newspaper was published in Chinese and staffed almost entirely by Chinese, Tang had a Western partner, a man he had met a few years earlier through common connections with student activists. According to a police report at the Shanghai Municipal Archives, it was this foreigner, the Russian-Jewish-American journalist George Sokolsky, who telephoned the police to report the hanging, a detail that was omitted in published accounts.[7] It may have been that Sokolsky was the highest-ranking newspaper employee on the scene. English-language letterhead for the *Journal,* which identifies Sokolsky as treasurer, survives in Sokolsky's archived papers at the Hoover Institution on the campus of Stanford University. It may have also been more convenient for Sokolsky—as a Westerner—to place the call to the International Settlement police than for a Chinese employee. Whatever the reason for his involvement at the scene, however, Xi's suicide rattled Sokolsky.

THE INQUEST

The day after Sokolsky's telephone call to the police, the Mixed Court of the International Settlement convened an inquest into Xi's death. The Shanghai Municipal Council, the peculiar governing structure that exercised delegated municipal powers in the Settlement, held only limited jurisdiction over Chinese nationals. In 1868, to manage Chinese legal jurisdiction within (foreign) Settlement boundaries, the Mixed Court was created for the judicial administration of Chinese, who had come to con-

席上珍慘史圖

席女士上吊

D.1 "**Miss Xi Hanging Herself.**" Reproduced from Cheng Pengling, ed.,
   Haishang nü shuji: Xi Shangzhen canshi (Shanghai female secretary:
   The tragic history of Xi Shangzhen), (Shanghai, Shenheji shuju, 1922).

stitute the majority population in the Settlement but remained subject to Chinese law. It was an unusual tribunal in that, to accommodate the co-existence of foreign extraterritorial jurisdiction and (partial) Chinese judicial sovereignty, it featured a multinational array of officers at the bench.[8] Because the *Journal of Commerce* was located within the Settlement, the case fell within the jurisdiction of the Mixed Court. At the inquest, Chinese Magistrate Lu and British Assessor (Vice Consul) Mead jointly heard testimony from the coroner, the police (one Western and one Chinese, who had been dispatched to investigate after Sokolsky's call), and the principals in the case.

The accounts of the police detectives, coroner, and witnesses provided the basis for the presiding judges' verdict of suicide. The judges' unanimous conclusion notwithstanding, the principals in the case presented ambiguous and contradictory accounts of the events preceding, as well as the circumstances surrounding, Xi's fatal act.

Xi's family accused Tang of immoral behavior and two transgressions that corresponded to crimes specified in Chinese law: (1) defrauding Xi of money (*zhaqi qucai*) and (2) compelling her to commit suicide (*weibi renming*).[9] They also revealed that Xi had attempted suicide twice previously, both times at the office. Thus, contrary to Sokolsky's retrospective insistence that her choice of location was accidental, her actions evinced deliberation. Xi's mother (née Fang) testified that Tang had borrowed a considerable sum of money and had failed to return it, causing her great financial difficulty. Xi's elder sister (whose married name was Wang) elaborated on her mother's story in an illogical and contradictory statement that suggested both an investment and a debt:

> In May 1921, Mr. Tang [spoke to] Xi of the benefits of purchasing stock. He borrowed 5,000 yuan from her, but he didn't give her any stock in return. When my sister asked for the money, Mr. Tang said the stock was already pawned, but things would work out. These were empty words, and my sister drank tranquilizers in [spring] of this year. Mr. Tang revived her with an injection. Her second suicide attempt occurred on an evening she didn't return home. Cherishing hope, we waited until dawn. Then the newspaper sent her home in a horse-carriage, saying that she had a fever. To our surprise, Sister refused to come out of the carriage, insisting that she was determined to die at the *Shangbao* office. . . . Sister also said [she] had taken tranquilizers because Mr. Tang had not returned the money. He said, "your money is with me, what is there to worry about?" [After Sister took tranquilizers,] Mr. Tang wrote out an IOU, stipulating three periods for returning her money. This was clearly an empty show as well, leading my sister to commit suicide.[10]

Xi's sister-in-law (who, like Xi's sister, quoted conversations at which she had not been present) stated further that after Xi's first suicide attempt, her family members noticed a swelling on her arm. She explained it was from the injection the medically trained Tang had given her. Xi also declared that she was determined to "wager her life" (*panming*) in her struggle with Tang. According to the sister-in-law, the most distressing feature of Xi's interactions with her married employer was that after her second suicide attempt, Tang had insultingly proposed that Xi should marry him. ("You belong to me. . . . How about marrying me?"[11]) When the outraged Xi exclaimed that she could not possibly think of becoming his concubine, Tang placated her with the IOU, agreeing to consider the 5,000 yuan a debt and promising to return the money in three installments. Thus, according to Xi's family members, Xi committed suicide for two reasons. First, Tang had devised various ploys to gain time without intending to return her money, and second, Xi's sense of virtue was aggrieved by Tang's suggestion that she, an educated woman, should become the concubine of a married man. His arrogant presumption and the crudity of his desires so exacerbated her despair over her financial losses that she took her life.

When called to the stand, Tang took exception to the Xi family's testimony. He dismissed the idea that he had borrowed money from Xi, explaining that she had given him the funds to invest on her behalf. He contextualized their financial relations in terms of the recent economic events. In spring 1921, in the heady bull market, Shanghai had seen the whirlwind emergence of more than 150 stock exchanges, a greater number than existed in total in the rest of the world. Seizing the moment, Tang had helped to found the China Commercial Trust Company. Excited and hoping for a piece of his venture, people in his office, including Xi, had clamored for shares in his new company. He had tried to accommodate Xi as he had done with his other employees, but unfortunately, the market collapsed and Xi's money was lost, a common, if devastating, experience at the time. He had given her some certificates when they became available; others he held for her in the office safe. Tang vigorously denied suggestions made by Xi's family that he had pressured Xi to become his concubine. "But even if she hadn't wanted to be my concubine," he asked, in ambiguously worded testimony, "why would she have done this?"[12] He explained further that when Xi's shares declined in value, he had given her a promissory note for 5,000 yuan in return for the shares (which no longer held that value). He stated that he did this, not to remedy an actual debt (since his note overvalued shares that were now worth considerably less than 5,000 yuan), but in a spirit of sympathetic generosity, to relieve his employee's financial distress. The idea was that the note, backed by his social prominence, would enable Xi to put off her creditors.

It was not the task of the Chinese and Western officials who presided over the inquest to reconcile the discrepant accounts. After pronouncing their verdict, they indicated that if Xi's family wished to pursue financial damages, they could lodge a civil complaint against Tang. In the meantime, they acceded to Xi's mother's request that the body be delivered to the Dongting East Mountain mortuary, which handled burials for Shanghai residents from Xi's home area.[13]

THE PRINCIPALS

Whereas Xi had lived and died in relative obscurity, Tang and his newspaper were stars in the Shanghai firmament. Tang's name appears, for example, in a 1922 list of Shanghai celebrities published by the tabloid paper *Crystal (Jingbao)*.[14] He had studied in the United States at a young age, returning to China in the last decade of the Qing dynasty. Foreign authorities in the city knew him as Fred C. Tong, a name he had used since his student days in the United States for the convenience of Westerners. After his return he studied medicine. According to British intelligence reports, Tang joined the Chinese army, attaining rank "in the medical branch of service," most likely associated with the Beiyang Army Medical Academy.[15] His name appears in the Tianjin newspaper *Dagongbao* in 1907 as a contributor to China's first veterinary hospital.[16] Sometime between 1915 and 1917 Tang moved to Shanghai, where he worked for the Xiang'an Insurance Company and the Zhong-Mei (China-US) Trading Company. British intelligence reports and Shanghai Municipal Police files identify him as an associate of Wen Zongyao, a diplomat and reform politician during the last years of the Qing dynasty, who was aligned with Song Jiaoren in the Guomindang prior to Song's assassination.[17]

In Shanghai, Tang rose to leadership in the powerful Shanghai Guangdong sojourner community. Capitalizing on their familiarity with foreign trade and their early mastery of English, people from Guangdong migrated from South China to Shanghai after the Opium War and established themselves as a leading trade group after the 1842 Treaty of Nanjing forced the city's opening as a treaty port. Tang's own route to the city some seventy-odd years later, after studying at the University of California and working as a physician in Beijing, reflected the draw of Shanghai's economy as well as the cosmopolitanism of well-placed individuals in the Guangdong community. Guangdong sojourners were resented by people from Jiangsu province (including Xi's Dongting Dongshan group) as rivals from a more distant region.

In the several years prior to Xi's suicide, Tang engaged in a civic movement to build popular sovereignty from the grassroots. A year before the 1919 May Fourth mobilization of Shanghai commercial society he joined a reform faction that democratized the Guang-Zhao Gongsuo, displacing the oligarchic leadership.[18] Tang then built on his influence as a leader of the reformed association to develop social connections with civic institutions beyond his "fellow provincial," or "native place" community (*tongxiang*) of Guangdong people in Shanghai.

In contrast to the student-dominated actions in Beijing, in Shanghai the May Fourth Movement found its societal clout in business circles, whose power to shut down the economy of the preeminent commercial city made Shanghai the most consequential arena for the movement. In June 1919, as the leader of the Federation of Public Commercial Associations (*Shangye gongtuan lianhehui*), Tang advocated republican citizenship and a politically mobilized business community. In this capacity, he helped to engineer a commercial strike, which served as an essential element of the "triple strike" of students, merchants, and workers and forced the hand of the more politically reticent Chinese Chamber of Commerce, which had opposed the strike. The one-week strike also forced the hand of the Chinese government, which reversed itself and instructed its representatives in Versailles to refuse to sign the treaty.[19]

Tang soon helped to mobilize a tax strike by Chinese shopkeepers against the Shanghai Municipal Council. When the strong-arm tactics of the Shanghai Municipal Police defeated this second strike, he threw himself into other campaigns for citizens' rights and Chinese sovereignty in the local, national, and international arenas. His growing influence soon enabled him to gain election to the reformed board of the powerful Chinese Chamber of Commerce.

During the May Fourth ferment, Tang began to associate with George Sokolsky, who positioned himself as an advisor to Shanghai students. Both men developed ties with figures in the Guomindang. A British intelligence report identifies the two as coorganizers in 1919 of a China Bureau of Public Information.[20] This was a China-oriented English-language newsletter for US institutions and media, a May Fourth venture that also involved the Columbia University–educated liberal philosopher and cultural critic Hu Shi.[21]

The connection to Sokolsky elevated Tang's profile in Shanghai's foreign community. Although Sokolsky habitually took credit for many things beyond his abilities, he did help Tang publish several speeches (in English)

DR. F. C. TONG, MANAGING DIRECTOR OF THE SHANGHAI
JOURNAL OF COMMERCE

0.2 Tang Jiezhi, June 1922. Reproduced
from Oong Zang-hyi, "Shanghai
Is Cradle of Press in China,"
Trans-Pacific 6:6 (June 1922): 77.

in the British-run *North China Herald*. Tang also rubbed shoulders with
prominent members of Shanghai's foreign community in the Good Roads
Association, a transplant from the US Good Roads Movement and one association that—unlike expat social clubs—featured Chinese as well as US
members. Tang's photograph appeared in foreign as well as in Chinese publications. (Figure 0.2)[22]

The creation in 1921 of the socially progressive *Journal of Commerce*
gave Tang a public organ for his political activism. In the same year, he was
elected president of the grassroots Federation of Commercial Street Unions
(*Ge malu shangjie zong lianhehui*). Through such media and associational
networks, Tang and his associates sought to create links across China's commercial cities, making preparations for a variety of national citizens' formations. The foreign police in Shanghai's International Settlement tracked
Tang's activism assiduously; Japanese officials also watched him closely,
labeling him and his newspaper as extremist anti-Japanese elements. [23]

Beyond his risky activism, Tang also engaged in risky business ventures.
Police files pointed to rumors that he had fled a financial scandal in Beijing, where he had been in charge of a hospital.[24] And in Shanghai, at the
height of the financial bubble that became known as the "trust and exchange storm" of 1921, Tang had founded his speculative China Commercial Trust Company.

As a social reformer, Tang had supported Xi's career at a time when few newspapers had female employees. By facilitating her purchase of stock, however, he was also, minimally, an accessory to her demise. As a poetic elegy for Xi put it, "The monetary affair with Tang was the cause of her misfortune."[25] The financial connection between Xi and a person who was behind the economically disastrous Western-style securities-trading institutions that had sprung up—and collapsed—in the previous year added to the moral resonance of her suicide. Many Shanghai residents had lost fortunes in their wake. Xi Shangzhen thus appeared as a symbol of human vulnerability, an individual swept into the whirlpool of financial temptations, in a city of untrammeled greed.

Despite the way her suicide propelled her life (and death) into public view, Xi Shangzhen the individual remains something of a cipher. She was observed to be a well-educated, intense, and unusually determined young woman. When a journalist interviewed her family, however, her brother insisted that there was little to say: "Sister just turned 24 this year, and then died. She had few accomplishments; there is nothing to recount. If in the future you want to edit a book about her, that would be difficult."[26] The brother's statement recapitulated the Chinese cliché that a mark of a virtuous (i.e., cloistered) woman was that nothing could be said about her. Despite her brother's reticence, a great deal more would be said, thanks to an inquiring press in an age when ideas of progress called for women's presence in public. Pressed by journalistic demand for a photo, Xi's family produced their sole (collective) family portrait. On failing to uncover an individual photograph, eager journalists cropped the family picture to construct a cameo that was reproduced in books and newspapers. Despite the effort to reveal Xi the individual, the enlargement and retouching had the effect of blurring her features (Figure 0.3).

Newspapers and books also published other visual evidence: extant examples of Xi's calligraphy were located and reproduced. Typically, more space was dedicated to her calligraphy than to her portrait. In China, brush-written characters were not simply words on paper; elegant calligraphy was the most exalted form of visual artistry. An attainment associated with the male literati elite in imperial times, calligraphic skill was considered especially notable for a woman. Calligraphy conveyed moral value, as a mark of disciplined self-cultivation and expression. Twentieth-century Chinese, like Late Imperial scholars, understood calligraphy as a gateway into character.[27] Practices of venerating paper with written characters and societies for "sparing the written word" and cherishing characters persisted into the Republican Era. Calligraphy was believed to offer spiritual communication with the deceased through traces of personality conveyed in lines of ink. Commemorations of the dead thus often included

0.3 **Xi Shangzhen.** Reproduced from Wu Yugong, *Zisha zhi nüshuji: Xi Shangzhen canshi* (Female secretary who committed suicide: Tragic history of Xi Shangzhen), (Shanghai: Zhongguo diyi shuju, 1922).

displays of "ink traces" (*moji*).[28] One sample of Xi's calligraphy that appeared in multiple venues is reproduced in Figure 0.4. Like other photographs of her calligraphy, it was not chosen to showcase her originality.[29] Rather than feature Xi's personal handwriting, all but one of six samples of Xi's calligraphy documented instead her ability to reproduce Han dynasty clerical script.[30]

Most accounts situate Xi within a formulaic pattern of virtue. She was quiet, diligent, and chaste. She was also frugal. To avoid the cost of the streetcars in the foreign settlements, she walked to the boundary of the Chinese city each day on her way home before hiring a rickshaw to take her over its rougher streets. This scrimping facilitated her filial support of her mother, to whom Xi turned over half her monthly earnings of 20 yuan. Her teachers, fellow students, and coworkers attested to Xi's studiousness, literary skills, and refinement and her efforts to further her education. Her English-language textbook was on her desk the evening she died. Her modern studies and newspaper work marked her as a "new woman."[31] In such details Xi emerged as an exemplar of virtue with an overlay of progressive values.

Despite media elevation of Xi as a new woman, there was oddly little public exploration of her writing. The largest corpus of Xi's writing con-

席上珍女士遺像及其墨蹟

惟三月三日月日石

中半震興立

左節刊表

□.4 "**Portrait and Ink Traces of the Deceased Miss Xi Shangzhen.**"
Reproduced from "Xi Shengzhen nüshi yixiang ji qi moji,"
Zhonghua xinbao, September 20, 1922.

sisted of unattributed "women's issues" columns and miscellaneous fiction
and poetry that she penned for the *Journal of Commerce* supplement
pages. These were briefly noted by an investigative reporter.[32] Had there
been substantial interest in Xi as an individual, these pieces might have
been probed for her concerns, writing style, and mode of thinking. One
such article in the *Journal,* possibly authored by Xi, was titled, "Optimism
for the Future of Women's Careers." It expressed cautious hope for "the
rising wave of advocacy for gender equality," but lamented that aside from
education and nursing, "there is nothing for women to do." To counter
dangers that lurked in public spaces and made women's professional employment risky, the author promoted education to boost women's knowledge and strengthen their morality.[33] Such sentiments were broadly characteristic of the May Fourth advocacy of gender equality by means of
educational advancement. Since these articles and other pieces were un-
signed, it is not surprising that they did not enter into public reflection,
though certainly journalists or some of Xi's acquaintances might have excavated them. There was considerable interest in the novelty of professional women.[34]

It is harder to understand the general public failure to consider the content of the posthumously published literary pieces that were unequivocally
authored by Xi. Several stories, notes, and letters were sent to a journalist
by a close female friend of Xi (identified only by her given name, Shufen),
who requested that he publish them.[35] Unlike her calligraphy, however, Xi's
fiction was not otherwise reproduced and was ignored in the social discussion of the case.

THE RATTLED MINOR CHARACTER

Although he played a minor role in the office hanging, Sokolsky's presence at the scene produced the accidental effect of leaving important evidentiary traces. Xi's death and Tang's imprisonment also marked a turning point in Sokolsky's chameleon life, a life that evokes some of the flavor of transnational interactions in the city. A sometime "flamboyant anarchist from a family of Russian-Jewish Bakuninists," the heavy-bodied, gregarious Sokolsky left Columbia University in 1917, before completing his BA, to seek adventure in revolutionary Russia as a writer for the English-language *Russian Daily News*.[36] Before long he abandoned Russia for China, where he marketed himself—an inexperienced though fast-talking American—as a journalist in the treaty port of Tianjin. He turned up in May Fourth Shanghai with two films, *My Four Years in Germany* and *Tarzan of the Apes,* for which he tried to drum up business. Soon he was attending Chinese student meetings and trading in news and gossip for Western and Chinese readers. He found work on Sun Yat-sen's English-language *Shanghai Gazette* and served as Song Qingling's amanuensis on the side. A letter from Song reveals that the Suns passed information to the students through Sokolsky, who persuaded Sun Yat-sen to contribute to the rental costs of the Student Union headquarters. Sokolsky also penned English-language letters on behalf of the students for publication in the *China Press* and *North China Daily News*. Tang, like Sun before him, soon came to serve as a benefactor to Sokolsky, who, as a Jew, was hampered in his ability to fully capitalize on Western privilege in the racialized social hierarchies of Shanghai's expatriate life.[37]

In the month after Xi's suicide, Sokolsky married his secretary, Rosalind Phang, the British-educated daughter of Charles Phang, a wealthy Jamaican Cantonese. Not long after the marriage, as Tang slipped into a legal abyss, Sokolsky left the newspaper. The cultivated Phang—who was the first Chinese licenciate of the Royal Academy of Music in London—was a close friend of Song Meiling and members of the wealthy Australian Chinese Kwok family (owners of one of Shanghai's premier department stores). The marriage embedded Sokolsky in the social life of Shanghai's transnational Chinese elite, elevating his political and journalistic capital and permitting him to cut his ties with the *Journal of Commerce,* which had become an inconvenience. He soon made common cause with Jiang Jieshi's (Chiang Kai-shek's) conservative wing of the Guomindang. In the 1930s, after returning to the United States, Sokolsky built a new career as an increasingly anti-Communist reactionary columnist and radio broadcaster. He famously debated Upton Sinclair on the topic of the necessity of capitalism for American democracy; later he became a mentor to Roy Cohn and a supporter of Joseph McCarthy.[38]

Some twenty-eight years after Xi's death and long after he turned away from the politics of the *Journal of Commerce,* in a peculiar aside in a speech he gave to the American Bankers' Association, Sokolsky was still attempting, as seen in the epigraph at the beginning of this chapter, to account for Xi's consequential choice of Tang's office for the location of her suicide.

THE UNFOLDING CASE IN PUBLIC PRINT

It would be peculiar, in this account of a newspaper-office hanging, if newspapers were not a large part of the story. Newspapers were also essential to the story because scandals rely on newspapers and newspapers rely on scandal. Within weeks, the incident had inspired hundreds of articles and the publication of three books, all bearing Xi's name. Chinese, Japanese, and Western newspapers in the city followed the case avidly.[39]

Chinese commentators declared from the outset that the tragedy exceeded normal bounds. In the words of one such account,

> In this world we often hear that people willfully kill themselves. But nothing has been like the recent death of Miss Xi Shangzhen, which has riveted society. . . . In today's world, people compete in admiration of killing. We find it unexceptional for commanders of great armies to kill thousands in a day. But the suicide [of this weak girl] has compelled the majority of people in society to mourn and sigh.[40]

Intellectuals across the political spectrum took up their pens. Among those who were anxious to respond—lest others draw improper conclusions—was Chen Wangdao, a translator of Marx and a founding member of the Chinese Communist Party. Chen analyzed the incident in *Women's Critic,* a supplement that he edited for the *Republican Daily* newspaper. In his analysis, he warned cryptically against unsavory rumors that had sprung from the "deep-rooted depravity of Chinese national character."[41] Prominent cultural figures, including film pioneer Zheng Zhengqiu, revolutionary dramatist Gu Jianchen, and a gamut of contemporary writers, including Zhou Zuoren, Hu Yuzhi, Bao Tianxiao, and Jiang Hongjiao, similarly intervened, in a variety of efforts to shape public opinion.

Narratives of the case unfolded in daily press accounts, drawing the literate public along as surely as the popular serialized fiction that attracted many Chinese to purchase newspapers. Publishers recycled choice articles in edited volumes that heightened their circulation, impact, and profitability. In the process, the dailies became vehicles for contending parties who enunciated understandings of law and morality before the reading public. Tang was one of the first. Responding to the shadow of legal vulnerability cast by the inquest and concerned about media-circulated rumors about his relations with Xi, Tang consulted a Western lawyer and published a front-page announcement in the major papers, which read as follows:

IMPORTANT DECLARATION OF TANG JIEZHI

In regard to Miss Xi Shangzhen's suicide, I make this declaration before society and my friends. The deceased purchased shares [from me] with money borrowed from others. I believed it was her money. She wished to buy additional shares but I refused, convinced that she was engaging in excessive speculation. [When] stock exchanges and trust companies began to collapse she became distressed and beseeched me for help, explaining that she had incurred heavy debt and was pressed by creditors. Twice she attempted suicide. Since she was an honest, diligent employee, I was motivated by a benevolent desire to ameliorate her distress. On August 19 I gave her a promissory note that stated I would give her a first installment of 1,500 yuan in 12 months; a second installment of 1,500 in 24 months; and a final payment of 2,000 in 36 months. The deceased gave this note to her family, which produced it at the inquest (it remains in the hands of the family). I undertook no further responsibility for the deceased. Any assistance I provided was in the hope of relieving her extreme difficulties. She was satisfied with the note and I do not know why she should have committed suicide.

Written in consultation with the lawyer [Stirling] Fessenden[42]

Tang published this statement as an individual paid notice, a genre that conveyed only limited credibility in a society that identified people through kin or other collective identities and in which public associations routinely spoke on behalf of individuals or guaranteed their trustworthiness. The collective declarations of groups thus enjoyed a more elevated status than an individual's statement. In the Xi affair, the pronouncements of interested associations featured as news; Tang's declaration, in contrast, appeared as a paid announcement.

Tang's damage control was swiftly challenged by the association of sojourners from Xi's home area. Borrowing language from popular knight-errant literature, the Dongting East Mountain association announced its intent to assist the Xi family by pressing the Chinese district court to initiate legal proceedings against Tang. Addressed to "all circles of Shanghai society," the association's manifesto was reported in all the major Shanghai newspapers:

DONGTING ASSOCIATION CRIES OUT TO REDRESS XI SHANGZHEN GRIEVANCES

When Tang Jiezhi established the [China] Commercial Trust Company in May 1921 he pressured Shangzhen, saying it was a good investment. Shangzhen naively gave him 5,000 yuan to buy stock. She also persuaded her elder sister to buy 1,000 and several hundreds of yuan of stock. Her sister received certificates. But Xi Shangzhen did not. Instead of handing over her shares, Tang urged her to marry him as his concubine saying, "I will pay all of your expenses." Thus, Shangzhen not only lost her money, but also suffered his abuse. In her fury she didn't want to live. [The money the deceased gave] to Tang consisted of family savings for the support of her mother and loans. When she realized there was no chance to recover the funds, she resolved to die. Before death she told her sister, "your sister's life is unlivable. I will write a detailed note of grievance. Please redress my grievances." . . . After she hung herself, her sister went to the Journal of Commerce office. But Tang had gotten there first. [Xi's] clothes were unbuttoned and the note couldn't be found. Now Tang has published a notice admitting that Xi Shangzhen entrusted him to purchase stock. But Commercial Trust Company stock never came into Xi's hands. He also describes his promissory note as [an act of benevolence.] Why doesn't he discuss turning over the stock? Why, instead of being grateful to Tang, did she three times attempt suicide at his office? [We] appeal to gentlemen of all circles . . . to examine this injustice, uphold public opinion, and redress her grievance.[43]

Other social groups convened meetings and produced statements in favor of Xi and against Tang. These included a women's suffrage association, Xi's former teachers and fellow students, a women's professional association, three kindred sojourner groups from Xi's home province of Jiangsu, and an office workers' association.[44] Their arguments evoked communal responsibility and the public demonstration of vital social connections. It was disadvantageous to Tang that his backers had not spoken out:

The Xi-Tang case is a major social incident [and] women's circles and several public associations have spoken. [But] Tang [is] director, manager, board member and supervisor [of various organizations] from which we haven't heard a word. . . . They should investigate. [If Tang's] behavior corresponds to newspaper reports, they must expel this mad horse from their organizations. . . . If investigation [reveals that Tang] has been slandered, they should intervene to protect his and their own reputation.[45]

In this fashion, the respective parties fought the matter out in the press, thus evoking and appealing to an adjudicating public. The war of words stimulated further print production. The social news that quickened the pulse of daily reportage in the first weeks after Xi's suicide soon morphed into poetry, fiction, and theater.[46] The incident's viral spread and mutation across genres attests to the vitality of literature in this moment—for the literate public—as a foundational mode of truth-making in a precarious world of meaning. The selection and renarration of social material that appeared first as news also transformed literature. Writers wove elements of the case into serialized short stories that filled popular literary supplements, enacting a shift in aesthetics that had been underway since the late Qing. In the process, new and old-style writers and editors modernized literature by engaging with news-based social issues.

Newspaper literary supplements opened up a space of interaction with the reading public. The influential *Eastern Times* (*Shibao*) encouraged readers to submit poetic elegies for Xi. Inspired by the pathos of Xi's fate, so many readers sent submissions that the editor could not keep pace, even as he published more than a hundred such compositions in the course of a week. Reader verses variously mourn the loss of a beautiful, intelligent, and modern girl; hail her ghost (in Tang's office, cognitively comingling the contemporary with the supernatural); and condemn Tang, capitalism, or the hazards of the city for a working girl.[47] One elegy compared Xi to the female revolutionary martyr Qiu Jin, who was decapitated in 1907 by Qing troops:

> Autumn wind. Autumn rain. Endless sorrow.
> The young lady at her death shed tears.
> Everyone clamors to tell stories of society's broken heart.
> Shanghai is stained with spots of blood.[48]

Other verses connected Xi to past heroines of exemplary virtue. Many writers implicated Shanghai as a site of impurity, corruption, and capitalism. If these poems were largely eulogistic in regard to Xi, this was not true of all the literary compositions inspired by the suicide. The small-format "mosquito" tabloid, *Crystal,* published savagely satirical comic poetry and an opera libretto that hinted, allusively, at sexual relations between Tang and Xi.

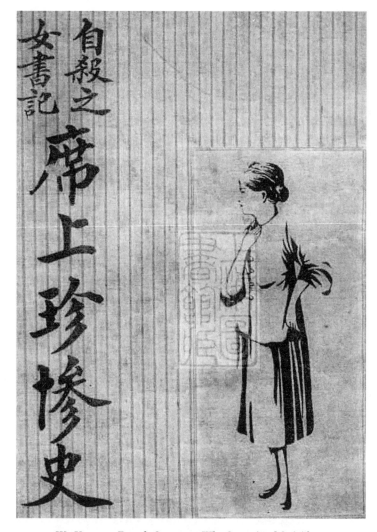

□.5 Wu Yugong, *Female Secretary Who Committed Suicide.*
Reproduced from *Wu Yugong, Zisha zhi nüshuji: Xi Shangzhen
canshi* (Shanghai: Zhongguo diyi shuju, 1922).

As publicity fanned public interest, several commercial newspapers published special issues devoted to the case. The three books that were published about Xi Shangzhen's suicide reproduced reportage and photographs along with new essays, evidence, and analysis. The first of these books, *Female Secretary Who Committed Suicide: The Tragic History of Xi Shangzhen,* was completed with stunning speed, approximately a week after Xi's death (Figure 0.5). As one commentator described the venture,

"Every day after Xi's death people visited her home for news. Among these, one person who was good at speculating in the book market assiduously interviewed the family. No doubt we will soon see the three characters: 'Xi Shangzhen' in the advertisements of a speculative publishing house."[49] Sales of this initial, hastily and modestly produced, lithographic volume, which featured a sensible-looking image of Xi on the cover, quickly confirmed the commercial potential for narratives of the unfolding Xi-Tang affair.

A stylish, heavily illustrated, more obviously commercial volume published by a rival press soon followed: *Shanghai Female Secretary: The Tragic History of Xi Shangzhen*. The imaginary Xi Shangzhen pictured on the red and blue cover bears more resemblance to a flapper than to the historical Xi (Figure 0.6).[50]

Despite its evident commodification of the suicide, press interest did not proceed simply from the profits to be garnered from a sensational case. The public realm that flourished in the interstices of Shanghai's jurisdictional confusion took seriously the idea that in the Republic, the press embodied and represented the public. In the absence of effectively functioning governing institutions, reporters, editors, and letter-writers called for direct public action to resolve social issues, with the newspaper as witness and record. Tang's politically outspoken newspaper was not alone in this sort of rhetoric. Wary of law and the institutional apparatus of government, the press constituted itself, and not the law or the state, as the appropriate arbiter of public behavior.

The introduction to the first book published about Xi's suicide made exactly this point. Because Xi's suicide was "a great problem for society," and not simply "a matter of one individual and one family," the editor declared that the matter could not be left to public officials or the law to resolve.[51] Indeed, any government resolution would be dubious. The book drew together interviews, newspaper reports, and other evidence for the explicit purpose of facilitating social research to "influence the legal process and temper justice."[52] Newspaper editorials that addressed the case conveyed a similar suspicion of official actions and legal process and suggested the need to look beyond the surface of the event to grasp its mysteries.

TANG'S ARREST AND TRIAL

By mid-October, the affair had migrated from the news and editorial pages to the literary sections, where it might have evanesced into didactic or elegiac remembrance. In November, however, a shocking development com-

0.6 *Shanghai Female Secretary,* ed. Cheng Pengling. Reproduced
from Cheng Pengling, ed., *Haishang nü shuji: Xi Shangzhen
canshi* (Shanghai female secretary: The tragic history of Xi
Shangzhen), (Shanghai, Shenheji shuju, 1922).

plicated the plot and shifted the storyline. Breathlessly, journalists re-counted the thrilling cloak-and-dagger spectacle of Tang's kidnapping arrest by Chinese police in the dead of night.

On November 13, newspaper readers belatedly learned of Tang's ex-traordinary secret arrest two days earlier. Tang's residence, on Alabaster Road, was located (like his business) within the International Settlement. It was therefore within the legal jurisdiction of the Mixed Court and the Settlement police.[53] The conventions of extraterritoriality held that the ex-ercise of a Chinese court warrant within Settlement boundaries consti-tuted illegal trespass on Settlement jurisdiction. The Chinese police justi-fied their action by arguing that the Gongyi Li alleyway on the side of Tang's residence, where Tang's bodyguard-driver parked his car, marked the boundary between the Settlement and Chinese territory. When Tang stepped from his car at 2 A.M., the police pounced, overpowering the two men, whom they delivered to the Chinese jail.[54]

Tang's arrest transformed what most commentators had considered an injustice and moral failure into a criminal case, to the surprise of the prin-cipals. The influential *Weekly Review of the Far East* compared Tang's unusual arrest to the recent framing on dubious charges of the finance min-ister, Luo Wen'gan, suggesting that it signaled a political sleight-of-hand. At a preliminary hearing convened at the Chinese court the next morning, Tang was ordered held without bail, despite an offer of security by his fellow-provincial association, the Guang-Zhao Gongsuo, to obtain his release.[55]

Once in the hands of the Chinese police, Tang's fate would be deter-mined in the Chinese courts. In short order, the Chinese judge pronounced Tang guilty of fraud and sentenced him to three years in prison.[56] Tang's trial, which took place a few months after the suicide, inspired a news-based play. In this type of theater, which was a break with older styles, each evening's performance was improvised from each morning's news. Such "new drama" (*xin ju*), or "civilized drama" (*wenming xi*), testified to the displacement of older genres and story lines by news-based content. No script survives.[57] After the trial, Tang's supporters mobilized a legal reform movement to contest what they decried as the exemplary fraudu-lence of China's corrupt legal system. But popular outrage over Xi's sui-cide led other groups—particularly women's associations and people from Xi's home province of Jiangsu—to assert that justice had been served.

Tang's newspaper became damaged property and was soon sold to the highest bidder. After Sokolsky's exit, it lost its protection under US law. Prize editors departed for other posts. Unlike Sokolsky, who successfully reinvented himself elsewhere, by the end of the decade, when Tang reentered Shanghai society as a broken man, his historical moment and the possibilities of his political world had vanished.[58] The public organs and aspirations that had breathed life into an urban Chinese romance of democracy in the early 1920s had been retooled to serve a vision of revolutionary modernity that was shared, in many respects, by the contending Communist and Guomindang Parties. In the new political climate, amid the power struggles of Jiang Jieshi's new disciplinary government, the once riveting Tang-Xi affair slipped into the dustbin of history and Tang became a nonentity. However, the vital democratic populism of the early Republic, which had emerged in the context of a fragmented and deconstructed state—the street democracy of Tang's May Fourth moment and the citizen democracy espoused in his newspaper—would nonetheless retain a ghostly presence in the decades that followed, lingering rhetorically and periodically erupting in ephemeral protests.

THIS LOST STORY—a scandalous and opaque legal case that emerged from the public agitation of the early 1920s in the aftermath of a financial bubble—reveals the public preoccupations of the early 1920s and everyday practices of citizenship, nation, and democracy that developed in this time and place. The Xi-Tang episode, which was generated within the new, sexually integrated office environment of the May Fourth Era, adjudicated across the landscape of extraterritorial and Chinese jurisdictions, and disseminated as a social issue through Shanghai's public print, provides a point of entry into quotidian negotiations of China's early twentieth-century passage through capitalism and democracy in a tenuous, if ill-fated, moment of possibility between empire and party dictatorship.

A genealogy of the ideas and institutions of the print public and the spaces they created for political maneuvering throws open a past that is relevant to contemporary Chinese engagements with capitalism, nationalism, media transparency, and the rule of law. The obsessive publicity of the suicide and its aftermath served perhaps to displace nagging concerns about underlying political machinations that could not be examined in print and paralleling matters that, in a similar fashion, cannot be illuminated today. In this sense, the suicide—in terms of both its surface significance and its political backstory—does not simply evoke its historical moment, in the early ephemeral experience of a Chinese republic, but also resonates with more recent, mysterious scandals that erupt from time to time in contemporary China.[59]

CHAPTER ONE

Shanghai Democracy and the Empty Republic

The state holds the empty title of Republic. . . . Speaking of finance, the state treasury is empty. In domestic affairs, nothing has been accomplished. Military men strive for power and position out of vanity. The business world favors speculation in empty enterprise. The parliament consists of fraudulent members who use the name for profit. In foreign affairs empty conferences are held in succession without successful proposals. . . . The emptiness dates to the early Republic. Every subsequent year has been empty.

—*Shenbao*, December 1921

On June 14, the Shanghai Federation of Commercial Street Unions issued a declaration calling to convene a national assembly to deal with national affairs. The Shanghai General Chamber of Commerce . . . has made a declaration to the entire nation that it is resolved not to recognize the parliament, which "cannot represent the people's will." It is moreover organizing a Committee for the People's Rule [*Minzhi weiyuanhui*] to take on the management of national affairs. . . . Judging from [their] actions, the Shanghai merchants . . . have discarded pacifism, taken up revolutionary methods, and mustered the courage to shoulder responsibility for national affairs. . . . The Shanghai merchants have arisen and begun to act.

—Mao Zedong, July 1923

XI'S SUICIDE TOOK place a decade into China's Republican Era. It illuminates a moment, after the fall of empire and before the rise of central party rule, when urban Chinese improvised practices of liberal democracy in public life. The tentative and fractious public that appears in the social ferment surrounding the Xi-Tang case constituted itself as a republican public, though not in the normative sense of the institutionalized participation of citizens in the state. Its proponents placed it—implicitly— outside the state because they held that the corrupt entity that masqueraded behind the name of the Republic had betrayed the foundational principle of popular sovereignty. In the breach, democratic institutions and practices took root in public associations and accidental interstices of power in a landscape that was riven by contending Chinese authorities and zones of foreign encroachment. On the ground, individuals and public associations noisily enacted citizenship and social reform, using language rife with neologisms (translated Western concepts, commonly represented via Japanese translations that redeployed Chinese characters in new arrangements of unstable meaning). These discursive shifts were characteristic of what Mary Louise Pratt insightfully called a "contact zone," defined as "social space where disparate cultures meet, clash, and grapple with each other, often in highly asymmetrical relations of domination and subordination, such as colonialism." The contact zone, in Pratt's influential conceptualization, is a space of "transculturation," understood not as a top-down process of cultural influence, but rather, creative cultural adaptation, even invention.[1]

Shanghai, with its commercial dynamism, mixed population, and multiple authorities and jurisdictions, was a crucial site for these democratic improvisations, which found institutional expression in the key venues of print (particularly newspapers and journals) and an abundance of public associations. These venues of the public connected Shanghai elites to a broader population of students, clerks, apprentices, office workers, shop hands, and other "petty urbanites" whose literacy enabled their livelihoods and informed their civic aspirations. They also provided physical and virtual spaces for the working out of the cultural and discursive transformations associated with the new ideas and desires of the contact zone.

The unfolding Xi-Tang scandal, which consumed and also stimulated this public, might be seen as a teapot tempest. On the scale of national history, it cannot be compared to the major events that framed the era: the revolutionary 1911 toppling of the crumbling Qing dynasty; the 1912 establishment of the fragile Republic of China; the 1913 political assassination of the brilliant revolutionary candidate for prime minister, Song Jiaoren. After this inauspicious start—and President Yuan Shikai's dissolution, in the next year, of the first parliament—the project of democracy in China would be increasingly detached from the state. In broad-stroke histories of China's republic, Song's death augurs darkening prospects for electoral democracy. The curtain falls on the project of republican governance at the level of the state, setting the stage for military rule, imperialist rivalries, political fragmentation, and contest between the two nationalist and anti-imperialist Leninist revolutionary parties (Guomindang and Chinese Communist Party), leading ultimately to the displacement of the earlier Republic by a "People's Republic" in 1949.

A few years into the first decade of the Republic, two events highlighted China's weak position internationally, throwing into relief the unbearable impotence of the Chinese state and stimulating popular mobilization outside it. The first event was the 1915 revelation of the infamous Twenty-One Demands, Japan's secret wartime ultimatum that aimed to entrench control over Northeast China and economic penetration of the Chinese economy. Public revulsion for the capitulating Chinese president, Yuan Shikai, stimulated the first anti-Japanese boycott. Popular nationalist protest against both Japan and the weak Chinese state reached an emotional peak in the second event, the May Fourth Movement of 1919, which directly framed the moment of Xi's suicide. The May Fourth protests, which began in Beijing and spread swiftly to Shanghai and other cities, vented popular urban outrage at the acquiescence of the Versailles powers to Japan's imperialist ambitions. The protests also crucially took aim at the failure of the Chinese government to support Chinese sovereignty in Shandong. Thus the era's emblematic democracy movement found expression as a revolt against the Chinese state, a feature that makes its commemoration politically sensitive and potentially volatile to this day.

The broader May Fourth Era, which extended from the late 1910s into the early 1920s, witnessed a tumultuous urban Chinese romance with democracy. Responding to the failed Republic (and to Yuan Shikai's ill-fated attempt to restore monarchy and state Confucianism in 1915, with himself as emperor), the revolutionary intellectual Chen Duxiu promoted democracy as an essential component of what became known as the New Culture Movement. Whereas late Qing proponents of "new learning" (*xinxue*) imagined that imported knowledge might be integrated with kindred elements of older knowledge and values,[2] New Culture intellectuals attacked Confucianism and hierarchical Chinese family tradition for instilling a "slave mentality" that doomed the project of a republic. Hope for transforming submissive Chinese subjects into free, independent, and equal citizens lay in cultivating science, democracy, and imported knowledge to break the chains of obsolete culture. Cultural critics like Hu Shi decried the rote memorization of a stultifying classical language and advocated using vernacular language to speed literacy and political progress. Democratic ideas and exhortations abounded in the expansive print and associational public of the period. In public rhetoric, codes of conduct, and vibrant associational activism, participants in new (or newly reformed) self-proclaimed republican formations imagined themselves rebuking and displacing the corruption of the existing state, thereby fulfilling an ideological desire for political participation.

Shanghai's economic dynamism and the strength of its commercial institutions intensified the propagation of these ideas and practices as they found adherents nationally, especially among urban students, professionals, and new-style intellectuals. Shanghai's commercial and associational connections and products (among them print) reached beyond the city through networks of communication and marketing. The time delays that corresponded to distance from Shanghai marked other places as behind or outdated in news, values, and behavior. Some critics looked askance at the way the city and its glittery distractions threatened customary communities, hierarchies, and morality and decried the ways that city life led Chinese to abandon their heritage. Even cultural critics like the famous writer Lu Xun expressed reservations about Shanghai and mocked its "Western fops" (*xizai*) and "fake foreign devils," by which he meant imitators of foreign culture who hung out in the foreign settlements. Others, however, believed they could reshape the city, and by extension the entire country, with new visions of radical equality.

The twin scandals of Xi Shangzhen's suicide and Tang Jiezhi's trial raise the question of what these contemporary social, political, and ideological concerns signified in terms of the everyday: in Shanghai's office spaces, print culture, associational practices, financial and legal calculations, the market, and the courts. The lives and fates of Xi and Tang were bound up with the vernacular developments of commercial society and the gendered social dynamics of democracy after democratic impulses became detached from the state. For a great many Chinese observers and residents across the political spectrum, the suicide of the young Xi Shangzhen exemplified the contradictions of Shanghai's modernity and the misbegotten Republic in which it was embedded, which had cast democracy astray.

A decade after the revolution it was manifestly clear that the Republic existed in name but not in substance. The name was most potent as an ironic invocation, raised to reproach the compound deficiencies of a government that had failed to uphold the aspirations of the revolution. A biting *Shenbao* editorial (the source of the first epigraph at the start of this chapter) described the years of the Republic as "Ten Years of Emptiness."[3] The term *emptiness* (*kongxu*) conveyed falseness as well as lack of substance. As Tang Jiezhi described the situation in the same year, the Chinese people suffered under a regime of illegitimate power exercised by a government "rotten to the core[,] . . . corrupt, mindless of its obligations to the nation, and incapable of insight into the future."[4] At other times he went further, stating that, "at the present time there is actually no government in China," only "two governments in name, one the government of the city of Beijing, and the other the government of the city of Guangzhou."[5]

Although the revolution created only the shell of a government, it succeeded nonetheless in destroying the legitimacy of the monarchy and enshrining in its place the *idea* of a republic. Recent studies by Peter Zarrow,

David Strand, Yves Chevrier, and others have emphasized the intellectual impact of the political reframing of the state, despite the "unfinished" character of the Republic (Strand), or, in key ways, precisely because of the "indeterminateness" (Chevrier) of the nominal republican order.[6] The new political polity, conceived literally as a "people's state" (*minguo*) in Chinese, shifted the site of the public (*gong*) from dynastic rule to the newly empowered people (*qun*, legitimate public community; *guomin*, literally "people of the nation," or citizens). In these formulations, the collectivity of the people exclusively conveyed the ideal of public norms or civic virtue (*gongde*). Henceforth, only a government that embodied popular sovereignty could possess political legitimacy. After the political revolution, however, the new (all-male) parliament betrayed the revolution's abstract aspirations for gender equality and the transformation of women ("slaves of slaves") into citizens by voting down female suffrage.[7] In the process male revolutionaries betrayed the very concrete demands of their furious female revolutionary comrades. It was left for Yuan Shikai to suppress suffrage altogether, at least at the national level. Yuan's dissolution of the parliament in 1914 foreclosed the possibility of parliamentary democracy, thus detaching the state from its link to the people. What then could represent the sovereign public?

Absent institutions of republican governance to connect the people to a state with a legitimate claim to represent them, it seemed to many that the people themselves were left to enact their own sovereignty. This led, as Strand observed, to a paradoxical "widening and deepening" of public life that encompassed both the political elite and broad sectors of the urban public (largely, but not exclusively, the literate).[8] With no working model of representative democracy, and worse, against the spectacle of the state's betrayal of republican ideals, people in the cities seized on circulating notions of democracy to call forth and represent the sovereign public of citizens. For about a decade, in the aftermath of World War I, ideas and practices of democracy emerged in print media and in public associations that went so far as to suggest the notion that—in the absence of a supportive state—popular sovereignty might be achieved outside a state.

SHANGHAI, THE ASSOCIATIONAL PUBLIC, AND THE PUBLIC IN PRINT

Since the late nineteenth century, in Chinese novels and the miscellaneous jottings of intellectuals Shanghai, for good or ill, has exemplified capitalism, transformations in material life, foreign influence and ideas, fashion, novelty, opportunity, and decadence. By 1920, Shanghai was China's pre-eminent city, with approximately 2.5 million Chinese residents (and fewer than 25,000 foreigners, most of them Japanese). A center of education, commerce, and print, Shanghai was foundational to the national dissemination of new visions and values. During the time of the May Fourth Movement, this included harboring in its commercial institutions a particularly radical vision of democracy, an impracticable and episodic but also powerful and recurrent impulse in China's modern experience. This vision found everyday sustenance in Shanghai's expansive press and public associations.

In the last several decades of the Qing dynasty, a Chinese periodical press, which was rooted in the city, rose to national prominence as the medium for the circulation of what was new, dynamic, and—to use a term that captures the distinctive modern combination of novelty and value— newsworthy. In the late Qing and early Republic, Shanghai newspapers and books—advertisements for desires generated in the contact zone— circulated nationally, stimulating and testifying to the market for Shanghai modernity among readers in coastal cities and the interior. Shanghai's printers also satisfied demands for more traditional fare, which remained substantial as offerings diversified. During the early Republic, the city was the national center of modern commercial publishing.[9]

With its foreign enclaves and zones of extraterritorial governance, Shanghai afforded spaces of possibility at the same time as it manifested global inequities, foreign privilege, and encroachments on Chinese sovereignty. Taking up shelter (and prime real estate) in the International Settlement, Shanghai's proliferating press and dynamic associational life—the twin milieux of Xi's employer, Tang—conjured an expansive public realm that shaped the new era. These institutions created spaces or staging grounds for ideas and practices of republican citizenship and democracy: nationalism, popular sovereignty, gender equality, and judicial independence.

Because the Xi case was enmeshed in the interconnected spaces of Shanghai newspapers, associations, and financial organizations, a few observations may highlight the ways in which ideological change and new and old behaviors animated these generative arenas of urban life. Western-style newspapers and organizations found footing in Shanghai daily life amid already robust offerings of Chinese print culture and associational life. Frames, names, and organizational structures that suggest Chinese or foreign origin (which might be taken to represent "old" versus "new" life-ways) distract from the shifting, interacting, and mutually interpenetrating substance of indigenous and imported norms in everyday experience. In this era of change, social activists engineered the reform of terms, behaviors, and forms of communal association, usually through imported procedures, names, and conceptual language. By the same token, adaptations of Western-style formats, associations, and institutions—shifts that were often viewed as concomitant to progress—necessarily relied on indigenous elements and found meaning in relation to local context. Print and public associations were mutually reinforcing in the Republic; not only did newspapers report summaries of association meetings all around town, but old- and new-style associations published their own journals, disseminating news of meetings and supplementing physical meeting rooms with virtual spaces of discussion that reached beyond city limits. Finally, despite the gradual emergence of specialized institutions and arenas of knowledge, intellectuals, journalists, and others whose ideas appeared in public print commonly conceived of knowledge more generally, without clear boundary lines of specialization. Many new associations engaged in what seem in retrospect to be a surprisingly broad arena of activities, casting wide social networks.

Examples of a few types of organizations that connected Xi and Tang to society beyond the workplace may serve to illustrate the intertwining of disparate old and new elements in the shifting fabric of urban sociability. In the first decades of the twentieth century, many indigenous social formations that might be considered "traditional" took up democratizing reforms, among them the powerful native-place associations that organized Shanghai's resident sojourners from other regions. Formerly managed by a small elite and focused on ritual functions (particularly the reshipment and burial of the sojourning dead), trade, and dispute management in the Republican Era, these associations proliferated, created constitutions and enacted more accountable governing procedures, including more transparent elections and record keeping. They also became more inclusive. Transformations that were underway in the Shaoxing association in the year of the Xi case convey something of these shifts. After a female member of the community embarrassed the association by pressing the issue in public, the reformed Shaoxing association pioneered the admission of women, promoting a gender-integrated ideal of citizenship that was denied by the state. The public vote of 87 to 53 that passed the measure expressed an associational shift, characteristic of the May Fourth Era, from an oligarchic, consensual style of decision making to an ethic of public voting that made disagreement newly visible.[10]

In the late Qing, Chinese and Western authorities relied on native-place associations to represent and manage their communities; in the Republican

Era, particularly in the foreign settlements, these functions became increasingly formalized. Because Shanghai regional associations were tied to both the native place and to webs of sojourners across China, and also because of the powerful commercial clout of Shanghai-based associations in these networks, change in Shanghai seeded change elsewhere. In the early Republic, like the progressive Shaoxing association, Tang's more powerful Guang-Zhao Gongsuo restructured itself through internal reform and external activism. Social activists also gained power in the Ningbo association, another deeply influential actor in local networks of power, which often found common cause with the Guangdong activists in Shanghai political movements.[11] The Guang-Zhao association did not have female members, but it sponsored a Guang-Zhao Girls' School, numerous charitable schools, and a night school for workers. Xi's Dongting association was more socially conservative.

In parallel fashion, reform officials and business and civic leaders appropriated imported forms, names, and formats (often Western-modeled elements that had undergone a prior process of Japanese adaptation) and "indigenized" them with familiar social units, behavioral conventions, and local cultural expectations. Chambers of commerce were ushered into being at the turn of the twentieth century by the late Qing "New Policies" reforms, a government effort to prioritize the commercial economy and bolster China's place in a globally uneven "commercial war" (*shangzhan*). The first Chinese Chamber of Commerce was established in Shanghai in 1904 to enable merchants to organize themselves, with the aim of loosening bureaucratic encumbrances in the interest of strengthening commerce. The governing structure of the Shanghai General Chamber of Commerce formalized representation of the older native-place and trade associations (which are often described in English as guilds) as constituent units in the new institution. The creation of an officially sponsored chamber of commerce that elevated commerce (and would form a national network of chambers of commerce), though inhabited by these older units, was nonetheless politically transformative. In the fragmented governance of the city, the Shanghai Chamber of Commerce—with its elected leadership structure—assumed a public representative and a governing function that transcended business and at times ignored Chinese authority. The Shanghai Chamber of Commerce was also at the activist center of a mobilized national network of chambers of commerce.[12]

A third type of illustrative organization is the Jingwu Athletic Association (*Jingwu tiyuhui*), a private initiative established before the revolution to promote Chinese martial arts. A mix of old, new, and sui generis elements, Jingwu transcended athletics. Indeed, its operations convey the protean character of well-resourced Shanghai public associations. Jingwu emerged into the Republic at a time when some moderns dismissed martial arts in favor of Western calisthenics and military drills. Purposefully reinventing martial arts under the national (and soon international) "Jingwu" brand, the association rebuked Western caricatures of Chinese weakness by remolding urban citizens and making effete scholars robust. Its corporate leadership criticized traditional martial arts for secretive transmission, superstition, and an unscientific character. Jingwu aimed to make public, scientize, and popularize martial arts in an urban setting. By these maneuvers, the Jingwu association both redressed the devaluation of the indigenous vis-à-vis the foreign, and resolved the problem, for nationalist identity, of preserving attachment to a fortified core of indigenous cultural tradition.[13]

Jingwu boasted connections to a number of Shanghai industrialists and financiers. It also encompassed influential native place and political connections, although it was not tied to any one group. Among its leaders in 1919 were the cotton mill magnate and Shanghai General Chamber of Commerce chairman Nie Yuntai (Nie Qijie), compradors of the International Banking Corporation, and the socially progressive Shanghai Guangdong businessmen Lu Weichang and Chen Gongzhe, two of a trio routinely referred to as "Jingwu's three corporations" (Jingwu *san gongsi*). Tang's associate Wen Zongyao (director of Pukow port) and another Guangdong businessman, V. Y. Kwauh, who was Tang's employer at the Zhong-Mei Trading Company, were among Jingwu's pillars. Jingwu networking, advertising, and fund-raising facilitated expansive activities. A renovated Jingwu campus provided Chinese and Western sports instruction, literary studies, English, Chinese painting, typewriting, photography, medicine, and debate. It also supported the first Chinese Western orchestra. In the May Fourth protests, its exercise ground accommodated a "commoners' meeting" (*pingmin dahui*).[14]

Tang had a greater connection to the Jingwu association than Xi, but Xi would nonetheless have encountered it at one of the girls' schools at which she worked.[15] Jingwu's modern platform encouraged gender equality. Its publications depicted female participants in martial pose. As one contributor exclaimed: "Citizens are male and female. . . . Women have hands and feet, ears and eyes, the same as men." The "era of democracy" had established gender equality, thus women were "equally capable of assuming professions." Bodily strengthening was recommended for "taking up such weighty matters."[16]

A May 1919 drawing by the painting instructor Shen Bocheng depicts an (unmistakably masculine) figure embracing the Jingwu crest, which is

1.1 **Society's Pillars "Upholding Jingwu."** Shanghai
Municipal Archives Q 401–2, Jingwu tiyuhui.

emblazoned with the motto, "Upholding Jingwu." He stands on a platform that is supported by the social pillars of "women's circles, military
circles, academia, business, government circles, and the press" (Figure 1.1).[17]
It is reproduced here to illustrate the depiction of the association as a cul-
minating emblem of the corporate strength of society, as figured by these
constituencies.

Sun Yat-sen presented an honorary calligraphic plaque for the tenth
Jingwu anniversary in 1919. The three-night celebration, which sold 4,000
tickets and was attended by the US consul, included a five-reel Jingwu film,
Chinese and Western music, "american dancing," and a performance of

the Encouraging the Workers Youth Orchestra (*Gongjie qingnian lizhihui*). Jingwu records note that board member Tang Jiezhi (who taught a medical hygiene class) sold 1,500 tickets.[18] Tang's engagement with the Jingwu association was of a piece with his broad and overlapping social networks. Influential figures in the early Republic characteristically embraced large public identities, multiplying their affiliations, patronage, and connections to increase the efficacy of their public interventions as they assumed quasi-representative functions.

If Tang was an associational man, he was simultaneously a newspaper man, an identity that enhanced his ability to maneuver within and shape the emerging public realm. Newspapers, which were formative in the creation of a modern print public, had coevolved with the associational public. The establishment of the first foreign-style Chinese newspaper in 1872—the long-lived *Shenbao* (*Shanghai Journal*), a commercial venture of the British businessman Ernest Major—created a virtual public space. This newly encompassing frame for Chinese print had consequential effects on readers' experience of time, geography, and authority. As the reformer Tan Sitong described it at the end of the nineteenth century, the newspaper uniquely brought together "writings of all times and places."[19] Not only did newspapers promote novelty, they also decentered the Chinese calendar, which measured time in the years of the reigning dynasty. The Chinese newspapers that emerged in the late Qing featured dual lunar and Gregorian calendrical notations in each page-top folio. Journalism marketed the value of the contemporary in Shanghai, China, and the world, the spatial categories expressed by the local, national and global geographic sections that framed Republican-Era newspapers. Newspapers lured readers with serialized fiction and writers turned news and newspapers into source material for the new social fiction of the early twentieth century, which dramatized the compelling issues of the day.

Just as they decentered an older calendrical unity, Chinese newspapers decentered political and textual authority. By the early twentieth century, journalists had begun to shed didactic literati assumptions of the authority of the classics and identification with a quasi-official sphere. Joan Judge's study of the early political reform journalism of *Shibao* (*Eastern Times*) showed that journalists at the end of the Qing understood themselves as mediators between the state and the public, whose role was to articulate the political interests of the people.[20] During the early Republic, journalists increasingly presented themselves "as practitioners of verifiable reportage" and representatives of public opinion (*gonglun*).[21] Republican-Era publishers, as Xu Xiaoqun observed, described newspapers as a public forum, a "public tool" (*gongqi*) to serve the public good.[22] With limited budgets and staff, newspapers also functioned as billboards for the associational life of the city, filling columns with the notices of meetings and manifestos that were sent to their offices for publication.

As the media landscape diversified, newspaper language, organization, and style conveyed novel notions of authority, identity, community, and political possibility. Editorials upheld the authority of the newspaper itself as the voice of public opinion. Claims to express public opinion and the people's will (*minyi*) gained greater credibility in the May Fourth Era, because—in this period between the press suppression and assassinations of journalists that took place under Yuan Shikai and prior to the press censorship and renewed violence that would be instituted after 1927 by the Guomindang state—newspaper expression was relatively unconstrained.[23] In this moment of relative openness, journalists in Shanghai organized the first newspaper association, under a platform that included protecting the freedom of speech.[24] These cumulative developments underlay the statement of the influential Columbia University–trained educator Guo Bingwen (Dr. P. W. Kuo) that the Chinese newspaper had become something new in the first decade of the Republic: "the newspaper has [changed] from the paper of literary style to that of reliable news, from the editor's paper to that of the people."[25]

If the presence of Shanghai's semicolonial International Settlement provided a degree of essential—if partial and not disinterested—extraterritorial protection, it was Shanghai's prosperity that fueled the expansive Republican-Era press.[26] This prosperity was facilitated by a degree of European retreat. The diversion of European business in World War I and the immediate postwar era created an exceptional climate for the growth of Chinese industry, banking, and commerce. In this "golden age of the Chinese bourgeoisie,"[27] which capped the first decade of the Republic, Shanghai's financial growth provided advertisement revenue to support growing numbers of newspapers. By 1922, at least seventeen Chinese dailies operated in the city.[28]

Shanghai wealth also filled the pockets of patrons and contributing members of new associations, multiplying available platforms for public political discussion and social mobilization beyond the more limited venues of late Qing society. The city's burgeoning market and media infused public culture with economic information and a scientific language of opportunity and profit, coupled with new modes of access to the market. As sojourners flocked to the city to try their luck, women and other individuals who had been formerly constrained by familial barriers, rural norms, or

occupational restrictions embraced information networks and associational ties in the city as pathways to profit, following "dreams of Shanghai
splendor" as phrased in the title of a popular turn-of-the-century serialized novel and its Republican-Era sequel.[29]

SHANGHAI COMMERCE AND
MAY FOURTH CULTURE

The capitalist economy animated a public realm that powered the city's
aura. Depending on the position of the observer, the city glowed, or glow-
ered, with the "light, heat and power" of capitalism, as depicted in Mao
Dun's famous 1930s novel *Midnight*. Recent scholarship on Shanghai commerce and consumer culture has supplemented older economic and business histories with heightened attention to the ways in which commerce
was culturally transformative. Wen-hsin Yeh has vividly depicted the elevation of "economic sentiment" in the early twentieth century. Entrepreneurs whose commercial, financial, and industrial fortunes built up the city
boosted the social prestige of moneymaking by presenting flourishing private enterprise as science-based, patriotic, and beneficial to the nation.
They thus imbued industrial wealth with May Fourth value. This "decisive materialistic turn" in discourse thrust economic concerns into a position of epistemological centrality, as manufacturers and financiers pushed
the imperative of economic growth higher on state and (in the breach) non-
state agendas. Commerce and economics gained prestige as categories of
knowledge, spawning new schools, study societies, and journals focused
on business and economics.[30] Tang's *Journal of Commerce* affirmed the
epistemological shift with its title, financial pages, and frequent exposi-
tion of the science of economics. So did another of Tang's journalistic projects, the *Journal of the Shanghai General Chamber of Commerce,* a
monthly that began publication in July 1921.[31]

Commercial culture, entwined as it was with a vision of national prosperity, was further elevated by campaigns for "national products." In October 1911, influential Shanghai native-place trade associations formed the
National Products Promotion Association (NPPA) (*Zhongguo guohuo
weichihui*) to support domestic manufacturing. By the 1920s, native-place
and commercial networks had replicated the NPPA in hundreds of similar
associations across China. In a consumer context of global inequality that
added value to the new and the foreign, the language of national products
helped Chinese entrepreneurs secure a market niche. Recent scholarship

by Eugenia Lean reveals how individual businessmen deployed the national products discourse in the production of competitive domestic versions of desirable global commodities.[32] As Karl Gerth has detailed, national products campaigns created "an ethic of nationalistic consumption" to compete against foreign competitors in the domestic market. In the process, the movement popularized and infused nationalism into China's consumer culture. At the same time, the purity of advertised national products was frequently in question. The challenge of nationalizing consumer culture created the negative categories of treasonous consumers and businessmen who betrayed China's economic interests with their connections to foreign products.[33]

Tang's journalistic and associational ventures, as bearers of enlightened Shanghai commercial culture, promoted both the science of economics and the nationalism of supporting Chinese products (despite the fact that economic science would soon fail his trust company venture and that in his legal troubles, he would be hoist with his own petard of nationalist loyalty). What is of particular interest for this study, beyond these more familiar aspects of Shanghai commercial culture, is the way in which commercial publications, networks, and associations also became arenas for democratic contestation, the institutionalization of self-consciously republican language and practice, and the exercise of May Fourth political activism. Tang's political career took the science of economics and Shanghai commercial culture into the less well-recognized direction of merchant democratic radicalism. As Mao Zedong wrote in an insufficiently remembered essay of 1923, for a moment in Shanghai, merchants "[took] up revolutionary methods and mustered the courage to shoulder responsibility for national affairs."[34] By the time Mao—an infrequent admirer of merchants after he became a member of the Communist party—made this observation, Tang was already in prison. But the Shanghai merchant-led People's Self-Determination Movement (*Guomin zijue yundong*), which Mao applauded as revolutionary in 1923, was the culmination of consistent, interlinked efforts of Tang and his associates in multiple popular campaigns.

In Shanghai, merchant activism developed from the public, quasi-governmental functions of native-place and trade associations, which expanded with the development of the foreign settlements in the final decades of the Qing. During the early Republic, these associations institutionalized cultural and behavioral shifts that have been more commonly associated with the writings and lifestyles of New Culture intellectuals and students. The Shanghai business community also played a decisive role in the May Fourth Movement.

Prior to the May Fourth events, Tang engaged himself in the restructuring or formation of a range of organizations; this is how he built his reputation and expanded his social networks. His path illuminates the working out of new understandings of the public and democracy in social practice, in the associations that structured community in the city. The May Fourth mobilization of Shanghai's commercial sector in 1919 catalyzed transformations that were already substantially underway in the language, institutional norms, and political speech of commercial organizations. These included the embrace of distinctive democratic norms of public culture, including an emphasis on representing a numerically superior public, an insistence on procedural clarity, the strategic deployment of public media, and a tendency toward associational multiplication.

Tang first emerged in Shanghai news in a 1918 reform struggle within his Guang-Zhao native-place association. He was joined in this struggle by Wen Zongyao and two colleagues, Feng Shaoshan, a titan of the paper industry, and Huo Shouhua (S. W. Fock), director of the Yufan Iron Mine. This group—all of whom also served on the board of the Jingwu association—orchestrated public meetings and used the press to embarrass the old leadership, thereby forcing democratic reforms.[35] What is striking in this and other reform struggles is the extent to which a sense of the new era of the Republic impacted the norms of associational life. In the Guang-Zhao Gongsuo conflicts of 1918, for which there is particularly good documentation, participants on both the reform and the "old guard" sides insisted on the need to manifest "the true spirit of the Republic" (*shiju gonghe zhi zhen jingshen*).[36] Battles raged, nonetheless, over what precisely this entailed. The imperative for public associations to manifest the spirit of the Republic was challenging in the context of a state that used the name of a republic without regard for the political ideals that had displaced the legitimacy of the monarchical order.

Tang soon emerged as a leading figure in a flurry of civic associations. Several of these would be prominent in the May Fourth Movement in Shanghai, where businessmen were major actors (in contrast to the more familiar student-dominated agitation elsewhere). Although narratives of May Fourth most commonly highlight student agitation in Beijing, the associational ground and the formation of activist commercial organizations in Shanghai—on which the strike would depend—predated the Beijing May Fourth events. Shopkeepers on Nanjing and Fujian Roads began to form unions organized by street as early as 1918 to organize urban residents to resist tax increases in the International Settlement.[37] In February 1919 seven activist organizations with commercial concerns, four of them native-place associations, collaborated to press the Beijing government to resist Japanese encroachment. In March, a larger assemblage of fifty-three (primarily native-place and trade) associations joined forces to form the Federation of Public Commercial Associations (FPCA) (*Shangye gongtuan lianhehui*). Tang was elected president. This group's immediate focus was to repair peace negotiations between the rival northern and southern governments, but the coalition endured as an organ of activists who were restive under the constraints of the politically reticent Chamber of Commerce. It was the FPCA that organized the urgent Shanghai "citizens' meeting" (*guomin dahui*) that convened after news of the May 4 events in Beijing. The FPCA also successfully pressed the reluctant Chamber of Commerce to agree to the business strike.[38] This FPCA activism attracted the early attention of the young Mao Zedong in 1919 as he looked about for the "requisite motive force for a great union of the popular masses of the country." Mao placed this "Shanghai union of 53 public bodies" in the category of recent "great unions" that had arisen from "the rise in consciousness that resulted from political disorder and foreign oppression."[39]

Absent a functional state that could represent the people, Shanghai activists redoubled their efforts to engage the twin imperatives of *representing* the public and *being* public. This entailed the intensified formation of capacious institutions of the people, following a logic that resonated with Mao's pre-Marxist hope for a "great union" of the people. Efforts along these lines included a remarkably named "Federation of All Circles in China" (*Zhongguo gejie lianhehui*), which included intellectuals, business, labor, journalists, women, and student associations, and conveys something of the national aspirations of these movements. Shanghai public associations also mobilized a street public, using newspapers to disseminate speeches and memorialize public meetings. Business circles, in coordination with other mobilized sectors, launched the decisive commercial strike on June 5 that ultimately secured the resignation of the "three traitorous officials" in Beijing.[40]

Tang's activism increased his leverage in a campaign to reform the Chinese Chamber of Commerce that followed the May Fourth tumult. After its establishment, the Chamber had served as a de facto, quasi-representative body for Chinese interests in the city. A progressive minority of members, including Tang, Huo Shouhua, and Feng Shaoshan, denounced the Chamber as elitist, unrepresentative, and lacking in scientific knowledge. They used a tactical and rhetorical repertoire honed in their earlier Guang–Zhao Gongsuo reform and FPCA activism. Their cause was aided by the political embarrassment of the Chamber in the May Fourth events.

Facing the May Fourth mobilization of Shanghai society, the politically cautious leadership of the Chamber of Commerce had sent a secret telegram on May 10 to the Beijing government suggesting direct negotiations with Japan. When this news leaked, the FPCA repudiated the Chamber leadership in Shanghai newspapers, in an unprecedented public airing of internal divisions. Taking up a characteristic May Fourth style of radical invective, activists denounced the Chamber chair and vice chair for traitorously close ties to Japan and subservience to the Beijing government. As they had done with the old *gongsuo* leadership, they attacked the officers' "aristocratic" habit of handling matters without consultation, arguing for democratic representation and procedures and pummeling the old guard with a public storm of criticism. The FPCA decried the parlous state of the nation ("China is called a republic, but in reality it is a military dictatorship.") It urged financial reform, the elimination of secret agreements with Japan, the prosecution of the "criminal Anfu clique" in Beijing, military disbandment, the revival of local self-government, and, perhaps most distinctively in terms of their conceptualization of democratic legitimacy, a new election and the re-creation thereby of a legitimate parliament that could restore the substance of the Republic.[41]

In the broad social mobilization of May Fourth, Tang and his associates participated in agitation for "urban citizens' rights" (*shimin quan*), in association with the grassroots formation of commercial street unions (*ge malu shangjie lianhehui*), which were groupings of shopkeepers organized by street. Activists coalesced in protests against a July 1919 tax levy by the Shanghai Municipal Council. Tang, the FPCA, and the street unions were behind the August strike of shopkeepers who demanded Chinese representation on the Municipal Council. The strike challenged the governing body of Shanghai's International Settlement, which excluded Chinese from membership. A pamphlet distributed by the FPCA linked property ownership with civil rights, explaining that "civilized countries" followed the principle of "no taxation without representation."[42]

The effort to create more popular or representative organizations—under the slogans of democracy (translated as *pingminzhuyi*, literally "principle of the common people") and egalitarianism (*pingdenglun*)—included an aspirational Commoners' Chamber of Commerce (an effort that gave way to a more powerful Shanghai Street Union Federation, or *Shanghai gelu shangjie zong lianhehui,* which united the already active street unions). Elements of the movement for more popular associations, including initiatives to mitigate social inequality and other capitalist ills with night schools and rent reduction campaigns, resonated with the utopian, anarcho-communist spirit that Arif Dirlik identified as at the heart of May Fourth social radicalism.[43] They also expressed radical populist understandings of democracy that circulated beyond anarchist circles. Edward Gu, who emphasized the salience of populist understandings of democracy, highlights Chen Duxiu's suggestion in 1919, that the common people, "consisting of students, merchants, peasants and workers," should implement democracy by "conquering the government," tolerating no political parties beyond associations organized by the common people, pushing notions of political equality and popular sovereignty toward a utopian embrace of direct democracy.[44] In Chen's exuberant evocation, political democracy was cast as "the active implementation of the autonomy of the people."[45] Such populist understandings of May Fourth democracy were strikingly prominent among Shanghai shopkeepers and merchants, people who, in another moment and context, might be identified with capitalist exploitation. This was not, however, how they understood themselves; rather, they identified as representatives of an expansive mobilized public of the common people, and they imagined the possibility that—through the mobilization of popular organizations—China might avoid the destructive social consequences of capitalism.

Associational innovations driven by Shanghai May Fourth merchant activists in this moment placed particular emphasis on elections and representation, particularly the representation of Chinese in the governance of the Settlement. Tang mobilized his Guang-Zhao association in combination with the influential Ningbo association to create a Chinese Ratepayers' Association that could elect Chinese representatives to the Shanghai Municipal Council. When the Municipal Council suggested, in summer 1920, that the Chamber of Commerce might appropriately oversee the selection of representatives for the Chinese community, the native-place associations protested. They articulated a civic, democratic, and nonparticularist stance, calling publicly for a general election to permit "every Chinese ratepayer, even those who are not members of organizations" to vote.[46] Shortly afterward, Tang was momentarily elected to a leadership position in the newly formed association of Chinese ratepayers, along with David Yui of the YMCA and C. T. Wang. In a parallel development, in August 1920, as Joshua Hill has noted, in one of the first public calls for voting based on universal adult suffrage, the Shanghai Federation of Commercial Street Unions called for the direct election of a national citizens' assembly.[47]

In this moment of escalating activism and multiplication of both ad hoc and more enduring public associations—associations which, at least in name, represented large sectors of society—Tang's faction of radicalized business leaders pressed to reform the Chamber of Commerce, accusing it of neglecting commercial circles at a time when the national economy cried out for protection. In a time of "commercial war," they advocated for science as well as democracy, proposing that the Chamber collect commercial information to scientifically guide policy and aid business. This included programs of research, statistics, and the regular dissemination of information in a specialized newspaper (to be called *Journal of Commerce*). To reform practice with scientific knowledge, they recommended bringing into the Chamber specialists in economics, politics, law, and commerce. They also demanded greater inclusiveness: doubling the board of directors, halving membership fees, and abolishing requirements for guarantors for candidates for office.[48] Riding the crest of his May Fourth fame, Tang was elected to the board of directors in a reformist sweep of the Chamber in August 1920. The progressive US-educated Shanghai cotton mill magnate Mu Ouchu (Mu Xiangyue), another Jingwu board member, was also elected.[49]

In September or October 1921, Tang was also elected to lead the more progressive branch of the grassroots Federation of Commercial Street Unions (*Ge malu shangjie zong lianhehui*) following a split in that coalition. This group loudly advocated democratic politics, declared the intent to foster equality by abolishing hierarchical titles like committee head and director, and adopted a new representative system (*daiyizhi*), which had been the slogan of the Commmoners' Chamber of Commerce. It also fostered free night schools and assistance in times of rice shortages, funded by the contributions of shop owners. In this position Tang gained an additional podium to press for national economic fortification, public welfare projects, and participatory democracy. The shopkeeper constituency of the street unions—its embrace of commoner democracy notwithstanding—made its case for rights on the basis of a liberal property-based logic of political participation, following the model of the foreign Shanghai Ratepayers Association.[50]

Throughout this period, Tang and his associates articulated a democratic vision that was grounded in Shanghai's flourishing civic institutions of urban commerce. They upheld the patriotic, politically engaged businessman as foundational to republican citizenship, a foil to corrupt bureaucrats and militarists, and an economic bulwark against Japan. In 1921 Tang's Guang-Zhao Gongsuo, Chamber of Commerce, and street union associates promoted a national conference of China's chambers of commerce, which focused on state affairs and tasks of national construction; a national citizens' convention; a national diplomatic congress; and the sending of "people's candidates" to represent China at the Washington Naval Conference (which took up the question of Japanese expansion in East Asia). It was in the context of a provisional national conference of China's chambers of commerce in late October 1921 that Tang elucidated the particular political mission of businessmen, which entailed "the creation of a government . . . that can represent the true will of the people":

> The students are still at the age of studying, preparing to work for our country in the future. We shouldn't sacrifice their valuable time. Most workers are unavoidably lacking in experience and without schooling. They haven't much time to sacrifice either. Thus those who can achieve things for the country, with relatively more time and experience, and at the same time [may inspire] the confidence of citizens, include ourselves: businessmen, educators, industrialists and bankers only. We must not evade responsibility for the construction of the country.[51]

In their efforts to mobilize a widening public of citizens, activists in these movements seized on Shanghai's burgeoning press as sword and shield. This was their key tool in a strategy of public maneuvering that might be counterpoised to Beijing autocracy and bureaucratism on the one hand, and on the other hand, the local military authorities, whom they held responsible for spreading the soldier-borne pestilence of predation and instability and for the trading away of railway rights and concessions for foreign loans. Through the press they called forth and disseminated news of public assemblies. After May Fourth, finding open space for citizens' meetings proved difficult. Large gatherings of Chinese were not permitted in the foreign settlements, so Tang engaged in periodic public contestations with the local military government over the use of Chinese public recreation grounds.[52]

JOURNAL OF COMMERCE

Tang founded the *Journal of Commerce* (*Shangbao*) in this climate of economic sentiment, nationalism, and activism that was grounded in commercial institutions and associations. It took up residence in the most desirable location for a newspaper: the intersection of Shanghai's "Fourth Road" (Fuzhou Road) and Wangping Road (now Shandong Road), a street unrivaled in China for its cluster of newspaper offices and publishing houses (Figure 1.2).[53] In the words of a Republican-Era Shanghai "bamboo branch" poem, "News concentrates on Wangping Road; newspaper offices line up east and west. Shops in other trades find they must move and hang their signs elsewhere."[54]

Tang advertised the *Journal of Commerce* as "the public opinion organ of industrial and commercial groups," established in order "to disseminate

1.2 **Wangping Road in the 1920s, facing the intersection with Fuzhou Road.**
Reproduced from Fuhui Wu, *Cultural History of Modern Chinese Literature*
(Cambridge: Cambridge University Press, 2020), 8.

global industrial and commercial news and promote the industrial and
commercial knowledge of national citizens."[55] His inaugural essay celebrated the *Journal* as a pillar of progress and called on citizens to promote the liberal values that were appropriate to "the city with the greatest
concentration of industry and commerce."[56] Rejecting the cliché that "those
in business should discuss only business," he instead articulated the higher,
liberatory aim of public political engagement:

> Our brothers in industry and commerce face political and economic pres-
> sure. . . . If people tell us of their oppression, we can deploy the power of
> public opinion (*yulun*) to save our countrymen and ourselves. This is our mis-
> sion. Our countrymen in industry and commerce are constituents of the
> national citizenry. As national citizens, we must formulate and uphold opin-
> ions about everything that relates to national politics. . . . We must not limit
> our outlook to just industry and commerce.[57]

The paper was not aligned with a political party. Although it was independent, the municipal police reported that it favored "the southern [GMD]
government and resumption of trade with Russia."[58] Under Tang's stew-

ardship, by fall 1921 the *Journal of Commerce* had become the third-ranking Chinese newspaper in Shanghai in terms of circulation, after *Shenbao* and *Xinwenbao*.⁵⁹ Now largely obscured from historical memory, its emergence in January 1921 impressed contemporary observers. As the newspaperman Zhang Jinglu wrote, "After May Fourth, a new newspaper burst forth like an army appearing ingeniously from nowhere. Although it had neither enormous capital nor an established reputation, its modern program and superlative personnel made it a revolutionary force in Shanghai newspaper circles."⁶⁰ One reason for the *Journal's* quick visibility was that Tang attracted prominent editors, among whom were Chen Bulei (who later became Jiang Jieshi's confidential secretary) and his brother, Chen Qihuai. Tang also hired Pan Gongzhan, who would later rise in Shanghai government circles.⁶¹

In Shanghai's fiercely competitive newspaper environment, the brash challenge of the *Journal* (with its initial run of 35,000 copies) incurred immediate resentment. In one particularly dramatic maneuver, the management of *Xinwenbao* reportedly bought up the entire first issue and dumped the bundled papers into the Huangpu River.⁶² Despite this inauspicious start, and after arranging publicity and distribution in cigarette shops, the newspaper gained attention and readers. Tang also disseminated his paper through the street unions and other associations. In its second month, the *Journal* established branch offices in Ningbo, Nanjing, Anqing, Beijing, Suzhou, Changzhou, Tianjin, and Zhenjiang.⁶³

Although it never attained the circulation of the two leading papers, the *Journal* was disproportionately influential among intellectuals and students and was acclaimed for its in-depth commercial and domestic news. The bold substance of its editorials contrasted with the anodyne pronouncements of the larger dailies. In Zeng Xubai's memory, Chen Bulei's columns created "shock-waves" among Shanghai's social and political leaders.⁶⁴ Former journalist Xu Zhucheng took Sunday walks as a middle-school student to the Wuxi City Library just to read Chen Bulei's editorials.⁶⁵ Literary scholar Hu Yuzhi called the paper the "star" of Shanghai newspaper circles.⁶⁶ Communist labor organizer Deng Zhongxia ranked it "of first importance" among contemporary newspapers and celebrated its outspokenness: "It opposes the Zhili [military] clique and imperialism, and supports a national people's revolution [*guomin geming*]." He described it as ahead of its time, since the capitalist class that it claimed to represent was still in its infancy.⁶⁷ The equally nationalist but less socially radical Hollington Tong described it as Shanghai's sole "progressive and independent" Chinese daily and asserted that it represented a new direction for journalism. It surpassed the two larger papers in influence, he suggested, because it provided "the kind of news which the people want [and] an attitude on political questions in accordance with the views of the people." A *Shangbao* cartoon presented the newspaper as the key to China's ills (Figure 1.3).[68]

Foreign observers attested to the *Journal*'s influence. The Tokyo-based expatriate *Trans-Pacific* hailed the *Journal of Commerce* for filling a need for a Chinese paper "devoted to commerce and finance," making it "one of the most popular in all of China." Owing to its rare independence, "liberal and impartial viewpoint," and lack of connection "to political factions or parties," it received "widespread publicity in other Chinese publications."[69] In his 1922 study of Chinese newspapers, University of Missouri professor Don Patterson tied the emergence of Tang's paper to Shanghai business prosperity. He pronounced it "devoted . . . to the interests of Chinese commercial circles and the various principal markets of the country" and commended its quality and "progressive attitude."[70] Japanese intelligence reports were less admiring, however. Recognizing the newspaper's influence, they reported closely on its anti-Japanese stance. The Japanese newspaper *Shanhai nippō* described it as "extremist," an anecdote proudly publicized by the *Shangbao* as testimony to its patriotic credentials.[71]

Tang's newspaper was supported by Shanghai businessmen who sought economic news and a self-conscious organ of the commercial sector, in a bid for an increased role for businessmen in the public realm. The newspaper was, in many respects, propelled into existence in 1921 by the dramatic "bid for liberalism" that developed in response to the disorders of warlord government in the failed Republic.[72] Activists in industrial and commercial circles joined intellectuals and provincial elites in advocating a provincial federalist or provincial autonomy movement (*liansheng zizhi*), an idea that gained popularity in 1920, joining ideas of provincial identity and autonomy that had emerged in constitutionalist politics to the democratic ideas of popular rights and self-governance. This federalism, widely endorsed by May Fourth intellectuals, expressed a distinctive form of democratic mobilization that aimed to preserve the autonomy and distinctive character of provinces against oppression from a central government. It was linked, as Prasenjit Duara has insightfully argued, to a political tradition of dissent from centralized power that would be firmly rejected by Republican Era-advocates of a strong centralized state. Federalism was embraced by many sectors of the Shanghai business community (which bore the strong imprint of sojourning associations and identities and was also influenced by the remarkable accomplishments of Jiangsu provincial government in the first years of the Republic) along with sectors of the conservative elites and militarists who strategically adopted the language of republicanism.[73] In the analysis of Marie-Claire Bergère, "The bourgeoisie

1.3 *Journal of Commerce* as the Key (keys are marked "Railroad Recovery," "Treasury Reorganization," "Maritime Customs Rights," and so on). *Shangbao*, January 24, 1921.

made use of this movement to try to further its own contradictory aspirations for both liberty and order. By encouraging the drawing-up of provincial constitutions and the reactivation of the organs of local government, the merchants hoped to consolidate their power in opposition to interventions on the part of the civil or military bureaucracy." The movement was also tied, as Joshua Hill noted, to ideas of "direct popular expression" and systems of representation "by occupational group."[74]

Through the *Journal,* Tang heralded society as an economic realm, lauded entrepreneurial desire, and argued that commercial activism was foundational to the new political order. He aimed to disseminate economic information, raise merchants' consciousness, and facilitate informed participation in government to meet the challenges of "economic society" (*jingji shehui*). Embracing a social category that reflected his US education, Tang argued that only a powerful middle class (*zhongliu jieji*) could "shoulder the great responsibility of rectifying the country in the disorderly politics of this time."[75] He advocated an enlightened "government of the urban citizenry" (*shimin zhengzhi*) that was empowered by speech, recognizing, at the same time, the political necessity of some modulation of expression:

> We may say the relation of words to society is like the arms to the body. This may be something of an exaggeration. But since we have this organ of speech, we must use it to contribute to the People, or we will waste our days emptily. We ponder this deeply and pace about at night. . . . We must use our knowledge to daily confront society. If we can't speak directly, we will speak indirectly. If we can't speak indirectly we will cry and sigh [to make our point]. There is not just one way to speak.[76]

Accounts of the newspaper attest that it took political risks. Tang managed to keep the intrusions of Chinese authorities at bay by registering the paper as a US corporation (a status facilitated by his partnership with Sokolsky). Foreign registration provided a cushion of extraterritorial security for Tang's intermittent use of the *Journal* as a podium to denounce the corrupt machinations of Defense Commissioner He Fenglin, the local military authority.[77] Such political boldness lay behind repeated court summons and attempts to execute search warrants for so-called indecent articles.[78]

TWO MAY FOURTH PERSONALITIES

Newspaper, associational, commercial, and police records make the formal features of Tang's public life knowable and give him a resume that embeds him in the urban social ferment of his time. He is easily identifiable as a May Fourth figure by his nationalism, civic activism, and persistent concern for rights, democracy, and action based on information and scientific knowledge. Beyond Tang's public and often bold political temperament, as evidenced in his political activities and periodic public manifestos, we don't know much about his personality. One anecdote recorded by Zhang Jinglu suggests that he sometimes flouted collegial etiquette and was something of a showboat. As a Shanghai Chamber of Commerce board member, Tang was a delegate to a national conference in October 1921 of China's Chambers of Commerce that was held in Shanghai. The conference produced a draft resolution for national political reconstruction, another aspirational initiative of commercial circles. Although reporters had agreed not to publish the resolution until after it had been formalized in a vote, Tang scooped his journalistic colleagues and published the statement in the *Shangbao*. Tang's audacity produced what Xu Xiaoqun has described as China's first journalistic boycott. Believing the conference organizers had given the *Shangbao* exclusive treatment, the reporters who were scooped walked out of the meeting and refused to provide any coverage until after the conference organizers apologized. The incident led to the formalization of the Shanghai Journalists Association, in November 1921.[79] The anecdote hints at Tang's sometimes impulsive (or calculating) character.

About other sides of Tang's personality—love, family feelings, or sentimental disposition—we know nothing. Love was, however, the modern and revolutionary May Fourth emotion.[80] It was imagined that through the realization of love individuals might break free from the bondage of parentally-arranged marriages and attain the self-actualization of self-determining citizens. We cannot know what Tang's wife meant to him, though she would later appeal to the court on his behalf. We also cannot know, beyond his exculpatory public statement, what he thought of the young woman who shared his office space.

In contrast to her employer, Xi Shangzhen's position at the *Journal of Commerce* involved considerably less public presence. The sources available for probing what the May Fourth moment meant to her are quite different from those available for Tang. As an urban, educated woman, Xi's social circles exceeded family and workplace constraints, but whereas Tang's social ties were largely male—and connected to influential networks of public record—Xi's circles were largely female, external to the male-dominated office, and less visible.[81] She attended gatherings with female classmates and teachers, as evidenced by their statements after her death; she may have also participated in the Professional Women's Association (*Zhiye nüzi lianxiu hui*), which published a letter about her in the press.[82]

This organization, which left no archives, may have sparked her friend-ship with another female secretary, her close friend Shufen, who was nei-ther a classmate nor a coworker. Because of this friendship and Shufen's preservation of Xi's private writings, we have exceptional source material for considering the ways in which Xi Shangzhen took up the formative ideas and circulating print of her time.

Xi's amateur fiction writing takes us into a rarely visible space of imagi-nation for a female office worker in that moment. Her imagination ranged across global geography, Chinese history, and the Shanghai present. Given Xi's modest background and the demands of her everyday existence, it is striking that she had the ambition to write and that she carved out some of her limited time to do so. She carefully copied her stories and gave them to her friend, suggesting the importance of this writing to her sense of self as well as its presence in her friendship. Upon her death, Shufen persuaded a reporter to publish this material. There is no print discussion, however, of the content of Xi's stories.

Two stories, which the reporter categorized as Xi's "jottings," evince a taste for popular fiction of the sort that was published in *Saturday* (*Libailiu*) and similar urban entertainment magazines beginning in the 1910s. These two brief melodramas, which are written in ornate classical Chinese, de-pict ill-fated couples. Both vignettes, which may have been based on nar-ratives Xi encountered elsewhere, are interesting in several respects. The first takes place in an imagined France during the Great War. The story's glorification of nationalist self-sacrifice might have appeared in a late Qing reform novel; the evocation of the recent war and the French location carry a hint of the May Fourth–Era context.[83] More striking is the absence of family or mediating social relations beyond the marital couple. The other vignette is set in the mid-Qing, a time, the author tells the reader, "When ships and railways were not yet built" and travel was unimaginably slow. This story's modernity lies in its stance of looking backward from the time-space compression of Shanghai economic development into a recent impe-rial past that appears already ancient. Both vignettes, Xi's prefatory nar-rative states, reveal "the arena of extreme passion" (*jiqingchang*). The imagined settings of France and an exoticized Qing past serve as backdrops for tales of a loyal woman's extreme bodily sacrifice for a higher virtue that is achieved by her male partner.

The first vignette, which drew on the popular genres of patriotic fiction (*aiguo xiaoshuo*) and military fiction (*junshi xiaoshuo*), describes the French cavalry captain Ironblood ("a valorous and praiseworthy man)" and his young wife, Julie (who is "pretty and full of feeling"). Their do-mestic happiness evokes the cliché of "lovebirds in intertwined branches."

The captain has to depart for war, to the sorrow of his wife, who "twisted her sleeves in the courtyard as he departed," like a Chinese heroine. Captain Ironblood understands that saving his country is more important than the "fragrance of his nuptial quilt"; Julie, however, cannot bear their separation and follows him. Knowing that the French military will execute any soldier who hides his wife in the barracks, the captain tries to reason with his wailing wife, who looks lovely in her dishevelment: "Do you think I don't understand the love in your heart? Military law is strict. . . . An intelligent woman like you must understand." Julie clings tenaciously to his left arm, "her tears like pear blossoms in rain and peonies in fog." Deadlocked for an hour in her grip and seeing that the sun is setting, the captain suppresses the pain in his heart, musters his courage, and reaches down with his right hand. Grasping his pistol, he shoots his wife in the chest. "Fallen, she appeared as a crescent moon or a withered flower, traces of smoke lingering in the air as her pretty soul returned forever to the land of the dead." Lingering briefly on the captain's sorrowful contemplation of the corpse of his wife, who failed to understand either patriotism or military discipline, Xi's narrative ends on a note of admiration: "His example shames those who dress as soldiers and depart from home but leave their hearts with women."[84]

The story set in the Qing draws on the popular genres of romance (*yanqing xiaoshuo*) and revenge fiction (*fuchou xiaoshuo*). It relates a courtesan's revenge throat-cutting of a corrupt official on behalf of a man who tried but failed to avenge his father's fatal persecution. The narrator (Xi) notes that "such an act is rare even among men, let alone among women." The story recounts the sacrifice of the courtesan Yingying, a beautiful and witty young woman who "fell into the mud" when her family was reduced to poverty. After a lengthy separation from her scholar-lover Sheng, who fruitlessly left his wife and children (and her) to find his father's tormentor, she reencounters him at a riverboat banquet. Reduced to working as a boatman, he tearfully relates his failed efforts. Yingying listens, smiles, and says, "You are alone and weak. How can you be an assassin? You have a person who understands you [*zhiyin*], who will die for you. Why toil as a servant?" Poor and eager to avenge his father, Sheng accepts her offer and her bracelet. The season turns from spring to autumn, and Sheng hears that the corrupt official has taken a new concubine. After running low on funds, Sheng moves to a temple to economize. One evening an old woman brings him a small sealed package that contains "a wisp of beard hair, freshly cut and tinged with blood." The next day he learns that the official has died after a meal with one of his concubines. The eyes of the corpse protrude like those of a poisoned ghost. Sheng burns the beard hair, makes pancakes with the ashes as a sacrifice to his father, and then eats them to celebrate his filial revenge of his father's persecutor. Because she executed the murder, Yingying is sentenced to death by dismemberment for the crime of a concubine's murder of her master. After Sheng arrives at the execution ground, the official's family requests that the executioner "proceed by fine cuts." Sheng prostrates himself, witnesses Yingying's exceptionally lengthy period of torture, and faints (fatally) as Yingying expires.

Although the two classical stories are quite different, both feature strong-willed women who make decisions that prove consequential to their male partners. Both female protagonists demonstrate the extremity of their commitment through bodily sacrifice. The plot of the French story, with its mixture of patriotic loyalty, twisted sleeves, and death by a husband's pistol, is somewhat unusual in its hybrid mix of elements; the second story has much in common with Late Imperial scholar-courtesan romances, in which courtesans at times evinced implacable devotion to scholars they often equaled or exceeded in talent.[85] This story speaks to female heroism and self-sacrifice in the service of a lover's performance of filial duty. Although the emphasis on the woman's determination and her bloodied corpse in each is striking, there is nothing that conveys the social or ideological concerns of the May Fourth moment. If these were Xi's only stories, they might merely indicate her literary taste and preoccupation with female sacrifice. There is no public in these stories, though their narration assumes a popular admiration for heroism.

Xi's third and longest story, "The Bitter Happiness of Little Love" (*Xiao'ai zhi kule*), is written in a different register and belongs in the realm of amateur May Fourth fiction. This suggests Xi's broader reading habits. This story hews to social realism and focuses on the ills and inequalities of contemporary society. It is the only story that the editor of the volume clearly categorized as "fiction" (*xiaoshuo*), and it is written in May Fourth vernacular. It is set in two locations: a village that (like Xi's) was not far from Shanghai, and Xi's contemporary Shanghai. The name of the female protagonist substitutes the character for the modern emotion of "love" (*ai*) for the older and more commonly used character for "sentiment" or "passion" (*qing*). Ai, as opposed to *qing*, invokes the New Culture reform of emotion.[86]

Little Love, like Xi, grew up poor in "an isolated and confined village," without a father. "There was nothing good to eat and no fun to be had." Her brother worked in Shanghai, "ate rich food, wore silk, spent money like water," and "even rode in a foreign car with gentlemen to watch opera." Exposed, by her brother, to the infectious desires of the city, Little

Love begins to find country life tiresome, suffers from her mother's scolding, and dreams of fashionable clothing. When she is thirteen her brother visits, bringing with him some beautifully patterned cloth. His stories of the city fall on her ears "like flowers from heaven." He says there is no value to country life and advises her to pursue her prospects: "Shanghai is a place where you can easily make a killing" (*laoqian de difang*). Little Love becomes so excited that it disturbs her sleep. When her mother hears that Little Love can earn money in Shanghai, "for the sake of the money, [her mother gives] permission for her to go."

After a year in Shanghai, Little Love wears beautiful clothing and fashionable jewelry and spends her evenings attending opera and visiting amusement halls: "everything she had wished for in her former rural life." However, this is because her brother has sold her to a brothel. It is not a first-rank establishment, and "her spiritual suffering [is] beyond description." She is controlled by the madam and has lost "her right to freedom" (*ziyoude quanli*). She does not even have ownership of what she wears. Clothing is shared by the prostitutes who can only touch it while they work; otherwise it is locked up. If she stains anything or if she returns alone the madam whips her flesh into bloody pulp. Soon she is entertaining guests every night, like a "public plaything" (*gonggong de wanju*). Her flesh is not just lacerated by her procuress's cruelty; it is cankered by sexually transmitted disease. She recalls her former village life, which is now a bucolic memory: "sitting in the shade of trees, singing folksongs at the riverbank, eating wild fruit in the woods."

One day, while strolling in a Shanghai park, her sores covered by fine clothing, she encounters a hometown acquaintance. She chats with him briefly but disappears before he can ask questions. When he returns to their village, his neighbors surround him, eager to hear of his time in the city. He tells them that he has seen Little Love wearing silk and beautifully adorned with gold rings, earrings, and a necklace. "I think she must have made a fortune. But she only spoke a few words to me and ran away. I guess she wanted to avoid being seen with a poor country bumpkin." Everyone thinks Shanghai must be "a great place to make a killing." and the women who listen envy Little Love's happiness.[87]

In this unusual amateur work of May Fourth fiction, Xi takes up the spaces of the city in which she lived, worked, and occasionally enjoyed a leisure outing with her friend Shufen. The alleyways in the vicinity of her office were full of brothels, which provided spaces for the banqueting that was a regular feature of commercial life.[88] Courtesans and prostitutes were everywhere in the city, rushing to banquets on rickshaws or lingering under streetlamps. Xi would have passed them frequently as she returned home in the evenings, dressed in her homemade clothes. They were ubiquitous topics in print, tabloid gossip columns, advertisements, fiction, and reportage, including news of a contemporary Protestant-led campaign to abolish prostitution in the International Settlement.[89] Xi's story speaks to the relentless economic pull of the city, the material desires of sojourners, female and male, and the commodification of women's bodies. Although some features of the story link it to late Qing Shanghai fiction (which is often set in brothels or offers catalogues of courtesans), the exclusive interior view of a single prostitute—with no authorial interest, exploration, or even identification of individuated male clients or potential love interests—is unusual.[90] Little Love does not seek to escape her position through marriage. The portrait dwells instead in bleakness and irony. There is no rhetoric of social equality or female emancipation here. Nonetheless, Little Love's strongly gendered individual perspective, desires, and pain; her consciousness of oppression (articulated in modern terms as "the loss of her right to freedom"); her concerns about individual ownership; and the dark portrait of her profit-seeking family speak to New Culture and May Fourth critiques and concerns.

THIS STUDY BUILDS on and draws together work by historians of Republican China, the May Fourth Movement, Shanghai, and gender, print culture, law, and finance in China's modern transformations, a rich foundation of scholarship that makes possible the interpretation here of the diverse elements of the Xi-Tang case and the broad range of primary materials required to fathom its mysteries. The primary sources for this study necessarily reach across Shanghai's newspapers (Chinese, English, and Japanese); associational and professional journals; women's associations and publications; Chinese commercial, police, native-place association, and court archives; and US, French, Japanese, and British commercial, diplomatic, and private archives.

This book traces the experiences and actions of Xi Shangzhen, Tang Jiezhi, and their social networks as they navigated the institutional and social changes of their time. The emphasis on the role of commercial culture in Shanghai's social and political transformation, the gendered commercial workspace of a newspaper, and the stock exchange as a product of the May Fourth moment offer a new perspective on this era. Attention to the vernacularization of new ideas in the activism of business circles that preceded May Fourth and informed its language invites reinterpretations of this movement that integrate, rather than ignore, the agency and ideational role of business and capitalism.

The chapters that follow excavate ideological arenas and flashpoints of the newly instantiated public of the Chinese Republic. The threads of the Xi-Tang case connect these historical themes to individual lives and events as they were experienced. The emergence and demise of Xi Shangzhen, an educated working woman whose suicide would be upheld as that of a "new woman" martyr, and of Tang Jiezhi, a now forgotten US-educated social activist who overstepped the bounds of what was publicly tolerable in China, were tied to the contradictory social, cultural, and ideological formations of the early Republic, which created expectations and spaces of possibility for working out the egalitarian categories of citizen, public, democracy, and national sovereignty. In this moment of public reckoning with financial capitalism, the stock exchange was marketed as a tool for national salvation. In the wake of the stock exchange bubble, Tang and his colleagues in finance were fatefully branded "fat bellied," and "traitorous merchants." The juxtaposition of these lives in this moment, as viewed through the medium of the social organizations and media that sustained the new public, highlights the interconnection of themes that are sometimes viewed in partial combination but rarely all integrated in a close reading of everyday life: gender transformation, nationalism and the stock market; judicial independence and human rights discourse; suicide and modernity; and the intertwining of Chinese and foreign lives, political institutions, and media flows in a semicolonial city.[91]

The activism and profuse social commentary aroused by the Xi-Tang affair coalesced around the two key venues of the imagined public that were associated with May Fourth democracy and modern cultural change: the print public and public associations. The boundaries and constituency of these public venues were in the process of definition in this era, as was their ability to represent the public. Mapping the traces of the republican public, this book excavates three contemporary issues of great sensitivity in the ferment of this era. Chapter 2, which follows, sketches transformations in gender relations accompanying the creation of a Chinese republic that constituted one essential lens of signification for Xi's suicide. Here the narrative reinforces but also complicates understandings of gender transformation in this period by examining how the suicide of a new woman revealed fissures in the modern category of "woman." The resulting account of gender transformation qualifies the broad narrative of gender progress that often characterizes the era, and darkens the picture. Chapter 3 tells the story of the 1921 Shanghai stock exchange bubble in which Xi's money disappeared. If elements of the financial picture remain murky, copious records and commentary on the financial bubble illuminate public understandings of the market in the context of a republic and the emergence of finance capitalism, comprising a second realm of signification for the suicide. The launching of the first stock exchange by prominent members of the Chamber of Commerce drew on the economic nationalism of this moment. The stock exchange, indeed, was introduced as a means of fending off foreign incursions into the Chinese economy. Like the Republic itself, the stock exchanges, though advertised as salvific, proved empty. Chapter 4 takes up the records of the legal case to probe public understandings of justice, both formal and informal, in the Republic, examining ideas of virtue, equality before the law, and the development of a modern judiciary; the realm for public understanding of the trial; and the brief judicial reform movement it engendered. Chapter 5 concludes the study by probing the character of these democratic ventures in the context of the indeterminacy of the Chinese state.

The arenas of gender, economy, and law were constitutive elements of the imagined democratic and more egalitarian nation that inspired the new public realm. These arenas also offered spaces for the redefinition of politically, socially, and culturally legitimate behaviors. In the multiple registers of the unstable virtual public in print and the public associations that claimed to represent the public, a growing number of voices would make themselves heard, all of them grappling with the failures of the new Chinese Republic, democracy, and capitalism, as they debated them in print culture and as they experienced them in everyday life.

CHAPTER TWO

The New Woman, the Ghost, and the Ubiquitous Concubine

Miss Xi. Miss Xi. For personhood and reputation you sacrificed
    your life.
Who among women does not sympathize with you and go forth to
    fight?
Exterminating those demons in human clothing,
Brightening the future for China's women.

—*Shibao*, October 15, 1922, reader poem

The bright sun must illuminate this dark injustice,
Hear the voices of the public, and uproot this evil.
Only then may we release [Xi's] regrets to the earth.

—*Shibao*, October 14, 1922, reader poem

AT FIRST GLANCE, in terms of sheer newspaper column space, public concern with the Xi case converged on disputatious issues relating to gender and sexuality. The multiple female figures—new woman, suicide, concubine—linked by media narratives to the historical Xi Shangzhen existed as both fantasies and real-life subjects of historical transformation. The contradictory associations of these female types, now bound up together in a perplexing case that implicated a politically outspoken man, made the Xi suicide a lightning rod for controversy over the promises and failures of the Republic.

Those who wrote about Xi Shangzhen's death wrestled with the conundrum of a suicide by an educated woman in a professional office. As the dramatist and film director Zheng Zhengqiu expressed it:

[Xi] was an educated woman, a woman who had been baptized in the new thought, who promoted women's careers, and set a model by her conduct. She courageously served others of her sex. How can it be that she has died, and moreover, not of illness, but that she hung herself while full of life, and with an electrical cord? [She] should have preserved her life for the sake of society, but instead she [cut off her breath] with the electrical cord. When this tragic news spread, it created shock waves in society.[1]

A woman who had been "baptized in the new thought" was the wrong sort of woman to commit suicide. Tang Jiezhi was also the wrong kind of man to get involved in this kind of trouble. Zheng Zhengqiu and the early Chinese Communist Party member Chen Wangdao intervened, in different venues, to soften public opprobrium against Tang and warn people not to believe rumors. Zheng prefaced his essay by firmly repudiating "voguish words of attack." ("This is very important!"). He insisted that commentators should "absolutely not smear people" or "wildly spread rumors."[2] Zheng and Chen both deflected analysis of Tang's behavior by foregrounding instead the challenges that an unreformed society posed for working women. Tang's critics preoccupied themselves, in contrast, with statements made at the inquest that seemed to blur or violate the distinction between a modern, sexually integrated workplace and an older domestic space of cloistered women, the traditional realm of wives and concubines. This was the focus of essays submitted to a special newspaper supplement, entitled "Deceased Woman's Edition," which showcased women's responses to Xi's death. (The editor noted in his preface, "These articles were all sent by women. This is a positive phenomenon.").[3] An article signed "Miss Hui Shi" explained the problem from this perspective:

> Tang's announcement says there was no such thing as his wanting to take her as his concubine. However, he said in court: "Even supposing she didn't want to, why would she take this drastic measure?" I want to ask for an explanation of the phrase, "didn't want to." Was she unwilling to be a concubine, or unwilling to receive Tang's aid of 5,000 yuan? When a person is in trouble and someone is offering a lot of money, would she kill herself? And especially why would she kill herself in the office of the great charitable Journal of Commerce managing director?[4]

Lust for concubines was out of place in the modern office. Another submission sarcastically mocked Tang as a pioneer of women's employment who should have borne no likeness to the polygynous master male (who was privileged in Chinese legal and literary tradition):[5] "The respectable managing director professes to modern learning. He directs a newspaper to promote public opinion. He hires female employees to promote women's vocations. Why would such a strange thing happen in his office?"[6]

Zheng Zhengqiu and Chen Wangdao were disinclined to implicate Tang. They were similarly disinclined to broach another disturbing feature of the story—an element that people who professed "the new learning" might dismiss as old-fashioned superstition. The event drew meaning from ideas of revenge suicide and widely held beliefs in ghosts, beliefs that were implicit in the logic of the essays in the "Deceased Women's Edition." According to popular belief in retribution, the suicide of a person who suffered unjust grievances created a store of bad *qi* (life energy). If the grievances went unredressed, the suicide became an aggrieved ghost. The suicide location determined the location of the ghost.

For New Culture intellectuals who were inclined toward a binary view of tradition and modernity, a creeping stain of the supernatural suffused the case, surfacing in the shadows of suicide and concubinage. If new-style women committed suicide and became ghosts and if men "who professed the new learning" were trying to turn educated women into concubines, how could such figures usher forth a secular and scientific future? Even more disturbing perhaps was the way in which details of the case revealed the time confusions of the Republic, the things that persisted in new guise amidst the aspirational figures of the new order. The everyday signaling of new women, new men, and new learning in newspapers and prescriptive literature served as a neon advertisement, a transporting pedagogy to convey travelers beyond the Chinese time-space distortions of the unfulfilled present into a future that was already familiar from circulating accounts of Euro-American experience. But the self-destruction of an imagined new woman suggested that the path to this future was unclear. The lights that promised to show the way were going out.

THE CITIZEN AND THE WOMAN IN TIME

In China as elsewhere, ideas of gender were central to ideals of equality, democracy, and the modern nation. Because the family figured as a microcosm of the state in Confucian thinking, reformers and revolutionaries aimed to retool the family as they reconceptualized the state. The intellectual architects of social equality accordingly attacked the gender hierarchy that was naturalized in traditional families. Although Confucian texts had always understood the family as deeply political, modern attacks on the traditional family heightened the political significance of intimate relations.[7] The print media of the Republic reinscribed the family with new political meanings, amplifying new pedagogies in news stories, fiction, and drama that stoked public fascination with gender, particularly the figure of the new woman (and her relation to the new man).

Styles of marking gender thus appeared as ways of marking time. Formative events—colonialism and the late nineteenth-century circulation of

European ideas in China; the collapse of the dynasty and creation of a republic; the New Culture call to reject Confucian culture—gave new meaning to categories of old and new. Particular acts, spatial locations (rural/urban; coastal/inland), or social types took on an imaginative connection to moments in progressive time. In semicolonial China, people who embraced an evolutionary vision of progress experienced the disorderly present as the "not yet" of an imagined future. Their compulsive labeling of old and new elements in the flux of the everyday facilitated a sort of mental order-keeping that undergirded belief in progress.

From the time Chinese intellectuals began to conceive of a new political order, the subject of women emerged as a key concern, as exhibit A, so to speak, of the new society. After Japan's shattering 1895 defeat of the Qing state, intellectuals denounced both the Manchus and the imperial order for turning the Chinese people into slavish subjects. As new spaces for the public materialized in the contact zones of treaty ports like Shanghai and in overseas intellectual networks, particularly in Japan, intellectuals called for the liberation of women as essential to the project of creating a republic of citizens. The transformation of women, and particularly the creation of the female citizen, emerged as a goal in itself and an emblem of the transformation of Chinese subjects into citizens on a new basis of equality.

Intellectuals who styled themselves as "new" identified the dynastic state and the hierarchical family as dual culprits in the production of a servile culture. As the modern categories of "the people" and "women" entered political discourse in the 1890s, gender inequality appeared as an obstacle to the sovereignty of citizens. Reformers thus fostered schools for Chinese girls. By the turn of the century, a small number of educated and vocal women had gained visibility as participants in the growing print public in China's cities and in sojourning communities in Japan.[8]

Late Qing reform intellectuals frequently compared women's historical victimization to that of the Chinese people. In his 1897 treatise *On Benevolence,* Tan Sitong called for ideological transformation to end the "master-slave relationship" between men and women in the interest of a new "self-sovereignty" that would enable women to contribute equally to society.[9] Liang Qichao described women as slaves and even parasites until they could contribute to the economy. (Both men assumed a male-defined standard of work.) As "slaves of slaves," oppressed doubly by nationality and gender, women required liberation.[10] Kang Youwei promoted self-sovereignty for all people, men and women, as a "law derived from geometrical axioms" and the basis for equality and independence.[11] Such arguments, which presented women as a universal national category (as Chinese women or female citizens)—a radical departure from earlier female kinship or generational identities (i.e. mothers, wives, or daughters)—anticipated women's placement into a newly proportionate relationship of equality with men. [12]

Once adopted, the ostensibly more egalitarian categories of citizens, people, and women revealed their own exclusions and fractures in the Republic. After the parliament denied women voting rights, a determined group of suffragists argued for this right on the basis of common membership in an educated revolutionary elite. These women's self-positioning as disadvantaged but meritorious citizens suggests the naturalized class hierarchies that lurked within the categories of both citizen and woman. To elite sensibilities, the vast number of illiterate women (like the broad mass of men) did not possess the requisites for modern citizenship.[13] Nor did these elite women articulate a common identity with nonelite women, whether urban or rural.

One exception to this rule was the anarchist He-Yin Zhen, who, in 1907–1908, questioned whether "women's right to vote should be concentrated in the hands of a few rich ladies." She criticized the subordination of gender equality to nationalism and the blindness of both to the subordination of laboring people. Her more radical (if marginal) feminism opposed, not only monarchy and colonialism, but also capitalism and the state. A dissenting voice against the nationalist stream of history, she insisted on women's liberation as a moral necessity in itself, one that, in breaking with foundational gender hierarchies, was key to the universal abolition of hierarchy and the liberation of all.[14]

He-Yin Zhen aside, most moderns identified with the progressive time of the nation and took for granted the elite character of citizenship. Imagining the future entailed the bifurcation of "woman" into two categories of time. Only women with a modern education shone a path to the future. Other women lingered in darkness as slaves and parasites. Coexisting in the present, they stuck out like wallflowers at the dance of modernity. Worse, like vampires, they threatened the lifeblood of the moderns. The discordant elements of Xi Shangzhen's suicide presented a puzzle. What sort of woman was Xi really, and where did she belong on the roadmap to China's future?

THE PRINT PRODUCTION AND ADJUDICATION OF THE NEW WOMAN

Xi Shangzhen reached young adulthood in the dawn of the "new woman" (*xin funü* or *xin nüxing*), a global figure who emerged in China with the new Republic. The appearance of women's journals, beginning with *Chinese Girls' Progress* (1898), marked the print production of woman as a subject linked to new conceptualizations of time.[15] The women's journals that multiplied rapidly in the first two decades of the twentieth century, the era of the female student, catalyzed a circle of elite literate women who sought educational, social, and political, engagement. The mainstream press, in parallel, filled columns with notices of women's meetings and editorials on "the woman question."

Late Qing reformers conceived of women's social value as mothers of citizens, women's educators, or women's physicians, activities that did not violate the separation of the sexes. Some reformers denied women's prior accomplishments. Liang Qichao, for example, championed women's education but derided the earlier figure of the talented woman (*cainü*) as dependent and idle.[16] In contrast, the female educator Xue Shaohui emphasized female self-cultivation, building on the *cainü* tradition. Revolutionaries envisioned more radical forms of agency, updating the figure of the female heroine (*nü haojie*), who appears in modern guise in widely-reproduced photographs of female revolutionary brigades in 1911.

Such bold promotion of female revolutionaries faded under the conservative politics of Yuan Shikai., who suppressed revolutionary radicalism. The nationally distributed reformist journal, *Women's Eastern Times* (*Funü shibao*, 1911–1917), which was edited by the prominent writer Bao Tianxiao, featured more modestly updated virtuous and talented women often in familial roles, comforting images that marketed well. To supplement the mostly male-authored articles, Bao solicited material from female writers. At a time of limited female literacy, he nonetheless estimated that 90 percent of his readers were male.[17] Bao promoted the new social category of woman in a commercial package embellished with portraits of delicate and elegant women. It was in this journal that the sixteen-year-old Xi Shangzhen published an early essay in 1914, this one with a byline that proclaimed its female authorship. Bao, her fellow provincial, also taught at her school and likely encouraged her submission. Xi's essay makes no reference to gender. It considers instead the character of Chinese writing at a moment when the classical language and ornate styles of writing were coming to be seen as obstacles to literacy.[18]

The more robust new woman figure, in formation at the inception of the Republic, emerged into full prominence in the proliferating New Culture and May Fourth press, displacing the talented, willowy *cainü*. Educated women gained public prominence in an increasing variety of women's associations.[19] Editors named at least eight journals for the new woman (*xin funü*), the first of which appeared in Shanghai (1920), followed by Beijing, Guangzhou, Tianjin and Nanjing. At approximately the same time,

Shanghai newspapers began to publish women's supplements. These evoked a growing female readership and brought women's rights, education, health, and Western-style scientific home management into everyday conversation.[20] In essays and social movements, men and women who would modernize China took on the public project of promoting or themselves embodying the educated and socially engaged new woman.

New Culture intellectuals indicted patriarchal culture for the Republic's failures, caricaturing the classical "three obediences and four virtues" that constrained women. The new woman was defined by what she was not: not traditional and especially not Confucian. If ubiquitous in public discussion, there was little consensus on her character. Hu Shi described the new woman in 1918 as someone who "wears unusual clothing and lets her hair flow long. . . . [Her] language is radical, [her] behavior inclines toward the extreme. She does not believe in religion and does not conform to ritual convention."[21] In 1919, the new editor of the widely circulating liberal *Ladies' Journal*, Shen Yanbing (Mao Dun), castigated an earlier "good-wife and virtuous motherism" and emphasized activism.[22] The socialist *Women's Critic* (*Funü pinglun*) stressed self-reliance and social activism.[23] The new woman's vessel of meaning contained an essentialized universal human being. Nonetheless, being marked female, she was inevitably sexualized. With few exceptions, a late Qing vision of future androgyny (shown in Figure 2.1) was not fulfilled. The new woman was recognizably feminine. Hu Shi would have her hair unpinned and long; radicals would have it short.[24] What was certain was that her hair would not escape notice.

There was also something elusive about the new woman. The thicket of translated Western and Japanese feminist writing abundantly featured foreign models, but less so successful contemporary Chinese women. Most Chinese discussion emphasized obstacles to women's liberation. The articulation of women's problems reached an apogee in 1922 when Zhang Xichen, editor of *Ladies' Journal* established the Association for Research on the Woman Question to examine economic, educational, and legal obstacles to women's rights.[25]

Real-life new women were scarce in Xi Shangzhen's brief adulthood, a small minority in the minority population of women in a largely male sojourner city.[26] It was still the case that few young women "of good family," to use a common euphemism, ventured forth in public. Guidebooks reveal women's exoticism for their target male audience. Late nineteenth-century Shanghai guidebooks promoted urban sexual opportunities, trading on imaginative connections between the city and financial, culinary, and sexual desires.[27] In the Republic, books on the etiquette of interacting with prostitutes multiplied in tandem with the city's brothels. Guidebooks offered practical advice and a vicarious taste of urban women and brothel culture for men who simply dreamed of Shanghai.[28] The expanding genre of "Shanghai fiction," which spanned the late Qing and Republican Eras and circulated nationally, fed the demand for such material.[29] Male voyeurism adapted to encompass new types of women, who provided fresh fodder for literary evocations of the city.

Illustrators took up women's growing urban visibility. A cartoon from 1909 from a series entitled "The Shop of New Learning" depicted women's spatial and sartorial accouterments past, present, and future, as indicators of social progress. In the image, a cloistered woman (past) peeks through her window blinds at a woman in a rickshaw on the street (present). Two androgynous figures in pants and hats walking directly on the street suggest the future (Figure 2.1).[30]

Attention to women's changing appearance continued in the new era, with a narrowed emphasis on past and present only, as if the future had arrived along with the Republic. A 1919 cartoon series published in *Crystal,* "Chinese Women Past and Present," contrasted the posture, bound feet, and hidden bodies of old-style women with the boldly striding new women, with detailed attention to individual body parts; for example, modern unbound feet or clipped fingernails (Figure 2.2).[31] Editions of the popular *One Hundred Views of Women* minutely described eighteen parts of women's bodies (hair, eyes, mouths, tongues, ears, necks, bones, skin, eyebrows, teeth, etc.) and mundane aspects of urban women's daily lives.[32]

In an era of stillborn republican institutions and a dishonorable state, the new woman was exalted for embodying new republican ideals that accorded with citizenship.[33] As advocates for women's rights called on women to help build the new society, they proposed that women should exemplify personhood (*ren'ge*). Modern personhood was what Chinese people needed to break free from slavish old culture. As Chen Duxiu diagnosed the situation in *New Youth,* the spearhead journal of the New Culture Movement:

> The three principles of the Confucians are the source of morality and politics. Ruler guides subject, father guides son; husband guides wife. Subjects, sons and wives are subordinates without independent autonomous personhood. [Thus] the virtues—loyalty, filiality, and chastity—belong not to the morality of sovereign individuals, but instead to the morality of slaves who are subordinate to others.[34]

Chinese interpreters of personhood evoked independent thinking, self-reliance, and individual moral integrity as universal values for citizens.[35]

2.1 Women as Icons of Progressive Time ("Women Yesterday, Today, and Tomorrow"). *Tuhua ribao* 10:9 (1909).

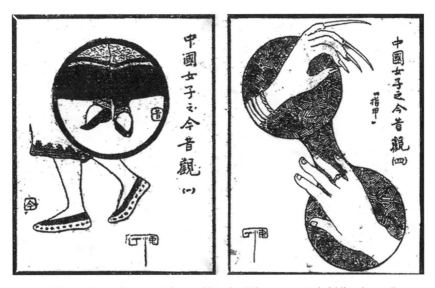

2.2 Illustrations of women's feet and hands. "Zhongguo nüzi zhi jin xi guan" (Chinese women past and present). *Jingbao,* March 21, 1919; April 6, 1919.

Personhood as a legal concept was at this moment under discussion by lawmakers; the concept acquired legal significance with the Republican Civil Code in 1929, which established a gender-neutral definition of personhood for all people, beginning at birth and ending at death.[36] As with other foundational notions associated with citizenship, in the early Republic the unrealized concept took on unusual rhetorical importance in public print.

Public concern for female chastity did not vanish, but it was rhetorically submerged and under attack by New Culture writers as obsolete.[37] The ideal of chastity nonetheless lurked in the shadows of personhood. The two concepts were entangled in the lingering contemplation of suicide, which had been a Late Imperial proving ground for female virtue.

SUICIDE IN THE TIME OF MODERNITY

Suicide, like virtue and family, required rethinking in the Republic. New Culture writers identified suicide as a failure of will, linking it to China's deficient culture and weak global position. As journalist Kang Qiuxin put it, "Alas! Suicide is a tragedy. Everyone knows this. But why do people today hasten toward suicide like a flock of ducks? Is it because the people of our country have a special disposition for committing suicide?"[38]

Journalists agreed that suicides were on the rise. Newspapers provided the evidence: "Alas! Witnessing so many recent suicides, we see they have become a contemporary fashion. If readers doubt this, please look at the latest Shanghai papers."[39] The press featured daily notices, with particular attention to female suicides.[40]

Even so, not all female suicides were of equal interest. Not long after Xi Shangzhen's death, Shanghai newspapers also reported the suicide of a daughter-in-law with the surname Guo, who had married into the Cai family. She hung herself from her bedpost after enduring her mother-in-law's abuse. Even though this was the second daughter-in-law suicide in the Cai family, the incident produced little controversy because it fit a typical pattern and location. A journalist contrasted the depressing familiarity of the Cai case with the shock of Xi's suicide: "Xi Shangzhen's suicide has rightly riveted society. [Now] another girl has committed suicide. [However] the details are extremely different. One is [a problem] for society. One is a family [matter]. One involves a new-style woman and one involves an old-style woman. It is nonetheless clear that suicide is women's only means of protest. How lamentable."[41]

This comment draws a categorical distinction between the suicides and their significance. An "old-style" woman's suicide was simply "a family matter." The girl's personal name is not given; only the natal and marital families. The suicide of a new-style woman, in contrast, was a unique event and a worthy social problem for analysis. Although New Culture journalism regularly criticized the cruelties of the traditional family, the individual suicides of old-style women were like background noise. By 1922, suicides of mistreated daughters-in-law conformed so obviously to critiques of tradition that they sustained little attention beyond confirming the imperative to overhaul the family. Xi's suicide was social news, in contrast, because the suicide of a new woman called into question the morality of Chinese modernity.

This differential treatment illuminates the reconsideration of suicide in accordance with the changing aesthetics of time, the individual, and morality. Female suicide had been an important site of a Late Imperial system of state-verified virtue that rewarded chaste suicide. Not all suicides met the standards of virtue. Bureaucrats investigated which families qualified for honors, classifying other suicides as hasty, deceptive, or forced. Male compilers of virtuous suicide narratives, often embellished with woodcut illustrations, variously illuminated virtue and garnered prestige, demonstrated literary connoisseurship, or profited from sales of entertaining, erotic, or edifying texts. In law and in popular understandings of ghostly agency, suicides—by disrupting cosmic order and engendering retributive violence—could express a powerful female agency, even if it necessitated self-destruction and the effects could only be posthumous.[42]

In the Republic, the exaltation of loyal or chaste suicides was called into question. But social sensibilities and state practice did not change immediately. Official rewards for virtue, which had been momentarily halted with the creation of a new state, were reinstated in May 1913 when the new parliament reasoned that renewed state promotion of chastity might correct the moral malaise of the young Republic. Honors for chastity and filial piety awarded in 1917 provided for the issuance to bereaved families of a commendatory plaque that was stamped in gold or silver with the presidential seal.[43] Public associations at times gathered to commemorate chaste suicides and promote individuals for state recognition. Such public ceremonies reveal the hybrid choreography of gender and virtue in the new era.

In August 1918, for example, 2,000 people gathered in Shanghai to honor the chaste suicide of seventeen-year-old Chen Wanzhen. The newspaper record reveals the meeting's improvisational mix of participants and ideals.[44] Organized under the auspices of the Shaoxing native-place association, women spoke first, with the mothers of several Shanghai notables signifying the public presence of "women's circles."[45] Included as guests were the feminist journalist Tan Sheying and several veteran female revolutionaries.[46] Shen Yibin, wife of the philanthropist Xu Jilong, chaired the meeting and delivered the eulogy. Senior women in the Chen family noted Chen's determination to follow her betrothed, Wang Jingshi, in death. Female students from the China Relief Committee for Women and Children (Zhongguo jiuji furuhui) sang a musical tribute. Businessmen and political notables subsequently spoke, including representatives of the Shanghai Garrison Command. Whereas some speakers praised Chen's chastity and the "positive impact of her death on social morality," Ge Pengyun, a nationalist activist, used his time at the podium to offer "bitter commentary" on the troubled relations between men and women. The meeting closed with band music and a display of elegiac calligraphy. The formulaic address of Shanghai Garrison Commander Lu Yongxiang was duly published ("Hers was the life of a very chaste woman . . . a noble example for all women in our society"). Ge's discordant speech was noted but not reproduced. Chen's Shaoxing compatriots obliquely registered the changed times by decoupling the suicide from old morality and emphasizing instead the newly sacralized nation: "This does not involve the rules or morality of the ancients. . . . For a girl to die for her fiancée is as noble as to die for one's country."[47]

The shifting moral status of suicide, which is hinted at in the heterogeneous speeches of this 1918 ceremony, is further evidenced by the relative paucity of such celebrations in the new era. These events were not uncontroversial. The Jiangsu governor saw fit to recommend that the Interior Ministry issue a plaque to Chen's family. In response, Hu Shi published an outraged broadside in *New Youth* in which he condemned the official encouragement of virtuous martyrdom as equivalent to the crime of murder. The landscape for virtuous male suicides (which were traditionally assessed in relation to political loyalty) was similarly shifting. Later the same year, when the former Qing official Liang Ji drowned himself to dramatize his loyalty to the fallen dynasty, he knew the public would no longer automatically read his suicide as manifesting virtue. Consequently, he drafted multiple testaments before his death to fix its meaning, expressing hope that his moral rectitude might reawaken that of the nation. Intellectuals variously condemned Liang's outmoded notion of loyalty, praised his integrity, or insisted that he was deranged. Nonetheless, his notoriety and deliberate fostering of anachronisms ensured public recognition of his agency. All the same, however, the new emphasis on the emancipation of the self-determining individual generally reframed suicide as abject behavior.[48]

Suicide continued to attract scrutiny as press-driven "public opinion" became an arbiter of value. Public discussion of suicide continued to probe individual morality, but the framework of the moral universe was no longer self-evident. Commentators also viewed suicides as a mirror of the morality of the new political order. Suicides that involved new social types, and particularly suicides by new women, attracted particular attention.[49] Public interest in Xi's death thus did not address female suicide in general. Rather, the suicide called into question the viability of the new woman, her agency, and the grip of the past on the present.

New Culture intellectuals described suicide as a symptom of the old culture or of the failures of the Republic to build a positive society. Suicide was the refuge of the wretched and victimized old-style woman, the foil to the public-spirited female citizen who would tackle social problems and build a better future. Literature that promoted the new criticized women's earlier ignorance, dependence, conservative and uncritical mindsets, vanity, passivity, and attraction to makeup and jewelry, echoing negative gender stereotypes. A full chapter of *Hundred Views of Women* focused on suicide, which it naturalized as female behavior: "Women's knowledge and reasoning are shallow and narrow. If they feel anger that has no outlet— either because they are ashamed of their dishonorable behavior or because they are unjustly wronged and cannot redress their grievance—resentment accumulates in their hearts and they think of suicide."[50] New Culture critics reformulated such gendered understandings in caricatures of old-style women, adding modern complaints about indifference to national progress as a key distinction between the old and the new woman.[51]

A *Shenbao* cartoon skewered the limitations of the old-style woman, depicting four options: (1) anger, (2) tears, (3) refusing food, and (4) suicide by hanging (Figure 2.3).[52] Like the guide to women, the illustration engaged readers in a shared voyeurism of female suicide, even as both expressed disapproval. As guidebook author Yun Shi opined, "The miserable conditions of these suicides are something that our ears cannot bear to hear and our eyes cannot bear to see. I just describe a few of them here for discussion over a cup of tea or following a cup of wine."[53]

Popular literature of this sort detailed cultural understandings that were not spelled out in other accounts. His narratorial delicacy notwithstanding, Yun Shi sketched the frequency, efficacy, and appearance of different suicide methods: throat-cutting ("infrequent in modern times"), hanging, starvation, drowning, poison, and firearms. Specific entries identified conventional locations and accessories as well as the appearance of the ghost:

2.3 The Suicidal Old-Style Woman. *Shenbao,* August 4, 1921.

Hanging is the most common means of female suicide. . . . It is extremely convenient, swift, and unlikely to be discovered before the deed is done. The usual location is the bedroom. A rope or waist sash is fastened around the neck and suspended from a high place, so the feet will clear the ground. The rope or sash constricts the neck, preventing breath. In an instant the woman enters the company of ghosts. If discovered quickly, the corpse is not notably different from life. But as time passes, the eyes open, the pupils protrude, the mouth opens, and a long tongue extends. . . . Therefore the ghosts of the hanged have protruding eyes and tongues.[54]

For New Culture writers who condemned Chinese tradition as suicidal, women's transformation betokened the creation of a new China. Advocates of new learning aimed to reform the family and engineer the new woman.[55] The new woman project began with a modern education that emphasized natural science as an antidote to "superstition" and skills as an antidote to dependency. The new woman achieved completion only when she emerged as an independent citizen. Contemporary illustrations typically

2.4 "Chinese Women Past and Present: Exercise."
Jingbao, June 30, 1919.

depicted an upright figure striding boldly forth, in a visual contrast with the stooped old-style woman, whose (invisible) bound feet necessitate the support of a maidservant (Figure 2.4). The new woman exercised her robust body to prepare for the purposeful work of citizenship.[56]

Although it was troubling when a new woman committed suicide, people still admired exceptional suicides. Indeed, from the moment of the new woman's conception there was something in her of the old-style woman. Late Qing narratives of new female exemplars—among them the French revolutionary Madame Roland and the Russian Sophia Perovskaia—tended to transpose the object of feminine sacrifice and loyalty from husbands onto the new nation. Stories of unconventional foreign women highlighted their selfless commitment and violent deaths.[57] Such tales, and stories about the Chinese female revolutionary Qiu Jin, implanted an ideal of willful martyrdom into the core of the new Chinese woman, as if to say that women's agency emerged most powerfully in their self-destruction,[58]

Xi Shangzhen's youth was nourished by such stories, a diet that may help explain the taste for female sacrifice in her stories. As a student at East City Girls' School (Chengdong nüxue), which was established in 1902 by the progressive educator Yang Baimin, Xi was exposed to a radical strain of nationalist feminism that rejected older beliefs as superstition and emphasized science and gender equality. The 1912 issue of the school journal *Female Student* opened with a fold-out photograph of female revolutionary soldiers. Pedagogical emphasis on female activism was bolstered by a sentimental appreciation of martyrdom. Chengdong students held a memorial ceremony for Qiu Jin, offering flowers, wine, and poetry to comfort the martyr's spirit.[59] Xi also studied briefly at Jingxiong Girls' School, which was founded after the 1911 Revolution by Qiu Jin's close friend, the political activist Xu Zhihua. The school's name, which translates to "Hero's Rival," was one of Qiu Jin's style names.[60]

Heroism and self-destruction entwined in such commemorations. At some point prior to her suicide, Xi penned a tribute for a chaste maiden with the family name Chen, who was betrothed to a man named Wang. This scrap of Xi's everyday handwriting was the only example to be chosen for posthumous dissemination in zincographic reproduction from among the various notes and letters preserved by her friend Shufen (Figure 2.5). The choice testifies to the social valuation of such tributes. Because the note is brief and undated and uses only family names, we cannot know whether this was Xi's response to the 1918 chaste suicide of Chen Wanzhen. Xi's admiration for the suicide is nonetheless striking: "She hanged herself twice and poisoned herself once, and was rescued each time. After she was watched for several days, she donned linen funeral garments and drowned herself in the river. She left a four-line poem beside her make-up case. . . . What a heroine!"[61] By this comment we may understand that in the eyes of Xi Shangzhen, a chaste and determined suicide called for acclaim.

In the Republic, suicide nonetheless posed problems for the agency of self-determining female citizens. The martyr Qiu Jin did not precisely commit suicide (though her refusal to flee capture ensured her execution). As a revolutionary, she could personify both modern agency and sacrifice. A similar commemoration of a suicide was more problematic for moderns, who strove to maintain the imagined fault lines that separated the new culture from the old. Suicide still commanded sufficient cultural capital to attract the admiration of radical iconoclasts. The interpretive challenge lay in the question of agency.

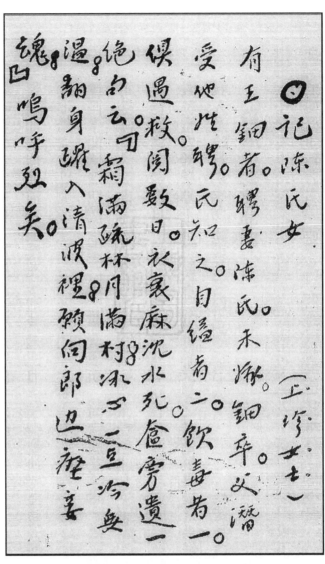

2.5 Xi's commemoration of Chen (Xi's name has been inserted in parentheses at bottom right). Reproduced from Wu Yugong, *Zisha zhi nüshuji: Xi Shangzhen canshi* (Shanghai: Zhongguo diyi shuju, 1922), 15.

FEMALE PROFESSIONS AND THE
EXCLUSIVITY OF PERSONHOOD

In 1919, the young Mao Zedong engaged in creative interpretation when he turned the suicide of a young Hunanese woman named Zhao Wuzhen into a modern social issue.[62] The novelty of his interpretation hinged on locating in Zhao's actions the elusive virtue of personhood (ren'ge), a term that was absent in the public discussion of Chen Wanzhen's 1918 suicide.

In contrast to those who praised Chen Wanzhen for exemplary chaste devotion, Mao embraced Zhao Wuzhen as a figure of protest against the patriarchal marriage system. Zhao slit her throat in a bridal sedan chair while being carried to the family home of her fiancé. In several short articles, Mao both affirmed her personhood and suggested its fleeting character. He acknowledged that Zhao's free will was constrained by her parents' insistence on her arranged marriage, but he disagreed that she was a purely passive victim. Choosing his words carefully, Mao argued that in her last moments, when "the snow-white knife was stained with fresh red blood[,] . . . her ren'ge also gushed forth, shining bright and luminous."[63] Her personhood was one with the flow of blood that took her life.

Tao Yi, a female member of Mao's New Study Society, elaborated on the logic of Zhao's personhood in her own article in Women's Bell:

> Though we should not say that Miss Zhao died "for love of freedom," we must recognize her as "one who sacrificed herself to reform marriage." If she were just a passive person trying to protect her freedom, why did she not commit suicide when she hid the knife . . . ? Why did she wait till she was in her bridal clothes, sitting in her bridal sedan chair? I doubt so many people would have known of her suicide or felt so troubled by her death if she had killed herself a day earlier, dressed as a regular daughter, sitting in a regular sedan![64]

Both Mao and Tao insisted that Zhao exercised agency and demonstrated personhood by means of her premeditated and strategically located suicide. Her action successfully inflicted financial damage on the families that oppressed her, and brought her name into public discussion.[65]

Though intent on endowing Zhao Wuzhen with personhood, Mao and Tao could make only limited claims for her agency because—like the Cai family's daughter-in-law—she lacked an independent existence in society. Had she been independent and employed, her carefully executed suicide would not have been the definitive mark of her personhood.

New Culture writer and educator Ye Shengtao, in responding to the animated public discussion of women's personhood in the same year, insisted that women should be entitled to personhood as human beings. However, he doubted that women historically possessed personhood: "Until recently there have been few independent women. Most women lacked authentic and substantial worldviews because they were cloistered. To say that women had inadequate or negligible personhood is no exaggeration."[66] Achieving authentic personhood in men's eyes was particularly hard for women. Writing in *Ladies Journal* in 1920, Shen Yanbing promoted equality as an evolutionary goal to "elevate women's personhood and ability, making them the same as men." Once women had been "raised up" they should enjoy human rights and the responsibilities of citizenship. In the meantime, he derided them as "totally lacking ability to reform the country, since they have none of the required qualifications." In short, he found it difficult to see how women could be made equal to men.[67]

Some female women's rights activists were more confident of women's personhood than their self-proclaimed male champions, but their writings nonetheless indicated that work remained to be done. Women's personhood needed encouragement and protection.[68] "Safeguarding personhood" was an explicit mission of the Association for Women's Suffrage, which was established in Shanghai in October 1922, a few weeks after Xi's death.[69] Wan Pu, a representative of the Beijing Society for the Advancement of Women's Suffrage, affirmed that such societies were needed to recover women's "lost personhood."[70]

The personhood that New Culture writers invoked was more an elite project or badge of distinction than a birthright. Women had to prove their agency before an adjudicating print public.[71] The recognition of women's personhood became an intellectual exercise, analogous to an earlier literary practice of celebrating female chastity (though personhood was recognized in the absence of state honors). Mao's essays on Zhao Wuzhen suggested that an exceptional young woman might demonstrate personhood from the confines of a marital sedan chair, but his comments were controversial. Most feminists aimed for women's *living* emancipation. This required education, without which women lacked discernment. Women's schools provided a necessary foundation—but education alone was insufficient.

New Youth editor Chen Duxiu had argued in 1916 that individual personhood depended on "the independence of individual property."[72] Confucian hierarchy and subordination obstructed both individual property and independent personhood. Women suffered from flawed personhood because of millennia of subordination and limited economic rights.[73] Only the economic self-sufficiency and status conveyed by purposeful occupations offered the freedom to act independently in public. Mature personhood thus required employment in society.[74]

New Culture advocates promoted women's professions or vocations (*funü zhiye*) as a transformational goal in the years just prior to Xi's death. Since women's vocations had just become a social issue, some commentators who tried to make sense of the uproar surrounding Xi's suicide tied it to this contemporary concern: "Since Miss Xi hanged herself in the *Journal of Commerce* office, the news has traveled far and near, and everyone has . . . published their views in the newspapers. . . . Why is this so? Isn't the reason that, at the dawn of women's vocations, there has been such an extreme setback?"[75] Xi's independent employment should have made her less susceptible to the self-destruction of suicide, but something must have gone wrong. One female essayist reasoned that Xi's suffering must have been exceptional:

> Xi Shangzhen was . . . a woman with a vocation. Now she has suddenly committed suicide. Furthermore she committed suicide at the *Shangbao* office. Whether or not you find this strange, this is not a hasty or insignificant [suicide] like that of a village girl who kills herself the instant she suffers an infinitesimal aggravation. I believe Xi Shangzhen's suicide reflects unusual pain and oppression.[76]

Assumptions about the liberatory logic of economic independence (and the suicidal character of uneducated women) suggested that only a great quantum of misery could explain the suicide of a woman with a profession.

Most circulating definitions of personhood and women's vocations restricted their achievement to a small minority. Not all jobs qualified. Depictions of the new vocational woman suggested that personhood was class exclusive. Concerns to protect personhood hinted further that modern women's personhood bore some resemblance to the older virtue of chastity.

In August 1922, a strike of Shanghai silk filature workers brought the economic plight of female factory workers to the attention of the urban public. The workers' dangerous conditions, poor pay, and long hours were sympathetically reported in many of the periodicals that covered Xi Shangzhen's suicide. Worker activism was crucial to the socialism advocated by journalists who wrote for the *Republican Daily,* for example. However, the language that such writers used to describe the two types of working women was quite different. Although female factory work was significant in other respects, it generally failed to meet the bar for personhood. Indeed, when writing about female employment in 1922, the sociologist Yi Jiayue identified female factory workers as slaves of capitalists. China's belated industrialization, compounded by oppressive culture, left women with only three options: they could sell their labor, prostitute themselves, or starve. For women, moreover, there was something about earning money that made factory labor and prostitution similar: "The former sells strength; the latter sells sex."[77]

The bar for personhood was high. As Chen Wentao explained in a special journal issue on female vocations, "Professions must be independent. Occupations not independent in character are only oppressed labor." He sketched four categories of female work: household labor, home handicraft production, factory work, and independent occupations (female shopkeepers or teachers). The first two types fell under the influence of husbands and family. Factory workers might exercise partial independence, but in his estimate only the fourth category (which described fewer than 1 percent of China's women) was fundamentally independent.[78]

Yi and Chen's typologies affirm the class-specificity of personhood and the critical role of independent vocations in determining women's social value. Ten years into the Republican Era, female suffrage remained controversial. Advocates invoked vocations as a prerequisite for this ultimate exercise of female citizenship. In the words of the Jingwu leader Chen Tiesheng, who also wrote for Tang's paper, only women with meaningful vocations could be granted the vote because only such women had attained independent personhood:

> Female doctors, female teachers, female secretaries, female businessmen and restaurateurs—only these count as independent and deserve the right to participate in government. As for those wives and daughters who ride in cars, play poker, mahjong, wear gold and diamonds and follow fashion, we absolutely cannot permit them to participate in government. They are only parasites on men, not themselves independent.[79]

Not only did dependence disqualify women from personhood, so did association with decadent lifestyles and female-identified consumption.[80] Added moral concerns threatened the personhood even of women who attained meaningful independent vocations. The comingling of men and women in a common workspace violated the canonical separation of the sexes. Women's education, like fashionable dress, could be contained in the home (in practice, most female students married and stopped work). Female careers, in contrast, threatened to muddy the separation of the sexes. This added a sexual charge to the public workspace and troubled concerns for female chastity, thus posing moral challenges to women's professional advancement. As explained in the anonymous article (which was possibly written by Xi) in Tang's paper :

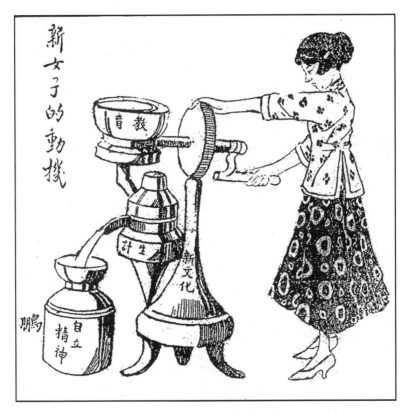

2.6 "How to Produce the New Woman." *Shanghai Gazette*, March 9, 1921.

To achieve equality there must first be an opening for women's work. At present this is difficult to speak of [because] the professional world is stubbornly closed to women. [But] there are two paths to progress. One is to elevate women's knowledge and morality . . . to enable them to take up professions without encountering abuse. The other is to break with old views that insist on the [sexually segregated] realms of "men outside, and women inside," so that women may be active in society and avoid being parasites.[81]

Newspaper illustrations (with the exception of titillating advertisements) commonly pictured the new woman alone or with female companions. One such cartoon shows the new woman operating a modern contraption with parts labeled "new culture," "education," "livelihood," and "self-reliance" (Figure 2.6). It was perhaps soothing to qualms about women's participation in a male-defined sphere that the process produced a liquid resembling milk.[82]

Even women's vocational schools rarely went so far as to envision women as actors in society. Most such schools, one author noted, promoted home economics rather than independent employment.[83] Although the goal of female vocations was broadly heralded, modernizers writing in *Ladies' Journal* and *Chinese Women's World* commonly elevated housework to the status of a profession, thus facilitating the maintenance of traditional gender boundaries while asserting equality and making professional work outside the home superfluous.[84] Others focused on women's "special endowments," naturalizing as particularly appropriate such jobs as teaching and nursing, which did not require mixing with men.[85]

Women who worked in male-defined spaces found their purity challenged. As one journalist opined, "All Chinese women's jobs—waitresses, saleswomen, movie stars—are no better than prostitution. Even respectable female schoolteachers cannot maintain their virtue. Talent and virtue cannot co-exist."[86] Personhood required that women work in society, but sexually integrated work stained their virtue with monetary and sexual desire. A 1921 *Shenbao* editorial celebrated the first female department store employees but worried that attractive women would be advanced over plainer ones. Their managers' motivations were suspect: "If you see women as rare commodities and hope to attract customers by using them, you will destroy women's personhood."[87] Writing in the leftist *Women's Critic*, Yang Zhihua decried the corrupting influence of workplace power relations. Some women attained high-quality jobs in banks, telegraph and telephone bureaus, but she questioned their ability to maintain independent personhood in the sobering sexual politics of the workplace: "Many . . . have no choice but to fan the farts of the men in charge."[88]

The New Culture press thus presented mixed messages. Recent scholarship has excavated a history of real new women: educators, physicians, writers, and political figures in the Republican Era.[89] Public discussion included the voices of many such women alongside the manifestos of their associations. The debate surrounding Xi's suicide featured the Women's Vocational Cultivation Society *(Nüzi zhiye lianxiu she),* the Society for the Advancement of Women's Suffrage *(Nüzi canzheng jijin hui),* a women's national products group *(Nuzi zhiquan gongsi),* and several women's schools. Their vocality prompted commentators to applaud the emergence of "women's circles," even as the suicide reinforced notions of female vulnerability.

The growing presence of actual new women suggests a disconnect between their existence and the tone of public discussion. The pessimistic fiction of the New Culture Era articulates a powerful critique of the traditional family but depicts an array of disturbing (and disturbed) bourgeois heroines—tubercular, suicidal, and lonely.[90] These heroines are rarely able to transform intellectual attainments into financial independence, happy relationships, or a meaningful public life. Whereas some female authors depicted the troubled psychology of new women, the new women created by male authors were often schematic or pitiable figures who reflected the morality of male characters rather than compel attention in their own right.[91]

Actualized new women enjoyed only limited portrayal in the programmatic New Culture press. A special "female vocations" issue of *Ladies' Journal,* for example, named just one contemporary Chinese career woman, Yuan Minfang of Hangzhou, who founded a private institute to teach poor girls handicrafts and literacy. Yuan depleted her family funds and was unsuccessful in attracting investors until her suicide prompted the Hangzhou gentry to support her school. The biographer's narration of her career merged the exemplary new woman with the virtuous suicide, concluding: "My greatest hope is that our nation's women might immediately take action to rival Madame Yuan's claim to fame!"[92] It cannot have been accidental that the author was drawn to an exemplary suicide, and moreover, one who reputedly swallowed gold, a mechanism of uncertain utility but familiar to Chinese readers of popular fiction. Despite the article's emphasis on personhood, the suicide elevated the portrait, as if a woman's accomplishment needed posthumous confirmation through inspirational self-destruction.

Yuan Minfang's virtue was confirmed by her death but also protected by the character of her work. A girls' school was a largely female space. Had her solicitation of male investors proved successful, that success might have undermined her hold on virtue. For women the modern virtue of personhood was not just fraught with qualifiers, but its achievement in practice could be nearly as inaccessible as state recognition for chastity in the Late Imperial Era.[93] The woman who worked in male spaces crossed a gendered boundary so imbued with virtue that its transgression made it nearly impossible to overcome the stain of the passage. Marked by association with men and the desire for money that employment entailed, the vocational woman was disturbing. As an exasperated reader expressed the problem of women's ambitions in the workplace: "When shall we sweep away such empty aspirations and forever make women trouble-free?"[94]

MODERN SOCIAL INTERCOURSE AND THE EROTICIZED PUBLIC

Although female vocations were hailed in Xi's time, professional women remained rare, perhaps no more than 1 percent of the adult female population.[95] Popular books like *One Hundred Views of Women* expressed their exoticism. Anticipating disbelief, the author wrote, "If you don't believe [such women exist, I provide] examples."⁹⁶ He fastidiously detailed the clothing styles, colors, and shoes worn by female students, teachers, and others, so that careful observers of Shanghai streets might recognize them. Because prostitutes, as a category of visible women, also increased in numbers in the city at this time, and because they mimicked the stylishness of female students, there was popular confusion.⁹⁷

Given this hyperattentiveness to women's visibility, it is not surprising that Xi's office suicide aroused fantasies of a sexualized workplace. The frisson of workplace intimacy sold newspapers. One observer described the case as an "injection of morphine" for newspapers and readers.⁹⁸ Newspapers sensationalized consideration of the desirability of female employment in male workspaces. Feminist responses to Xi's suicide highlighted the dangers of women's public intercourse.⁹⁹ As if visualizing one of his screenplays, Zheng Zhengqiu decried women's vulnerability in offices where the "lascivious thoughts" of employers "would be realized in lascivious actions, seducing the pure female."¹⁰⁰ Proponents of women's careers denounced gossip that exacerbated the awkwardness of the sexually integrated workplace, even when women were not subjected to sexual pressure: "When we see a female working among men its strangeness assumes a special character. If we don't say the woman is shameless, we say she has loose morals. If a male co-worker chats with her we suspect they have relations."¹⁰¹

Details of the Xi case were titillating, starting with the location of Xi's desk in Tang's office and the fact that she and Tang worked together in the evening. Tang telephoned Xi's family when she was ill; he was present at an earlier suicide attempt; their financial affairs were intertwined; her coworkers witnessed their violent arguments; and Tang himself called Xi's English teacher to cancel a scheduled session. Of particular concern was the testimony of Xi's family members that Xi stated she would wager her life in a struggle to make Tang yield. Most notorious was the claim that Tang's suggested Xi should become his concubine.¹⁰²

The mainstream papers steered clear of sexual gossip. The entertainment press, however, was less circumspect. A few days after Xi's death *Crystal* published a satirical poem depicting the social dynamics of Tang's office. The poem stands out for its explicit suggestion of office intimacy and its mocking portrayal of Xi as a dressed-up ingénue. The text features several terms for concubine to refer to the female secretary:

The Female Secretary: A Poem on Recent Events

The female secretary, beautifully aflutter
Enters, gripping pencil and pad,
Brightly dressed and lovely.

The boss adored you [concubine]. He invited you into his business.
You thought he was rich and sharp at finance.
You ransacked your storage chests and pockets.
You gave the boss your money.

Oh, the business war is rough and it shook the businessman.
Oh, the money is gone, never to return.
Oh, the boss lost his money and depleted his strength.
Oh, the woman lost her money and grew miserable.
Oh, she poured her tears in waves before the boss.
Oh, how could the boss face her again?

Smiling, the boss said,
"Please don't dislike me because I'm imperfect.
Your money is my money
I have a way to make amends.
Let me make you my concubine
In hunger I will feed you; in cold I will clothe you."

"What strange nonsense. What sort of employer are you?
What you say is madness. Don't be so crude.
Your concubine? I have no heart to be your concubine.[103]
But what can I do with empty pockets and money gone?
Let me to gulp down my sobs and end this with death."

The boss liked you so much.
But now that you are dead, the boss finds you unworthy.
Alas, the female secretary.[104]

The scandal of this poem lay in its unsentimental exposure of the sexual calculus of male employers and female employees. It punctured the chaste ideal of female careers by eroticizing Xi's secretarial get-up and her financial gamble. The office romance drew upon the canonically proscribed desires for sex and money (*se* and *cai*) that feminists avoided in order to preserve the new woman's virtue and keep her sex-free. The poem's devastating logic presented the career woman as complicit in workplace sexuality and unable to chart an independent course that might enable her to escape becoming a benighted concubine or a corpse.

A few days later, *Crystal* took the innuendo further with a piece by Zhang Danfu, a humor editor also employed by Tang's paper. Zhang cloaked his commentary in literary guise, a familiar strategy in a print culture in which news flowed across genres. Readers read fiction as an alternate mode of truth telling, seeking roman à clef details. In Zhang's riff on the Yuan dynasty play, "Prefect Qian Wisely Bestows Favor on Xie Tianxiang" by Guan Hanqing, readers were alerted to the real subject by the gratuitous appearance of Tang and Xi's surnames in a subtitle. In the original, the upright Prefect Qian takes the singing girl Xie as his concubine but does not sleep with her, and Xie sings a poignant aria complaining that she is lonely in her empty bed. In Zhang Danfu's version, the aria is hilariously rewritten in Tang's voice. Tang is thus made to complain that after an office romance turned unexpectedly serious, he now sleeps alone. He speculates that his office companion is keeping her distance—after the stock market crash—because she finds his straitened finances unattractive.[105] Among several humorous takes on the case, Zhang's stands out for cynical portrayal of Xi's character (comparing her cupidity to that of a courtesan or concubine).[106] Zhou Zuoren, the essayist and translator of Japanese feminist texts, denounced Zhang's mocking portrayal of Xi.[107]

For feminist commentators, an account that sexualized Xi or blurred the line between a new woman and a concubine was an outrage. Ideologically speaking, for the elites who articulated the ideals of the Republic, there was no place for concubines. As figures of oppression and male privilege, concubines were antithetical to the equality of citizens.

THE UBIQUITOUS ANACHRONISM: THE CONCUBINE IN THE REPUBLIC

In the last year of the Qing dynasty, the influential *Eastern Miscellany* published a critique of concubinage, a practice that was never uncontroversial. The editor, Du Yaquan, mused that Europeans viewed women's rights as an index of civilization, whereas China had only begun considering the question. Concubinage violated the modern principle of equality between men and women and had to be abolished. Otherwise, he said (naturalizing a globally circulating figure of European orientalism), talking about equality or women's rights "was as ridiculous as discussing . . . republican governance with Chinggis Khan."[108] Du's critique of concubinage was nonetheless most concerned with inequality among men. He advocated gender balance because inequality deprived poor men of access to women, creating social instability: "Unmarried men may be seen everywhere, while others have multiple women to satisfy their lust." Polygynous men, he warned, enfeebled Chinese society with the "poison of concubinage," making China's political arena like "a congregation of Mormons."[109]

Jurists of the Republic, hastening to construct a legal system that accorded with the globalized model of a nation-state, promulgated interim legal codes that prescribed an imported Western emphasis on monogamy. Earlier legal codes formally distinguished between wife (*qi*) and concubine (*qie*); nonetheless, in late Qing legal practice concubines were effectively treated as secondary or minor wives.[110] In Republican rhetoric, concubinage, like suicide, cast a shadow on the new era. As with other intentional demarcations of rupture between past and present, modern caricatures of concubinage entailed considerable distortion of a minority practice in a complicated and dynamic landscape of marriage and sexuality.[111]

In the first years of the Republic, when Western diplomatic intercourse rendered the public presence of a spouse desirable for Chinese officials and others, the concubine system enabled some prominent men to attain educated women to serve as public spouses without divorcing older, illiterate or domestically bound wives, as Xia Shi has shown. Public exposure of diplomatic travel with concubines, however, proved scandalous. The concubines were stigmatized and their public visibility was decried by critics as a national embarrassment.[112] Republican-Era print increasingly portrayed concubinage as a decadent and shameful holdover of the old family system. Protests against the imposition of "single-wife-ism" appeared occasionally in the entertainment press, but were far less prominent in the rhetorical battle.[113] Legally defined out of marriage (though not out of existence) in the Republic, concubines lost their former status as a type of wife, becoming only household members. As an "old-style" female type, the concubine was particularly problematic. Whereas the dependency of unemployed wives disqualified them from New Culture notions of modern personhood, wives nonetheless commanded respect because their (reproductive) sexuality was framed within the state-sanctioned framework of monogamy. Prostitutes, traditionally the most debased women, had no claim to virtue but posed less of an embarrassment for the Republic: prostitutes were hardly unique to China. Moreover, they remained outside the home. In contrast, as two centuries of Western missionary efforts to "Christianize Chinese sex" had emphasized, concubines were a problematized category that distinguished China from most Western societies.[114]

Republican-Era pundits commonly portrayed concubine ownership as typical of elites in imperial times. Family reformers also linked concubinage to powerful and corrupt figures whose decadence had enfeebled the

Republic: "officials and politicians, tyrannical landlords and dishonest businessmen, thieves and bandits." In common caricatures, such greedy and immoral types, addicted to opium, competed to acquire the ostentations of concubines and Western-style houses "to manifest their wealth and status."[115] Chinese suffragists were embarrassed by Yuan Shikai's possession of nine concubines. The Shandong warlord Zhang Zongchang, reputedly acquired some thirty to fifty numbered concubines, too many to remember by name.[116]

Concubines thus appeared in two guises: as remnants of the old society and also as a public measure of men in the new society. But their acquisition was not limited to the sorts of men identified in popular caricatures. In July 1921 an article in *Crystal* compared the owners of four Shanghai newspapers in terms of their fashionable possessions: clothing, cars (who rode one first; who preferred horse-drawn carriages), eyeglasses, and concubines. The men's habits (and their imputed characters) varied in respect to clothing and cars. None of the four wore glasses. However all of them, according to the *Crystal* report, possessed concubines.[117]

This item of social gossip raised for public contemplation the polygynous households of newer sorts of male figures: men at the helm of the print media that framed the public culture of republican citizenship. The vast majority of men, needless to say, could not afford concubines; many poor men, as Du Yaquan attested, could not even afford wives, a Late Imperial concern that was if anything exacerbated in the disorders of the Republic.[118] Nonetheless, the aura of the polygamous male maintained a powerful grip on the urban imagination.[119] Shanghai guidebooks, which were written for both practical and vicarious uses, provided advice on how to acquire concubines. Given the abundance of available women in Shanghai's numerous brothels, editors took for granted that men would travel to the city in search of potential concubines (for whom concubinage served as a primary means of escaping prostitution). Such books estimated costs for the purchase of women of assorted backgrounds and their willingness to accept concubinage. One of these guidebooks—even as it offered useful tips—also moralistically registered the shift in public attitudes, noting that "purchasing a concubine was unexceptional in the semi-enlightened past. However, in today's enlightened world, this kind of filth is out of place."[120]

In his testimony at the inquest, Tang had vigorously denied that he was the type of man who desired concubines, something that would have been at odds with his public reputation. But as his critics noted, this denial appeared to be contradicted by the rhetorical question he posed immediately afterward, "Even if Xi didn't want to become my concubine, why would she kill herself?" Tang's peculiar formulation of this question set off red flags at a moment when concubinage was particularly politicized. The legal redefinition of marriage under the Republic had done little to change the sexual imbalances of Chinese families. Whereas early critiques, like that of Du Yaquan, approached the issue largely in terms of the excessive sexuality of powerful men (and poor men's sexual starvation), new critiques emerged that placed greater emphasis on equality between men and women.

The politicization of the concubine question reached a high point in the May Fourth Era in the context of the second-wave women's suffrage movement. Increasingly strident critiques of concubinage appeared that were authored by overlapping actors: women's rights groups; male feminists; legal and family reform activists. Political agitation surrounding the issue in the year prior to Xi's suicide comprised what became known as an anticoncubinage or concubine abolition movement (*feiqie yundong*).

In contrast to the *Crystal*'s mocking poke at the era's guardians of public opinion, the rhetoric of contemporary concubine abolition leaned toward the humorless and hyperbolic. Women's suffrage groups were significant actors in, and authors of, this movement (some of these made public statements in the aftermath of Xi's suicide).[121] These activists, who commonly drew their leaders from the small elite of wealthy and often foreign-educated professional women, were known for their rhetorical sharpness and guerrilla tactics. In some cases they demanded the expulsion of legislators with concubines, blocking their access to meetings.[122] Critical of hypocritical men and at times disparaging of their wives, such activists could be merciless in their criticisms of actual concubines.

This movement, which was tied to women's campaigns to gain suffrage in provincial constitutions between 1919 and 1923, made the news during Xi's brief career and comprised the immediate context for sensitivities about concubines in the Xi case.[123] Xi would certainly have encountered the language of the anticoncubinage activists while working at the newspaper. This rhetoric suggests how concubinage fractured the newly emerging universal category of "woman." One anticoncubinage manifesto, for example, compared the divisions among women to the divisions between classes, paraphrasing Marx: "The history of all hitherto existing families is the history of struggle between wives and concubines." The manifesto's author called for concubines to become self-determining: "Concubines, quickly awaken your consciousness!" In the same gesture, however, she excoriated their cupidity and denied them personhood, asking "Can diamond jewelry compensate for your loss of personhood?"[124]

Activists decried concubinage as "the shame of the Chinese nation."[125] Abolitionist Lin Meijing, writing in 1922, insisted that all civilized nations were monogamous. She expressed an evolutionary assumption that concubinage was fading naturally from the Chinese landscape: "At the dawn of the Republic, people's minds embarked on a new course. All social matters . . . necessarily followed the footsteps of the Euro-American powers. Thus people upheld monogamy and the trend of taking concubines gradually diminished."[126]

In this characteristic formulation, Lin conceptualized concubinage as an anachronism, comparable to other prerevolutionary social ills that re-emerged in the political disarray of the Republic. New social and political associations articulated a common disgust at the persistence of concubinage, which they considered an embarrassing time lag in China's march to the future. In efforts to foster self-determining, independent citizens, the New Culture press promoted new relationships based on romantic love.[127] It also publicized the suicide protests of women threatened with concubinage.[128] With the exception of a few advocates of unfettered sexuality as the apogee of individual freedom, most male feminists who exalted new women spoke for monogamy and against concubinage.[129] New men risked exposure for hypocrisy if they kept concubines, and yet such exposure was not uncommon.[130] A contemporary cartoon lampooned a recognizable and pervasive type: the hypocritical man who mouthed slogans supporting gender equality while consorting with a concubine with bound feet and a child prostitute (Figure 2.7). The man is appears physically depleted by his polygynous sexuality and unable to stand without a cane. The caption identified this as a national, not an individual problem.[131]

The contemporary discussion of the anachronistic concubine suggests how the category of the new woman entailed a status beyond the reach of the majority. The idea of kindred identity between the concubine and the new woman was unthinkable because the new woman was defined—and defined herself—against the fundamental inferiority of other women. Suffragists, as claimants to the status of new women, policed the boundaries of categorical distinctions among women. Identifying concubines as former prostitutes, servant girls, and performers, they emphasized their unhealthy habits. As one concubine abolitionist put it, "Their personhood is inevitably flawed."[132]

Women's associations in Shanghai, Guangzhou, and Tianjin barred concubines from membership. The Shanghai Women's Association disqualified "anyone bound in concubinage."[133] These feminists considered that women who bore the moral stain of concubinage were out of step with the Republic. In the intermittent elections of the new era, the (elite male) individuals who qualified as the new electorate exercised the emblematic practice of representative democracy. Voting enacted the abstractly egalitarian (if nonetheless exclusionary) equation of one citizen,

2.7 "The Common Illness of Chinese People: Words and Actions Do Not Match." *Shanghai Gazette,* July 29, 1922.

one vote. Female activists chafed at their exclusion from the suffrage rights of citizens. However, they did not extend their indignation to embrace, or even ponder, voting rights for concubines.

The republican nuclear family, like the Republic, expressed a radical formulation of equality that was at the same time exclusionary. The modern monogamous family was named in terms of numerical proportionality: "one husband, one wife" (*yifu yiqi*). Its exclusionary character was evident in the contrast with the old family, which was identified by a phrase that rendered its inequality visible: "one husband, multiple wives" (*yifu duoqi*). Under the new law, concubines were excluded from marriage and could no longer be approximations of wives. In the early Republic, the supreme court defined the concubine as a special contractual relation, with no right to property but with a claim to maintenance. Now categorically different from wives, concubines lost any potential claim to state recognition of virtuous behavior or status corresponding to that of a wife.[134]

The legal redefinition of marriage and their growing legal invisibility did not resolve the problem of concubines' continued existence. Abolition literature often blamed men for oppressing women by purchasing concubines to satisfy their sexual appetites or fulfill their unenlightened filial desires to produce offspring.[135] Female activists also unrelentingly caricatured the women they ostensibly sought to liberate, holding concubines responsible and complicit in their own degradation: "When a woman is willing to abase her personhood and humiliate herself to become a concubine-toy, her motivation is nothing more than an obscene desire for wasteful extravagance."[136] Exculpating elite men who purchased concubines (who were, after all, the new women's presumptive marriage partners), female abolitionists had a tendency to endow their concubine-rivals with a destructive agency.

Verses from a concubine abolition collection typify female activists' denigration of concubines and their own self-exaltation. One such poem contrasts "the woman who is free" (and "stands high in the clouds") with the concubine (who "tumbles into the fiery pit").[137] There is no literary ambiguity; the poem simply asserts unequivocal difference between the self-actualized new woman and the concubine. Another addressed concubines directly, rhetorically alerting them to their lack of modern virtue:

> Concubine! You are so powerful.
> You who violate humanitarianism,
> You who injure human personhood.
> [How can you] ensnare men's hearts?[138]

Such venting better fits popular burlesques of wife-concubine struggles than the ostensible goal of gender equality. Their authors uncritically repeat popular caricatures of "arrogant, lazy and wanton" concubines (a guidebook description).[139] Indeed the abolition rhetoric at times suggests more of an anticoncubine movement than an anticoncubinage movement.

This ill-tempered condemnation of concubines may also have reflected the shifting demography of concubinage in the Republic. Social mobility and urban property arrangements loosened wives' former authority and economic control. Sojourning men could leave their wives in their hometown; they could also set up concubines in autonomous urban apartments outside the supervision of their wives, thus undermining in practice the legal elevation of wives.[140]

Some observers noted that despite the legal redefinition of marriage, concubinage had increased in popularity. Zhu Caizhen, the male editor of a collection of these anticoncubine essays, poems, and fiction published in the year of Xi's suicide declared that the Republic had become "a world of concubines."[141] Some observers attributed the perceived increase in concubines to the economic dislocations of the Republic. Poor families sold their daughters, creating a buyers' market: "From the inception of the Republic, because of economic pressures, prostitution flourished. Any sort of man with cash would quickly acquire three wives and four concubines."[142]

Disregarding the long history of a robust commercialized market in women and sexual services at all levels of Chinese society,[143] some contemporary commentators suggested that concubinage was compounded by capitalism, in which "the evil of money, like fungal spores, spread throughout society."[144] Mei Lu, writing in the journal *Life,* similarly linked the moral contamination of concubinage and capitalism, characterizing capitalism as a modern time, "when men rob women with money, [and] dishonest, inhumanly fat businessmen and people who are up to no good have concubines. . . . The more harmful and evil a person is, the more concubines he obtains."[145]

Other critics of concubinage adopted the neologisms of liberal economics (without reference to the term capitalism) to bolster their arguments, portraying the concubine system as a symptom of economic imbalance. The healthy, balanced sexual economy of the monogamous family, in contrast, fostered national prosperity. Family reform advocate Guo Xun, for example, emphasized the national economy in his description of the evils of the old family system. Concubines drained the husband's energy and distracted him from work. The concubine's extravagance diverted the flow of currency in the market. Only a loving and monogamous union enabled the family economy to flourish, to the benefit of the nation.[146]

In this fashion, preoccupation with concubines permeated and absorbed modern knowledge and new political apprehensions of the world. Even as the ubiquitous anachronism of concubines shamed the troubled Republic, the new principles of economics and democracy failed to fulfill their promise. Concubines gummed up the works, and in counterintuitive ways. Zhu Caizhen prefaced his collection of anticoncubinage writings by suggesting that the egalitarian ideals set loose by the revolution had mutated in Chinese society:

> People have become infected by an epidemic: "concubine-taking madness." The idea of taking concubines has been popularized. In the Qing dynasty, concubine acquisition was restricted to a certain class. But this is not so in the Republic. There are innovations in form. The concubine virus has been disseminated into commoner society. Everyone harbors the desire to acquire concubines. Look! Small merchants, shopkeepers, principals, and schoolteachers all keep concubines; college students, . . . lawyers, and artists keep concubines; miserable poor scholars [win lotteries and] take concubines.

Most egregiously, legislators who preach Marxism also take concubines, and graduates from Women's Normal Colleges marry below them into warlords' families as concubines.[147]

Zhu despaired that voting rights and popular education remained unrealized in Chinese society. The egalitarian economic ideal of equal distribution also remained an empty promise. Only the evil of taking concubines had been popularized. Concubines had become equally distributed.

If the Republic had perversely succeeded in democratizing concubine acquisition, Zhu also suggested that polygynous formations were themselves changing, particularly among educated New Culture elites. Young women found themselves in murky new-style love affairs outside the bounds of monogamy and marital fidelity. Facing limited options, many new women became sexually involved or cohabited with married men. To observers, their situation resembled the old concubine system. A clear vocabulary for these relationships did not exist. Zhu Caizhen coined the term "new-style concubine":

> Relations between men and women are in a state of extreme instability. People vigorously advocate freedom in love, freedom in marriage, and freedom in divorce. But people with freedom in divorce cannot leave their spouses, and people choosing free marriage cannot marry. Social intercourse between men and women is not publicly acceptable and it is remains difficult for people to have unconcealed love relationships. Because the old custom of considering men superior [persists] many new-style concubines have appeared. The old-style concubines have not yet been abolished. How can we bear to add new-style concubines?[148]

The complexities of new domestic arrangements thwarted the construction of sexual equality. New women were caught between the universal vision of New Culture equality, and the particular (and unequal) experiences of women in a society that retained polygynous practices. Women who were inspired by ideals of public social intercourse and freedom in love, or simply desired self-determination, often became entangled with men who had submitted to parentally arranged marriages in their teens.[149] It was easier for men to remain married than to reject parental arrangements and abandon their wives.

For new-style individuals and relationships, despite efforts to throw off the old, the inheritance of polygamy proved protean, creating new-style concubines. What, indeed, was Xi? And what was at stake for men in her demise?

A NEW WOMAN NARRATIVE FOR XI SHANGZHEN,
OR THE FAILURE OF THE MODERN MAN?

Once her suicide catapulted her into public view, Xi was acclaimed as a
new woman. Fragments of her life fleshed out the narrative. Her education emphasized female employment and engagement in society. East City
Girls' School sent student lecture teams into the countryside to educate
poor women, "to prevent the nine thousand ninety-nine uneducated
women" (out of 10,000) from being "useless people."[150]

Xi's employment identified her as a pioneer. Office work for Chinese
women was novel, dating to the end of World War I and still rare in society. Female department store employees would still be considered a new
innovation a decade later in 1930, when the influential Wing On Department Store began to place women in sales.[151] The *Journal of Commerce*
hailed the opening of various professions to women.[152] Identified as "female" secretary, "female" copyist, or "female" clerk (the qualifier necessary for male-identified positions), Xi's monthly salary of twenty yuan,
though minimal, permitted a degree of economic independence[153] For the
adjudicating public, Xi's personhood may have been confirmed by one unequivocal act of will: she had broken off a parentally arranged engagement and vowed never to marry. No doubt this decision was facilitated by
her money-earning role in her family.[154]

Public embrace of Xi as a new woman is key to understanding the media
focus on the contradiction her suicide posed for her personhood. Feminists
found her suicide incomprehensible. Xi was presumed to be "someone who
experienced women's inequality and wanted to realize liberation and economic independence."[155] Her employment was heralded as a brave achievement. Her suicide appeared to shatter the facade.

Several commentators concluded Xi was not an authentic new woman,
but simply someone who had achieved the outer likeness while failing to
"cast off her traditional woman's mindset."[156] One writer wondered, "If
one rushes to suicide when one encounters a problem, what kind of independence is this?"[157] Some attempted to control the fallout by pointing to
Xi's imperfections as a modern woman. But whatever Xi's shortcomings,
Xi the individual was a sideshow for what was at stake for the men who
memorialized her in death. They understood her death to be emblematic
of a larger issue—it called into question the creation of modern citizens
through female employment.

New men who promoted women's vocations were vulnerable to blame
if things went wrong. This vulnerability drove male architects of female

vocations to defend themselves from responsibility for thrusting young women into dangerous spaces. One group of New Culture intellectuals, Zheng Zhengqiu among them, jumped to stave off attacks on "the modern movement" resulting from Xi's suicide and organized a Society for Research on Women's Vocations. This group swiftly published a two-volume compilation of essays and reportage on Xi's death.[158] The most substantial of the three books that bore Xi's name, it parsed the commentary on her suicide and attempted to condense its meaning. The editors avoided discussion of Tang Jiezhi, their confrère, while hailing Xi as a gender pioneer who was victimized by an insufficiently reformed society. As Zheng presented the issues: "It was rare that the *Journal of Commerce* was willing to employ a woman, and it was rare that Miss Xi was willing to take this step. Who would think that the result would be so tragic? The future of woman's vocations has been struck a great blow. Doesn't this give conservatives an excuse to oppose liberation? Won't women now see vocations as dangerous?"[159]

Conservatives duly attacked women's vocations, suggesting that feminists had "aimed to draw a tiger but managed only to sketch a dog." The suicide constituted proof that female employment was socially irresponsible: "[Xi] was intoxicated with employment . . . if [she] had not worked at the newspaper . . . [s]he could have achieved happiness within women's quarters and avoided today's tragedy."[160]

For men who despaired that "the average stubborn person who opposes modern thinking will use the suicide to attack new thought and advocates of the women's movement," Xi's life was not the main issue. "Xi's suicide, in terms of her own body, is a small thing. However, the influence on society . . . is very great."[161] Much of the obsessive concern and self-examination in the Shanghai press that accompanied the suicide of a vocational woman may be explained by the understanding of Tang's associates that their reputations were called into question. Their print effusions over Xi's death defensively displayed their own male modernity.

Other participants in the controversy, including women's groups and Xi's native-place association, placed greater blame on Tang. Female commentators were commonly disinclined to see Xi's body as "a small thing." Indeed, they upheld her body as jade.

Suffrage activists often merged the figure of the new woman with older images of exemplary women. Such associations underlay their presentation of Xi as a chaste victim. Xi's feminist champions insisted on her traditional virtues: "Her character was retired and tasteful [*youya*]. She liked to study and rarely mixed with others. She stayed home and didn't go out."[162] Her calligraphy, which adorned the essays published by the Society for Research on Women's Vocations, identified her with the key concept of *ya* (elegance), as opposed to *su* (popular, vulgar).[163] The women's groups that took up Xi's case understood that her virtue was in question and defended her honor, repeating the unsubstantiated claims of Xi's family that Xi resisted her employer's insulting lechery. They thus demonstrated that in 1922, as earlier, a woman's act of self-destruction could be still be interpreted as evidence of her moral purity.[164] In this awkward logic, which still strained to separate new from old, the new woman might only be distinguished from a virtuous old-style woman by the added deliberation that tempered her suicidal impulse:

> Suicide is abject behavior, but in today's society, what support does a woman have? Even if she hadn't killed herself and had persevered, I doubt she could have achieved success. Now that she is dead, people of conscience will redress her grievance. . . . She died partly because of Tang's insulting desire to make her his concubine. . . . To protect one's body as jade is always a good thing. Her body was pure. [Therefore] when she heard Tang's [suggestion] she felt ashamed. . . . Naturally she killed herself. Had she been an old-style woman, she would have killed herself sooner.[165]

Poems by newspaper readers celebrated Xi for "dying to preserve chastity," compared her purity to "flawless jade," and hailed her "chaste ghost."[166] Zhou Fengxia, recent head of the Society for the Advancement of Women's Suffrage, emphatically defended Xi's choice of suicide, associating her education with propriety and chastity: "Tang dealt with her frivolously, he insulted her to her face. Since she was an educated woman and could understand propriety, if she could not protect her reputation, why should she live?"[167]

Preoccupation with Xi's chastity among the broader public reveals the enduring moral salience of chastity, though social and rhetorical frameworks were highly dynamic. The melancholy aesthetic through which many Shanghai readers understood female suicide may be glimpsed in a Qing collection of poetry by cultivated young ladies that was republished in Shanghai by the New Education Press in the year of the Xi case. One poem in the collection, "Chaste Girl Yang" by Fan Huzhen, commemorated a faithful maiden who followed her fiancé to the grave. The poem suggested that (through the intervention of the female poet) a chaste suicide created a (posthumous) path from boudoir obscurity to literary immortality:

> The girl died, but isn't dead–
> her name is on everyone's lips.
> We could say it's because she doesn't live

that she hasn't really died. Oh, woe and alas!
At her throat was a white silk sash
like a "white rainbow suspended";
it lifted up those "dark and moth-like brows"
onto the pages of history.[168]

The aestheticization of female suicide is striking: the "dark moth-like brows;" the silk sash (the instrument of death) "a white rainbow suspended." That such poetry was reprinted in 1922 reflected the vitality of this aesthetic in the literary marketplace in the Republic. That it was published by the New Education Press suggests the ambivalent reception of the new woman and new morality of citizenship in the wider print public.

Newspaper publication of poetic elegies penned by readers reveals the protean character of the genre and the ways in which the literary apprehension of events infused the transplanted medium in China. The newspaper—and the idea of a republican public of citizens—also changed the character and content of poetry. The poems written on behalf of Xi Shangzhen transposed elements of the older aesthetic onto the new political project of female citizenship. Such poems, which were solicited and published daily in the month after Xi's death, take us into the imaginations of the Shanghai readers and suggest how they integrated the news of Xi's suicide into their understandings of gender, morality, and history.[169] The diversity of the hundred-odd published poems evinces continuities with late Qing poetic imagery as well as the linguistic ruptures of the vernacular. One poem suggests that classical language created no impediment to the expression of new sentiments:

> Don't say women's hair adornments can't rival men's beards and
> brows
> [Xi's] determination clarifies the chaos of these times
> As heroic and unyielding as Madam Roland,
> Her grievance sinks like Jingwei's stones;[170] her anger cannot be
> appeased.
> With fortitude, she relinquished her life at its peak.
> Snowflake pure, intelligent and unsurpassed in beauty,
> Her action makes famous intellectuals die of shame.
> Why not turn and contemplate this event?[171]

The chastely heroic imagery of this poem alludes to modern female martyrs and evokes the exemplary female citizen, while also inscribing the virtues of gender equality and citizenship onto Xi's aestheticized image.[172]

Other sincerely reverential, if at times poetically clumsy submissions, composed in the plain speech of the vernacular, may have been penned by readers with limited experience in composition, individuals who would not, in the past, have seen their writings in print. A first example expresses striking sympathy for Xi as a "flower, sullied in mud," (normally a reference to a loss of virtue).

> Lady! Your death fills my heart with tragedy!
> Making me tremble with fear.
> Lady! We didn't know each other.
> I cry for you in sympathy.
> I sympathize with the flower
> Sullied in mud, that still is fragrant.
> Oh deceased lady! Can [my feelings] be known to you?[173]

A second, more militant poem, this one in a female voice, defended Xi's personhood and vilified Tang:

> Miss Xi. Miss Xi. Your suspicious suicide
> Made society reverberate with discussion.
> Alas! Cheated by the evil demon
> You sacrificed yourself for your personhood.
> Once the news spread, who could fail to admire you?
> Who wouldn't take up your anger?
> Your death is the glory of women.
> Exposing the fiend's false face,
> offering a lesson about women's conduct in society.
> Miss Xi. Miss Xi. For personhood and
> reputation you sacrificed your life.
> What woman does not sympathize with you
> and go forth to fight,
> exterminating fiends in human clothing,
> making our women's future bright?[174]

If the first poem voices horror at Xi's death and sympathy for a downtrodden educated woman, the second composition adopts personhood like a code word for chastity, raised like a shield against the evil world of men as women strive for a better future.

The poems hint at the way that speculation over the intimate details of the case destabilized the new woman image and tarred Tang's reputation, tantalizing readers with the compromises of an actual working woman's life. The ideal of the virtuous suicide coexisted with the imagination of the suicides of the impure. Such figures lurked in Late Imperial judicial examinations and in literary depictions of passionate women who took their lives in heartbreak or revenge. These flawed women, portrayed in opera and fiction, unsettled the virtuous martyrs that were upheld in didactic pedagogy.

Impure women were everywhere in the Shanghai guidebook literature. *One Hundred Views of Women* contains a section entitled "Women Who Die Unjust Deaths" that articulates popular and prurient understandings of suicide. The account, which ostensibly explained urban women to male readers, took up the question of why young women committed suicide. The answer was illicit sexuality: "Usually it is because they have illicit relations. Once the secret is divulged they are ashamed to face their families. [If] they carry on with pleasurable assignations and become pregnant, [they] calculate that this will make their future difficult, and realize only suicide can resolve the problem."[175] Such vernacular knowledge, invisible on the surface of the news, created an important subtext for public fascination with the case. Xi's defenders' protested her virtue in the face of assumptions about the desperate calculus of women (or their families) to cover up behavior that might otherwise cause a devastating loss of face.

Similar assumptions are conveyed in the short story, "Suicide," written several years later by the leftist Shen Yanbing, under his literary name Mao Dun. The story was likely inspired by Qin Dejun, his lover and muse, who attempted suicide after a rape several years earlier (and who made two more unsuccessful attempts after Mao Dun abandoned her). The story features a melancholy young woman who hangs herself after an affair with a revolutionary. Unable to cope with her pregnancy alone, she also fears public revelation of her affair.[176] Mao Dun suggested that family dynamics and modern print culture conditioned his flawed heroine's mental state: Her relatives gossiped. She browsed social news only to read sensational stories about suffering women betrayed by men, tropes repeated in the fiction that surrounded her.[177]

The explicit imagination of illicit sexuality animated several of the *Shibao* reader poems. These suggest how readers drew together images of disparate women that coexisted across literary genres and print media of the Republic. Here we may observe that—beyond the parties eager to preserve the reputations of Xi and Tang, or the feminist cause more broadly—many people assumed Xi's death was linked to unhappy romance and tarnished virtue. One poet said of Xi that, "she staked everything [but], failed to attain marriage."[178] Another asked how Xi "could have paired herself with such a person." A third referred to Xi's "unreasoning passion" (*zhiqing*).[179] The poems compare Xi to an assemblage of historical tragic lovers, including the beautiful imperial consort Yang Guifei ("you sacrificed your life, like Concubine Yang"), who was killed after distracting the emperor from state affairs.[180] A prose submission elucidated a lesson about purity for China's female citizens ("our sacred circle of women") in Xi's sexual indiscretion:

> Misfortune knows no door, it is invited in. Could it be that Miss Shangzhen herself incurred her death? Was she obliged because of secrets? . . . Although the trouble didn't begin with her, she brought trouble to herself. [There] is no doubt Miss Shangzhen was not sufficiently scrupulous in this tragedy. I sigh and regret her folly. . . . What unspeakable secret led you to this act? . . . I [advise] discretion for our young women fellow-citizens. May our sacred circle of women take this case as a warning.[181]

If Xi had indeed engaged in an intimate relationship with her employer, as these readers believed, this could explain her choice of suicide as a strategy. An unequal relationship with her married employer may have led Xi to demand greater assistance, feel more bitter about her position, and hold Tang responsible for her financial losses and more, leading to her revenge suicide in his office. Such a relationship might also render comprehensible Tang's handling of Xi's financial affairs, his promissory note, their quarrels, his presence at a prior suicide attempt, and his puzzling choice of words at the inquest. Such a hypothesis also helps explain an account of the Xi incident that appeared two decades later. In contrast with earlier narratives, this one (which appeared in a retrospective publication of her native-place association) states that Xi hung herself because Tang reneged on a promise to make her his concubine.[182]

The reader poems, like Yun Shi's chapter on female suicide, both exploit and narratively quiet the disturbance of female sexuality or female transgression of the gendered division of space by means of their contemplation of the female corpse. Although Yun Shi titled his suicide chapter, "Unjust Deaths," his narrative implied instead the appropriateness of women's violent ends. By his account, excessively sexual, morally lax women, owing to the fault of their own actions, resorted to suicide and became ghosts. The reader poetry in *Shibao* is more sympathetic, but the sympathy relies on Xi's self-destruction. In death, Xi Shangzhen's imperfections could be memorialized as a fated urban tragedy:

> The young lady wept at her death.
> Everyone clamors to tell of society's broken hearts.
> Shanghai is stained with spots of blood.

Your keen eyes pierce the urban void.
Your life cut short with electrical cord.
Where now is your beautiful hair?
Women's circles have lost a talented person.
Your fragrant ghost has fled to heaven.
The regrets of this life remain.[183]

Another reader-poet framed the suicide as the price of women's emergence into public space:

Social intercourse between the sexes should be transparent
But he dared the opposite. . . .
Who knew the perfect jade would be ground to dust?
Conflict arises when bird and rat cohabitate.
A price must be paid for women's empowerment.
What a pity to sacrifice such talent.[184]

Such commemorations suggest the public appeal of tragedies associated with new women. Death balanced the disturbance of their ambivalent associations, desires, and boundary transgressions. By replacing the bitter compromise of life with the purity of martyrdom, suicides cleansed transgressions and made women "trouble-free." Thus the aspirations and failures of the new equality, its temptations, and its dangers found reckoning in this poetic accounting of the unsavory bargains of modern society.

THE NEWSPAPER AS MORAL RECORD
OF THE REPUBLIC

If, in 1922, Xi Shangzhen—like the "Chaste Girl Yang" of the Late Imperial poem—was thrust by her suicide "onto the pages of history," much had changed in the interim. In the Late Imperial Era, exemplary female suicides were traced in a limited number of genres—poetic, historical, theatrical, judicial. These identified chaste death with virtue and promoted a moral order in which the maintenance of gender hierarchy naturalized the hierarchical political order. In the Republican Era, suicide remained a template for the production of moral truths. But the absence of the monarchy and the New Culture promotion of citizenship based on gender equality, opened virtue's powerful legacy of meaning to radical but tenuous redefinition.

The new vehicle of historical record was the newspaper. In a new republic that lacked a state with the machinery to enforce moral meanings, the expanding realm of the commercial press became a medium for the circulation of history, a history now composed of contemporary newsworthy events and ideas intermingled with cultural memories and new moral value. Newspapers also became an adjudicating mechanism and the medium for public rectification of wrongdoing, a kind of moral bulletin board of public accusations, responses, and position taking. Heterogeneous in language and form, this serial medium was open to professional and amateur writers. Its multiple genres knit together a literate (and to some extent petty-urbanite) public out of the print interactions of intellectuals, journalists, public associations, and readers, both male and female. In a climate of commercial competition, newspapers struggled to capture and profit from readers' attention, purveying novelties of news and newness and mixing new language and ideas with older words, texts, and reformulated memories.

The newspaper's remix and reframings of the historical and the contemporary, and the array of judgments the medium rendered—as public opinion—on the confusions of the present were captured in one reader poem :

> Examining [China's] five thousand years [of history],[185]
> How many people died for five thousand pieces [of money]? . . .
> Five thousand expressions of opinion—
> This is today's morality.[186]

Commentators seized upon public interest in the truth value of suicide to press particular concerns. Newspapers transformed public apprehensions by turning suicides into news and presenting serial records of suicides to an increasingly broad public, amid reportage of local, national and world events. Information morphed across the boundaries of juxtaposed genres blurring the narrative and moral frameworks of the news, literary, and advertisement pages. The vitality of the urban press facilitated a broadening—if still elite—public discussion, in which participants spoke in the name of the people and in which the people were imagined to be the arbiters of a new public virtue (*gongde*). The newspaper's self-proclaimed mission of bringing the voice of the people into being was taken up by a broad range of actors as essential to the development of an active citizenry.

The profusion of voices in the newspapers and the details of reportage, not to mention the multiplicity of linguistic styles and ideological frames, ensured that the meaning of an emblematic event like Xi's death resisted assimilation into any universal model of virtue, whether old or new. In the unsettled language of newsprint, instabilities of meaning propelled sensational events into controversy. Because new ideologies lacked familiar cultural and institutional anchors—particularly in view of the moral failures of new claimants to state authority—the moral role of the press appeared particularly urgent.[187] As one reader-poet described the newspaper: "The bright sun must illuminate this dark injustice./Hear the voices of the public and uproot this evil."[188]

Xi Shangzhen's afterlife in print was excessive (even obsessive), multi-vocal, and capricious. The suicide of the new woman resonated with the ambivalence of social and economic progress. Herself an unstable construct infused by older virtues and new ideals, the new woman was expected to be a live participant in, as well as a sacrifice to, the republican civic order. Her provocative emergence into public in the raw, compromised, and conflicted human form of Xi Shangzhen, an office suicide, fed popular imagination, rumor, and risqué satire. Public fascination with the Xi suicide reflected the agonizing everyday decisions of men and women caught up in the casualty-strewn process of reimagining gender norms.

The Xi case fascinated the Shanghai public for other reasons as well. These had to do with its connection to an outspoken public figure like Tang, who was also enmeshed in the machinations of the stock market (the subject of Chapter 3). Suicide resonated as a template for the production of truth, but—when loosened from familiar frameworks—it opened to a broader range of interpretive associations. The poignant spectacle of female self-destruction stood as an accusation, not simply against one immoral man, but rather against a diffuse range of social pathologies, and even against the immorality of modernity itself.

Participants in the print public took for granted China's embrace of an aspirational national future (as emblematized by the idealized creation of the new woman) even as they voiced ambivalence about the morality of social and economic change, and in particular, the changing cultural value of money. The deepest apprehension about the Western-modeled world of the new, however, was about the apparent failure of its realization in China, despite the revolutionary creation of the Republic. The view from 1922 was troubling. Despite what Marie-Claire Bergère termed the "golden age of the Chinese bourgeoisie," by 1922, the economic terrain had begun to shift. Faith in economic development was haunted by the specter of financial speculation.[189] Prior to Xi's suicide, Shanghai had been rocked by city-wide strikes, another reminder of the failed promise of the liberal republic. Capitalism, meriting the social qualms it aroused in China, was failing to deliver. The press, the medium for the dissemination of the desires, visions, and vocabulary of modernity, served also as the moral record of modernity's historical imperfections in China.

If the new woman spoke to the fantasies of the Republic, the new men who heralded her creation and betrayed her promises were ultimately to be held accountable for its failings. In the moral vacuum of state and society at large, media focus on the suicides of new women poignantly dramatized the failings of new men. Accordingly, the particular interest of Xi's suicide for writers and readers at the time was not to be found in Xi's character or actions so much as in the character of the man who was illuminated for judgment by the spotlight of her suicide. Given Tang's public visibility as an advocate of cultural reform, commerce, democracy, and the stock market, he was a perfect target for public rumination over the immorality of the new order. Xi Shangzhen's suicide, which evoked social and economic contradictions specific to 1922, may be contextualized within a pattern of public discussion of scandalous men. Their moral trespasses were illuminated by an array of female corpses, which stretched across the timeline of the Republic.[190]

CHAPTER THREE

Long Live the Republic, Long Live the Stock Exchange

> Under this unhealthy economic system, Miss Xi's desire to achieve wealth was naturally difficult to restrain. At the peak of the trust and exchange storm, when things were at their most fierce, even famous scholars were inevitably sucked into the whirlpool. To criticize Miss Xi for speculating unto death is really too harsh. In my opinion, even if it is appropriate to use Miss Xi's death to persuade people to abjure financial speculation, it is incorrect to say that Xi brought the harm upon herself through her own evil behavior and does not deserve sympathy.
>
> —Zheng Zhengqiu, "Lessons from Miss Xi's Suicide," 1922

> How could she stake everything on a bad venture?
> An incorrect move leads to failure.
> He cheated her because of her wish to be in a gold chamber.
>
> —Reader poem in *Shibao*, October 14, 1922

IN A COMMERCIAL CITY that was recovering from a ruinous financial bubble, Xi Shangzhen personified the human casualties of speculative investment in the stock exchange. Her death also emblematized the financial and political impotence of the Republic and the ethical deficits of the new capitalist order. Even those who focused on sexual morality or the challenges of establishing a sexually integrated citizenry understood that Xi's suicide was inextricably entangled with a story about money. A death for "five thousand pieces" of money, in the words of the poem, enmeshed with as many opinions, comprised the new morality.[1]

Xi's suicide thus drew attention to the liberal marketplace—its promise of public access to finance and moneymaking and to national wealth—and its failure to deliver. Promoters of the new Chinese stock exchanges and trust companies presented them as essential for national economic survival. The Shanghai public leapt to invest. When the bubble collapsed, moralists attacked the exchanges and their proponents as more evidence of a corrupt Republic. Tang Jiezhi had established his *Journal of Commerce* in the interest of promoting liberal, market-based values that called for an activated citizenry. His ideals and his activism were discredited by the market crash, which also belied his newspaper's promotion of new financial institutions. Xi's failed investment in Tang's trust company and her suicide transformed Tang's ventures into targets of suspicion—not simply suspicion of the market—but also of liberal governance and the hypocrisy, greed, and corruption it concealed.

The press, the site of "five thousand opinions," was foundational to ethical and economic reckoning. As a key source of economic information, it was crucial to the financial backstory of the bubble. Financial news and advertisement lubricated popular engagement with the market. Newspaper columns, literary supplements, and cartoons lofted the promises of investment. By the same token, the newspaper was critical to its exposure as a scam. It was thus ironic—and perhaps to some observers entirely fitting—that the *Journal of Commerce* office became the site of a stock exchange–tinged suicide.

The scandal intensified public discussion of money, economic opportunity, new financial institutions, governance, and—as is common in revelations of fraudulent finance—hand-wringing astonishment over business morality. Financial theory and economic morality also played an important role in Tang's trial, which subjected the new financial institutions to the harsh light of judicial examination. Tang's conviction rested on a verdict of financial fraud, a judgment that entailed inquiry into the vanished 5,000 yuan. What indeed had become of Xi's money? What lay inside the mysteriously opaque trust companies and stock exchanges, in which Xi had reportedly purchased and pawned shares? What was Tang's responsibility as a board member of the China Commercial Trust Company, in which capacity he had sold Xi shares? What responsibility did businessmen bear for the economic crisis? What was the responsibility of the Chinese authorities? And what, finally, was the responsibility of the commercial press, which fed on advertisement revenue from the proliferating exchanges that it publicized?

Public discussion of these questions lamented both the parlous economic state of the Republic and the phantasmic financial institutions that had sprung up on Shanghai's streets in the year before Xi's death. Most of the exchanges had just as quickly vanished, leaving a trail of economic desolation, and, as many told the story, suicide. The trial and cross-examination of Tang Jiezhi, who was implicated as a financial manipulator, promised to shed light on the matter. Once in custody—unlike the many exchange entrepreneurs whose machinations would never come to light—Tang could be held responsible and punished for a measure of the human carnage of

Shanghai's "trust and exchange storm." Tang aside, the exchanges at the heart of the matter were upheld as symptomatic of a broader problem: the unbalanced finance and empty economic foundation of the new Chinese state.

THE DISTORTED ECONOMICS OF THE CHINESE REPUBLIC: TROUBLE AT THE FOUNDATION

Writing in early 1922, the US-trained journalist Hollington Tong (who was later vice minister of propaganda under Jiang Jieshi) characterized the previous year as "one of the worst since the establishment of the Republic." The state was politically fragmented and in disarray. The (internationally recognized) Beiyang government in Beijing faced regional challengers, including the Guangzhou-based Guomindang government established in 1917 by Sun Yat-sen. The young nation lacked the resources to address the domestic and international problems that menaced its survival. Financially, the government had reached "a low ebb." Ignoring the fiscal predicament of the state, "the gambling spirit of the public ran high," fueling Shanghai's "mushroom growth of stock and goods exchanges." As many as 150 exchanges had materialized in that year, speculative ventures that the Chinese Ministry of Agriculture and Commerce had been reluctant to sanction and unable to control. Nearly all these "losing propositions" had already dissolved by the publication of Tong's essay, with catastrophic losses to individual fortunes and a resulting waste of capital that might have been invested in productive enterprises that served the nation.[2]

Hollington Tong's account of China's troubled finances emphasized the dysfunction of the state, the preeminent actor in Chinese conceptualizations of economic matters. By mournfully contrasting inadequate state resources with the speculative excesses of individual investors, he also drew attention to the alienation (and economic malfeasance) of "the public," which was the presumptive foundation of the new Republic.

The skewed financial flows that threatened the national economy drew significance, in Tong's narrative, from their dissonance with long-standing ideas of statecraft. Over the course of imperial history, scholars and scholar-officials elaborated an ethic of statecraft (*jingshi*) that associated the state with economic management. Successful statecraft depended on astute financial governance, concern for the population, and meticulous probity. These ideals were expressed in the key phrase, "governing the realm and nourishing the people" (*jingshi jimin*). In this focus on ethical governance by the state, the term *licai* (literally "managing wealth") conveyed both state responsibility and a domain for prudent financial policy making that was necessarily tied to the state. Preoccupation with the economic policies of the state remained foundational in modern Chinese reformers' appropriations of Western economic theory. Indeed, traces of classical statecraft ideals were sedimented into the modern term for economics (*jingji*), a "return graphic" import from Japan that truncated the older Chinese four-character statecraft notion to create a two-character translation for the Western social science.

The cascading military defeats of the late nineteenth century, capped by the ruinous financial indemnities imposed by the Sino-Japanese War (1894–1895) and the Boxer Protocol (1901), eroded faith in the sufficiency of the accumulated corpus of statecraft tradition. Turn-of-the-century Chinese reformers imported foreign knowledge as a tool for the recovery of national wealth and power. Western conceptual vocabulary frequently arrived by way of Japanese translation or Japanese elaboration, because of Japan's earlier modernization and adaptation of Western developmental concepts into Chinese-character based language. Once imported, Chinese thinkers' readaptations of foundational economic texts like Adam Smith's *Wealth of Nations* were dominated by concern for the Chinese state. In his early introductions to economic theory, Liang Qichao conceived the realm of the economy in the frame of the state. Accordingly he elided or dismissed ideas of laissez-faire in favor of mercantilism and the German historical school of national economics, which emphasized the role of the state. For Liang and other popularizers of Western economic theory, the state was the presumptive economic actor whose effective action ensured the livelihood of the people. It was from this state-oriented perspective that economic reformers in the first decade of the twentieth century pressed for the adoption of Western financial institutions.[3]

In the Republican Era, notions of finance continued to emphasize national economic strength, but they also took on the attributes of a liberal republic, celebrating property rights and an engaged citizenry. In his 1916 essay, "The Way of Confucius and Modern Life," Chen Duxiu (who would, in a few years, co-found the Chinese Communist Party) embraced the importance of private property as a foundational right. His discussion of independent personhood (*duli ren'ge*) as the core of modern citizenship connected personhood to economics and recognized the mutually constitutive relation between capitalism (though he did not name it here) and liberalism: "The pulse of modern life is economic, and the fundamental principle of economic production, according to economics, is individual independence. [The] independence of the individual in modern ethics and the independence of individual property mutually constitute each other."[4] When financial institutions that embodied the promise of market-based liberal democracy failed, they would tarnish the aura of the Republic.

SHANGHAI'S FIRST CHINESE EXCHANGES: NATIONALISM, RIVALRY, AND LEGITIMACY

A multitude of impulses fueled the establishment of the first two Chinese stock exchanges in Shanghai, which emerged in July 1920 and January 1921. After Japan's notorious Twenty-One Demands, fears of Japanese economic penetration added urgency to Chinese developmental aspirations. Entrepreneurs seized upon the language of economic nationalism. In the meantime, the trade disruptions of World War I had contributed to a glut of uncommitted Chinese capital.[5] Competition between two groups of stock exchange initiators fostered intrigue, deception, illegality, and betrayal of avowed nationalist and nation-building goals.

Telling the story of the Shanghai-centered financial bubble that developed in 1921 requires a brief sketch of shifting notions of political economy after the Opium War and the changing climate for Chinese investment. Starting in the late nineteenth century, the aura of Western knowledge and power—and the presence of Western financial institutions in China's semicolonial enclaves—opened new possibilities for investment. Perceptions of Chinese weakness, by the same token, discredited or effaced awareness of earlier modes of financial organization that had developed in various Chinese institutions, among them lineage trusts and Buddhist organizations.[6] In the 1860s, Chinese compradors and clerks who worked in foreign companies speculated profitably in foreign shares. Chinese capital soon comprised some 40 percent of the total in foreign companies in the China trade, among them, Jardine Matheson and Dent and Company. An ephemeral Chinese shares market emerged in the early 1880s, along with a short-lived company that specialized in stock trading.[7] In the wake of this development, a *Shenbao* editorial published in fall 1882 chided Chinese investors for excessive enthusiasm for speculation and failure to invest as knowledgeably as Westerners were imagined to invest:

> Chinese rush to buy stocks as soon as they hear the price rises. This is the difference between Westerners and Chinese. Today the Chinese who buy stocks do not even ask about the strengths, weaknesses, or profitability of the company. Instead, they compete to buy as soon as they hear there is a company that is selling shares.[8]

This first Chinese share-trading company quickly met its demise in a speculative bubble in 1883, but this did not diminish the aura of stock trading as a financial principle that writers associated with Western wealth and power. By the early twentieth century, Chinese company shares were traded among guild representatives at regular "teahouse meetings," so named because they took place at the Huifang Teahouse in the International Settlement. As early as 1907, a group of Shanghai businessmen proposed the creation of a Chinese stock exchange, modeled on the successful Tokyo Securities Exchange (established 1878), which appeared integral to Japan's successful modernization program. The envisioned Chinese venture failed to secure government support. In the meantime, informal Chinese trading coalesced into a Shanghai Stock and Bonds Trading Association, which listed approximately twenty securities in 1914. Individual trade guilds established offices and formulated regulations for the buying and selling of securities.[9]

Outside the guild communities that traded shares at these venues, Chinese investors gained experience in securities trading through the contemporaneous (and profitable) foreign shares market, which formalized into the Shanghai Stock Exchange in 1904–1905. This Western exchange operated under the extraterritorial legal framework of the International Settlement, creating a loosely regulated venue that was rife with speculative forward transactions, price manipulation, and other abuses. In 1909 the burgeoning automobile industry created the expectation of a vast global demand for rubber. Many Chinese speculated heavily, investing in dubious British plantations in Southeast Asia.[10] When rubber prices fell in July 1910, half the approximately one hundred Chinese native banks fell into bankruptcy when they tried to cover their losses and Shanghai's foreign banks refused to accept rubber shares as security on loans.[11] A financial settlement that was brokered, weakly, by the Shanghai circuit intendant (the local Chinese official who mediated with Shanghai's foreign authorities) favored the Western banks. The outcome highlighted the prejudicial power relations of the semicolonial city. It also cast a temporary shadow on Chinese trading on this exchange. For some years after this traumatic episode, Chinese newspapers refused to print stock prices in order to avoid inciting speculation.[12]

Excluded from membership in the Western exchange, hurt by the fraudulent rubber schemes of British companies—and having witnessed the crippling vulnerability of Chinese financial institutions in an economic realm dominated by foreign interests—constellations of Chinese businessmen, reformers and revolutionaries again took up the banner of the creation of a Chinese stock exchange. Straddling the last years of the Qing dynasty and the first year of the Republic, the reform intellectuals Liang Qichao and Kang Youwei (whose earlier advocacy of constitutional governance initiated the "Hundred Day" reforms of 1898) extolled the benefits of stock exchanges. In their analysis, China suffered from a lack of capital. Imported Western financial knowledge and institutions suggested a path out of national impoverishment. After Chinese rubber-investment losses through the Western exchange, Liang Qichao lamented in 1910 that Chinese businesses were disadvantaged without their own institutional framework "for stocks, trading, and corporations." He described stock exchanges as the "hub" of a new financial dynamism that resulted from share circulation and predicted that, if China could grasp this mechanism, the nation could benefit from "a several hundred-fold increase in the efficiency of its capital."[13]

In 1913, Kang Youwei published *Saving the Country through Finance,* a treatise that compared Chinese losses to foreigners to "racing a watermelon-rind boat against a forty-thousand-ton iron frigate."[14] Kang argued that only "the way of finance" could restore fiscal strength and national dignity in the Republic. "If correctly wielded," he predicted, in ten years the way of finance could make China "wealthy and powerful, without comparable competitors." Exchanges were essential to capital creation: "Stock trading enables [an increase in] paper money [and] huge profits. . . . Business profit is calculated [on a yearly basis]. But profits from stock trading can be gained on a daily basis, with rapid increases. Yearly and daily profits differ by a factor of 360."[15] Kang (who had engaged in speculative investment in Mexico)[16] straightforwardly addressed the question of risk. He did this through a logic of pretty good odds: "If we take New York as an example, on average, of those who purchase stock, 75% are winners and 25% losers. . . . Winners prevail. . . . [We] should choose the option with more benefits."[17] Kang was sanguine about economic crises: "[Every] thirty years, banks will definitely become bankrupt. The Americans understood this early on. In winter 1907 . . . US banks were exhausted and became bankrupt [creating panic]. Even so, [the exchange] is where huge profits lie, and Europe and the U.S. still [maintain exchanges] and prosper. You can't stop eating because you once choked on some food."[18]

Kang acknowledged that finance was a gamble, and that the wealthy would benefit disproportionately, but he argued that there was no other way to create capital in an impoverished national economy: "I understand the harm of gambling," he wrote, "but this is needed at this moment when China is extremely poor." In small print he appended a revealing comment: "At first, I did not want to include this passage because it might make me seem like an advocate of speculation, but I could not persuade myself to [remove it]."[19]

Kang's optimism regarding the profits to be made from stock exchanges was echoed in other quarters. In the first year of the Republic, the revolutionary Wang Shijie (who would study political economy at the University of London and law at the University of Paris before teaching constitutional law at Beijing University) edited a new *Journal of National Economy,* which advocated financial revolution.[20] *Independence Weekly* and *Life Weekly,* established in the same year, similarly emphasized the centrality of finance for the new nation. Both published a manifesto, possibly written by the journalist Zhang Shizhao, who was influenced by British liberalism. The essay celebrated economics as "the key to the rise and fall of nations and the extermination or survival of peoples." The stock exchange played an important, even predictive, role in this calculus:

> For economic development and prosperity there is one essential mechanism. What is this mechanism? It is the stock exchange. What is the function of the exchange? [It] creates balanced prices for trade. Commodity costs follow the definite principle of supply and demand. [The exchange] can aid government, economy, and society, now and in the future. To be able to know the future in advance benefits not only business but also social welfare. This is precisely the purpose of the exchange. Without this mechanism, investing in commerce cannot escape the character of gambling. By concentrating competition, the exchange enables rational [and fair] pricing, [following] economic principles. [In European countries exchanges have] kept interest rates low, controlled usury and reduced fraud. Whether or not our country's economy will develop depends on the exchange—that is all. . . . The benefits of the exchange outweigh the harms. You may know this from the relative positions of Eastern and Western countries.[21]

The manifesto celebrated the rationality of the market. This distinguished the exchange from gambling. The science of economics reduced the risk of commercial losses and panic, ensuring that the new financial tools would benefit society and "eliminate fraud." Science and social welfare provided touchstones of legitimacy, modern and traditional, respectively.[22] The argument drew rhetorical force by reference to the historical success of European economies. The Western-identified economic mechanism of the exchange would ensure China's future and make that future knowable. As with Kang and Liang, the author took for granted the statecraft assumption that finance was foundational to governance, and that new financial institutions properly served as tools of governance.

In the first years of the Republic, as political authority gradually fragmented into regional power bases, those who would establish Chinese stock exchanges had to grapple with diverse actors and interests: the Beiyang government; contending regional authorities (including foreign consuls and enclaves); and business groups with interests of their own and little faith in China's military governors. At a national meeting in 1913, the Ministry of Agriculture and Commerce considered a proposal to establish a stock exchange in each major port, a framework advocated earlier by Liang Qichao. Under pressure from the business community and facing severe fiscal challenges, the Beiyang government promulgated a Securities Exchange Law in 1914 that stipulated that just one exchange of any given type could be established in any given locality. Drawing protective lines around the national economy, the law prohibited foreign shareholders and excluded non-Chinese from exchange employment. From the perspective of the state, the primary purpose of this law was to facilitate the marketing of government bonds. Lingering questions over the extent of government or merchant control prevented the immediate approval of an actual exchange.[23]

In 1915, Sun Yat-sen embraced the stock exchange in hopes of financing his revolutionary movement. After conceding the presidency to Yuan Shikai, Sun watched Yuan's dictatorial regime with dismay and established a new revolutionary organization in Japan. His associate, Dai Jitao, collaborated with sympathetic Japanese businessmen to create a Sino-Japanese exchange in Shanghai. In the next year Sun recruited the prominent Shanghai banking comprador and shipping magnate Yu Xiaqing to this venture. Leader of the powerful Ningbo sojourner group and recent chair of the General Chamber of Commerce, Yu was arguably the most influential civic leader in the city. Tang Jiezhi would have repeatedly worked (and wrangled) with Yu in the course of his May Fourth activism.[24] Tang would also have reckoned with Yu's enormous commercial influence in the city. (Yu's name would soon appear some years later alongside Tang's, in 1921, on the board of Tang's trust company.)

Yu energetically took up Sun's stock exchange project, proceeding with absolute determination and mobilizing local, national, and overseas networks of associates. After securing the support of the Jiangsu provincial governor, Yu and his surrogates pressured the Ministry of Agriculture and Commerce in Beijing for the approval of a joint securities and commodities exchange.[25] Yu also collaborated with Kobe shipping magnate Mikami Toyotsune, "a supporter of the Chinese revolution," who offered capital in return for a division of profits in a Sino-Japanese exchange.[26]

In the meantime, a separate group organized a Japanese government–supported exchange (*Shangye quyinsuo*), which began construction in Shanghai's International Settlement in late 1917 or early 1918 under the English name Oriental Trust Guarantee and Exchange Company. The intrusion of this exchange on Chinese soil heightened fears of Japanese penetration of the Chinese market and strengthened arguments for Chinese financial institutions to protect the national economy.[27] With the law in place and the political climate conducive, Shanghai entrepreneurs aimed to secure acceptance for their exchange initiatives with rhetorical claims to serve the national interest.

Disingenuously cloaking the Japanese interests in his own exchange, Yu argued that the creation of a Chinese exchange was the only way to prevent Japanese manipulation. In a public relations campaign waged via Shanghai newspapers in April, he borrowed the logic of the national products movement, arguing that "if we do not establish the exchange ourselves, foreigners will overpower us and establish their exchange. Foreigners would gain the upper hand, destroying [Chinese] sovereignty."[28]

The challenge of obtaining a license from the Beiyang government (for an exchange that would operate beyond the range of its effective territorial control) was not negligible. Yu and his colleagues began an intense two-year campaign to win Ministry approval. These Shanghai Ningbo people found Beijing politics tricky ("a trip to a tiger's den").[29] In 1920, after much travel back and forth, Yu's collaborator, yarn magnate Wen Lanting, took up residence in Beijing to lobby for official approval. His remarkable correspondence with Shanghai colleagues documents months of fruitless politicking, costly banqueting and gift giving, and efforts to go around the Ministry. Meanwhile, back in Shanghai, the exchange initiators, who had little knowledge of exchange operations, hired Japanese instructors for a training school (*yangchengsuo*). Guo Waifeng, a former employee of the Yokohama Russo-Japanese Bank, worked full-time as an interpreter in the Japanese-language based class.[30]

The Ministry of Agriculture and Commerce approved a securities exchange in principle but objected to Yu's proposal for a *combined* securities and commodities exchange (which violated the 1914 law). On July 1, 1920, Yu preemptively opened his Chartered Stock and Produce Exchange (hereafter the Chartered Exchange) within the extraterritorial jurisdiction of the International Settlement.[31] Not abandoning the effort to gain approval, he continued to pressure the Ministry, using a tactical repertoire of deception, wrangling, and bribery. Although operating his exchange without a license (which he lacked until June 1921) risked official displeasure, Yu was determined to monopolize Shanghai exchange business. He feared that bureaucratic delay might facilitate the licensing of an exchange that had been proposed by members of the Stock and Bonds Trading Association. His rivals viewed themselves as the rightful claimant to a license, given their association's established expertise. They were also suspicious of Yu's monopolistic scheme.[32]

The establishment of a Chinese exchange in Shanghai thus aimed for legitimation in respect to national law and nationalist cultural sensitivities. The badge of legality was desirable but not essential in the fragmented political terrain. Even if Yu had a license, this would not have dispelled the question of social legitimacy for a private Chinese exchange, given its separation from the public virtue of producing revenue for governance. The foreign origin of the stock exchange and the awkwardness of its recent association with financial instability in China made it necessary for proponents of the first exchanges to reassure the public that exchanges served the Chinese nation and that individual profit making would be tempered with moral concerns for protecting the people's livelihood.

The carefully orchestrated opening of the Chartered Exchange on July 1, 1920 was designed to awe critics with a display of grandeur and social clout, while also papering over Yu's preemptive bravado with ceremonial humility. The ostentatious ceremony drew a crush of vehicles and bystanders as well as copious coverage in Shanghai newspapers. Capital, nationalism, cosmopolitanism, and political power were all on show. In a symbolic gesture at the end of 1919, Yu had purchased the property of the Japanese stock exchange, displacing it from the site.[33] The hastily remodeled three-story Western-style building was located at the prominent intersection of Avenue Edward VII and Sichuan Road. At the time of the opening, the flags of Shanghai's numerous consular powers festooned the upper balconies. Larger five-bar flags of the Republic of China were draped prominently above the entry (Figure 3.1). The exchange publicized a capitalization of 5 million yuan, with one quarter paid up. Celebratory telegrams and calligraphic scrolls from patron officials and notables filled interior exhibit spaces, testifying as well to the organizers' political capital. To compensate for the lack of a license, Yu displayed congratulatory scrolls from former president Li Yuanhong, a suggestion of legitimacy that he reportedly purchased with a gift of 50,000 shares.[34]

Three thousand Chinese and foreign guests attended the opening of the Chartered Exchange. Among them were diplomat and statesman Wang Zhengting (C. T. Wang, the former vice minister of industry and commerce, who would soon launch his own exchange); businessman and philanthropist Wang Yiting (who would also soon launch an exchange); the Jiangsu provincial governor; the circuit intendant; and officers of the

3.1 **The Chartered Stock and Produce Exchange, July 1920.** Photograph provided by Shanghai Archives.

Shanghai General Chamber of Commerce. At the striking of a gong, a choir from the Door of Hope (a refuge for trafficked girls) sang the national anthem. Six hundred employees, brokers, and representatives of the exchange executed three ritual bows before the national flag. Three times they shouted: "Long live the Republic of China! Long live the Stock Exchange!"[35] Yu spoke following these ritual gestures to the state, social welfare, and the exchange. His oration affirmed a classical as well as a patriotic pedigree for the exchange. He also wrestled with market morality. Having beaten his rivals to the punch, he now exhorted compromise and unity:

> The moment has arrived for us to make speeches for our fellow citizens. The ancient *Book of Changes* says, "[people gather goods at the market], exchanging and retreating, each receiving what he needs" [*jiao yi er tui, ge de qi suo*].[36] Business fluctuates day and night, rising and falling. Many prosper but some struggle financially. Some fall bankrupt. Just as bodies have mouths, people contend and snatch food from others. Some squeal in joy; others weep. How may we say that each receives what he needs? Is [inequity] the fault of businessmen? Or is it the fault of a lack of balance and compromise? How may we aid people in distress? [If we] find the source and moderate its flow, maintaining solidity at the root, the branches and leaves will flourish. As with business, so with the country. And as with the country, so with the world. [A prosperous economy] is the responsibility, foundation, and mission of the stock exchange. This [is] beneficial for China. We aim for balance and compromise, [the] basis for trust, [and] encourage our patriotic, business-loving colleagues [to help] each another.[37]

That the new institution was introduced under the classical imperative of improving social welfare suggests the awkwardness of a public embrace of the stock exchange as a core feature of capitalism. Insofar as it could be claimed that the exchange served the nation by moderating disproportionate private moneymaking, its contributions might be publicly cerebrated. Yu's deft classical allusion—and his recognition of the moral deficits of capitalism—exhorted business unity in the project of national uplift.

Yu's evocations of equality, mutuality, trust, and balance (and his classical references to solidity, flourishing, and flow) notwithstanding, his action betrayed willful disregard for Chinese legality, laying the foundation for the speculative bubble that ensued. Just as Yu deployed newspapers and social connections in a public relations campaign for his exchange, so did his competitors, who saw no reason to respect its legitimacy. The powerful Nantong industrialist and educator Zhang Jian (who was connected to the rival effort) published a circular telegram denouncing the illegal preemptive opening of Yu's exchange. Together with the influential educator Huang Yanpei, Zhang pressed the Jiangsu Provincial Assembly to suppress the unlicensed exchange.[38] In November, Shanghai newspapers reported that Jiangsu Assemblyman Huang Shenxi had called to abolish Yu's exchange, accusing it of circumventing the Securities Exchange Law by quietly adding "commodities" to its name, whereas the Ministry had only entertained approval for a securities exchange. Huang charged, moreover, that the exchange had created a lethal form of gambling, cloaking its evil with newfangled economic terminology:

> Under the fiction of 'fixed-term trading,' the exchange masks speculative, 'empty buying and selling' [*maikong maikong*, buying on margin and selling short]. In the months since it opened, newspapers have reported Shanghai businessmen's bankruptcies and suicides. The looming disaster will exceed the damage of *huahui* and *fantan* gambling. . . . Cunning businessmen, coveting profit, will spread this plague to the nation's interior.[39]

From the moment Yu opened his exchange under the extraterritorial shield of the International Settlement, his rivals exposed his vaunted patriotism as a sham. They claimed he was in the pocket of the Japanese and that his exchange was contaminated with Japanese capital. Rumors circulated that a Japanese expert secretly "resided in the exchange."[40] Opponents charged that Yu had mortgaged 80 percent of shares to Japanese partners in return for a loan. In early November 1920, the widely circulated English- and Chinese-language newspapers, *China Press* and *Xinwenbao*, reported that the Chartered Exchange had hidden ties to a

Japanese corporation (the China Enterprise Society) and camouflaged Japanese shareholders with Chinese names.[41]

Amid this nationalist hyperventilation, the *Xinwenbao* offered the rare observation that fears of foreign influence distracted from the fundamental question of whether an exchange would benefit the Chinese economy:

[T]he question of having foreign shareholders is of no great importance and can be settled afterwards. Of course foreign shareholders should be eliminated, but the question to be settled first [is]: Does Chinese commerce require such an exchange? . . . [W]hen such an organization is unsuitable to Chinese methods and also detrimental to Chinese business, there is no justification for its existence. To preserve business conditions, the exchange . . . should be abolished.[42]

The question of the utility of an exchange for China's economy went largely unheeded. Nationalist fears of Japanese infiltration—compounded by specific concerns about the Chartered Exchange—had more traction (and more usefully bolstered competing claims to legitimacy). The controversy damaged the business of the exchange. Initially it listed staple commodities (cotton, yarn, cloth, gold and silver, grains, oils, furs and hides). As suspicions increased of Japanese connections and other improprieties, particular commodity groups withdrew and organized their own exchanges. By January 1921, *Millard's Review* reported that the Chartered Exchange was "fast disintegrating," but "doing everything in its power to convince the public that it has been financed by the Chinese, managed by the Chinese, and operated for the benefit of the Chinese."[43] Critics, including Chamber of Commerce chairman Nie Yuntai (who held that it was "financed by alien capital and established to serve alien interests") substantiated their accusations with evidence from the Japanese press.[44]

Yu had tried to co-opt members of the Stock and Bonds Trading Association by bringing them into his exchange, but was rebuffed. Instead, led by Fan Jimei and Sun Tieqing, this group launched their rival China Merchants' Securities Exchange (*Huashang Zhengquan Jiaoyisuo*), the name evidently chosen to assert its national purity. Both the rival exchanges ultimately secured licenses from the Ministry of Agriculture and Commerce, each working out separate deals with officials. The result exposed the faction-ridden and disorderly governance of the Beiyang government. By licensing two securities exchanges in one locality the Ministry violated its own law.[45] China Merchants', with fewer resources than Chartered Exchange, established a capital target of 250,000 yuan, with one quarter of the capital paid up by association members. It opened for business in January 1921, six months after Yu's exchange and the same month as Tang launched the *Journal of Commerce*. China Merchants' members were at once organizers, shareholders and brokers, a "three in one characteristic" that was as conducive to speculative manipulation as the workings of the Chartered Exchange it attacked.[46]

The improvisational and uncoordinated bureaucratic procedures governing this new terrain of finance, compounded by the factional complexity of Chinese politics, complicated the enforcement of the Securities Exchange Law. The 1914 law, in any event, had been largely cribbed from an 1893 Japanese stock exchange law. Many of its identical articles, bore little relation to Chinese reality. Because of Shanghai's fragmented jurisdictions, there was, moreover, no effective regulatory or supervisory agency.[47]

Each of the two newly licensed Chinese ventures issued stock in its own exchange (in addition to shares in represented companies). Share prices in the exchange stock soared, exceeding expectations and outdoing other trading. In the first six months of operation, the Chartered Exchange earned profits of over 500,000 yuan. By early 1921, China Merchants' and a new Flour Exchange proved similarly profitable. Their experience incited imitators. By spring, "a forest of exchanges rose up, sucking up huge sums of capital, diverting most of the savings in Chinese and foreign banks into speculative investment."[48] By this point, Tang's newspaper had leapt into the fray with a full-throated defense of speculation in the new financial institutions.

TANG JIEZHI AND *THE JOURNAL OF COMMERCE* IN THE PEDAGOGY OF FINANCE

Tang's newspaper began publication shortly after the first two Chinese exchanges in the city had opened for business. In this moment of relative commercial prosperity, Shanghai business interests pressed for rights vis-à-vis foreign powers while also gaining influence in the local and national political arenas.[49] Tang established his *Journal of Commerce* in this climate, in the interest of not simply reporting on business news, but also—as an extension of his earlier May Fourth commercial activism—calling for civic activism.

As Chen Bulei later recounted, Tang was unable initially to raise sufficient capital to publish the paper. The Chen brothers resolved the problem by enlisting contributions from Zhao Linshi "and other organizers of the Shanghai Stock Exchange."[50] The newspaper was thus indebted to the stock exchange from its inception. After its creation, favorable economic conditions for Chinese business contributed to unprecedented reader interest in commerce and finance, boosting circulation.

The *Journal*'s combination of commercial news and its outspoken political stance attracted readership. But the path forward was not smooth. In January 1922, Tang lamented that in its first year his newspaper had failed to achieve its goals. China's problems were more complex than he had imagined. He had initially identified Chinese and foreign authorities as the culprits in China's dilemma and had held them responsible for depriving the middle class of rights and capital. He still aspired to the day, "when we will take the reins of government," however, he was no longer confident in the morality of the business community he would place on the saddle. Honest criticism required doing more than simply targeting the usual suspects— foreign imperialists and domestic militarists. The industrial and commercial classes themselves had to be held to account for their hypocritical failure to reform the financial system. This first anniversary editorial reflected that, "capital has lost its stability and society has lost its balance."[51] With these evocative phrases, Tang referenced the financial crisis that was gripping the city. The financial crisis was particularly embarrassing for Tang's newspaper, which had been bullish on the stock market. It had also been personally mortifying and financially ruinous for Tang, who had initiated one of the evanescent trust companies that collapsed in the crash.

A year earlier, shortly after publishing its inaugural edition, the *Journal of Commerce* had invited Zhu Zongliang (an editor of *Republican Daily*) to weigh in on the ongoing dispute between organizers of the two rival stock exchanges. Zhu spoke first to the utility of stock exchanges for China, and second, whether they should be organized, like Chartered Exchange, by businessmen outside of particular trades, or whether, like China Merchants', they should be organized by representatives of the trades at stake. Given that Chartered Exchange and the *Republican Daily* had links to the Guomindang, it is perhaps unsurprising that Zhu upheld the importance of an exchange for China and expressed a preference for the Chartered Exchange. He dismissed lingering questions about the foreign character of stock exchanges and their appropriateness for China. Instead, noting China's history of financial sophistication, including futures trading, he found domestic precedent for the practices of the new institutions: "China had already developed [guilds], with characteristics similar to exchanges in Europe and in the U.S." However, the personalistic and insufficiently capitalized guilds needed updating:

> The relationship between the old guilds and the new exchange is like the relationship between the old native banks and modern banks. Trust is based

on people. But firm guarantees are based on concrete things. If transactions are based on people, they may be endangered. A more concrete foundation is more reliable. The old guilds are thus naturally becoming obsolete, and must be replaced by an exchange, organized through a stock shares system. This trend is an empirical necessity.[52]

After asserting the necessary evolution of guilds into exchanges along Western and Japanese lines, Zhu argued on behalf of the Chartered Exchange. His logic relied on the force of global example: in other countries, he stated, exchanges were not managed by manufacturers themselves. China Merchants' organizers argued that, as the relevant trade representatives, they would protect China's manufactures and avoid manipulation of the market by businessmen external to the trades. Zhu countered that global principles required separation of financial institution personnel from manufacturers. The resulting economic order would benefit the manufacturers. The contrary creation of an additional exchange like China Merchants' would endanger the system: "The exchange facilitates the flow of goods and stabilizes the market price. This is beneficial for agricultural and factory enterprises. Producers can profit too. Starting another exchange is not only unnecessary, it would create chaos. This is not merely my own opinion. All precedents from other countries point to the same conclusion."[53]

Even as Zhu's article warned against the "bad trend of exchange crowding," the *Journal of Commerce* championed the exchanges' economic functions. In February, the newspaper published a half-page editorial in full-throated defense of "speculative enterprises" (*touji shiye*):

> Disappointed people publicly castigate exchanges as speculative enterprises that harm society. They try to abolish them. In fact, the term "speculation" has different meanings. The average person views speculation as a "poisonous snake and ferocious monster." But this is not the scholarly understanding. People say that the exchange promotes speculation, therefore the exchange itself is speculative. But those who liken this to gambling and say it is harmful to society are ignorant and cannot distinguish green from red.[54]

Claiming the authority of specialized knowledge, the author cited foreign economists to assert that economics and finance relied fundamentally on speculation:

> [In English] "speculation" is any action that anticipates extra returns based on hopes for the market price to change in the future. [Accordingly] there is almost no difference between speculative trade and regular business. The

German economist Friedrich List stated that speculators evaluate information to predict future commodity prices. This is how major enterprises allocate resources. . . . Speculation conducted in an organized exchange [is equally] a matter of predicting changes in a market price, and earning profit on the price differential. This type of speculation should not be compared to "Asian-style speculative manipulation," which is too extreme. Many businessmen in our country do Asian-style speculation, but this is not correct speculation. Based on the [French] *Economics Dictionary,* speculation is defined as a rational and necessary function. Rational means that it does not contravene conditions of social survival. "Necessary" means it does not waste money nor is it unplanned. Exchange speculation is [rational and necessary]. Asian speculation is the only great enemy for people in the economic world. Exchange speculation is not the enemy.[55]

This argument is striking for its cosmopolitan nationalist stance and its deprecation of excessive speculation as a specifically Asian cultural problem. In both respects, it was consistent with New Culture advocacy of Western ideas and institutions as modern, and rejection of customary behavior as backward. The author advocated a special role for Chinese intellectuals in disseminating new financial knowledge: "Opposition to the stock exchange that emphasizes drawbacks and ignores benefits is not unique to our country. [However], everywhere else conservative suspicion quickly receded. Mass psychology indicates that people . . . do not want to change old habits. When a new idea emerges, people are [suspicious]. Our scholars bear responsibility to examine new ideas [and] confirm their truth."

Western experience confirmed that the stock exchange was a global evolutionary necessity:

It became established after proving itself through successful performance [and] no longer raises suspicion. The exchange has three important economic functions: 1) mediating supply and demand; 2) adjusting market prices to market situation; 3) clarifying commodity price and facilitating liquidity. Not only is it not harmful to society and economy, it guarantees their safety. The average person should not imagine that the stock exchange will exhaust society's finances. It vitalizes capital and benefits society. This is why more exchanges are being established. The trend is unstoppable [and] necessary for a society such as ours.[56]

In view of what was happening on the ground, such emphatic endorsement of the abstract economic functions of exchanges, even many exchanges, is remarkable. It was, however, consistent with the liberal economic viewpoint of the newspaper. The multiplication of Shanghai's exchanges was indeed "unstoppable." By July, the proliferation of exchanges created a shortage of commercial office space and raised Shanghai rents.[57] Newspapers reported that construction workers were killed in accidents that resulted from frenzied exchange construction.[58]

EXCHANGE FEVER, EXTRATERRITORIALITY, AND GOVERNANCE

As one analyst recalled two decades later, "at that time people were crazy about stocks. If they heard of an exchange being created, they booked shares in advance, as if getting hold of shares equaled getting hold of wealth." Ambitious entrepreneurs, aiming at the source of wealth creation, "hit on the idea of starting stock exchanges themselves. [Even] those without a specific trade created exchanges out of the blue."[59]

The surge in stock exchanges was enabled by extraterritorial jurisdiction. Exchanges rented offices in Shanghai's foreign concessions to avoid Chinese legal regulation.[60] According to one report, up to 10 exchanges claimed registration with the Chinese Ministry, 2 claimed registration "with the defense commissioner of Shanghai; 16 with French authorities; 11 with the Spanish consulate; and 2 in the Mixed Court." In regard to 4 that claimed US protection, the American Chamber of Commerce in Shanghai stated the US Court for China found that "none of the stock exchanges purporting to be American were locally registered"; thus, "they were not entitled to American protection."[61] The complexities of tracking such exchanges in the International Settlement often meant that, in practice, they evaded regulation by any authority.

Stock exchange fever permeated the city. Between spring and fall 1921, the front pages of Shanghai newspapers swelled with scores of advertisements for exchanges and trust companies, institutions that captured city residents' imaginations with intimations of wealth. By late summer newspaper readers had to turn through four or five pages of exchange advertisements before reaching the news (Figure 3.2).

Exchange advertisement conveyed rather superficial information. A full front-page announcement in *Shenbao* for a Chinese Cotton Goods Exchange, for example, provided the name and address, a general rationale, and a few specifics:

> Organization: Operated in accordance with the Company Law
> Character: Entirely Chinese

3.2 Advertisements for Stock Exchanges. *Shangbao*, July 5, 1921.

Objectives: To protect the safe operation of business and facilitate trust
Type of business: Machine spun cotton yarn
Total capital: 3 million yuan[62]

It additionally listed personnel (director, board, and supervisors, in large print; in small print, 120 brokers). Most advertisements stated the name of the exchange, address, amount of subscribed capital, initial share price, and names of prominent Shanghai businessmen who served as officers. As the exchanges proliferated, the advertisements made a powerful impression. Aside from showcasing the capital of the exchange, the main function of these advertisements appears to have been to highlight the exchange's connections to business celebrities and other social notables. The *North China Herald* reported on one exchange formed by a group of Chinese that were "reputed to be substantial men," which listed "over 50 of their names . . . in the advertisements in the Chinese papers announcing the formation of this institution." Informants suggested that "this was done for the purpose of investing the scheme with an appearance of solidity it would not otherwise have obtained."[63]

Contemporaneous stock exchange fiction confirms the impression that trust was generated, not by economic information, but by the social connections behind particular exchanges. Jiang Hongjiao's novel, *Exchanges Unmasked*, related that "when people saw that shareholders were identified by name and address, and the majority were Shanghai celebrities, the public was instantly and unanimously convinced [and] the company's credit was established."[64]

Even as the upwelling of exchanges in 1921 fueled premonitions of a bubble, new exchanges did not cease to materialize. Many exchanges restructured, combined, vanished, or otherwise shifted shape or name. The journalist Xia Juhou sketched the features of the new institutional landscape in October. Excluding exchanges that dissolved shortly after their founding ("night-blooming cacti"), he located addresses for 71 exchanges that appeared in June ("the most memorable month for the economic sector in national history"), July, and August 1921.[65] Seventeen exchanges were in full operation, 6 of which had secured licenses from the Ministry of Agriculture and Commerce. Others were unlicensed or registered with foreign authorities. Fifty-three exchanges were still raising capital or constructing offices. Fifty-nine exchanges had publicly announced their operating capital (ranging between 200,000 and 20 million yuan), which amounted to a collective total of 510 million yuan. The author musingly invoked the maxim that, "once things reach a peak they can only weaken," wondering rhetorically whether exchanges could escape this rule of nature. His numbers indicated some slackening in September, when just 3 new exchanges were reported.[66] But the exchange establishment frenzy was not over. A January 1922 investigation by Hamada Minetarō, editor of the economics page of the Shanghai *Nichi Nichi Shinbun,* reported that in October and November 1921 over 80 Shanghai exchanges had registered in foreign consulates, a late surge that defied imagination. As of November 1921, Hamada counted a total of 130 exchanges, with combined capital of 200 million yuan. The *Chinese Engineer and Contractor Bulletin* reported 142 exchanges before the end of 1921, with aggregate capitalization of 200 million.[67] No definitive count of these exchanges exists. My attempt to count exchanges by comparing advertisements from 1921 with extant partial lists from the period yielded a total approaching 160, but name similarities among exchanges made precision impossible.

Scattered surveys of the exchanges at particular moments, with their uneven figures, confirm an impression of duplication and reduplication in an unstable landscape of rapid institutional formation. Of the exchanges the Chinese journalist tracked, 4 specialized in securities (Hamada found 8). Twenty-eight listed securities and commodities. Three named cotton and cotton yarn. Another 3 listed mixed grains and oil-cake fertilizer (Hamada found 6). Two identified flour and bran. Four named cotton cloth; 3 named gold bars; 7 named currency. Hamada found 5 identified with cigarettes and liquor. Other individual commodities—sugar, coal, cocoons, and bricks—were represented by 2 exchanges each. The exchanges used various names to designate their function, suggesting the newness of the institutional concept. Most adopted a neologism for "exchange" (usually *jiaoyisuo;* also *jiaohuansuo*). Other terms simply conveyed markets (*shichang, shangchang, jingmaichang*). Some names evoked a locality or region (Shanghai, Pacific Ocean, globe, Great Western, Eastern, global/international, Southeast Asia, inland, China, and China–United States). Some indicated times of operation (daily, weekly, evening, day-and-night).[68]

A sampling of exchange advertisements illustrates their creative naming strategies. All of the following concerns, advertised in Tang's newspaper, were distinct from the first two licensed exchanges, despite similarities in name. None of these names specifies what people could actually purchase at these exchanges. All exchanges listed only Chinese officers. Hyphenated place names (China–United States) conveyed a foreign aura, like fairy dust on a Chinese concern. The listing of actual foreign officers would, in any event, have contravened both Chinese law and the economic nationalism that necessitated the imagination of nationally pure Chinese exchanges.

EXCHANGE NAMES IN NEWSPAPER ADVERTISEMENTS (1921)

China Securities Exchange	中國證券交易所
Shanghai Night Market Commodities Coupon Exchange	上海夜市物券交易所
Shanghai Product Coupon Exchange	申市貨券交易所
China-France International Product Coupon Exchange	中法合辦萬國物券交易所
Shanghai Securities Exchange	滬海證券交易所
China Merchant China-Foreign Exchange	華商中外交易所
China National Product Exchange	中國國產物券交易所
Shanghai China-Foreign Investment Share Exchange	上海中外投票交易所
China-US Securities and Commodities Exchange	中美證券物品交易所
China Securities Exchange	中華證券交易所
China-Western Weekly Securities and Commodities Exchange	華洋星期證券物品交易所
Global Commodities and Securities Day and Night Exchange	環球物品證券日夜交易市場

Although the confusing names of these exchanges suggested they would trade in company shares and/or commodities, it soon became evident that such trading, when it took place, was tangential. The hot-ticket trading involved stock in the exchanges themselves. The primary business of most exchanges was exclusive trade in exchange stock. In other words, the exchanges created a speculative market in an opaque form of derivative.[69] *The Trans-Pacific* highlighted this peculiar and "extremely bad" characteristic, predicting "wild-cat speculation . . . which will [destroy] the stability of the China market":

A strong element of speculation has been injected in the business world. The success of the Chartered Stock and Produce Exchange has resulted in the founding of exchanges to cover almost every phase of commerce and trade. In Shanghai there are more than 39 exchanges. Tientsin, Hankow, Nantongchow, Ningbo and many of the smaller cities have also opened exchanges.

These bodies are not organized as exchanges or bourses are in America and Europe. They do not have members who are subject to the rules of the exchange. They are corporate bodies financing themselves by the sale of shares upon the open market. . . . Anyone can buy shares in an exchange whether or not he is associated with the trade in which the exchange specializes. . . . The exchange makes a profit through the transactions which take place within its rooms and therefore puts a premium on the sale of shares. The exchange encourages speculation in shares or in commodities so that it will make a profit.[70]

By spring 1921, the banking community had become deeply concerned, mindful of the financial crisis that had consumed native banks in 1910. In May, the Bankers' Association appealed to the (national) Ministry of Agriculture and Commerce and (local) Jiangsu provincial authorities, urging the dissolution of the excessive exchanges: "Greedy people rush to buy and sell, throwing the country into [disorder.] Stock prices rise unceasingly. . . . When prices fall, there will be unthinkable disaster, worse than the rubber chaos. Of all market sectors, the financial sector will suffer first, so we cannot remain silent. [We] hope the Ministry [will intervene] to stabilize the market."[71]

A June editorial in *Native Bankers' Monthly* despaired that "the country has gone crazy and public opinion heightens the folly." China had departed from global economic trends. Whereas initial economic prescriptions had assumed the universality of Western-modeled evolution, Chinese deviations now required rethinking, readjustment, and castigation of the Chinese people for bad speculative habits. Correction was necessary to rescue the Chinese economy from dangers posed by the "speculative mindset:"

So-called exchanges have been established in almost every sector, with multiple exchanges competing even within the same sectors. Recently trust companies have formed. Their share prices rise before they even open. [Other] countries impose limits of one exchange to one locality, unlike the deluge in our country. [Society] seeks instant success and profit, to the great harm [of the people]. Safe investment brings prosperity and abundance; risky investment shakes the foundations of society. How may we lead investors to the correct path? [If] we use these financial instruments wisely, we may resist foreign economic invasion. But exchange organizers seek only to speculate. . . . If the exchanges fail, foreign capitalists will step in and our economy will fall into ruin. [Already] there is a silver dollar shortage and widespread speculation. Once crisis occurs, even capable people will be unable to remedy the situation.[72]

The Beiyang government attempted to constrain unregistered exchanges, but lacked jurisdiction in Shanghai's foreign settlements, where most of the exchanges were located. The municipal councils of the two settlements were disinclined to help. The French established a licensing scheme that created a revenue stream from exchanges in their jurisdiction.[73] A Chinese journalist, writing in late summer, asked what could be done in the context of mixed jurisdictions, weak Chinese sovereignty, and poorly developed laws:

China has no central bank that can [regulate rates to control speculation]. . . . Shall we rely on the government to ban [speculative activity]? . . . Despite the promulgation of an exchange law, exchanges have been established without constraint. We predict that a law on trust companies would be similarly useless. [China] has multiple administrations; foreigners interfere. [If] exchanges are banned in Chinese territory they find shelter in the International Settlement, invoking the freedom to do business.[74]

He reflected that in the absence of a political solution, the banking sector must step in: "If banks suddenly awaken and resolutely unite to deny funds to the exchanges, [we may save the economy]." Ultimately, Shanghai's modern Chinese banks announced they would no longer accept loans that were secured by stock.[75] After losing funds to employee speculation (and discovering employees moonlighting as exchange brokers), native banks adopted similar tactics and deployed guild mechanisms to mitigate damage:

Qin Runqing, director of the Native Bankers' Guild, invited the native banks [to discuss solutions]. Managers and staff have taken positions as exchange brokers, dangerously linking our business and exchanges. . . . It is resolved that from the tenth month no native bank will permit managerial or staff involvement in exchanges. Individual banks should surveil each other to prevent future disasters. If anyone is exposed [as a violator] punishment will be imposed in an open meeting.[76]

These tactics moderated the effects of the crisis on the finance industry. The tightening of capital was felt by October and November, when the proliferating exchanges were clearly irresistible to speculators.

"DRUNKEN WITH ILLUSION" AND "BLINDLY CHASING TRUST COMPANIES"

Once banking associations began to constrain the flow of capital to exchanges, observers began to register that exchanges had begun creating their own bank-like structures. *Shenbao* deputy editor Yang Yinhang worried about a "poisonous" mechanism that facilitated speculation with funds from deposits.[77] He described the problem:

So-called trust companies have suddenly arisen like storm clouds on the horizon. Their scope is excessive. They encompass major operations like banking and insurance. They also broker minor things like antique-dealing and gift-purchasing. This is ridiculous but we won't dwell on it. We should be concerned, however, that stock prices for these companies have doubled, even before these companies they have formally opened or have issued stock. This is unbelievable. Their quotas for raising capital are oversubscribed before business has begun. By business or economic logic, this is incomprehensible. A trust company's prospects cannot be known before it has opened. There is no basis for the rising share prices.[78]

Outside China, he explained, trust company business involved neither brokers nor speculators. Chinese, in contrast, were "intoxicated with illusion," "in defiance of all economic principles."[79]

Trust companies were less familiar to the Chinese public than stock exchanges, which had functioned in Shanghai in various forms since at least 1905. In Shanghai, news of trust companies in Europe, the United States, and Japan began to appear here and there in the press shortly before the stock exchange bubble. Their advocates introduced them in the context of a general promotion of Western financial institutions, the introduction of which, many assumed, could lead China to wealth and power. The character of US trust companies—as legally constituted fiduciary agents that administered assets for individuals or businesses or facilitated their transfer—was relatively unexplored.

An early Chinese introduction to trust companies, published in 1919 by Xu Cangshui, editor of the new *Bankers' Weekly,* ventured a remarkably enthusiastic account of the little-understood institutions: "At a time when the idea of savings in our country is still undeveloped, the method of using trust companies offers an extremely favorable path for saving funds and multiplying capital."[80] His advocacy hinted darkly that, without Chinese trust companies, China's businessmen would lack access to the financial resources that were enjoyed by Japanese competitors. If its financial institutions could not keep up, China could lose precious business capital to Japanese institutions.[81]

Precisely because trust companies were unfamiliar, if not entirely unknown to the Chinese reading public,[82] the first Shanghai trust company organizers went to considerable lengths in spring 1921 to construct a pedagogical language of economic plausibility and promise. An early, eye-catching ad for a planned China Trust Company attempted to dispel readers' concerns by simultaneously identifying the company with Western trends and Chinese traditions, all the while conveying proximity to foreign wealth:

> The trust company [facilitates] trade between China and other countries and introductions for businesses in industrial circles. In the big cities of Europe and America, many people run these companies, and they are all wealthy.

The business includes buying and selling merchandise, mortgages, cash deposits, savings and loans, banking, insurance, purchasing and selling construction sites, property rentals, and tax collection. Government bonds, company stock, manufactured goods, and mineral products may all be entrusted to trust companies for management. Once entrusted, trust companies will not disappoint. They enable giving and receiving parties to peacefully enjoy the pleasures of ownership and use without exhausting their minds and strength. Modeled after European and American trust companies, with modifications to suit [Chinese] customs and economic realities.[83]

What followed assured readers that investment served the national economy and upheld moral and civic order. The company's departments— Commercial Trust, Finance Trust, and Social Unity Trust—bridged the global and the local, the foreign and the familiar, "purchasing foreign goods, promoting Chinese products, and collecting ancient Chinese artifacts, handicrafts, and unique natural products." Offering loans, transfers, and deposits, including savings for the elderly, the company "nurtured social frugality," "independent and autonomous citizens," and enabled "businessmen and industrialists, Chinese and foreign, to benefit from exchange and trade, as if they are in the same hall doing business, even when separated by thousands of miles."[84]

Such advertisements immersed readers in a warm bath of associations that blended economic functions with national strength, wealth, and a harmonious and cosmopolitan future that retained traditional virtues and avoided risk. The earnestness of this language (and of Chinese adaptations of the trust company) did not always persuade. The entertainment newspaper *New World* elegantly ridiculed the new institutions in a mock advertisement of its own that was styled as a classical poetic offering. It was ostensibly signed by thirteen poets and prose writers of the Tang and Song dynasties, among them Wang Anshi, Su Dongpo, Han Yu, Ouyang Xiu, Du Fu, Li Bai, and Li Qingzhao. (Some of the humor survives translation):

> This is the Year of the Chicken. The hen cries:
> "One thousand thousands, an infinity of exchanges."
> The cock cries: "How many have transmogrified into trust
>   companies?"
> All of you gentlemen and friends
> Viewing the announcements in the gateway of advertisements,
> See that each trade has an exchange, and most organize trust
>   companies,
> Arousing colleagues' envy and desire.

We spellbinding lyricists of past dynasties are invited sponsors.
We have collected 999999999.999999999 yuan,
Together creating a large nine-nine, a small nine-nine, a small nine-
    nine, a large nine-nine . . . each share of nine expanding to become
    ten. . . .
The [capital] quota is already oversubscribed.
Outsiders cannot gain insiders' knowledge;
Foreigners absolutely cannot think of participating;
Even wealthy people find it difficult to squeeze their hands in.
We are establishing an office to complete the preparations.
As the opening approaches, fearing this news is not well-known,
We post this notice.[85]

The joke was that it took the greatest of China's poets and statesmen to concoct the wordplay that sold trust companies to a gullible Chinese public. In Chinese numerology, multiple nines, the highest odd numeral, invoked the supreme masculinity of the emperor, amplifying the potency of the exchanges and trust companies.

By July, when Tang's China Commercial Trust Company published its first paid announcement, arrangements for as many as six other trust companies were underway in hastily thrown-together planning offices around the city. By this point, the mockable verbiage of the first trust company advertisements was streamlined. Detailed discussion of trust companies had moved onto the pages of the daily press, which unfolded a spirited debate over the function of this still poorly understood financial institution.[86] In the meantime, trust companies, like the Semper Augustus tulip in the Dutch Golden Age, had become all the rage. As the *Shenbao* reported in the same month: "When the name 'trust company' was first heard in Shanghai, the people who run around the market were all abuzz and competed to buy shares. Remembering how [early investors] got rich at the moment of exchange establishment, they thought they would regret it if they missed this new opportunity. This was the time of blindly chasing trust companies."[87]

Twelve trust companies would be established in all. The China Trust Company, which had so elaborately crafted its advertisement in the spring, had dissolved by midsummer. Of eleven remaining in the fall, two were initiated in May, five in June, and four in July.[88] The first would formally open in September. This was the context for the establishment of Tang Jiezhi's China Commercial Trust Company (which was among those that began preparations in June).

For the investing public, the foreign aura of trust companies may have conveyed a magical potency akin to the numeral nine, or simply looked like the next hot thing, as the *Shenbao* journalist understood the situation. We cannot know the precise motivations of their creators. It may be, as one Republican-Era financial writer suggested in retrospect, that the trust companies developed as a fallback for "those who failed to create exchanges or couldn't get their hands on stock exchange stock."[89] But if we lack evidence of individual motivations, trust company promoters did not spare ink in their efforts to naturalize and economically legitimate these obscure institutions.

The editorial line of Tang's *Journal of Commerce* is clear. In May and June 1921, as Tang was launching his company, his newspaper emphasized the accomplishments of US trust companies and affirmed their positive role in fostering economic growth.[90] A late June article found trust companies essential to national development and economic sovereignty and key to resisting "the oppression of foreign capital." This new financial product, which had facilitated the economic development of North America, would flourish in the similarly expansive geography of China's new Republic.[91] A July editorial, published when Tang's trust company was raising investment capital, insisted on the economic legitimacy and necessity of Chinese trust companies:

> Two criteria govern evaluation of enterprise development: 1) they should meet society's actual needs; 2) society must have sufficient human and financial resources. . . . In the past two months eleven trust companies have been established. [This] expresses the vigor of our society's industrial and commercial economy. . . . The legitimate need for trust companies cannot be doubted. Moreover, their capital approaches 80 million yuan. Therefore financial resources are not necessarily insufficient.[92]

As expounders of the gospel of trust companies, *Shangbao* editors agitated for the swift promulgation of appropriate legal regulation by the Chinese Ministry of Agriculture and Commerce. "How could it be," one asked, that the Ministry "is only now drafting a trust company law?" Already numerous trust companies were underway. The interests of Chinese businessmen were imperiled, once again, by the ineptitude of the Chinese state:

> If the law is delayed another day, business losses will increase by a day. If business losses increase, the progress of economic society will be stifled. The bureaucrats do not consider what helps or harms businessmen, who are forced

to await the digging of a well when they are already parched with thirst. . . . Officials only know how to suppress and control businessmen, while obstinately refusing to promulgate a basic law.[93]

Foreign observers were less sanguine about the future of Chinese trust companies. *The Trans-Pacific* noted that the peculiar institutions were already disrupting business:

[T]here is no similarity between the trust company in China and the institution of a similar name in America. A trust company in China is really an investment company. It is financed by the sale of shares on the open market. . . .

When the trust company begins to operate it purchases large quantities of shares in other enterprises, on the chance of a rise. [O]ne of the trust companies in Shanghai made considerable profit on the purchase of the Peking Tramway shares before it was fully organized. Therefore its own shares rose. It speculated not only for profits in the shares purchased but also to inflate the value of its own shares. . . . [It] is doubtful such companies can be successfully managed, for when the enthusiasm of the speculation is over, the trust companies will seek other fields.[94]

In addition to functioning as speculative ventures, the trust companies appear to have served exchanges as a work-around, displacing the administrative complexities of dealing with banks. As time passed they became a means of replacing the banking functions lost to exchange entrepreneurs by their ostracism by the banking sector. The economic historian He Xuyan described the remarkable transfer of capital their creation entailed: "within a few months, tens of millions of yuan were invested in this completely new financial industry."[95] Key organizers of the trust companies were, tellingly, not in the financial sector. Instead, as the *Trans-Pacific* observed, in Shanghai, "Practically the same individuals are active in exchanges and trust companies."[96] Key figures who initially organized the exchanges (among them Yu Xiaqing and Wang Zhengting) appear as initiators of trust companies. Several of these individuals simultaneously served as officers or major shareholders in multiple exchanges and in trust companies. The closely intertwined founding of trust companies with exchanges facilitated capital flows that fueled speculation: "Exchanges turned to trust companies to obtain funds and the trust companies bought and sold their own stock through the exchanges."[97]

When the first Chinese trust company formally opened on September 1, 1921, the *Journal of Commerce* marked the event with both celebration and lament:

Trust company business in Europe and the United States began in the early nineteenth century. In Japan it was later, in Meiji 38. . . . Today all the major cities of Japan and the U.S have trust companies. The same is true of England and Germany. . . . But our country has delayed so long that the first gurgle of China's wellspring of trust companies is bursting through the earth only now, in the tenth year of the Republic. We can only sigh at this slow progress.[98]

By this point, Tang's newspaper, in cooperation with the Commercial Press, was marketing a popular reference book on trust companies, one of several that were assembled and published at this time.[99] Reading these books offers an experience in cognitive dissonance. The economic abstractions they describe bear no connection to Chinese economic institutions and transactions on the ground. Instead they summarize foreign texts that explicate idealized foreign practices. One hastily produced volume, *Guide to Trust Companies,* published in February 1922, devotes the entire text to detailed description of US trust companies and state-by-state regulations. Only on the final page does the compiler note, without clarification, the challenge of extending foreign theories to Chinese circumstances.[100]

The most scholarly of the new books on trust companies was edited by the London School of Economics–trained economist Yang Duanliu. He prefaced his *Introduction to Trust Companies* by expressing bafflement that, "trust companies are the latest pressing concern in our country's business circles." As he drily observed, "Everyone wants to create trust companies, and everyone, equally, has no idea what a trust company is!" Yang queried whether trust companies were "appropriate to the time" or corresponded to the needs of China's industry and business. He posed several pointed questions for trust company initiators: "First, what exactly is your goal? Second, do you have sufficiently trained personnel? If you take people who are unfamiliar with law, accounting, and economics and position them in this work [the future is] difficult to predict."[101]

Tang's own company, the goals and expertise of which remain obscure, was short-lived. At the moment of its founding, it announced that it would raise 5 million yuan, setting a preliminary target of one quarter of that sum. An advertisement dated July 12, 1921, which prominently displayed Yu Xiaqing's name alongside Tang Jiezhi at the top of the board of directors, indicated that 1 million had been raised by that date.[102] By September the company announced it had reached its target of 1.25 million and would establish two departments on Fuzhou Road once office renovations were complete. By this date, only six of the fourteen individuals listed on the original board of directors remained. Yu Xiaqing, perhaps sensing the wisdom of an early departure, is notably absent from the list.[103] Hamada Minetarō lists the trust company address as Wangping Road, the location of Tang's newspaper.[104] By this point Xi Shangzhen, her sister, and many of Tang's employees and their relations had squandered family savings on stock in Tang's trust company. Most of them, like Xi, had invested in June. Actual stock did not become available until late fall. The trust company did not open officially until November or December 1921. By spring 1922 it was in bankruptcy and under liquidation.[105] Xi's money was gone, and her stock was virtually worthless.

THE IMPROPRIETY OF THE FEMALE INVESTOR AND THE PROMISCUITY OF THE EXCHANGE

Contemporary commentators on Shanghai's market bubble drew imaginative connections between female investors like Xi and Shanghai's traumatic investment experience. There was something about a stock exchange that was out of bounds for women. According to the 1914 Exchange Law, women were disqualified from serving as brokers, officers, or employees of an exchange. Women topped the list of excluded categories, which also included criminals of various types and foreigners.[106] In contrast, the fiction of the stock exchange that emerged was full of women. Not a few of the stories published about the "trust and exchange storm" detailed riveting stock exchange-induced female suicides. These, like the real-life suicide of Xi Shangzhen, served as fodder for didactic moralism.[107]

In his treatise on Xi's suicide, the playwright and pioneer filmmaker Zheng Zhengqiu highlighted gender inequities in law and the placement of women beside criminals in unfitness for exchange employment. ("Can this be fair?" he asked.)[108] He contextualized women's exclusion in terms of historical legal discrimination against female inheritance and property ownership in China.[109] Long-standing social habituation to male control over family property made the idea of a female investor inherently suspicious. How, after all, had Xi come by 5,000 yuan? How could she prudently manage such a sum? Didn't the episode demonstrate that female investment threatened family morality and compromised the security of family property?

Older models of business and social networks took for granted age and gender hierarchies and relied on connections with known associates, commonly reinforced by kin or native-place ties. Stock exchanges (and the similarly configured Chinese trust companies), in contrast, offered outsiders greater access to financial instruments and facilitated transactions that transgressed family and business hierarchies or community boundaries. The exchanges made possible for women a new kind of transactional anonymity with money, opening an avenue for economic investment for a group that still enjoyed only limited ability to engage in public social intercourse. Conservatives maintained long-standing suspicions of women's selfish expenditures of family money, which threatened the proper order of family and marketplace. Not only did women's financial transactions facilitate the intrusion of amoral profit making into the interior of the family, but female investment also exacerbated financial risk.

Such concerns were grounded in widely held understandings of female character. Even a feminist like Zheng commented unselfconsciously that a female investor like Xi must be by nature impulsive and find it difficult to resist the temptation to invest. Xi's sympathetic eulogists lamented her inability to resist the lure of money.[110] Their prejudicial assumptions were compounded by imaginative associations between monetary greed and illicit, excessive, and disorderly sex. Most investors were undoubtedly men (and they were undoubtedly impulsive); nonetheless, portraits of the exchanges seized on a variety of female types—wives, new women, concubines, and prostitutes.[111] In the logic of the market, as investors, it was hard to keep these categories of women separate. For moralists, connection with money equally tainted the normally differential claims to virtue of different categories of women. Conservatives depicted stock markets as iconic sites of boundary transgression and virulent moral contamination. In these accounts, women's aspirations for economic liberation exposed them to moral deterioration. This happened as quickly as the new exchanges and trust companies "turned what was formerly gold and silver into paper with characters on it," ultimately transforming it "into wastepaper."[112] One stock market exposé writer used the spectacle of corrupt exchange practices to condemn feminists who wanted to integrate women into male arenas of moneymaking:

> Fashionable people sing of liberation and equality between men and women. [One] exchange director fancied himself a modern man. He raised a strange proposal for hiring both male and female exchange employees. . . . The female exchange employees [were] like a certain female short story writer in Shanghai, or one of her characters. Or like the physical education graduates of a certain school. Most comically, they were like someone's concubine. In short order, they were transformed from female students to prostitutes and from prostitutes to concubines.[113]

Although the 1914 law banned women's employment in exchanges, female exchange employees appeared in fictional accounts of the Shanghai bubble. Whether or not female stock exchange employees had some basis in reality—this study found no trace of such figures—their ability to fascinate was certain. The juxtaposition of money-stained employment and disordered gender relations epitomized the impropriety of women's entrance into male arenas. Morally, all women were degraded by association with the corruptions of the exchange.

Some conservative writers insisted that "women were not permitted to enter exchanges to conduct trade, even if their husband or family head granted permission."[114] This claim may have reflected conservative assumptions or social practice in some cases, but it was not a matter of law. The law neither anticipated nor proscribed female investors. Nor did exchanges discourage their business. The accessibility of the exchange and the logic of stock exchange proliferation called female investors forth. As the numbers of exchanges multiplied, they competed for investors. This led to the development of niche markets. The so-called evening exchanges aimed to induce petty urbanites to invest after work. Several exchanges were located in amusement halls, where exchange gambling presented itself as a novel form of entertainment. Some of these exchanges operated on-site pawnshops aimed at women. A description of such an exchange is preserved in the archives of the French consulate, in the letter of a Chinese resident who appealed to the French authorities to suppress such practices:

> Among the exchanges in the French Concession, there is one in particular that operates at night and is more nefarious than the others. In addition to its exchange business it has installed a pawnshop with the intent of facilitating mortgages on the jewelry that women normally possess, inducing women to abandon themselves to all sorts of speculative activity. Since women are generally ignorant, they fall into these traps more easily than men. . . . This exchange seeks instant profit and is oblivious to the disorder it creates in families and in society."[115]

Concern about the improprieties of female investment, based on assumptions of women's ignorance and susceptibility, was heightened by satirical descriptions of nighttime exchanges that played on double-entendres for "exchange" (*jiaoyi*, which meant both exchange and sexual intercourse). One example is a mock advertisement in *Crystal* for a "Carnal Trade Exchange." The exchange was conveniently located in entertainment halls and hotels. Operating hours were midnight to six A.M. Young men and girls ("older than six years of age") were invited to train together. Prominent prostitutes were named as "exchange organizers." Stock could be purchased at low-class brothels (*xianrouzhuang*, literally, "salty meat shops").[116]

Fictional tales of the stock market appeared in print, many of them serialized in newspapers at the same time that exchange announcements filled the advertisement pages. In these stories, respectable women who invested were often enticed by disreputable brokers. In one fictional vignette entitled, "The Suicide Hanging of a Woman Who Failed," the writer Lu Shouxian portrayed women as natural targets for manipulation. The broker in the story understands that "women's money was easily loosened from their grasp with promises of profit." This story depicts a broker's financial seduction of an insufficiently guarded wife. Her husband periodically traveled for business, unaware of her secret—and ultimately disastrous—financial relations with the broker. The story presents what might have been understood as the *impersonal* economic consequences of the woman's speculative market activity entirely as a result of the *interpersonal relations* between the woman, Madame Hu, her broker, and the exchange director: "She had to sell her clothing and jewelry, and borrow money to repay the debt. Early and late the broker demanded payment, not permitting a slight postponement. Madame Hu begged the broker for mercy." In desperation she visited the stock market director and knelt down humiliatingly before him. Although the fictional Madame Hu was not sexually promiscuous, her financial transactions were depicted as marital improprieties.[117] Such mutual associations of the exchanges and sexuality drew upon earlier cultural critiques of commercial society and the evils of lasciviousness and greed, now depicted as features of Shanghai modernity.

Given the social concerns surrounding female investment, compounded by a lurid social imagination of women's financial and sexual entanglements, it is not surprising that Cheng Pengling's book on Xi's suicide places special emphasis on the fateful moment of Xi's investment. It memorializes Xi's financial relationship with Tang in a full-page illustration that would have appeared provocative to Chinese readers.[118] The delicately carved woodcut depicts Xi and Tang perched together at the corner of a table in the office, with nothing but an abacus between them. An onlooker peeps in from the hallway, a common motif in erotic depictions. The detail heightens the message that this is a scene of seduction. Tang is fancifully pictured wearing both glasses and a Western suit, accouterments that signaled his suspicious foreign style. (Extant photos show him without spectacles and in Chinese dress.) His hand manipulates the abacus, indicating his calculating nature. Xi's fashionable skirt reveals alluring small feet and exposed ankles. Underneath the table, the tip of Tang's pointed Western shoe touches the leg of Xi's chair (Figure 3.3). Readers understood that the woodcut depicted a deadly negotiation. Lest there be any lingering

信记
公司
存款
交涉

3.3 "Discussing Placing Money in the Trust Company."
Reproduced from Cheng Pengling, ed., *Haishang nü
shuji: Xi Shangzhen canshi* (Shanghai female secretary:
The tragic history of Xi Shangzhen), (Shanghai,
Shenheji shuju, 1922).

doubt, the illustration was paired with the woodcut illustration of Xi's suicide by hanging (see Figure 0.1) on the opposite facing page. The pictorial logic showed Xi's suicide as a direct consequence of a seductive and lethal economic transaction.

SHADES OF THE WUTONG CULT, AND WEALTH IN THE VERNACULAR IMAGINATION

Contemporary fiction about finance commonly figured stock exchanges as an occult mechanism for the production of wealth.[119] Because the exchanges and trust companies were opaque, popular understandings of their link to wealth drew on vernacular beliefs about access to money, profit-making, fortune, and gambling.

In the popular culture of the Jiangnan region (which encompassed Shanghai and Xi's home area) one stream of ideas about wealth drew upon the cult of the god, Wutong. The cult of the demonic Wutong spread in the late Ming dynasty, when money surged into daily life in the heavily commercialized region. Understood to govern the dispensation of wealth, Wutong embodied the vices of lust and greed, linking the acquisition of riches to the sexual possession of women. In thrall to his appetites, Wutong tempted and defiled women, leading weak (but materially desiring) individuals into tragedy. In the prurient tales of storytellers and vernacular literature, Wutong's wealth whetted the appetites of impressionable girls. Bestowing gifts, he ravished their bodies. But the magical gold that Wutong offered turned to paper. The despoiled women met sad ends, madness, and death, at a time when the cult of female chastity suggested that women cleanse stains on their virtue through suicide.[120]

In popular religion, riches were thus personified by a disruptive demonic entity that threatened the normative order and the morally appropriate distribution of material goods. In an increasingly commercialized Jiangnan, merchants presented lavish sacrifices to Wutong, attributing business success to loans from the deity. In this and other strains of vernacular thinking, wealth and fortune were a matter of individual destiny or supernatural intervention. Fortune created a karmic debt that needed to be requited through offerings to Wutong. Monetary transactions to repay Wutong's favor may be understood as a metaphor, as historian Richard Von Glahn suggested, of the vulnerability of people caught in a volatile money economy.

Over the eighteenth century, Wutong metamorphosed, possibly in association with his appropriation by urban shopkeepers and merchants, groups linked to an entrepreneurial ethic. The unsavory Wutong was sanitized through a merger with a better-behaved god of wealth, Wulu Caishen, who embodied the business virtues of industry, integrity, and thrift. Analyzing the emergence of this more modern god of wealth, Von Glahn suggested that after the insecurities and anxiety of an expanding money economy gave birth to Wutong, the greater stability of the market in the eighteenth century engendered more positive figurations of wealth. Nonetheless, the Wutong cult and its associated ideas about wealth persisted in the Jiangnan region throughout the nineteenth and early twentieth centuries.[121]

Notions of unsavory access to wealth that were associated with the Wutong cult appear to have become relevant again in the expansive commercialization and economic instability of the Republic. Even if the demonic Wutong didn't precisely rise again, his cult persisted in the Jiangnan countryside. For the people of Suzhou, Mount Shangfang was renowned as a pilgrimage site for its Wutong Shrine. Xi Shangzhen's hometown of Dongting Dongshan was not far from Mount Shangfang. Her extant writings suggest vivid awareness of the Wutong cult.

Xi's posthumously published poetry and her story, "The Bitter Happiness of Little Love" highlighted the twin topics of money (or poverty), and the plight of poor women, themes she knew from her own experience. One of her three surviving poems is entitled, "Borrowing a Covert Loan" (*jie yinzhai*). The idea of a "covert loan" arose from the predicaments of belief that an individual's maximum lifetime attainment of wealth was both finite and fated. Any disproportionate desire to enjoy prosperity in the present threatened to diminish one's lifetime allotment. Those who chose to "borrow" against their allotment needed to "replenish fate" (*buyun*) with deposits of spirit money at an appropriate shrine. Such ritual practice aimed to secure good fortune by redeeming the spiritual debt.[122] Penned by an educated new-style woman who, with her classmates, had made offerings to the spirit of the female revolutionary Qiu Jin, Xi's poem "Borrowing a Covert Loan" reveals her ambivalence about offerings to Wutong and her suspicion of the monks who profited from poor people's devotions:

> At Mount Shangfang in Suzhou,
> There is a god called the Creditor of the Dead.
> He is said to be the source of wealth.
> Poor people flock there; their numbers reveal their bewitchment.
> Temple priests prepare paper money, like businessmen stockpiling goods.
> From far and near, people compete in prayerful supplications.

Fragrant incense fills the temple
[The deafening throng] silences soft voices.
People borrow sacrificial money,
Placing it in the ritual vessel before departing.
Keeping some to put before their kitchen god at home.
Each year they increase their offerings of money to repay the god.
Their lives are filled with hardship.
Greedy people hear and hope to become rich, dreaming of money.
The key thing is to make a living.
Otherwise you are bullied by that god.
The temple monks are fraudulent.
False gods cheat ignorant people.
How can you ask for wealth? What is the use of prayer?
Who goes to the mountain temple just to hear words of the Buddha?
How may a greedy heart be restrained?
The only answer is to be content [and face] poverty through diligence.[123]

Although she expressed contempt for "stockpiling" priests ("like businessmen") and "fraudulent" monks, Xi's poem poignantly sympathized with the poor. Her assertion, "the key thing is to make a living," echoed her own path to modest employment. But as the poem flows, this claim is less than confident. Xi's question, "How may a greedy heart be restrained?" stands out. Might we read the poem's concluding line, which advises contentment and "facing poverty through diligence," as a nostrum that Xi hoped that she herself could swallow? In retrospect, her desperate investment gamble belied her own poetic counsel and suggests her challenges, as she struggled to make ends meet, in the face of the temptations of a booming stock market.

The thoroughly monetized Qing economy gave rise to an abundance of verses about money, a source that illuminates Late Imperial vernacular ideas of money. Both "grand themes" of wealth and secondary concerns "like financial transfers for the dead" preoccupied Qing poets with an intensity that the historian Mark Elvin suggested was "unparalleled in any other society or age." Such verse depicted a world of "remorseless present day financial calculation," in which greed comprised "the fabric of life," and the market was a proving ground of life or death.[124] Ensnared in webs of money, human life was commodified in a commercialized world that forced bodily labor to redeem debt or simply to maintain livelihood. Even as she registered her skepticism of clerics, Xi's poem drew on this extensive tradition of monetary verse that depicted the life-bestowing and denying powers of money and fate.

STAKING EVERYTHING ON A BAD VENTURE:
CRIMES OF GAMBLING AND SPECULATION

Gambling (another topic in Late Imperial poetry) occasioned a stream of associations in vernacular thinking about fate, fortune, and access to wealth. Mencius identified gambling as selfish, unfilial behavior that interfered with a son's duty to maintain his parents. Moralists condemned gamblers, as violators of ethical obligations, for a wasteful and self-destructive vice that prevented the ability to think rationally or sustain family bonds.

Organized gambling was illegal in Late Imperial China. Prohibitions appear in the Great Ming Code and the Great Qing Code.[125] Gambling was nonetheless popular, even ubiquitous as everyday pastime and entertainment. Condemnation of gambling grew shrill in the Republic, as New Culture propagandists held an array of "traditional" habits and character flaws responsible for weakening the Chinese nation. Chief among such flaws were the linked vices of visiting prostitutes and gambling, which dissipated family wealth. Reformers aimed to extirpate gambling from Chinese cities. The May Fourth press is awash in editorials attacking the evils of lotteries and advocating suppression of all forms of gambling.[126] As seen in the following example, which found approving translation in the English-language press, gambling was often depicted (following a New Culture susceptibility to Western caricatures of Chinese "pathology") as a cultural addiction:[127]

> The Chinese may be the most ardent gamblers [making] gambling an indispensable supplement to wedding feasts, birthday parties, and even funeral feasts. From the highest official down to the laborer, gambling is a regular occupation. . . . Those in power have never tried to suppress this widespread gambling habit. On the contrary, everything is done to encourage it. Lotteries are a form of official gambling . . . The Zhejiang lottery, "benevolent lottery," Hubei lottery, and Anhui lottery continue in full swing. Under the pretext of public welfare, some persons have surely become rich by this means. With the exception of a handful of men who actually benefit, no one derives any good. In our view, all lotteries should be suppressed.[128]

Promoters of new financial institutions endeavored to differentiate modern speculative investment from discredited gambling, as we have seen. Their carefully elaborated distinctions were mocked in fictional depictions of the exchanges, which commonly characterized them as gambling dens and presented readers with the same tableaux of death and family ruin that appeared in didactic lessons about the consequences of gambling.

In Shanghai and the adjoining provinces of Zhejiang and Jiangsu, the most notorious and popular form of gambling was called *huahui* (to which Jiangsu Assemblyman Huang Shenxi compared Shanghai's exchanges). *Huahui* involved a complicated sort of roulette or lottery in which gamblers placed bets on thirty-six "doors" (cards with named figures on them). One of the figure-cards was secretly concealed in a tube-like receptacle or roll of cloth. At an appointed time, crowds gathered and the tube was dramatically opened, or the cloth unfurled.[129] The game was operated throughout the region by professionals (itinerants in the countryside) who accepted bets of all amounts, luring rich and poor to the game. Winners received nearly thirty times their wager. In Shanghai the game was known for attracting women, as depicted in a 1919 cartoon of *huahui* as the number one evil of Shanghai's "evil society" (Figure 3.4).

Women are shown running into the roiling sea through an ingot-shaped gate, marked "*huahui*." Chinese police reports from the 1920s frequently identified women's losses in *huahui* as a cause of suicide.[130] Because Shanghai game operators sent runners to people's homes to collect wagers and deliver rewards, this form of gambling was convenient for women who found it awkward to go out. Throughout the 1920s civic groups agitated for the prohibition of *huahui*, but the goal proved

3.4 "Shanghai's Evil Society, Number One: *Huahui*." *Jingbao*, October 27, 1919.

consistently elusive.[131] Imaginative linkages between gambling and Shanghai's exchanges help to explain particular concern with female exchange investment and suicide.

Gambling evils and the cosmic retribution they incurred may also be tied to depictions of the stock exchange. An illustration of the evils of gambling shows a female-identified demon-like figure (a *yaonie*) in a black cape emblazoned with a death's head. The figure holds aloft a scale that contains gold bars and coin (on the left). Labeled "life," "reputation," "family," and "property," these are consumed by flames. The right-hand basket contains an item labeled *huahui,* together with dominoes, dice, and other gambling devices. The scale tips slightly to the right. The transfixed gamblers (at right) turn into leering skulls (left), as lives, family, and property go up in smoke (Figure 3.5). An accompanying article on *huahui* emphasized its popularity, especially among women who were known to consult diviners and burn incense, praying for good fortune before placing bets.[132] This illustration assembles elements of vernacular visual culture that were redeployed in cartoon depictions of the stock exchange.

Images of exchange speculation shared the iconography of gambling, with its concern for dangerous play, suicide, and destructive female behavior. A cartoon entitled "Speculators" shows enraptured children, eyes fixed on lucky chickens (*ji,* a pun for the *ji,* in *touji,* literally, the target that is hit) that are identified by the neologisms "stock exchange" and

3.5 The Evils of Gambling. *Jingbao,* April 24, 1919.

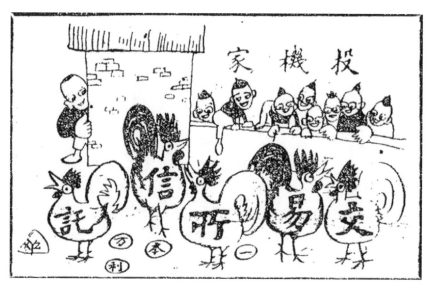

3.6 "Speculators" (*Toujijia*). *Jingbao,* October 27, 1921.

"trust company."[133] Whereas the cartoon depiction of gambling in Figure 3.5 gave minimal textual explanation (its warning about gambling dangers would have been obvious to readers), the graphic representation of exchange speculation in Figure 3.6 performs the function of translating economic neologisms with familiar visual cues and verbal idioms. The tempting eggs laid by the wondrous chickens are labeled with a familiar phrase that conveyed extraordinary profitability: "immense profit from a bit of capital" (*yiben wanli*).

The "Speculators" cartoon focuses on the element of play and profit, barely hinting at the dangers of speculation. The lethal character of exchange gambling is fully manifest in a second cartoon, "The Evils of the Stock Exchange," which appeared shortly after Xi Shangzhen's suicide. The term used for evil is *nie*, which conveys karmic sin and its inevitable punishment as moral retribution. The death-scape of skulls is captioned "Stock Exchange Product Exhibition Hall." Individual skulls bear tags identifying modes of suicide (drowning, poisoning, hanging, etc.). The largest skull is identified as "The latest arrival, Miss Xi" (Figure 3.7).

The two realms of gambling and securities speculation may have also been linked by government fund-raising practices and personnel. Histories of Chinese gambling note its popular character and the dynamism of lotteries in China's modern transformations.[134] Although lotteries were frequently proscribed, late Qing and early Republican regional governments

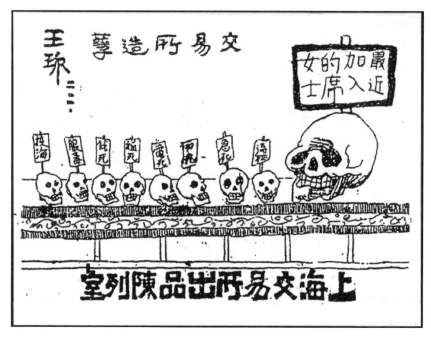

3.7 "Evils of the Stock Exchange" *(Jiaoyisuo zao nie)*. *Jingbao,* September 18, 1922.

operated charitable lotteries (among them, Hubei disaster aid lotteries and Zhejiang dike lotteries). These conveyed the promise of great returns while connecting lottery gambling to social welfare. The immensely popular "surname-guessing" lottery *(weixing)* was linked to the late Qing examination system, which was the primary mechanism for achieving bureaucratic position. At the turn of the twentieth century, lotteries were not only drawn on by financially strapped provincial governments, but were also used by foreign companies to help sell foreign products in China. Indeed, because of the frequent suppression of Chinese lotteries, some Chinese accounts suggest that lotteries, like the later stock exchanges, were a foreign import, dating to the turn of the century.[135]

Fortune in the form of lottery tickets (many of them imprinted with the phrase "immense profit from a bit of capital") was a more tempting form of investment than savings banks. At the time of the Shanghai bubble Chinese banks competed with "lottery savings companies" and used lottery tickets *(caipiao,* also *jiangquan)* as an inducement for opening savings accounts.[136] People in convenient service occupations—for example teahouse attendants—sold lottery tickets as a sideline occupation. The lotteries, advertised in Shanghai papers that had national distribution, were popular and drew people from the interior to Shanghai to purchase lottery tickets from brokers. Identifying these people as Shanghai's first securities brokers, historian Yu Laishan noted the hiring of lottery ticket brokers by the China Merchants' exchange as it scrambled to hire brokers with relevant experience.[137]

Although only fragmentary traces of such direct connections may be found, imaginative connections between lotteries and the exchanges are easily documented. For example, the cartoon "Both Are Speculation" depicts lotteries and exchanges as two methods of fishing, differing only in technique (hook or net) (Figure 3.8). In a similar imaginative linkage of lotteries and exchanges, in spring 1922 Jiangsu sojourners in Beijing, unable to "bear the heartbreak" of people's financial troubles in their native province, sent twin petitions to the Ministries of Finance and Agriculture and Industry to ban and strictly supervise lotteries and exchanges in Shanghai, "two new types of speculation that proliferated in the past two years in Shanghai." The petition stated that although "the exchange [balanced prices in foreign countries and] was not originally a harmful institution," the speculative character of Chinese people and Shanghai's prominence as a gambling center had led to the speculative creation of more than one hundred exchanges. The resulting bankruptcies, fraud, and self-inflicted harm demanded government intervention.[138]

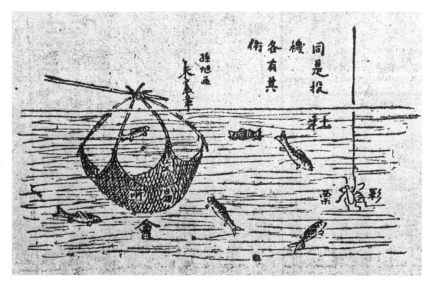

3.8 "Both Are Speculation; Each Has Its Technique" (The fish hook is labeled "lottery" 彩票; the net is labeled "exchange" 交易所). "Tong shi touji; ge you qi xian," *Shenbao,* August 2, 1921.

THE MORAL EQUIVALENCE OF THE EXCHANGE, LIBERAL DEMOCRACY, AND THE FAILED REPUBLIC

The imagined and real linkages of the exchanges to popular beliefs and practices helps to explain the role of the "exchange and trust storm" in the developing pedagogy of the market in the early twentieth century. The historical lessons that observers took from these institutions of finance capitalism did not bode well for supporters of market liberalism. Economics and finance were understood, not as discrete realms, but as tied to abiding ideas of statecraft, in a pervasive atmosphere of concern for the uncertain project of state-building in the new time of the Republic. This broader conceptualization of things economic meant that failures or malfeasance in the marketplace had wide resonance. The Shanghai financial bubble accordingly stained perceptions of associated institutions of liberal democracy.

As their wake of bankruptcies widened, exchanges and the trust companies they spawned were exposed as a swindle. Financial experts who had promoted exchanges as a tool that could guarantee fair and accurate prices seemed to have taken people for a ride. Not only had market information proved unreliable, but newspapers, the heralded medium for public dissemination of financial information, looked as corrupt as the exchanges. Newspapers served throughout this episode as a venue for exchange news, economic pedagogy, and public reckoning. But they had not been transparent. Satirists portrayed financial reportage as a smokescreen or "dark curtain" that obscured insider dealing, market manipulation, and speculative intrigue (*heimu*).[139]

At the height of the bubble, *Crystal* published a biting critique of newspaper complicity, entitled "Major Newspapers and the Exchanges":

> Shanghai newspapers receive innumerable advertisements. . . . Thanks to the beneficence of the exchanges, even financially stressed newspapers now survive. Although they know that exchanges will create economic panic, newspaper personnel hope the numbers of exchanges will increase daily. Ideally, of five newspaper pages, four and a half will be filled with exchange advertisements, and only half a page will be reserved for news.[140]

In Jiang Hongjiao's novel *Exchanges Unmasked* (which drew on the author's intimate knowledge of recent events) the fictional *Plain-talk News* operated as an economic parasite that preyed on new financial institutions.[141] It specially raised its advertisement fees for exchanges, aware of their particular dependence on publicity. It also seized the opportunity presented by the rhetoric of the national products movement and nationalist fear-mongering to blackmail the first exchange by spreading rumors that it harbored hidden Japanese employees.[142]

Some of the more intriguing fictional characterizations of the exchange likened its operations to old and new governing mechanisms in the Republic, which appeared in vernacular commentary as another venal realm of speculation. The old and new regimes were linked, in literary imagination, by the titles of the two most substantial literary works that depicted the exchanges. It was no accident that Jiang Hongjiao's serialized novel and Lu Shouxian's lurid "dark curtain" exposé of the exchanges shared the same title, *Exchanges Unmasked.* The choice of title placed these works in the lineage of Li Boyuan's earlier, genre-defining novel, *Officialdom Unmasked (Guanchang xianxingji)*. Written between 1901 and 1906 and filled with extensive details of financial transactions, Li's novel illustrated the transactional character of office purchasing and official culture at the twilight of the Qing dynasty.

The stories Jiang and Lu told of the exchanges presented the ideals of republican governance as a mask that obscured familiar, corrupt machinations, and particularistic ties. One of Lu Shouxian's chapters, "Forming Parties and Struggling for Power," described bizarre doings and unprincipled "filth" (*wochuo*) within a fictional exchange that was run by a judicial official whose career straddled the revolution. Before the revolution he had manipulated his government post for power and profit. In the new Republic, he watched the rising share prices of the first exchange and adapted his skill at "seizing government positions" to grab an official post in the exchange. He quickly imported relatives and people from his native place and took over the operations.[143]

In another chapter, an exchange organizer named Shi fell prey to a colleague who similarly employed the method of "seizing government positions." While Shi recruited people with expertise in Shanghai, his cunning colleague Zhang recruited relatives and friends from his village. Zhang hid his retinue temporarily in a hotel while he secretly relocated the exchange preparation office. By the time Shi discovered the new location, Zhang's men had occupied all the desks. A final anecdote took up the tendency of late Qing officials to use birthday celebration invitations to solicit bribes from candidates who sought official positions and suggested that such practices had simply shifted location in the Republic. Now former officials set up exchange preparation offices and sent birthday invitations to solicit contributions from board members, sponsors, and staff.[144]

This fictional transposition of the commodification of Qing officeholding onto the economic engine of the exchange placed blame on cultural habits as well as on the way monetary transactions had brought about a crisis in an earlier system of governance that was formerly legitimated through an examination system. This raised questions about the novelty and legitimacy of political economy in the Republic. As speculation ran rampant, commentators did not simply deride exchanges and their inhabitants. Some writers more broadly targeted capitalism and the language of economic nationalism, which served as a cover for rapacious moneymaking. A satirical essay written by Yang Yinhang that described a "fertilizer exchange" for example, used the pungent stink of the business as a metaphor for the corruptions of capitalism. Whether business involved the indisputable "national product" of night soil or foreign products, the odor was the same. In each, "businessmen chase after something rotten and stinky, and government officials emanate the stink of money."[145]

The polluting stink of money and speculation permeated the entire package of liberal economics and democracy, in a process of importation that began in the late Qing reforms. Exchange speculation and election manipulation were coined in the same mint, so to speak. The venal character of elections was a common element in satirical depictions of corrupt practices in the Republic.[146] A cartoon captioned "China's New Business," for example, depicted the fluctuating daily market price of election ballots in the context of troubled practices and legal questions surrounding the March 1921 national parliamentary election and July 1921 Jiangsu provincial legislative elections (Figure 3.9). Reflecting on the corruption of elections in the Republic, as Joshua Hill has recounted, a Suzhou journalist wryly suggested that they be discarded and replaced by lotteries, which—in a twist on the legitimacy of gambling practices—had greater appeal in that they might at least create revenue streams for the government.[147]

The words for "election" (*xuanju*) and "exchange" (*jiaoyisuo*) came together in references to "election exchanges" (*xuanju jiaoyisuo*) that emerged in newspaper editorials and literary supplements at the height of the exchange bubble. This compound neologism reflected assumed linkages between the foreign financial and political institutions that had so rapidly gained currency in China. If peculiar-sounding today, the phrase highlighted a logical association of the time, confirming Chinese suspicions of elections as a speculative vote-purchasing mechanism:

> [The price of a vote] fluctuates according to market conditions. Those who campaign for a candidate deduct a percentage as their service fee. This resembles the customs and rules of an exchange. . . . [T]he profits people gain

3.9 "China's New Business." *Shenbao,* July 26, 1921.

from this process are more evenly distributed than bonuses among share-holders. All that people are capable of doing in exchanges may also be seen in an election. The only difference is that what is bought and sold in an exchange is a commodity. What is bought and sold during elections is the integrity of citizens.[148]

The editorial was unsparing in its depiction of the role of the market in the new governing order: "Legislators and politicians collude with moneyed interests and live by selling off railroads, mines, and all types of Chinese rights. How is it that selling votes should be considered 'illegitimate?'"[149]

A second satirical example is a mock advertisement for an "Election Ballot Exchange." It began by comparing financial instruments ("Government bonds are quite profitable, but costs eat 40% of the gains. Lotteries provide lucky chances, but not everyone reaps high rewards.") Investors were counseled to abandon these inefficient paths to fortune for the newer instrument of the election ballot exchange. The wealthy might thus "compete to buy their way into parliament," manage "discrepancies between supply and demand," and "corner the market on a rare commodity":

> This [election exchange] holds good credit [and] facilitates business, with the acquiescence of the government. . . . High-class clients should not hesitate to invest. Together we can manipulate the world. For those with limited capital, we will take limited profits. Whether you are from South or North China, you are all welcome at the exchange, we provide package services.[150]

If this writer intermingled ideas of nondiscrimination and equal access with manipulation and "cornering the market," another spoof tied exchanges to the myriad ills of the failed Republic:

> Several types of enterprises should borrow the name "exchange." Politicians . . . brag about the capital they have for elections. They hire people to vote for them and treat democratic elections as a business. . . . This is why an election exchange should be established. [There should also be] bribery exchanges and [kidnapping and female trafficking] exchanges. Do financially enlightened families not agree?[151]

The humor in these passages played upon the multiple resonances of neologisms. Neologism, as a process, created unanticipated or discordant meanings by juxtaposing characters in new ways to represent imported concepts. Just as *jiaoyisuo* (exchange) suggested a place for sex (as highlighted by the "carnal trade exchange"), the name for trust company (*xintuo gongsi*) had a peculiar ring to it. The trust company concept was murky in itself, but the neologism that named it turned the cardinal Confucian virtue of trustworthiness (*xin*) into a marketable commodity. This upended foundational notions of public good and private interest, as suggested by a mock advertisement for a "Trust Private Company":

> Trust among people should be considered "public," and yet Chinese trust alone [is now] "private." Any wealthy merchant, businessman, magnate or high official may enjoy our "trust private company" (*xintuo sisi*) with their property, money, treasure, and other precious items. . . . Although we share the same aspiration [of taking money] as unfilial sons and fierce robbers, we operate in a peaceful fashion without threatening lives.[152]

This playful essay, written while prices were still rising, highlighted the inversion of values, the commodification of human trust, and the way that capitalist institutions and advertisement betrayed the sincerity of language itself.

Six months later, a mournful meditation on language appeared in Tang Jiezhi's newspaper amid an urban landscape of bankruptcy and disorder. On January 1, 1922, accompanying Tang's sorrowful accounting of his newspaper's first year, the *Journal of Commerce* published a lengthy essay by Chen Qihuai (former revolutionary, educator, and brother of Chen Bulei). Chen offered his new year's essay for the benefit of the "badly diseased speculative businesses"; the benefit of the "not yet sick speculative businesses"; and the benefit of "average ambitious businesses." The essay excavated the meaning of speculation (*touji*), which Chen tied to governance by means of an exercise in linguistic genealogy. He began with the character *ji*機 (chance, opportunity, crucial point, intention), and explained that it referred to the "initiation of the pivot" (*shuduan fadong*). Chen thus linked speculation to classical notions of the cosmos, or the heavenly mandate, which conceived of the ruler as a balancing pivot for the state. Chen criticized the speculators of his day, who, "driven by profit," had "lost both their timing and their ability" and "abused the power engendered by their resources." His essay aimed to alert readers to shifts in social thinking: "Originally people identified the appropriate moment by measured judgments; now they identify with wild ambition." Chen concluded his lengthy and often obscure essay, which is dense with philological meanderings and philosophical abstractions, with a reflection on the first decade of the Republic, in which men roved about in vanity, madness, and mediocrity. He described the Republic itself as infused by "speculative fever" which, if unchecked, would lead to darkness and doom.[153]

FETISHIZED BY THEIR associations with Western power, the financial science of economics and its peculiar institutional offspring, stock exchanges and trust companies, seemed initially like a pretty good bet. Because he imagined their potential for increasing capital to be "exceptionally huge," Kang Youwei and his successors in the early Republic dismissed critics who identified the stock market with harmful speculation. Kang had appealed to a logic of good odds, arguing that, based on Western experience, "winners predominate."[154] Abstracted of connection to local specificities and historical practice, Western and Japanese-styled financial institutions and ideas, with their foreign names and terminology, served as icons of development. For reformers in the first decade of the Republic, they promised access, not simply to wealth, but also to an imagined package of rational governance that was associated with liberal democracy. Without the ability to conjure essential institutional and informational infrastructure, however,—not to mention adequate law and legal sovereignty—price predictability and economic rationality proved chimeric.

The story of the exchange bubble that is recounted in this chapter may be the story of a con game (by organizers), but it is certainly also the story of a gamble (by both organizers and investors). It was not that observers failed to point out that economic jargon and nationalist language cloaked illegal machinations and risk. Certainly Western economics and institutions conveyed an aura of wealth and power. But while they were deployed to dazzle, there is little evidence to demonstrate that investors believed that modern speculation was fundamentally different from gambling. Everything pointed to it being a gamble, and possibly an improved type of gamble, being modern. Like Kang Youwei, they may have figured they had pretty good odds. Kang, like the Chinese investors who soon flocked to the exchanges, was rather clear-sighted about the fact that exchange speculation was a gamble.

Aura notwithstanding, the new institutions ceased to pay out, and, on going bankrupt, they lost their ability to persuade. Introduced and promoted by Chinese entrepreneurs, when the gamble failed, these institutions brought on a crisis that delegitimated the Chinese who made the bad bet, the Western science that served as window-dressing for the bet, and the liberal modernity that had failed to pay off in the gamble that was the Republic. Chinese economists would soon cast away the norms of liberal finance and borrow authority from the imagination of a new indigenized science. In the 1930s, Chinese economists would reject liberal economic theories and argue that Chinese conditions required the development of a state-driven "controlled economics" (*tongzhi jingji*) or "national economics" (*minzu jingji*)." This turn to party control could easily mobilize the memory of market trauma, even images of karmic punishment, in the interest of a new financial discipline. Exchanges remained, and they remained corrupt, but they largely traded in government bonds and served the state.[155]

The language of liberal economics promoted by Tang's paper was exposed in the aftermath of the exchange bubble. Its foreign cachet lost its sparkle along with its legitimacy as science. In the tumultuous aftermath of financial devastation, many would concur that a crime had taken place. As Zheng Zhengqiu phrased the key question in his introduction to a book that was inspired by the suicide of Xi Shangzhen, "Whose crime is this? It is the crime of economics."[156] Not everyone, however, was satisfied with the targeting of an abstraction, when the opportunity presented itself to judge a flesh-and-blood villain. Indeed, there was no consensus about the character of the crime, the appropriate mode of its adjudication, or the means of achieving justice.

CHAPTER FOUR

Morality and Justice in an Unsettled Republic

A constitutional nation emphasizes law. The written law is imprecise. Vicious cliques adopt fake law, which harbors a thousand murderers and ten thousand evils. . . . A republican nation emphasizes public opinion. Public opinion is based on the will of the people. If public opinion expresses the true will of citizens, it doesn't matter if the law is clearly written. Public opinion must eventually prevail. By this means the incompletely prepared law will ultimately be corrected by public opinion.

—*Shenbao* editorial, October 15, 1921

The arrest of Dr. F. C. Tong and of the Minister of Finance, Lo Wen-kan, and the warrant issued by the president for the arrest of Mr. Fu Siao-en should have more than a passing interest for the younger Chinese, who are keen for the relief of China from the umbrageous position in which she now is. The law, when it is capricious, political and uncertain, can do more to disturb the nation than the depredations of banditry. Dr. Tong was arrested at two o'clock in the morning by men not in uniform and has been held without bail. . . . Despotism in any form is harmful to the free development of a nation and in China today, every petty official is a despot who can do whatever he pleases without any regard for the rights of those whom he governs.

—Editorial, *The Weekly Review*, December 2, 1922

B EGINNING IN FALL 1922 and stretching into 1924, the Xi-Tang case wound its way through diverse, overlapping, and potentially conflicting laws, legal institutions, and judicial cultures. From the perspective of everyday practice, the Chinese judicial process was patchwork and improvisational, of a piece with the early Republic. Chinese and foreign newspapers served up a variety of frameworks for thinking about law and justice, which were fraught topics at the time. Newspapers editorialized on the ideal relationship between law and the political frame of the Republic, criticized the imperfections of laws and legal institutions, queried the efficacy of distinctive legal models, and contemplated public opinion as an alternate mechanism for achieving justice. The legal twists and turns of Tang's arrest and trial served as a touchstone for public reflection on these themes, variously arousing hope, bafflement, skepticism, and fury.

The creation of a republic repositioned people as citizens in a state that was to be governed by law, rights, and the protection of property, aspirational ideals that took shape in language long before they could find expression in practice. Chinese jurists began to revise the Qing code and the administration of justice in the last decade of the dynasty, making changes that would extend into the Republic. But whereas Qing law was an instrument of the state, administered under a Board of Punishments, law in the Republic was administered under a renamed Ministry of Justice. The theoretical adoption of popular sovereignty necessitated changes in terminology and legal procedures. Legal language and procedure in the Republic affirmed citizens' rights, legal representation, and separation between the administrative and judicial realms.[1] Practices of judicial torture and corporal punishment—stigmatized by Western powers as barbaric—were replaced by incarceration.

The reformed legal system was thus modeled on Western practice, the universal validity of which appeared to be confirmed by its adoption in a rapidly modernizing Japan. Japan offered both advisors and templates for adaptation.[2] At the same time, the revised law retained features of indigenous tradition that reformers considered appropriate for the Chinese nation. Shen Jiaben, the leading Qing jurist in the legal reform, ensured significant continuities with the indigenous legal corpus. These extended into the Republic Era.[3]

Like other aspects of the conceptual and institutional landscape of the Republic, the confusions of law that emerged in this process of rapid transformation had everything to do with nineteenth-century encroachments on Chinese sovereignty and the power that accrued to Western ideas and institutions. From the 1860s, the Western treaty powers justified extraterritorial jurisdiction with the claim that Chinese law was uncivilized and unacceptable for the citizens of Western nations. Ross Browne, the US minister to China, backed by his British counterpart, Sir Rutherford Alcock, stated that China needed to enact "a code of laws based on principles of justice, recognized and accepted by the comity of Western nations." A retrofitted Westernization of Chinese law was thus stipulated as a prerequisite to any rescinding of extraterritorial privilege. As Shen Jiaben described the situation: "Consular jurisdiction was [imposed by foreign powers] in China under the pretext that our judicial system was defective. Initial

British [pressure] was followed by Germany, while Japan even set up courts of law in [the Northeast]. Our sovereignty has been undermined day by day. The current situation makes it imperative to reform our legal system."[4]

Under what Li Chen has termed the "epistemic violence" of this juncture, after several decades of the translation and study of Western and Japanese law, the Qing government initiated a process of legal and judicial reform that would give shape to the revised law of the Republic. Chinese legal reformers, working with Japanese scholars, completed a draft criminal code in 1907. The draft drew on the modern Japanese criminal code, which was modeled initially on Napoleonic law and had been revised on the basis of German law.[5]

Yuan Shikai enacted a slightly modified version of the 1907 draft as the Interim New Criminal Code of the Republic of China in 1912. Differences of opinion persisted concerning the selection of Chinese and Western features. If the Republic made do with a partially contested and provisional criminal law for sixteen years, it managed with even less of a civil law, which remained aspirational. The absence of explicit civil law may have been less unsettling for Chinese jurists than a provisional criminal code since a civil code lacked indigenous precedent.[6] A draft civil law had been equally a project of the late Qing reforms, but it was still incomplete by the time of the Revolution. Thus, in spring 1912, the Ministry of Justice advised, with characteristic ambiguity, that civil adjudication should follow useful provincial customs but should also refer as appropriate to relevant Japanese commercial and civil laws. Portions of the Qing code that were relevant to civil matters also retained validity.[7] Ten years later, in 1922, Zhang Yaozeng, the head of a commission on judicial practice, still looked forward to a time when judges no longer faced "the awkward process of relying on customs and usages" since "different places had different customs."[8] The profusion of Chinese and foreign guideposts and the paucity of written law illustrate the ideological flux of the judiciary in this interim era.[9] The civil law of the Republic, relevant for enterprises, trade, and finance, would not be promulgated until 1929–1930.

The challenges of creating and staffing new courts compounded the unsettled character of judicial administration. To speak simply of the shift from traditional magistrates' offices (*yamen*) to new courts of law (*shenpanting*), there was neither sufficient funding nor adequately trained personnel. A five-year plan mandated the creation of 2,000 courts: 500 each year from 1914 to 1917 (and 40,000 new judges).[10] More courts were established in major cities where they were visible to foreign authorities. Inland, the administration made do with traditional *yamen*s, with the result that traditional and modern judicial institutions coexisted for much of the Republican Era.[11] As government fragmented, some provincial authorities took it upon themselves to abolish newly established courts. One such case in 1922 involved the governor of Zhejiang province. When chastised by the Beiyang government for dismantling new courts, he reportedly opined that "the central government should never have established the courts in question."[12] The new legal culture remained tentative, spatially delimited, and subject to local authority.

The rise of local militarists diminished the authority of both old and new Chinese courts in the Republic through the growing exercise of legal exceptionalism. Insofar as exceptionalism had a legal foundation, it was based on a 1914 "Law on Punishing Robbers and Bandits." The law allowed for temporary extraordinary measures to preserve order in provinces infested with bandits while maintaining the formal judicial process in other realms. Its practical consequence, however, was to affirm the potential applicability of exceptional measures anywhere, without regard to time or place.[13] Military authorities interfered in or sidestepped regular law and judicial proceedings and instituted summary justice—executions, displacement, and imprisonment—without representation or appeal. Military justice and penal institutions (which were not within the purview of the reforms) have passed largely under the radar of Chinese legal history research,[14] but they served as wild cards in the deck of formal Chinese legal institutions that dealt justice in the Xi-Tang case.

This collection of Chinese institutions was complicated by a thicket of foreign courts on Chinese soil, novel hybrids that sprouted in Shanghai's semicolonial terrain. The multiple extraterritorial jurisdictions that divided the city obstructed the enforcement of Chinese legal authority. Shanghai's Chinese jurisdictions were bisected by the International Settlement and French Concession. In Chinese-governed spaces, Chinese judges presided. In the foreign settlements, the Mixed Courts provided for both extraterritorial privilege and Chinese sovereignty (the framework for the inquest that followed Xi's suicide).[15] By the time of the Xi-Tang case, Mixed Court practice had evolved a complex choreography:

> Under the present rules of the court, Chinese magistrates, appointed by the Peking Government, sit with foreign assessors having equal power. Two assessors appointed by the British Consul-General, sit on Mondays, Wednesdays and Fridays; two assessors, appointed by the American Consul-General, sit on Tuesdays and Thursdays; and one assessor each, appointed by the Italian and Japanese Consuls-General, sit on Saturday. In the French Mixed Court, French assessors only sit with the Chinese magistrates.[16]

Consular courts and extraterritorial courts for foreign nationals (for example, the US Court for China) added to the legal assemblage. Such foreign courts on Chinese soil—the stigmata of impaired sovereignty—were understood to disadvantage China in globally asymmetrical relations of power. At the same time, they created accidental spaces and opportunities that could be manipulated in practice.[17] It was not unusual for Chinese litigants to pursue suits in foreign venues, despite their foreign taint. Some took up lawsuits in both Chinese and foreign courts to maximize their options.[18] Lawyers who practiced in the city needed expertise in multiple legal systems.

JUSTICE BEYOND FORMAL LAW AND LEGAL INSTITUTIONS

Beyond formal law and institutions, the production of justice in China relied on customary mechanisms of justice making by mediating social institutions like lineages, trade guilds, and native-place associations. These were encompassed in references to local custom in guidelines on civil matters. In the Late Imperial Era, the magistrate's *yamen* coexisted with and relied on the rules and adjudicatory procedures of manifold self-governing associations that organized Chinese society. Magistrates' legal reasoning combined the citation of law with reference to communities of rules beyond formal law. Magistrates also made reference to feelings (*qing*) and reason (*li*), terms that signaled the relevance of emotions or the exigency of poverty in particular cases. Rather than follow the strict letter of the law, magistrates often sought to achieve community compromise and avoid polarizing labels of right and wrong that might deepen social enmities within a community.[19]

The early Republic saw as much continuity as rupture in these judicial aesthetics and mediating practices. Chinese judges at all levels continued to evoke "custom" (*xiguan*) and "social norms" (*qingli,* combining the words *qing* and *li*). These terms referenced normative community morality and dispute resolution. New commercial institutions (like Chambers of Commerce), themselves a mechanism for societal transformation, were similarly consulted by Republican courts as authorities on local contractual and commercial practices.[20]

The diverse assemblage of urban legal offerings, jurisdictions, and the "interim" or "provisional" designation of new laws complicated the ability of judicial mechanisms to convey legitimacy. New judicial concepts and practices that refashioned or discarded older imaginaries of law coexisted with older notions. Readers encountered the language of Republican law, judicial independence, and citizens' rights in daily reportage. The literary pages of the same newspapers serialized fiction that gave play to old and new virtues, values, and conceptions of justice. New Culture insistence on new legal frameworks and science-based approaches coexisted with continuities in popular practices and ideas of justice.

Denigrated by New Culture thinkers as "superstition," cosmological beliefs in a moral universe were woven into daily life and intertwined with ideas of human law. Crime and sin were linguistically merged in the same term (*zui*), which blurred distinctions between secular and cosmic wrongdoing. Beliefs in cosmic resonance or response (*ganying*) and moral reciprocity and retribution (*baoying*) held sway in popular opera, crime fiction, court case ballads, and everyday rituals of popular religion. Ideas of retribution and destiny-shaping good and bad deeds were concretized in morality books that expressed an economy of virtue. These "ledgers of merit and demerit" were widely printed in the Late Imperial and early Republican Eras and consumed by the literate and semiliterate classes. Notable Shanghai businessmen found solace and sought merit in their printing and distribution.[21]

The theory of cosmic response held that bad deeds disturbed the flow of *qi,* the vital force that permeated heaven, earth, and human bodies. Criminal acts provoked heavenly retribution (as seen in images of gambling and the stock exchange), through which cosmic balance might be restored. By the same token, human justice was of cosmic importance, being necessary to repair dangerous imbalances that had been unleashed by crime. Injustice or grievance (*yuan*) suffered by victims of crimes created an imperative for redress. Criminals might thus be punished by both human law and vengeful ghosts. The challenge of restoring balance, for legal administrators, was expressed by the twin challenges of "avoiding injustice" (*wuyuan*) by preventing incorrect judgments or, if an injustice had been done, "washing away injustice" (*xiyuan*) by punishing the criminal.[22]

NAVIGATING THE JUDICIAL TERRAIN

Judges thus enjoyed considerable leeway to interpret law and social norms in this time of rapid social change and new knowledge. How then did people who were not legal specialists navigate the thicket of legal arrangements that surrounded them and formulate their concerns for justice in everyday life? In practice, residents could only negotiate the maze of institutions and jurisdictions with help from Chinese and foreign lawyers. New categories of law, transitional codes, and new courts added to the confusion of frameworks, terminology, and jurisdictions. Seasoned Shanghai observer Yao Gonghe estimated in 1917 that "eight or nine of ten average citizens" did not grasp the conceptual distinction between a civil and a criminal complaint. Yet the ability to differentiate was critical to determining venues and filing legal paperwork.[23]

Jurists and popular writers in the New Culture Era battled legal ignorance with a new emphasis on legal literacy as part of an effort to instill common knowledge (*changshi*).[24] A decade into the Republic, newspapers offered remedial legal pedagogy, explaining distinctions between civil and criminal law, and identifying new courts and terminology:

> All regulations governing private matters between individuals are considered civil law. Those that stipulate punishment of criminals are considered criminal law. Civil law is non-interventionist. Civil lawsuits must be brought by the victims. After litigation there is family and lineage mediation. In criminal law cases, the victim does not file a lawsuit. The procuratorial court must file the suit after the victim informs the prosecutor of the crime. No mediation is permitted. Criminal law is thus interventionist. In civil cases the victim is called the *plaintiff*. In criminal cases, the prosecutors are the plaintiffs or originators. Victims are only called victims [or accuser, *gaosuren*]. Civil laws are national laws that are required to recognize individual rights, placing people in the primary position. Criminal law is public law that governs relations between the state and people. The state is in primary position.[25]

The Commercial Press published popular guides that were premised on the assumption that citizens required basic legal knowledge:

> All litigants, civil or criminal, need basic legal knowledge to avoid the torturous pain of engaging the law without preparation. Today the complexity of laws and decrees is extreme. Legal scholars continue to lack knowledge. How much more so the common people! . . . This book specifies [costs, timing, and procedures for appeals]. . . . For criminal cases [it covers] reporting, accusation, confession, surrender, appeal, and all basic items. . . . The low price of this brief guide for citizens and merchants enables wide circulation.[26]

Such books introduced readers to law and legal institutions in theory. Their brevity and national orientation ruled out an examination of the extraterritorial complications of judicial procedure. The practical and formal focus elided the question of how readers made sense of law and justice or how they might deploy their social networks in interaction with legal institutions.

In the course of a Shanghai workday, residents who traversed cultural and administrative boundaries encountered diverse notions of justice in newspapers, fiction, morality books, opera, and temples. In the welter of formal and informal practices, jurisdictions, and legal institutions of multiple nationalities, the individuals and groups caught up in the Xi-Tang case faced choices. Public commentary, legal maneuvering, and documentary records from the scandal's legal aftermath reveal how differently positioned individuals, groups and institutions understood and enacted justice and law. Participant perspectives are sketched here to indicate contending strategies for achieving justice in the legal terrain of the early Republic.

XI SHANGZHEN AND THE COSMIC
LOGIC OF SUICIDE

We may begin with Xi Shangzhen, whose choice of suicide provoked informal and formal interventions. As a student and teacher at East City Girls' School, Xi encountered a language of female independence and self-sufficiency that both heralded the late Qing female revolutionary Qiu Jin and incorporated sacrifices to Qiu Jin's ghost. In her newspaper work Xi had exposure to New Culture ideas and occasionally authored articles on women's issues. Her private writings admired women who died tragically, some by their own hand. Xi's fiction and poetry mixed the modern imperative for opposing superstition with a taste for melodrama and a degree of supernatural imagination. After her suicide, individuals attested to earlier words and behavior that revealed a sense of grievance. By the logic of retribution, Xi's suicide, as an unnatural form of death, created a store of bad *qi*. If a suicide's grievances remained unredressed, the disturbed *qi* threatened to assume the form of an aggrieved ghost, and the suicide site determined the ghost's location. Unexpiated grievances endangered the community. The threat of an aggrieved ghost encouraged offenders to make amends. Concern for the tormented ghost—and the need for a balancing act of retribution to restore social balance—compelled family or community members to take action.

The language of grievance and retribution was ubiquitous in everyday life, by no means dislodged by critiques of superstition. Ghosts lingered in contemporary fiction, poetry, and theater. Popular books like Yun Shi's *Hundred Views of Women* described, not only the appearance of the corpse of the female suicide, but also the appearance of her ghost. Towering figures of ghosts, particularly hanged ghosts (*diaosigui*)) with protruding tongues, paraded through the Chinese areas of the city during the late summer Hungry Ghost Festival and appeared in many Daoist and Buddhist ceremonies.[27] The Hanged Woman (*diaonü*), a figure of grievance who demanded justice, as Gloria Davies recounts, was described in a late essay by Lu Xun:

> a specter radiant with unbridled hate for those who had wronged her in life; who had chosen an unnatural death to end her suffering. She powdered her face chalk-white and dressed in bright red before hanging herself, thereby clearly signaling an intent to metamorphose into an avenging ghost. [She] was bent on haunting her persecutors and instilling fear in others. [The] Hanged Woman had such force of presence in local Shaoxing culture that women intent on ending their lives of misery often copied both her mode of suicide and her dress.[28]

Ghostly shadows haunted the Xi case. Newspapers disseminated the knowledge that Xi had attempted three times to commit suicide in Tang's office. Her determined focus on this location was universally recognized as evidence of her grievance and its logic in her strategy for justice. As one editorial reasoned:

> Tang Jiezhi cannot escape responsibility in the matter of Xi Shangzhen's suicide. Three times she attempted suicide, each time in the manager's office at the *Journal of Commerce*. In the end she finally managed to hang herself there. If she did not harbor extremely great resentment against Tang, why would she so determinedly implicate him?[29]

Another newspaper comment expressed similar logic of grievance and revenge, elaborating an economy of virtue and moral debt:

> Xi's suicide attempts were in the *Shangbao* office. If she didn't have any grievance against Tang, she wouldn't have selected this place to die. Otherwise, if she brought trouble to the *Shangbao*, speaking of virtue, she would then owe a debt to the *Shangbao*. But I have heard that Xi was especially virtuous. Therefore her intentional suicide at the *Shangbao* makes us conclude that it was her great anger at General Manager Tang that led her to do this.[30]

Her family members reported that, before expressing her determination to die at Tang's office, Xi said she would risk her life (*panming*) in her struggle with Tang. Xi made multiple attempts, beginning with the less definitive method of drinking sleeping medicine while other people were about. The fact that she didn't shift to the more decisive act of hanging until her third try, suggests that, initially, she may have hoped to force Tang's hand, rather than await posthumous (and supernatural) justice. Her actions suggest a form of negotiation known as "gambling with *qi*" (*du qi*), a risky but often successful way to gain leverage by wagering a suicide threat. The term and the tactic, as a deadly means of struggling to achieve justice, are familiar in China today.[31] More a covert than explicit form of knowledge in public print, the familiarity of the concept and its logic at the time is evident from a comic question and answer that appeared in the *Shenbao* shortly after Xi's suicide: "Q: How do you gamble without losing money? A: Gamble with *qi*."[32]

We may thus imagine that Xi may have preferred to live (if Tang had conceded to her wishes) rather than rely on posthumous revenge. Beyond these options nothing in her words or behavior suggested that she envisioned another means of achieving justice. Nothing indicates that she sought formal or informal mediation. Although some critics faulted her for not pursuing a more modern form of redress, others understood that as a woman of modest means, Xi may have chosen the most efficacious route to punish Tang.

THE JUSTICE OF MEDIATING SOCIAL ORGANIZATIONS: THE CHIVALRY OF THE DONGTING ASSOCIATION

After the fact, Xi's family members swiftly availed themselves of the mediating leverage of the Xi lineage and the Dongting native-place association. As a Xi family elder explained to Wu Yugong less than a week after Xi's death:

> The deceased was truly pitiful. Her household had only an elderly mother and Xi's brother. The mother is just a woman [*nüliu zhi bei*]. How could she have the wherewithal to instigate a lawsuit? Her brother has had tuberculosis for more than a year. He doesn't have strength to redress the injustice. . . . However, the Dongting sojourner association can be indignant on their behalf [*daibao buping*]. It has already convened a first meeting to consider a response to the incident. Yesterday it published a letter calling upon the authorities and people in every circle to examine [Xi's] hidden grievances and uphold public opinion [*gonglun*]. . . . As for what will happen next, we can't know.[33]

For sojourners in Shanghai, the transplanted sojourner community of the native-place association served as an extension of the family. Because the Xi lineage was influential in Shanghai, the Dongting association (with numerous Xi family heads on the board) often acted as an extension of the lineage. A public scandal that affected a member of its community reflected upon the reputation of the sojourning community.[34] Action by family, lineage, or, native-place group offered a socially sanctioned means of washing away grievance.

In a relatively noncontroversial case, the way this might work may be seen in the example of the contemporaneous suicide case of Miss Guo (the young woman Xi's age who was mistreated by her mother-in-law in the Cai family). Miss Guo's suicide disappeared quickly from the news, not simply because it was "old-style" news, but also because the social rift created by the suicide was effectively mended through the mediation of the Chaozhou native-place association (Chaozhou *huiguan*).[35] In the Cai-Guo case, both families were from Chaozhou. Association records provide details: an influential Chaozhou elder called a meeting "to express indignation and redress the profound grievance (*xue shenyuan*)" After publicizing the young woman's ill-treatment and demanding punishment of the Cai family, the *huiguan* registered a legal complaint at the Mixed Court, creating a plausible threat of legal action. This tactic applied the necessary degree of pressure to cause the Cai family to request a *huiguan* settlement. After investigation, the association ruled the Cai family should pay 500 yuan to build a tomb in Chaozhou for the deceased Miss Guo and cover the costs of returning her coffin for burial. Finally, the *huiguan* contacted the local Chaozhou court. Following the initiative of the *huiguan* as the mediating agency, the court ordered the Cai family head to convey his son (the girl's husband) to offer formal apologies to the Guo family. In this case, unofficial and official institutions, working in concert, effected monetary and ritual sanctions that cleansed Miss Guo's grievance and repaired the social rift created by her suicide.[36]

A similar internal mediating dynamic involved the Dongting association in the Xi case. Xi's mother sent a letter begging the association to redress her daughter's grievance. A Xi lineage elder took up the matter in the association. Repeating the mother's account, he stated that Tang had tricked Xi into purchasing trust company shares and had pressured Xi to be his concubine, thus provoking her death. Dongting association directors pronounced Tang's insult to Xi Shangzhen "an affront to the [Xi] lineage and our [Dongting] people" (*guanxi tongxiang tongzu bewu*).[37] Meeting minutes hyperbolically record outrage at the gall of Tang's published statement, which proclaimed that he bore no responsibility. Tang's American lawyer, Stirling Fessenden (whose name appeared at the end of Tang's statement), was one of the most influential figures in the International Settlement, dean of the Shanghai American Bar and the presumptive new chairman of the

Municipal Council.[38] Tang's statement aimed to intimidate with the borrowed mantle of foreign authority.

From the outset, the Dongting association understood that the matter presented severe challenges. Tang was an outsider to their community, a member of the powerful, competing Guangdong group, and an influential public figure with broad connections. Things could not be easily contained, nor would resolution be simple. Several Dongting leaders, Xi lineage elders among them, were businessmen and bankers in the city; one owned a rival newspaper. Despite their clout, they could not force Tang to submit. Tang had already rejected any ameliorating public acts of recompense. The Dongting association improvised tactics that escalated the controversy. In the process, Xi's individual grievance was thus transformed into a public struggle that would be characterized by appeals to different ideas of justice. Tang asserted the authority of formal law and brandished his ties to foreign authority; the Dongting association appealed to an older moral calculus and righteous community valor.

The association resolved to defend Dongting reputation and moral integrity (*mingjie*) by confronting Tang. As people from Dongting told the story, the community recognized that Tang was a fierce character (a "tiger with a cap") and sought a fearless champion to fight him. Zhu Xianhuai, an influential businessman, stepped up to spearhead the investigation. The proprietor of numerous silk warehouses and an enamel factory, Zhu was known for his erudition, martial skill, and chivalrous sense of justice (*xiayi*). His handling of the case would augment this reputation. A retrospective account lauds him as a "chivalrous knight-errant" who "achieved justice on a grand scale."[39]

Zhu's swiftly forthcoming analysis of the suicide inspired Dongting association members to record their unanimous indignation over the injustice (*gongfen buping*). Silence became a moral impossibility.[40] The association raised a public battle by "crying out to redress Xi Shangzhen's grievances," denouncing Tang in newspapers so that "people of every circle" might know his perfidy. Their media-amplified letter asserted that Tang had cheated Xi of money and explicitly linked Xi's suicide to Tang's desire to make her his concubine.[41] It also repeated the claim of Xi's family members that Xi had written a note explaining her grievance (*yuandan*) but that Tang had arrived earlier and removed the note. This claim contradicted witness testimony that Xi family members were the first to arrive at the scene of the suicide.[42]

The Dongting accusation (that Tang bore responsibility for Xi's suicide because of his financial and sexual appetites) presented moral crimes, not legal ones. The association did not immediately consult a lawyer, nor did its initial statement refer to law or a lawsuit. This leaves the impression that the association aimed initially to shame Tang into making amends. An anecdotal account from "a gentleman close to Miss Xi's relatives" stated that after Xi's death, Tang promised to pay 500 yuan for Xi's coffin and funeral (the same penalty as in the Cai case, which hints at a common customary standard of recompense). Such a promise would have satisfied social conventions and norms of mediation that aimed at compromise. However, according to this gentleman's account, "because Xi's sister testified that Tang wanted Xi as his concubine, he became furious and went back on his word." [43] If the Dongting association had intended to persuade Tang to heed community norms, it miscalculated. The public affront of its letter so enraged Tang that he refused absolutely to concede. Thus the dispute escalated.

THE SHIFT TO FORMAL LEGAL PROCEEDINGS

For his part, notwithstanding his emphatic nationalism, Tang exhibited faith in the pragmatic utility of Western lawyers, law, and institutions to defend him. In a brash and widely publicized response to the Dongting accusations, Tang brought libel suits against the highest-circulation Chinese and English-language newspapers, *Xinwenbao* and *China Press,* for extraordinary damages of $200,000 (altogether). Both had published the Dongting document, as had other Shanghai dailies. Tang's targets suggest his confidence in Stirling Fessenden's ability to maneuver on his behalf under US judicial authority. Both these newspapers were registered under US ownership; thus, the cases could be litigated in the extraterritorial anomaly of the US Court for China. [44] In the meantime, Tang's refusal to compensate Xi's family made him vulnerable to public opprobrium. In response to his legal pursuit of monetary damages to his reputation, he was denounced as a "speculator" who aimed to swindle more money from the affair. [45]

Whereas it appeared advantageous to Tang to initiate proceedings in a US court, the Dongting association had reason to obstruct Tang's recourse to extraterritorial justice. The association thus shifted course and pressed for legal action against Tang in the Chinese procuratorial district court (*jianchating*). [46] In this tactical shift from communal to formal justice, the records of the association reveal a degree of linguistic self-consciousness. The phrase "all members of the association are righteously angry" is crossed out of the meeting minutes and replaced with the more modern, rights- and law-oriented sentence, "in order to protect human rights [*baozhang renquan*] . . . we unite all circles from our native place to bring a lawsuit to arrest the principal offender." The association now pursued Tang under the framework of criminal law, however, it habitually referred to Xi's "unredressed grievances" (*yuanyi*).[47]

Association members worked behind the scenes to facilitate Tang's November 13 dead-of-night abduction from the International Settlement. A commemorative history of the Dongting association later explained that Zhu and Xi lineage members, "disguised as peddlers, helped the [Chinese police] arrest Tang." As police staked out the alleyway where Tang parked his car (at the boundary of Chinese jurisdiction), they served as lookouts.[48] The police seizure of Tang displaced the problem of redressing Xi's grievance from society onto the formal Chinese judiciary. Once the Dongting association had decided to exact revenge through Chinese legal mechanisms, the native-place group became a peripheral actor in what would follow: transformation into a criminal trial of what the inquest had judged to be a potential civil suit. Surprise was registered across the social spectrum, including the foreign community, at the spectacle of Tang's arrest.[49] Adding to the mystery, newspapers soon reported that new charges had been brought against Tang, who was now "implicated in the purchase of arms for opposing political cliques."[50] According to the *China Press*, these charges were made in the office of the local military authority, Defense Commissioner He Fenglin.

CONSULAR JURISDICTION AND JUDICIAL INDEPENDENCE

Tang now awaited trial in a Chinese prison. The *China Press* published an indignant description of the conditions of his captivity, comparing his persecution to that of the Ningbo businessman Fu Xiao'an, whose recent spurious arrest by Chinese authorities for conspiracy and treason had created a stir. This Western account depicted Tang's ill-treatment, as well as Fu's arrest, as justification for the retention of extraterritoriality in China:

> Dr. Tong is in a cell in which there are seven persons, criminals and coolies of various descriptions. He sleeps on a plank four feet long which is covered by straw. The place is dirty and the odors are disgusting. Whether Dr. Tong is guilty or not—and it is preposterous to believe that he is—it is unjust that a man of his standing in the community and one who has done such public service, should be treated in this way. It is also unpleasant to think of what

would happen to a public-spirited citizen like Fu Siao-en if the politicians who are scheming against him got him into that prison. The Chinese who seek for the abolition of extraterritoriality . . . should think carefully and clearly about cases of this sort—in which men are suddenly and without legal process arrested, thrown into horrible prisons, and held without bail.[51]

Although Tang's Chinese associates may have been glad for sympathetic publicity of Tang's ill-treatment, they would surely have been mortified to see Tang deployed as "exhibit A" in an argument for extraterritorial jurisdiction.

The peculiarities of Tang's arrest by the Chinese police and his appeal to US authorities on Chinese soil necessarily focused attention on the intertwined questions of extraterritorial jurisdiction, Chinese legal sovereignty, and the quality of Chinese legal reforms. However, few Chinese would explicitly endorse extraterritoriality as a solution. May Fourth activism had fueled an urban movement for the abolition of extraterritorial privilege and the restoration of Chinese legal sovereignty. The discussion of the issue intensified at the time of the Washington Conference of 1921–1922, at which the Chinese delegation lobbied for full legal and territorial sovereignty.[52] The United States, Belgium, Great Britain, France, Italy, Japan, the Netherlands, and Portugal stated that they would reconsider extraterritorial rights only after the Chinese government reformed its judicial system "[to] bring it into accord with that of Western nations."[53] Chinese newspapers served as public billboards for these issues, enunciating the catchwords: "sovereignty," "Mixed Court rendition," and "withdrawal of consular jurisdiction." Tang's newspaper characteristically denounced consular jurisdiction as an imperialist intrusion that "afflicts all citizens with shame and regret."[54] Chinese frustrations at the conference, together with criticisms of the Chinese legal system, were vented at length.

Influential social institutions in Shanghai and other cities publicized the issue of legal reform and pressured the Chinese Ministry of Foreign Affairs to raise the issue of Mixed Court rendition with the Diplomatic Corps. Newspapers printed in their entirety speeches delivered and telegrams dispatched, amplifying their audience. In May 1921 the Shanghai Chamber of Commerce convened a conference on legal affairs, ostensibly to advise the government on legal reform and to strengthen legal organizations.[55] The Shanghai, Beijing, Hangzhou, and Wuchang lawyers' associations convened a meeting, also in May, to discuss judicial reform, in preparation for a 1922 national meeting. The street union federation agitated vociferously for legal sovereignty as integral to national economic rights.

Speaking for "the residents of the entire Settlement," the street unions unanimously pressed for return of the Mixed Court to Chinese control.[56]

Emphatic endorsement of Chinese legal sovereignty was often combined with equally emphatic denunciation of the flawed Chinese judicial system. New Culture criticisms of the despotic corruptions of Chinese "tradition" heightened concern for human rights and judicial reform to safeguard republican citizens. Eminent Chinese lawyers called for the urgent protection of human rights and the independence of the Chinese judiciary. In particular, speakers castigated the inquisitorial procuratorial system (in which one official had authority for both investigation and prosecution) as a consequential error resulting from China's hasty adoption of Japanese judicial models. The jurist Chen Zemin decried the authoritarian character of the procurators. The spirit of a republic, he argued, called for citizen participation and respect for rights. He advocated a jury system, following the US and many European states.[57] These themes were showcased at a national judicial conference in September 1922 (the month of Xi's suicide). Here the Shanghai Lawyers' Association advocated for the abolition of the procuratorial system and the unconditional rendition of the Mixed Court.[58]

Some commentators noted that the problem of judicial reform was not simply a question of the legal model. The root problem was the absence of financial and political safeguards. Judicial independence was salient as a deeply felt imperative in the Republic, but the political circumstances of Chinese law in this period rendered the ideal elusive.[59] From the foundation of the Republic, politicians understood judicial independence as a threat to power. After the first tremulous flutters of "judicial revolution" in 1913–1914, Yuan Shikai cut the judicial budget. Availing himself of the rhetoric of the new political economy, he pronounced judicial expenditures as "non-economic funding."[60]

As central government control devolved, extraordinary military jurisdiction expanded. Tang's newspaper criticized the intrusions of He Fenglin's military court in Shanghai judicial proceedings. An editorial comment complained that "little remained of judicial independence." The takeover by the local military court of the 1920 sentencing and execution of Yan Ruisheng (who notoriously murdered the courtesan Wang Lianying for her jewelry) and its appropriation of other cases, "made the [Shanghai district] court superfluous."[61] Such a travesty as the Law on Punishing Robbers and Bandits, the author lamented,

> exists in our country only. Each day this law remains, we cannot say that rule of law exists in China. . . . When ordinary criminal cases are transferred

to military jurisdiction—since the military court has no compunction about handling them and the local court is unashamed about losing authority— there is no possibility for the restoration of legal sovereignty.[62]

Tang's arrest by the Chinese police and his appeal to the foreign consuls placed him in an awkward position. For Chinese nationalists like Tang, legal sovereignty was an unquestionable good. The weak state of the Chinese judiciary nonetheless stood in the way of this goal, particularly as foreign powers made judicial reform prerequisite to relinquishing extraterritoriality. Practical concerns for achieving sovereignty added rhetorical force to calls for judicial reform. For Chinese who were concerned with the rights of citizens and for those in politically delicate circumstances seeking justice, judicial reform and an independent judiciary were essential. In the interim, however, it was embarrassing for nationalists to seek extraterritorial jurisdiction to escape the reach of Chinese courts.

After he was taken into custody, Tang's lawyers, Fessenden and Holcomb, notified Italian Consul-General De Rossi, senior consul of the Consular Body (the multinational assembly of consular officials in Shanghai). The lawyers reported that the Chinese police had violated extraterritorial jurisdiction by arresting Tang within the boundaries of the International Settlement. De Rossi upheld the account of Tang's lawyers and took up the matter with the Chinese police but was unable to secure Tang's release. The Chinese police insisted that the alleyway where Tang was arrested was within Chinese jurisdiction.[63] Matters remained at a diplomatic standstill and Tang remained in Chinese prison.

The wheels of extraterritorial justice moved slowly. Nearly two months later, in January 1923 (after Tang had already been tried and sentenced), the case was taken up formally by the Consular Body. The meeting minutes clarified the jurisdictional questions, as well as the improvisational character of power negotiations in Shanghai's semicolonial contact zone:

> Senior Consul Chevalier de Rossi said the Shen Pan Ting sentenced Dr. Tong to three years imprisonment on a charge of obtaining money by fraud. In the absence of reliable information as to the exact place where the arrest had taken place there seemed no grounds for a protest on the ground of his arrest in the Settlement. But as the crime, if any, was committed in the Settlement, the proceeding should have been instituted in the Mixed Court, and he was of the opinion that the Consular Body should enter a strong protest against the action of the Shen Pan Ting in assuming jurisdiction. This was agreed to [by the Consular Body].[64]

From the perspective of the diplomatic community, the location of the arrest (the focus of the Chinese police) was tangential to the jurisdictional question. The rules of extraterritorial jurisdiction precluded Chinese police action within the International Settlement. However, the key jurisdictional question that had bearing on the appropriate judicial venue was the location of the crime. Since Tang's transactions with Xi and Xi's suicide had all taken place at the Journal of Commerce, the appropriate venue was the Mixed Court of the International Settlement.

The sedate pace of consular discussions ensured that the exercise of extraterritorial jurisdiction was imprecise. The Chinese authorities that had gone to such lengths to arrest Tang were not inclined to give him up. It was no accident that Tang was repeatedly denied bail. Without possession of the accused, extraterritoriality could not prevail without substantial effort. Such effort—on behalf of a nationalist activist who had led a tax protest against the Municipal Council of the International Settlement—was not forthcoming. Shanghai Municipal Police records suggest more concern over Tang's nationalist political activism than his arrest by Chinese authorities.[65] Beyond the formal registration of a protest by the Consular Body, the foreign police and the consular archives contain no additional action or discussion of the matter.

FRAMING THE CASE

On November 25, the Chinese procurator indicted Tang in the Chinese district court on criminal charges. The indictment summarized perplexing details of Xi's interactions with Tang that had been in public discussion since the inquest and reframed them in terms of criminal law. Tang's handling of Xi's shares might have been adjudicated under applicable civil law governing the sale, purchase, and delivery of stock. The Chinese court instead charged that Tang had fraudulently induced Xi to purchase shares that he had no intent to deliver. According to the indictment, in spring 1921 Tang persuaded Xi to purchase 360 shares of China Commercial Trust Company stock. Tang was also accused of inducing Xi's purchase of 50 shares of Hu-Hai Exchange stock (but this claim was dropped once it was plain that Tang had never been in a position to sell Hu-Hai stock).

This judicial accounting relied on a process of selection, exclusion, and distillation of the facts as presented by Xi's family (with the assistance of the Dongting association, which documented the story and paid the family's court fees). The indictment also streamlined the cast of characters involved in the suit. The Dongting association, though in the shadows, was erased in the lengthy indictment narrative (and transcripts of the trial). There was no role for the association in the modern criminal procedure.

The indictment explained that Xi's mother had reported her daughter's death to the procurator. According to her account, Tang Jiezhi had defrauded (*pianqu*) Xi of a huge sum of money; he had lured and coerced (*you bi*) Xi to become his concubine; he had schemed to force (*ji po*) Xi to commit suicide, and he had stolen and destroyed (*dao hui*) Xi's note of grievance. On the basis of this report of a crime, the procurator ordered Tang's arrest. Investigation determined that Xi Shangzhen hanged herself because she had been defrauded of a huge sum of money. Other accusations were dismissed for a lack of evidence or uncertain legal status:

> As for the matter of inducing and coercing (*youpo*) Xi to be his concubine and stealing and destroying Xi's letter of grievance, there is no clear evidence. As for [Tang] saying, "Marry me as my concubine," and "my money is your money," when Xi asked for the money . . . , it is difficult to know what type of crime this constitutes [*zi nan renwei ling cheng hezhong zuiming*].[66]

To indict Tang, the court needed to translate the accusations into a criminal case. The court's decision to pursue a criminal indictment required the identification of a crime that was specified in the interim criminal code. "Compelling suicide" like financial fraud, was specified in the code.[67] However, the court seized on the economic crime of financial fraud (*zhaqi qucai zui*) as more promising in terms of evidence.

The indictment highlighted two key pieces of evidence, making inattentive or inconsistent references to units of currency. The first was a personal receipt that Tang gave Xi for 2,000 Mexican dollars on June 6, 1921. The receipt acknowledged payment for 160 shares of China Commercial Trust Company stock. It was marked with Tang's chop (a seal customarily used in lieu of a signature), and it was in the possession of Xi's mother. The second document was the promissory note that Tang gave Xi in August 1922, after her first two suicide attempts. The note acknowledged "receipt of valuable securities" from Xi, valued at 5,000 yuan, and promised in return payment of 5,000 yuan to Xi without interest in three payments over a period of three years.

Both sides in the case acknowledged the authenticity of these documents. The question was how to interpret them. The indictment asserted that the two documents substantiated the claim that Tang intended to defraud Xi of her money. Although Tang gave Xi a receipt for her first payment, he did not provide receipts for two additional installments (2,000 yuan and 1,000 yuan). The indictment claimed that after Tang received the total payment of 5,000, he did not give Xi her shares but made excuses. Xi's two suicide attempts at the office worried Tang, thus he wrote the promissory note. The indictment interpreted the promissory note as a strategy that enabled Tang to defer repayment of his debt to Xi. Xi hung herself on September 8, 1922, when she realized that Tang never intended to pay. The indictment reasoned:

1. Xi's mother provided compelling testimony that Xi bought stock because Tang tempted and induced her (*quanyou*).

2. If Tang had given Xi her shares, he would have taken back his receipt. The receipt remained in Xi's mother's possession, proving Tang did not give Xi the shares.

3. Tang's explanation that the promissory was written to help Xi cope with creditors was not credible. He only produced the note after Xi's suicide attempts created pressure to repay the money.

4. Tang's claim that Xi pawned her shares at the Shangbao bank was unverifiable. The bank stated that an employee of the newspaper served as guarantor for a "Xi Shangji," who pawned 50 shares of China Commercial Trust Company stock for 400 Mexican dollars. ("Whether Xi Shangji is Xi Shangzhen we cannot know.")[68] Moreover, Tang said the items pawned were stock receipts, whereas the mortgage at the bank was stock. Thus there was insufficient proof that Tang handed over the shares.

The indictment concluded that Tang had committed financial fraud, a violation of article 382 of the criminal code.[69] The crux of the criminal case for fraud, as outlined in the indictment, involved the procurator's claims that (1) Tang had lured Xi to purchase stock; (2) he had not delivered, and had no intention to deliver, the stock; and (3) his promissory note was fraudulent and designed to mislead her. If Xi had freely purchased stock, Tang would not be guilty of inducing Xi to buy. If he had delivered the shares, it would be difficult to insist that he had defrauded her of her money. The court lacked hard evidence for the first point beyond the mother's testimony. Evidence for the second point was unclear since Xi's apparent pawning of stock suggested that she had at least received some certificates. As for the third point, the promissory note presented a challenge. It therefore had to be explained and discounted as deceitful. The trial thus adjudicated various forms of financial instruments (Tang's promissory note among them), commercial transactions, and the means by which they might be authenticated.

VOICES AT THE TRIAL

Tang's trial took place in the Chinese district court on December 2 and December 8, 1922. The courtroom was reportedly "filled to capacity by friends of the accused and the Xi family, Japanese lawyers, Japanese journalists and spectators, Chinese newspapermen and curious spectators."[70] Among those attending the first hearing as spectators were the theater manager and actors from the Diyitai Theater on Fuzhou Road, who were preparing for their anticipated theatrical production, *Xi Shangzhen.*[71] In a measure of exceptional public interest, all the major Shanghai Chinese newspapers printed transcripts of the two public hearings.[72]

The first hearing lasted between four and five hours and featured the divergent testimony of Xi's mother, older sister, and sister-in-law (as complainants and witnesses) and Tang Jiezhi. The procurator served as plaintiff in the criminal proceedings. The court refused Tang's request for a foreign lawyer.[73] Three eminent Chinese lawyers represented him instead: Qin Liankui, Li Shirui, and Xu Huilin. Du Fuyao presided as judge. The procurator did not request the presence of any additional witnesses at this hearing.

Questioning began after the procurator read the indictment. Xi's fifty-four-year-old mother, a healthy, vigorous, and full-faced woman,[74] repeated her earlier inquest testimony and added that after Tang had induced Xi to buy stock, family members pooled their money, which they paid in three installments. After writing a receipt for the first 2,000, Tang stated that further receipts were unnecessary since the stock would soon be available. Subsequently, however, Tang made excuses and never turned over the stock. On the day of her first suicide attempt, Xi arrived home with a bottle of medicine that she said Tang had given her for mosquito bites on her arm.[75] On further questioning, however, Xi reluctantly explained that Tang had given her an injection to counter an overdose of sleeping medicine that she had taken. Xi's mother testified (as Xi's older sister stated at the inquest) that Xi said she would risk death in her struggle with Tang. The suggestion of suicide made her mother anxious, and she asked her daughter how she would survive without Xi's support. Xi responded that she would leave a note that would explain. When she was sent home after her second suicide attempt, Xi resisted getting out of the horse-drawn carriage, saying that she wanted to die at the newspaper office. Xi's mother added, furthermore, that Tang's words revealed his evil character: "When Shangzhen was at the office, he often said, 'You don't need to worry about your dollars. Your dollars are my dollars. Your body is also mine." Reciting these words as if she had heard them herself, she rested her case: "You can see that he wanted to cheat her of her money and also her body."[76]

The twenty-five-year-old wife of Xi's tubercular brother was next. She testified that on the day of Xi's suicide, she had rushed to the office only to find Xi hanging, "without spirit." When she checked the clothing on the corpse it appeared that the buttons of Xi's undergarment had been opened, she stated, hinting at the removal of a suicide note. The interior undershirt was untouched.[77]

Unlike the women in the Xi family, who focused on details that were extraneous to the crime of economic fraud, Tang addressed the specific charges in the indictment and the relevant financial evidence. He dispassionately explained financial details, relevant context, and conventional practice to refute conclusions drawn in the indictment. Tang testified that the China Commercial Trust Company, which had been established in late 1921, was dissolved by June or July 1922, after only seven months. Xi had approached him in summer 1921, while the company was still being organized, and purchased 400 shares of company stock, and in no way had he persuaded her to buy them:

> At this time masses of people were vying to buy shares in exchanges and trust companies. There wasn't enough company stock to satisfy demand. Seeing how prices were going up, Miss Xi urged me to buy even more shares [for her]. There weren't shares since the company hadn't issued sufficient stock. This was when [the market] was hot. Relatives and friends were all purchasing, Xi among them. It is simply not the case that I defrauded her of money, as I am accused.[78]

Tang explained that he was not present for Xi's first suicide attempt in summer 1922, when share prices plummeted. On the evening of her second attempt, however, he noticed her unusual pallor and rushed her to the hospital, where she was revived with an injection. When he asked her why she had tried to kill herself, she talked to him about her family's poverty and asked for help, explaining that the money she had used to buy stock was borrowed and that she was under pressure to repay it. Repeating his earlier testimony, he stated that since Xi's shares were now worth considerably less than face value, he gave her the (more valuable) promissory note for the original sum to help her out. The idea was to provide her with sufficient credit to fend off her creditors.

Tang's narrative, which detailed his activities on the night of Xi's suicide, conveys the mix of business, networking, and leisure that filled his evenings. After attending to a business matter at a tobacco company, he visited the Guangdong Club. His chauffeur then drove him to the Grand

Theater, where he was watching an opera performance when newspaper staffers spotted his car and entered the theater to report the suicide. By the time Tang managed to get back to the office, Xi's sister-in-law and others were already there. These details, which were corroborated by others, contradicted the Xi family's suggestion that Tang arrived first and destroyed a note. Tang also stated that he had called the police.[79]

Most crucially, Tang reviewed the documentary evidence and refuted the procurator's interpretation. Tang stated that the moment he received the stock, he had delivered Xi's stock to her at the office on August 18, 1921. He didn't bother to get his receipt back from her since the receipt was at her home and he was busy. He contextualized this casualness in terms of their work: "We worked in the same office, so I wasn't worried that she wouldn't give me the receipt. This was honest negligence on my part." The key point, however, was that there was definitive evidence that Xi had the shares: she had mortgaged some shares at a bank and used other shares to qualify to purchase Hu-Hai exchange shares. This evidence exculpated him from what was clearly a false accusation:[80]

> She pawned this stock. I want to call your attention to this. The plaintiff's statement is illogical. Xi had someone mortgage the stock on her behalf at the Shangbao Bank.[81] This is sufficient proof that I turned over the stock. The plaintiffs say I never turned over the stock. This is incomprehensible. They say that she gave me 5,000 dollars, but that I pawned the stock and said I couldn't give it to her until I redeemed it. . . . Moreover, at this time the Hu-Hai Stock Exchange had opened and was trying to attract investors. . . . .Because so many people wanted to purchase Hu-Hai shares, they limited investors to people who had ten shares of trust company stock. This qualified them for one share of Hu-Hai stock. Now we see that Xi Shangzhen owned Hu-Hai stock. If she didn't receive the trust company stock, how could she get Hu-Hai stock? This point is proven by the newspaper advertisement of the Hu-Hai exchange at the time.[82]

Tang's lawyer Li Shirui provided a copy of the Hu-Hai advertisement, which corroborated Tang's testimony. Li further emphasized that Xi gave her stock certificates to Tang in return for the promissory note, as specified in the language of the note. After furnishing the court with several of the certificates Xi had given to Tang in that transaction, Tang asked the judge to examine what was written on the back of the shares. Several bore the characters "*yi ren*", indicating that the trust company shares had been used to purchase the Hu-Hai stock. Other purchasers who had similarly used shares could attest to this practice. As further proof that Xi had received shares, Tang's lawyers provided photographs of records from the

Shangbao Bank recording the pawning of Xi's shares receipt. Li explained that the shares receipt had the same function as the actual shares (thus people easily confused the two, particularly as the formats for certificates and official receipts were not standardized at this time). He requested that the court call specialist witnesses who could easily attest to this type of transaction.[83]

The evidence presented by Tang and his counsel—and their insistent requests for expert witnesses who were familiar with financial transactions—raised questions about the credibility of the indictment and impeded the prosecution's ability to swiftly demonstrate guilt. The judge adjourned the hearing pending further investigation.

The trial resumed on December 8 with Judge Du and Procurator Yang presiding. A large contingent of the Chinese bar crowded the courtroom to hear the arguments of Tang's celebrated legal team. Three witnesses now joined the three female plaintiffs and Tang in the courtroom, two of them summoned in response to defense request. Two other requested defense witnesses were out of town, unable to return on the court's very short notice.[84]

Records of this second hearing suggest that, despite formal procedural attentiveness, the judge was disinclined to consider Tang's evidence. Ignoring crucial financial details, the procurator focused on tangential and seemingly extraneous questions. Statements of witnesses who corroborated Tang's delivery of stock certificates to Xi were struck from the record as "confusingly irrelevant."[85] Exculpatory documentary evidence was summarily declared counterfeit and tossed aside by the judge without expert examination.

The first witness called to the bench was Lu Weiqing, a former cashier at the Shangbao Bank, who was a witness for the prosecution. Lu testified that the *Journal of Commerce* employee Ying Jishen had mortgaged fifty shares of China Commercial Trust Company stock at the bank on behalf of Xi Shangzhen, an employee of the *Journal of Commerce*. However, since Miss Xi did not visit in person, he did not see her. He could not verify that the characters "Xi Shangji," which appeared on the documents, referred to Xi Shangzhen. The procurator did not ask about the conventional usage of the character *ji* (記) for account names, which he could easily have confirmed. The procurator also did not consider the unlikelihood that "Xi Shangji" could refer to any other employee at the *Journal* who had also mortgaged China Commercial Trust Company shares.[86]

Qiu Youxin, an editor at the *Journal* and the first of the two defense witnesses, was up next. The trial transcripts don't record any questions relevant to the interpretation of the financial evidence. When the next defense witness, Shen Zhonghua (also an editor), was called to the bench, the procurator took up an unexplained line of questioning concerning Xi's calligraphy.[87] He asked whether Xi could write clerical script (*li zi*). Shen said she could not. The examination then considered the precision of Xi's brushwork in standard script (*zheng kai*) style, followed by her proficiency with seal script (*zhuan shu*). When he was given the opportunity, Tang's lawyer Li Shirui redirected the questions to the evidence, enabling Shen to corroborate key points of the defense. Shen stated clearly that the market was flourishing and a great number of employees all purchased and received shares from Tang, including himself. Xi purchased her shares in this giddy investment climate, without any urging from Tang ("everyone was contending to buy"). He related several conversations he had had with Xi at the office. She often asked him about the price of shares. When share prices dropped, he said, "she lamented and sighed." As the market began to fail, she asked what Shen thought of Hu-Hai shares. He told her the prospects were dim. He also reported that once, when entering the office, he had seen a stack of share certificates, including Hu-Hai shares, on Xi's desk, and asked Tang about them. Tang explained that Xi was pressed by creditors and wanted to return the shares. Shen told Tang that the dispute over Xi's shares was not good for the Journal of Commerce and advised him to quickly settle the matter. Shortly afterward, Tang assured him that he had "taken care of the Xi business." Tang explained that he had given her a note in return for the shares, providing for the original purchase price. The judge cut Shen's testimony short and asked him to step down.[88]

The procurator then had Tang return again for three quick questions. First, he asked Tang to verify the regulations of the China Commercial Trust Company. The rules stipulated that promoters who sold and delivered shares should clearly note the name of the purchaser, a step that Tang had evidently neglected. Second, the procurator asked about Ying Jishen's position. Tang explained that Ying worked at the business office of the Journal. Third, the procurator asked Tang why Xi remained unsatisfied, if Tang wrote the promissory note to help her. "Xi was not a girl from the countryside," he said. "Why would she repay your virtue with revenge (*yi de bao yuan*)? After making this final rhetorical point (which relied upon cultural stereotypes of rural and modern women and also assumed the relevance for the case of the moral economy of virtue and the logic of suicide as retribution), the judge called again on Xi's mother.

At this point the trial took a dramatic turn. The judge held up the photos of Hu-Hai exchange records that had been submitted by the defense. He asked Xi's mother whether a square imprint of the characters for Xi's name on the documents reflected the authentic chop mark of her daughter.[89] In what journalists took to be a rehearsed move, Xi's mother stated that she had never previously seen this mark. She testified that her daughter had just one chop, and that it was oval in shape. Like a magician she produced from her sleeve an oval-shaped seal which she identified as Xi's authentic and exclusive chop. Declaring the square chop a counterfeit and the imprint forgery and evidence of Tang's fraud, she turned to Tang and delivered an emotional address:

> If my daughter had had the shares or the receipts of the trust company, she could have disposed of them at a profit. Why should she die? Why should she die in Tang's office? She should be grateful to Tang. So why should she cause him all this trouble by dying in his office after two unsuccessful attempts? Answer me! Answer me! You say she was pressed by creditors. She had no creditors. It was you who pressed her to death! You and your crowd at the *Journal of Commerce*![90]

Nonplussed, Tang's lawyer asked the judge how it happened that Xi's mother had known to bring the chop to court. The procurator explained that he himself discovered the seal on the previous day when he personally visited Xi's house.[91] The procurator had gone to extraordinary lengths to discount the exculpatory financial records that inconveniently bore Xi's name.

The defense meticulously returned to the documentary evidence and corroborating testimony. Tang also stated that he sympathized with Xi, but it had to be recognized that she had speculated, for which she was herself to blame. He pointed out that his note enabled Xi to assure her creditors that money was forthcoming. (His prestige carried more value at that point than the shares.) He emphasized that Ying Jishen's testimony was vital, since Ying, as Xi's agent in the pawning, could verify that Xi indeed possessed the shares, and moreover that Xi Shangji was Xi Shangzhen. Tang requested a few days' postponement. The judge refused.

The Chinese procurator and trial judge held formal authority. However, the presence of defense counsel, as permitted in the reformed criminal code, allowed for an alternative articulation in the courtroom, by authoritative legal professionals, of the law and the evidence. Speaking to the packed courtroom, in proceedings that were transcribed in the press, Tang's defense lawyers—public figures in their own right—challenged the court, criticizing the judges' grip on the law and pronouncing the case to be a false accusation. They described the judges as ignorant of commercial practice and market behavior, willful in their disregard of evidence that evinced lawful contractual behavior and confirmed Xi's possession of stock. The court had blindly accepted the uncorroborated statements of Xi's family. The accusation failed to grasp the financial context. If Xi had wanted stock certificates at the time of her suicide attempts, Tang could have easily supplied them. He had more than a thousand certificates of his own. The key problem (which Xi's mother could not comprehend) was that all of these, like Xi's shares, had lost value on the market. By the time Xi asked for help, her shares were worth substantially less than his promissory note.[92] Even if Tang had violated a commercial agreement, the defense explained, this would constitute at most a breach of contract, a matter for civil law. Tang's defense refuted the illogical, unsupported, and unwarranted criminal prosecution, ridiculing the court's arguments point by point:

1. The charge of "luring" was completely inappropriate. Shen Zhonghua contested the assertion that Tang persuaded Xi to buy and instead described Xi as unusually eager (*qingre yichang*) to buy shares. In terms of law, no responsibility could be adduced.

2. As for Tang not taking back his receipt: Tang was manager; she a clerk; they worked in the same office. They didn't need to be so formal. To take this as proof that he defrauded Xi of 5000 yuan misinterpreted the evidence. No evidence supported the groundless claim that Tang didn't turn over stock or that Xi demanded it. There was only the testimony of three women who colluded to testify in unison, empty words with no evidence.

3. It was illogical for the procurator to argue further that Xi's failure to use her stock to qualify for election for office at the trust company constituted evidence that she didn't receive shares. The purchase of 200 shares only conferred the *right* to be elected; purchasers were not *required* to run for election. Moreover no election was scheduled.

4. As for the pawned shares, it was essential to have Ying Jishen's testimony on the pawned shares to establish the truth, a matter of waiting three days. The fact that Shangbao bank could not verify that Xi Shangji was definitely Xi Shangzhen did not prove Xi Shangji was *not* Xi Shangzhen.

5. The claim that Xi's seal imprint was inauthentic was not proven. Rather than accept the complainant's word, the court should have examined third party evidence of the seal's authenticity.

6. As for the promissory note, it constituted a formally drafted and signed contract that showed both sides in agreement. There was no swindle. Moreover, the text specified, "*received Xi's valuable securities* for a price of 5,000 *yuan*." Witnesses corroborated that the accused

gave Xi the note in return for the securities, which had lost value. The securities were now in the hands of the court. The note provided evidence entirely in favor of the accused, in no way contradicting his statement.[93]

The defense summation was closely argued in terms of financial and social context, evidence, and law.[94] In closing remarks, Qin Liankui emphasized the court's inattentiveness to law and legal procedure and warned against the distraction of suicide and the public attention it had engendered:

> This case has aroused the discussion of society, which has shown extreme interest. But one must be discriminating. Social attention is riveted because Xi killed herself at the Journal of Commerce office. But the fact that she committed suicide [does not mean that] Tang swindled and defrauded her of money. The court has already determined that the matter of suicide does not raise a question of law [the court discarded the potential charge of "compelling suicide"]. It is not permissible to arbitrarily substitute another crime [by which to charge Tang]. Society doesn't understand the reality of this case. Once the reality is understood, the misunderstanding may be eliminated.[95]

THE TRIAL AND THE PUBLIC

Qin's concluding remarks, which were addressed as much to the public as to the court, recognized the influential adjudication of the case that was taking place outside the courtroom, in the virtual public of newspapers and in the meeting places of the city. In the Late Imperial Era magistrates at times endeavored to appease community sentiment as articulated by lineages, village elders, and guild associations. Jurists understood the interventions by these groups as integral to the customary adjudication of disputes. In the last Qing decades, lineages, guilds, and urban intellectuals made use of newspapers to amplify their interventions.[96] Extending this trend and also engaging ideas of civic participation in a new republican public of citizens, a broader sort of adjudicating public arose in the first decades of the twentieth century. Newspapers facilitated an increasingly heterogeneous and participatory print public that fed on, discussed, and acted on news. The early articulations of rights and citizenship that emerged in the reforms and revolutionary mobilization of the late Qing flourished in the widening public culture of the Republic and in the publicity of theatrical trials such as this, in which the lawyers of defendants could chal-

lenge the authority of procuratorial narratives by the authority of a reconceptualized legal process.

The new public lacked the unified architecture of a national representative organ (following the demise of the parliament). But in the proliferating
May Fourth press, a virtual public enunciated its rights in both individual
and collective speech, deploying concepts associated with republican citizenship. These included popular sovereignty, a politicized citizenry, rule
of law, and new forms of association based on the political interests of new
social categories, including women, students, and shopkeepers. New categorical identities appeared in invocations of "the people" alongside older
forms of identity. Old and new voices and vocabularies mingled in urban
print.[97]

Reportage of Xi's suicide and Tang's arrest and trial, like other social
scandals, created a staging ground for this increasingly participatory, discerning public. Because Shanghai's major newspapers located themselves
in the International Settlement, this print public took root in the interstices
of jurisdictional division and fragmented governance. Similarly protected
by the confusions of extraterritoriality and coexisting and contending authorities (local and national), a growing number of voluntary associations
gathered in urban spaces, convening assemblies and disseminating public
pronouncements. Tang's trial, like other crystallizations of local and national issues, set such spaces abuzz, connecting discrete circles of association with threads of common interest.

As one commentator put it, Xi's suicide "threw public associations into
a state of public indignation" (*ge tuanti da dong gongfen*).[98] Heterogeneous
forms of association and frames of reference were manifest in the first
volley of public statements by the Dongting association and several women's
associations. If the (traditionalistic)[99] Dongting association instrumentally
added the new vocabulary of human rights into its rhetoric of grievance
and righteous chivalry, the women's associations that spoke on behalf of
Xi Shangzhen blended female virtue and retributive logic into their articulations of women's rights and feminist concern for a female office worker.

The machinery of the trial, which had been set in motion at least in part
by the first wave of public response to the suicide, stimulated in turn a
second wave of public agitation, this time social mobilization on Tang's
behalf. Whereas the actions by the Dongting and women's associations on
Xi's behalf appeared natural and unexceptional in journalistic discussion,
the situation was different for Tang as a public figure. Xi had little public
identity to speak of aside from her lineage, gender, native place, school,
and workplace, the key frameworks that "placed" her in society. Gender
and social status worked differently for Tang. Because Tang had a public,

political persona, the entanglement in the case of organizations with personalistic ties to Tang conveyed a different signification. At this moment of the construction of a public realm that was imaginatively defined by impersonal bonds of citizenship, Tang's personal ties with associations that claimed to represent sectors of citizens made them vulnerable to accusations of masking private connections as public opinion. Although it surprised no one that these organizations spoke out, ties to Tang called into question their claims to operate according to the ideals of an impersonal, rational, democratic and transparent public. In contrast, the concerns of public associations for Xi, as a young female and moreover a suicide, in contrast, appeared righteous, charitable, and appropriate.

Tang's defenders thus took care to create broad civic coalitions, which mobilized under the banner of judicial reform, judicial independence, and human rights, making ample use of the platforms of the press and public associations. Associations and individuals close to Tang initiated this mobilization, but—as they took care to insist—their connections to Tang transcended the personal. Tang's political activism had already engineered structural transformation in a number of associations, including his native-place association, enforcing greater transparency and connection with other progressive reformed associations in urban struggles for Chinese representation, sovereignty, and democratic governance. Those who stepped up to defend Tang had also been engaged in civic causes and struggles consistent with reform of the judiciary.

On December 9, immediately after the second hearing, one week before the court would pronounce its guilty verdict, the Guang-Zhao sojourners' association, which had not previously spoken out about the case, addressed a public letter to the Chinese Chamber of Commerce requesting its intervention in the case. The letter detailed the procurator's failure to respect legal procedure and law and his willful pursuit of a false charge, noting the jurisdictional violation in Tang's arrest; the spurious logic and investigatory techniques of the court; and the discounting of exculpatory evidence. The association particularly ridiculed the notion that Tang had lured Xi to invest when everyone in the city had experienced the summer of 1921—when Xi invested her money—as a moment of collective speculative irrationality (*huangmiu yi da jidian*).

As the Guang-Zhao Gongsuo made its appeal, it emphasized that the key issue at stake was not Tang, but the broader threat the trial posed for Chinese businessmen and the nation:

> If Tang, who has a reputation in business circles and is a board member of
> this esteemed association, can be harmed by such false accusations, how will

other businessmen defend themselves in similar situations? All nations are watching Shanghai at this time of [anticipating] the return of legal sovereignty. The two judges [trampled] on human rights [and damaged] the reputation of the judiciary, harming the future of the country. Thus, whatever the result for Tang, it is necessary to [rectify] these judges.

In a gesture that aimed to bolster its credibility as a modern civic association and distinguish its actions from the early interventions of the Dongting association, Gongsuo affirmed its reluctance to intrude in legal proceedings for narrow interests:

> The Guang-Zhao Gongsuo does not recklessly intervene, especially in the judiciary, which we respect. . . . But seeing with our own eyes the bias of the judges and their violations of law, we could not bear it. This is not simply a matter of decrying an injustice to the one individual, Tang. [We call upon] the Chamber of Commerce, as the organization of businessmen, with responsibility to protect businessmen's rights.[100]

The *gongsuo* requested that the Chamber uphold justice (*zhuzhang gongdao*) and intervene, "to protect the rights of all businessmen."[101] It hinted that—despite the court's failure to consult the Chamber—the Chamber might publicly attest to normative commercial behavior, to correct the misconstrual of evidence.

The Chamber temporized, its leadership torn by disagreements over a case that was highly political. It would not respond publicly until December 29. The meeting minutes in the Chamber archives illuminate the questions of commercial behavior raised by the case. They also reveal the members' understandings of law and legal procedure and their concern to avoid legal entanglements resulting from potential liabilities in the financial bubble. The *gongsuo* letter was immediately taken up in a meeting that was convened on the day it was received (December 9). Chairman Song Hanzhang delegated to the Guangdong businessman Feng Shaoshan the task of presenting the case. Feng had joined Tang in the reforms of the *gongsuo* and the Chamber, as well as in social mobilization for Chinese sovereignty. A member of the Chamber board, Feng had just returned from a meeting of the Federated Union of Chambers of Commerce, a national organization that Tang had helped foster. Feng stated that the judges' bias, ignorance of "common knowledge," and willful misconstrual of commercial practices demanded action. He based his case for Chamber intervention on the precedent of business mobilization in an earlier miscarriage of justice at the Shanghai district court, in which Fujianese students involved in street protests were imprisoned on the basis of a false accusation:[102]

In the case of the arrested Fujianese students, it took the [collective] struggle of many public associations to affirm their innocence [and secure their release]. But by then two of the nine students had already died . . . The Tang case was initially considered by the procuratorial court to involve the charge of "compelling suicide," but this was dropped. Then the procurator claimed "financial fraud," again without firm evidence. . . . The sacrifice of Tang the individual doesn't matter. But if judicial officials cannot uphold justice this is of wide concern and a matter of the protection of human rights. The Fujian student case served as a warning to us all [of the need for swift collective action]."[103]

The discussion that followed reveals members' uncertainty over points of law (the criminal-civil distinction), tactics, public sentiment, and the status of the Chamber as a leading public organization. Several participants worried that the financial crisis had damaged the Chamber's reputation. Others noted that many members, among them Wen Lanting, had engaged in ad hoc economic transactions in the heat of speculation, but that testifying was awkward.

Song Hanzhang asked the members to consider the question of how, precisely, to "uphold justice," wondering whether it was legal to interfere in the case before the verdict was pronounced. Ningbo shipping businessman Yuan Lüdeng argued that intervention didn't accord with the law and that, moreover, the case raised strategic concerns:

Social feeling [*shehui qingli*] finds Tang rather repugnant in this case. There are still people demanding that the Chamber expel him as a member. Although the court's verdict can't be known, the result will likely be "guilty." If the Chamber protests, it will surely be criticized. . . . Excessive outcry on behalf of Tang before the verdict might anger the judges, which could hurt Tang's case. In any event, before a verdict, intervention cannot free him from custody. His suffering would be the same.

Yuan counseled that to avoid the appearance of partiality, the Chamber should not act alone, but "should only follow actions by other groups."[104] Others were similarly inclined to wait until the verdict was in. Fang Jiaobo, the vice chair, pointed out the uselessness of an appeal to Beijing in view of the independence of the local courts. Out of caution, disagreement, and the uncertain efficacy of action, the matter was postponed.

In the meantime, individuals and organizations associated with Tang orchestrated a broad public response. *Journal of Commerce* editor Qiu Youxin published an editorial that argued that judicial behavior in the trial harmed the prospects for Chinese legal sovereignty:

Let us despair of the cancellation of consular jurisdiction. [What] kind of courts are the Shanghai courts? . . . If the procurator and judge of the Shanghai court do not follow law in civil and criminal cases, we cannot expect the return of our legal sovereignty. If they don't understand the workings of the market, and if they don't understand customs, they should not be judge and procurator. . . . If they hold biases, fail to grasp the complexities of legal detail, and deviously register a guilty verdict, the result is not simply grave for the single locality of Shanghai. [Foreign countries are watching]. Thus, we cannot tolerate such judges. . . . On behalf of Shanghai's 1.2 million people, How can we not loudly protest and call for punishment of these worms in our legal system?[105]

Qiu wrestled with the challenge of appearing impartial in view of his relationship to Tang:

This is not a matter of protecting [our employer] but of representing public opinion and discerning true from false. According to the arrest and procurator's investigation, the matter may be judged as fraud because, as the court alleges, stock was not turned over. . . . In both hearings Du Fuyao openly favored the complainants. Should a judge arbitrarily deny the reasonable requests of the accused? Collude with the complainants to produce a chop in court? Deny clear evidence of the Shangbao bank pawning? There are many such travesties, all brazenly committed. The sacrifice of Tang and his family are regrettable. How may the human rights of 1.2 million people [in] Shanghai be protected?

He urged readers to adopt a civic identity that transcended regional groupings: "Don't permit the Guang-Zhao association and the eight Fujian associations to take up the burden of justice by themselves."[106]

The next day, the Guang-Zhao Gongsuo gathered together politically kindred groups, including the influential Ningbo sojourner's association, and the Federation of Commercial Street Unions.[107] The *Journal of Commerce* announced a new stance of public activism in the case. It acknowledged the awkwardness of connection to Tang and interference in the legal process before unleashing its denunciation of the court:

Because we were close to the matter, we couldn't but investigate. We did this in good conscience, avoiding motivation by personal feeling. . . . That we adopted [an attitude of silence] reflected our faith in legal officials and the administration of justice. [Other] powerful organizations, feeling similarly, maintained the same attitude. Thus we waited patiently for the matter to be correctly handled through the judiciary, and we avoided making criticisms or engaging in discussion.

[However] since the procurate violated law in arresting Tang and the judge violated trial procedures and did not permit bail, we doubt the judge knows the law. The indictment deviously manipulated words to assert guilt. . . . In two hearings the judges demonstrated ignorance of the trust and stock exchange turbulence of last year, the market, and the nature of stock. . . . With such minds how can they responsibly investigate? . . . We know that Xi Shangzhen pawned stock at the Shangbao bank. But the judge insisted that Xi Shangji was not necessarily Xi Shangzhen, suggesting this was suspicious. Obviously the judge doesn't understand pawning practices. . . . We are not like the confused judge who can't distinguish stock receipts and certificates, making the audience laugh at his stupid talk. . . . We regret our premature respect for the judiciary.[108]

On the day this editorial was published the Guang-Zhao Gongsuo convened a "federated" meeting in its great hall, with more than eighty individuals from twenty-five public associations in attendance. Huo Shouhua, Tang's comrade in earlier civic causes, chaired the meeting. Huo decried the false accusation and prejudicial court proceedings, but emphasized that the gathering should not focus on "Tang's individual affairs," but rather "rectification of the judiciary and protection of human rights." Speakers placed Tang's arrest and the judges' financial ignorance and rejection of evidence in the context of "the dark underside of China's judicial world." Li Shirui reviewed judicial irregularities in the case and proposed judicial reforms that included: (1) abolition of the procuratorial system; (2) adoption of the jury system; (3) payment of damages from the national treasury for those denied bail.[109] Rhetorically linking human rights and national sovereignty, Tang's supporters argued that the judge's actions injured Chinese sovereignty:

If Tang, a prestigious Chamber of Commerce board member is subjected to such abuses, how will ordinary merchants be treated by these butchers? In this moment of concern for judicial sovereignty, when the Shanghai court is being scrutinized by foreign countries, [these] judges dare to trample on human rights, [making] China a global laughingstock.[110]

The assembly fired off strongly worded telegrams to the president, cabinet, and Ministry of Justice in Beijing, civil and military authorities in Jiangsu, the Jiangsu Provincial Court and the High Procurate in Nanjing, calling for firing and punishment of the Shanghai judicial officials. Following Republican-Era strategies of "being public," the texts of these circular telegrams appeared in the newspapers. In the fragmented political landscape, the telegrams' scattershot dissemination reflected uncertainties over lines of administrative authority.[111] The assembly described a pattern of "judicial tramplings" that "enraged the people, making their hair stand on end," and called for swift action to "save the spirit of judicial process [and] protect our international status."[112] Participants selected representatives to visit the court, created a Committee to Reform the Judiciary, and invited "all Shanghai associations" to a larger meeting to reform the judiciary. All votes were recorded as unanimous.

After the meeting, the Guang-Zhao association sent a second letter to the Chamber of Commerce, detailing these developments and pressing for Chamber intervention on behalf of Shanghai businessmen.[113] The *Journal* amplified public pressure with an editorial that lauded the "mass rebuke" of the court, stating that the misdeeds of the judges, "threatened the lives of the people," and justified extreme public anger and direct citizen action to correct judicial corruption: "When judges don't follow law . . . their poisonous harm exceeds that of soldiers and bandits. How is this? This is because the people may flee soldiers and bandits, but they cannot escape the illegal behavior of judges [and] fall prey to their harm." Only dismissal of the judges and adoption of a jury system could remedy the problem, "giving the people the right to directly participate in judgment and to supervise judges."[114]

The next days saw fresh initiatives to pressure the court and shape public opinion. In the spirit of direct participation, twenty-some delegates proceeded in a motorcar caravan after the meeting to visit the Chief Justice of the Shanghai district court, Mei Yiguo. According to a police report, the delegates delivered the meeting resolution, discussed the evidence, asked about Tang's treatment, and offered bail for his release. The unusual audience lasted two hours, a substantial if awkward and improvisational encounter that likely reflected the lack of judicial preparedness for such a visit as well as the elevated social status of the visitors and their ability to capture publicity. Judge Mei was polite but made no concessions. He patiently explained that no one could intervene; thus he could not interfere with Judge Du's case, whether or not the proceedings were fair. The question of Tang's right to bail remained murky.[115] The delegates espoused a kind of direct, improvisational democracy based on their informal status as representatives of a larger public. Their arguments failed to penetrate the wall of legal procedure held up by Judge Mei. A journalist who interviewed the delegation afterward quoted them as stating that they were "not disappointed in Justice Mei and came to understand that we have insufficiently studied the law."[116]

As the participants reflected on this lesson in Republican legal order, the legitimacy of their federated meeting did not go unchallenged. The swiftly organized meeting had reflected the need to create a public coalition that might "represent" a public that transcended narrow interests and personal ties in order to challenge the court. It was reported, however, that various members of street unions—seeing the newspaper texts of the telegrams from the federated meeting—themselves held an extraordinary meeting that raised "questions of representation":

> Participants held that before the re-organization of the street unions themselves as a recognized body, no representatives should have been sent to the [federated] meeting. The street union members that attended the meeting did so on their own initiative, and thus without the proper authorization of the street unions.[117]

Commentators explained that the Federation of Commercial Street Unions was engaged in a process of recombination and members wished to avoid entanglements "in external affairs" until matters were settled. Four street unions (Nanjing, Shandong, Xinzha, and Haining Roads) reproached the Street Union Federation, complaining of reports that their association was a signatory to telegrams [of the federated meeting]. They asked, "What people, with what qualifications, represented our association and exercised association prerogative?" The problem was not simply that the Street Union Federation, a conglomerate of contentious individual street unions, was in a state of factionalization, though this was certainly the case. Other groups faced similar dissent over the question of representation, as one report explained it, for "failing to be meticulous in their procedures." Four members of the Ningbo association published their own protest letter opposing use of the Ningbo association name as a signatory to the telegrams. They demanded that the directors "make known at once to the public on what day, by what collective decision, these delegates were authorized to represent the association." The protesters insisted that the Ningbo association print a formal response in the newspaper for all to see.[118] Facilitated by the accessibility of the press, these disputes opened the internal dynamics of formerly oligarchic associations to public view, with the newspaper as public record. In the process, organizations claiming to represent the public were forced to grapple with the procedural requirements of the democracy they espoused as well as the double-edged character of the press.

The Dongting association, organized its own "federated meeting" in response to the agitation orchestrated by Tang's defenders. This meeting included members of ten associations: four Jiangsu associations (Dongting East Mountain, Dongting West Mountain, Suzhou, and Wujiang); three girls' schools (Chengdong, Bo'wen, and Nanyang), and a women's business association. Also present were members of the Xi family. More than one hundred people reportedly attended, declaring support for the court verdict under the banner of judicial independence. Highlighting the embarrassments of the Guang-Zhao federated meeting, this meeting resolved to await formal approval by each association before sending any telegrams.[119] Newspaper coverage was minimal.

Protests escalated after December 14, when the judge pronounced the anticipated guilty verdict and sentenced Tang to three years in prison for fraud.[120] The verdict gave narrative weight to the suicide attempts, including the reported conversation in which Tang proposed that Xi become his concubine, despite the fact that the court's own indictment had questioned the relevance of these claims. Most crucially, the verdict ignored or dismissed the evidence introduced by the defense that demonstrated that Xi had possessed and pawned the shares. The verdict also ignored witness testimony that corroborated the defense's explanation of the financial transactions at the heart of the case, stating simply that "it is obvious that Tang intended to take possession of Xi's money for himself." This conclusion was based (1) on the personal receipt Tang gave Xi for her first investment; (2) the absence of Xi's purchase information in the dissolution records of Tang's trust company; (3) uncertainty as to whether Xi Shangji was Xi Shangzhen; and (4) the fact that Xi's suicide refuted Tang's claim that his promissory note was not fraudulent, but generous. ("If so, Xi should have been grateful. Then why would she want to kill herself?")[121] Tang announced in court that he would appeal.

POST-VERDICT DISCUSSION, IN AND OUTSIDE THE PUBLIC

The evening the verdict was pronounced, a second federated meeting with representatives of seventeen organizations formalized a "judicial reform movement." These were largely the same groups as before, with the exceptions of the Ningbo association, the four protesting street unions, and one representative from the Federation of Commercial Street Unions. Huo Shouhua announced that the meeting was "for the purpose of reforming the judicial system, not for continued discussion of the Tang case." He reviled China's judicial system as "unsuitable for modern life, at this time of contesting foreign control over Chinese courts." It belonged to a tradition of "authoritarian government to which Chinese have been subjected from ancient times," in which judges "trampled on the human rights of the majority" and "inflicted hardship on the body of the people."[122] The goals were the judicial reforms advocated by the Shanghai Lawyers' Association: abolition of the procuratorial system, adoption of a jury system, creation of a commercial court, high court supervision of lower courts, and compensation for improper arrest and detention. Tang's lawyers, Qin Liankui and Li Shirui had participated in earlier advocacy of these reforms as leading figures in the Bar Association.[123]

The following weeks were rich with gatherings, news, and commentary on the case, the courts, the question of judicial independence, and the declared movement to reform the judiciary. On December 23 the Guang-Zhao Gongsuo published a statement in major newspapers and sent yet a third letter to the Chamber of Commerce. The association's statement was mindful of the public imperative to embrace the civic and impersonal cause of judicial reform (notwithstanding a degree of condescension in regard to the women of the Xi family). It also articulated an alternate scenario behind the Xi family suit:

> We cry out in pain before our countrymen and demand protection of natural human rights. . . . Judicial reform is the first step in the people's demand for human rights. We witnessed the Shanghai judges' despotism in the Fujian student case. [This time] Judge Du Fuyao ignored evidence and failed to check facts, abruptly sentencing Tang to three years prison. Xi Shangzhen, in difficult circumstances, having failed in her investment, was blamed by her mother and elder sister. Oppressed by financial circumstances, she committed suicide. Her family was pained by her death and hated Tang for not providing cash compensation. They were falsely led to claim that he had not turned over stock. We forgive this type of behavior, coming from women. We pity their misfortune. However, Du Fuyao, a judge, convicted Tang entirely on empty words. Is this not evidence of judicial trampling of human rights? . . . Fellow-countrymen, let us not lose this opportunity to reform the legal process![124]

Facing new appeals by the Guang-Zhao and Dongting associations, the Chamber of Commerce renewed its discussion of the case. At a moment when any group might seize on decontextualized elements of republican ideals when it suited, the Dongting association, which had not previously focused on the topic, took up the rhetoric of judicial independence and denounced the judicial reform movement's call to dismiss the judges as a shocking "obstruction of the administration of justice." It derided the movement's authenticity, given the disputes over representation, as only "the private idea of a few people" and not a genuine expression of public sentiment.[125]

The Chamber of Commerce was thus faced with the daunting task of managing the divergent demands of two powerful constituent groups. The board members' discussion was confidential, but it was recorded in detail as a result of the Chamber reforms two years earlier, when Feng Shaoshan had successfully institutionalized the practice of verbatim meeting minutes in the interest of greater transparency. These verbatim minutes, a short-lived novelty of the May Fourth era, preserve the actual discussion. They thus expose language, habits of mind, and associational practice in a fashion that would not have been visible in the consensual abbreviated summary records that were maintained prior to the May Fourth agitation (when Feng and Tang's critiques of oligarchic practices mustered sufficient force to amend Chamber practice). Some board members expressed concern that by siding with either party, the Chamber's reputation as the organ of Shanghai businessmen might be compromised by an accusation of bias. Feng Shaoshan, for his part, argued that a rebuke by the Chamber of the judges' "commercial ignorance, dismissal of evidence, and neglect of human rights," could be a consensual action that supported the rights of all and prevented "court officials from bending law to frame the innocent." It was thus not an expression of bias.

On the topic of the court's handling of the financial practices exposed in the trial, several board members noted that in the period of surging investment, the type of improvised receipt that Tang had given Xi was not unusual. However, since such receipts did not comply with formal rules, this was disadvantageous in a lawsuit. The only solution, given the delicacy of Tang's position and the Chamber's situation, was to see whether the court might ask the Chamber for information about common practice. This might allow the Chamber to provide context. Given the awkwardness of Tang's case in terms of law and public sentiment, several members expressed preference for a less public solution. As Zhu Jinqing explained: "It is very difficult to engineer an informational request from the judge to the Chamber." He recommended that the Guang-Zhao Gongsuo should instead "make arrangements with Xi's family to stop them from agitating further," noting that "many approve of resolving the situation with money."[126]

Feng Shaoshan objected, referring to matters that were evidently understood by those present, but which appear cryptic a century later: "Xi didn't commit suicide over the 5000 yuan. There were other circumstances (*shi ling you bie qing*)." He stated that the Guang-Zhao Gongsuo was unwilling to engage in a private payoff to the family and was committed instead to the public movement to reform the judicial system.

In a statement that highlighted the challenge of appearing impartial, Fang Jiaobo recounted a thorny situation that had recently confronted his own Ningbo association when a female worker had been accused of kidnapping and sentenced to imprisonment:

> To avoid the suspicion of native-place bias [created by overt intervention], the association charitably engaged a lawyer to serve as her legal counsel. Later her innocence was demonstrated by evidence that proved that she had worked in the factory on the days in question. There is a way to save Mr. Tang, but we must carefully weigh our response . . . and our testimony.[127]

The discussion turned to the question of legal advice. Because of the awkwardness of "unanticipated trouble at the moment of foreign opposition to the return of legal sovereignty to China," the body ruled out a foreign lawyer, settling instead on the Chinese lawyer Wang Zhongdan as a consensus choice and delegating an investigative committee to meet with him. The venture was understood to be precarious: three of five board members initially declined the honor. The others present were sworn to secrecy about the plan.

When he met with the board several days later, Wang counseled caution. First, he ruled out bail, which he pointed out was only a possibility at the Mixed Court (confusion persisted over the right to bail and the rules of the Chinese court). Second, he counseled refraining from testimony unless consulted by the court. He recognized that the Chamber could verify several of the financial transactions and documents at issue in the case as not uncommon during the exchange bubble, including Tang's explanation of the receipt he gave Xi and her purchase and pawning of Hu-Hai shares. However, he argued that it was risky to admit to such anomalous practices. They were not in the category of "customary practice" that was recognized by law but were, rather, improvisations called forth in the rush of the stock fever. Hence they had no legal standing. Wen Lanting concurred that it was best not to "hastily stand out and testify":

> There were many anomalous practices during last year's stock market surge. Should this Chamber testify to each in turn? While it might be all right for another body [to give such testimony] it is inappropriate for the Chamber of Commerce, which should have been responsible for the rectification of anomalous practices. It is therefore inconvenient to admit to them. The reality is that such deviations were not limited to [Tang's] trust company alone. I fear new requests for the Chamber's testimony in similar cases. . . . Indiscretion in this instance could make the Chamber vulnerable to criticism.[128]

Emphasizing the importance of differentiating established custom from temporary, if common, improvisations during the exchange bubble, Fang Jiaobo argued that, "while justification of such practices is inappropriate, Tang will suffer if the Chamber does not attest to them." Such practices were not invented by Tang. "In testifying to this, the Chamber must, on the one hand bring no trouble to [itself]; on the other, we should not create problems for Tang's case. If testimony helps the case but harms the Chamber, we should reconsider testimony. The most difficult thing is crafting a [public] response to the Guang-Zhao association." Fang referred to an earlier case in the Mixed Court in which the Chamber attested to customary practice. In that case the Chamber confirmed practices that did not correspond to law and requested that the court use the information as the basis for its verdict. Feng suggested that in this case the Chamber could both attest to the common reality of improvised practices during the financial bubble and at the same time exculpate itself by stating that the Chamber was opposed to such practices.[129]

Wen Lanting pointed out that there were greater risks for the Chamber in the Chinese court than in the Mixed Court of the International Settlement. Moreover, the social atmosphere surrounding the two cases was quite different and there were divisions within the Chamber leadership:

> People on the outside have asked us why Tang hasn't been expelled [from the Chamber]. . . . Even some board members are displeased. Given the awkwardness within the Chamber, we shouldn't disregard objections from the outside. [Moreover,] we cannot ignore whether or not a transaction conforms to the law. If we hastily attest to the [commonplace occurrence of] practices that did not conform to law . . . this may cause problems for us in the future.[130]

Wen argued that—in terms of appeasing both the judges and public feeling—Tang might best be served by a light sentence in return for a cash payment to Xi's family. In contrast, whereas Feng recognized that "protest may anger the court by embarrassing the judges," he countered that such tactical concerns reflected a misplaced understanding of justice: "if judges act on the basis of their emotions, this endangers the people."

The lawyer shifted the discussion from the board members' various concerns about social strategies and rational administration of justice back to the legal crux of the case. The key point was "that Tang actually turned the stock over [to Xi]. The other issues are of little relevance." He stated that he was quite familiar with "the defects of the Shanghai district court." Nonetheless, he advised that the Chamber avoid confronting the judges by criticizing the handling of a specific case: "the Chamber should make only abstract criticisms."[131]

Fang Jiaobo expressed dismay that the judge had visited the Xi residence without witnesses. He stated that he would personally help Tang. However, in his role as an officer of the Chamber of Commerce, he asked Wang to draft a general statement concerning judicial reform, without referring to the Tang case. Attesting to anomalous financial practices was unwise. He also alluded to things that were understood but not explicit: "Tang has aroused resentment for other reasons. The death of Xi Shangzhen also has another origin. Unfortunately for Tang it happens that the two [unrelated matters] have coincided."[132]

In the face of arguments for institutional neutrality, safety, and regard for judicial independence, Feng Shaoshan restated the case for intervention to uphold human rights. His speech is of interest for his radical articulation of popular sovereignty as the foundation of a republic and its implications for the function of the judiciary. He argued that all powers of the state were given by the people, a principle that should not be brushed aside on the excuse of judicial independence, which might protect the malign exercise of power. The judge had revealed his partiality by making the groundless claim that the chop was counterfeit (and likely colluded in the production of an alternate chop). Should people not protest such astounding miscarriages of justice, which visibly angered the audience of more than 100 people who attended the trial? "If the receipt that Tang gave to Xi Shangzhen is taken as proof of guilt," he asked, "might not anyone who handles money and engages in the common practice of providing a temporary receipt be held guilty?" A sovereign people could not accept such trespasses.[133]

Feng's and Fang's remarks hinted at a political backstory to the case. Feng provided a few more clues, stating that there were two causes for "outside" resentment toward Tang, neither of which had to do with the Xi case. The first was an opaque lawsuit over the China Merchants' Steam Shipping Company, in which Tang was a shareholder. The other involved a summer 1921 controversy over Japanese munitions that were transshipped through Shanghai at the behest of the Beiyang government to aid Guangxi militarists against the Southern (GMD) government. In this latter case, Wu Tingfang (foreign minister in the south) and leaders of the Shanghai Guangdong community, Tang among them, created sufficient public outcry that Shanghai Defense Commissioner He Fenglin (who, as one commentator remarked, "theoretically takes his orders from the war department dispatching the munitions") was pressured to seize and halt the shipment, despite his close ties to Japan.[134]

The board members who heard him out did not dispute Feng's points about Tang's mistreatment in court, or its coincidence with He Fenglin's enmity toward Tang. Nonetheless, Feng failed to persuade the board to intervene in the case. Those present sought to justify their delayed response to the Guang-Zhao Gongsuo and to craft an appropriate response. Ultimately the awkwardness of the situation led them to choose the embarrassment of further delay.[135]

Frustrated in its efforts to muster the public legitimacy that might have been conferred by the sympathetic intervention of the Chamber of Commerce, the Guang-Zhao association continued to improvise a public. It convened a third federated meeting, this time drawing representatives of twenty groups. This last-ditch effort to influence the course of justice dispatched telegrams to officials in Ningbo, Suzhou, and Shanghai; the Beijing government; and Sun Yat-sen (who was in temporary residence in Shanghai, having been forced from leadership in the southern government in 1918). These telegrams reprised a history of abuses and likened Shanghai judicial cruelty to the barbarity of warlords.[136] Although the responses of other recipients are unclear, the out-of-power Sun seized the occasion to position himself with the people and against the arbitrary exercise of power: "Law must do justice to all the people. The people of the entire nation rely on the protection of the law. . . . This case is extremely significant [and] affects all citizens. [I] will try to prevent legal officials from depriving people of human rights."[137] In the meantime, the Chamber of Commerce board arrived at sufficiently anodyne wording for a response to the *gongsuo* that suited the delicacy of the occasion:

> We have three times received letters from your esteemed association. The aspiration to protect human rights is more powerful than may be expressed in words or countenance, and we deeply admire your [efforts]. Because of its significance, our Chamber gave this matter serious discussion. . . . We also organized a special investigative committee for this case. Among the points you raise, in regard to reforming the administration of justice, we believe it necessary to research a fundamental means of reform. After we find a concrete means of reform, we will make a proposal to the judicial authorities. Aside from this, we write this response to appease your concerns. . . . We beg your forgiveness for our belated response.[138]

For its part, the Society for Women's Participation in Government convened its own meeting "to insist on justice" in the Xi case. Zhou Huanfang, who spoke to the assembly, explained that the association was distressed to learn from newspapers of efforts "to interfere" with justice in the Tang case by calling into question the court's punishment of Tang. Such pressure on the court by Tang's defenders, she argued, called for a response from the women's association. She testified that "Xi's mother, sister, and sister-in-law are all womankind [*xi nüzi*]," and that the matter "involved the question of women's personhood [*yu nüzi ren'ge you guan*]." Those present affirmed their determination to support the execution of justice, by which they meant the court's verdict and sentencing of Tang. Thus the banner of protecting female personhood, as an abstract principle, was raised in opposition to the (male-identified) assertion of human rights.[139]

POWER AND LAW

Alone in prison, Tang appealed the verdict. Not only did his multiple appeals fail, but he was unaccountably transferred to a military jail under the vague charge of involvement in illegal arms trading, a charge for which he never stood trial. This result had been foreshadowed by a brief report in the fiercely nationalist Japanese newspaper, *Shanhai,* which disseminated the rumor shortly after Tang's arrest (quite possibly at the behest of He Fenglin) that Shanghai Defense Commissioner He had received "accusations" that Tang had violated military law by abetting a seamen's strike, smuggling weapons, and corresponding with members of a political party. Japanese interests in Shanghai had long identified Tang an anti-Japanese extremist, and must have welcomed the discrediting rumors as well as Tang's arrest by He.[140] Tang would not emerge from the military prison until 1928 (under the GMD), three years after the expiration of his original sentence and long after He Fenglin's departure from office.[141]

In the meantime the Xi-Tang case was preserved for prosperity as a chapter in a textbook for lawyers who aspired to understand case history, not just legal code. In 1923 the legal scholar Zhou Dongbai published his *Compilation of Famous Cases of the Nation's Lawyers.* His preface characterized the relation of the people to law and political power with pessimism:

> The people have the duty to comply with the laws. However, people do not fully know the law. . . . Looking at the history of law [it is obvious that] law has been the personal tool of the powerful and the victorious. . . . [If] those who establish law do not know what actually happens in society and create law based on theory, even if the law that is created is good doctrine and does not contain errors, the law will still not work [in social reality].[142]

Zhou's chapter on the Xi-Tang case, like his other chapters, consists entirely of court documents. Zhou limited his own analysis to a two-sentence preface. Here Zhou stated that Tang's defense by "the great lawyer, Li

Shirui, is extremely brilliant and worthy of note, so well written it should be studied." "As for the question of the appropriateness of the verdicts, identification of facts, and application of law," he observed tersely, "this serves amply as material for our study."[143]

On the face of the evidence, as Zhou's praise for Li Shirui's brilliant defense suggests, the outcome of the case was surprising. Public opinion, as Li noted, was stirred by Xi's suicide, and stood against Tang. Even so, the nature of Tang's critics' interventions and their inability to frame a compelling legal case suggest that they may not have been confident of the outcome. Tang's supporters, in contrast, clearly believed in a fact-based approach and imagined the evidence would vindicate him. They only belatedly organized meetings and protests after the second trial, in which crucial evidence was dismissed. It is unlikely that the individuals and organizations concerned in these efforts would have gone to such lengths to defend Tang (given the social scandal that surrounded the case) had they not felt a credible argument could be made for his innocence. Zhou Dongbai's emphatic praise for Li Shirui's defense summary, which dismantled the legal reasoning behind the verdict, reinforces this impression.[144]

The court verdict is only surprising, however, if one dismisses the political realities behind the case, the convenience of public distraction with issues tangential to the law, the judge's manipulation of public opinion, and the power relations that governed the administration of justice. In other words, as Zhou Dongbai warned his readers, it is necessary to grasp, not simply points of law, but what actually happened in society. Bringing into the picture the power of the local military authority over the Chinese court—though this crucial relationship was largely invisible—is essential to understanding the disposition of the case. It also explains the determination of the Chinese police to place Tang under the jurisdiction of the Chinese district court and why the procurator pursued a criminal case that precluded bail. Commentators generally avoided mention of He Fenglin in public discussion of the case. Tang's defenders nonetheless understood that the judges were his pawns. In his campaigns for citizen's rights before Xi's suicide, Tang had repeatedly clashed with He and had embarrassed him on the pages of his newspaper. His public mortification in the Guangxi munitions shipment case can only have added to He's enmity for the outspoken Tang. One can only imagine He's delight when Tang was delivered into his hands by means of a scandal that destroyed his social reputation.[145] Tang's sentencing may thus have been a foregone conclusion for the judges who ultimately served at He's pleasure, obviating their serious review of the evidence. This "backstory" to the trial proceedings did not deliver them of the need to maintain public deference to legal procedure, nor did it protect them from criticism on these grounds. Proper legal procedure was not, however, the primary concern of public discussion that enveloped the case.

JUSTICE IN THE VERNACULAR:
MORALITY AND LAW IN PUBLIC OPINION

Despite the efforts of Tang's legal defense and his various defenders, only a portion of public comment focused on matters of law or legal procedure. The first volley of publicity highlighted the morality of female vocations, the corruption of money, grievance, and even ghostly retribution. Observers invoked Tang's responsibility in terms that attest to the paternalistic character of office culture in this era: "[As employer] Tang bears moral responsibility for protecting Miss Xi. [She] belongs to the junior generation. Therefore Tang is responsible to guide and protect [her]. . . . If he thought she might benefit from purchasing stock, he should have helped her to profit and avoid failure."[146] The societally affirmed logic of Tang's moral responsibility for a revenge suicide was also explicit in the court's reasoning, which interpreted the suicide as evidence that Tang had not delivered the stock, even in the face of the contrary evidence that Xi had pawned the shares.

The pervasive language of grievance and retribution was joined in print discussion to ideas of public opinion (*yulun, gonglun*) that infused the self-described republican public of newspapers with culturally resonant communal norms. At the same time, in this period, public opinion was joined to the idea of an activist and amateur investigative public. Investigation was not the exclusive preserve of judicial professionals. Public investigation—by associations, journalists, and newspaper readers—was necessary, preferable, and linked to the desirable dissemination of public information and negative exposure of wrongdoers. Public justice, not the law, was the solution: "Only public opinion circles can punish him in terms of his reputation."[147] In this radical formulation newspapers served the sovereign public as a tool of transparency and direct democracy while at the same time extending older practices of community shaming.

By the same token, the social production of justice, which interacted unevenly with the formal administration of justice, was collective, not an individual or impersonal affair. Social groups that weighed in on the case publicized their own investigations and pressured court officials in collective statements and actions. Although journalists and letter writers indulged in individual analyses of evidence as a part of the production of rational and impersonal (science-based) public opinion, individual statements also risked the taint of personal ties with the accused. As Tang's defenders crafted human rights arguments, they did so within the framework of communal associations that could speak for a public. Arguments for the rights of one individual were necessarily crafted in terms broader collective identities, "the people" (or "womankind"). Operating outside of representative governing structures in the empty shell of the Republic, associational agitation followed a logic of coalition politics that proceeded from the impossible-to-realize imperative to represent the larger public, not merely a self-interested group.

In vernacular discussion, morality trumped law; indeed there was little appreciation of the role of law in democratic practice: "It is a problem of human integrity. The legal issues are secondary."[148] The strict provisions of law served to exasperate: "As for him angering [Xi] unto death . . . how can this remain beyond the law?"[149] Some insisted that morality must be key to the law. As the feminist Zhou Fengxia, argued, "Law protects people's rights, and justice is in people's hearts. Since law proceeds from justice. . . . If you have justice, you have law." Law was nonetheless a secondary concern: "His behavior is absolutely not upright." If Tang had been a good employer, "he should have taken care of things for her."[150] Like others, Zhou combined moral judgment with disregard, misunderstanding, or refusal to accept the impersonal logic of market mechanisms.

In this climate of opinion businessmen and economists faced rough seas. Legal maneuvering and recourse to lawyers generated suspicion:

> [Tang] has now printed his statement in [newspapers], in consultation with Lawyer Fessenden. This intimidates people with the power of the law. . . . However, law is one thing and virtue is another. I personally don't dare speak of law, and so I will speak of virtue. . . . Since Xi died tragically, Tang, should have the conscience to charitably help her family.[151]

Xi's family's recourse to law was met with surprise: "It is said that Xi's family members are innocent and timid people. But [Tang's arrest] seems rather sharp and goes beyond normal expectations."[152] Denounced also for his libel suit, Tang was advised instead to bend to public criticism and compensate Xi's family: "Where justice exists, you can't lightly pass over it. Newspapers are the organ of public opinion. . . . The greater the uproar, the more useless it is to resist."[153] From this perspective, Tang's arrest suggested a rare correspondence between public opinion and law that might boost the reputation of law by the association. As one commentator exulted after Tang's arrest, "Previously law had no efficacy; it simply supported people with power and property! [But] Tang Jiezhi's arrest [suggests] that lawfulness may still be discerned in the law."[154]

Distrust of law and legal proceedings was ubiquitous. Even Zhou Dong-bai's legal casebook expressed this, stating at the outset that "most sociologists disdain and attack the law [as a tool of the powerful]. There is nothing strange about this." Zhou's justification for publishing a legal case-book was remarkably apologetic, reasoning that in China's current situation, "even those most intelligent and most strongly opposed to the law would still not go so far as to argue that law may be abandoned altogether. [Thus] study of law retains some value."[155] He expressed the hope that study of the actual functioning of law in society through the examination of cases would facilitate the improvement of the law, suggesting that his book might facilitate research by sociologists who criticized the legal system.

If suspicion of law and the administration of justice varied in its reasons and its strategic application, its pervasiveness reflected the chaotic and conflicting legal patchwork of the early Republic and the realpolitik of legal reform in a time of global inequity. Some writers characterized law as an "empty form." Others expressed distaste for Western legal culture as a model for China. One article that was reprinted in several venues criticized both the corruptions of Chinese culture and the lack of virtue in Western society, finding law impotent in both cases:

> Chinese society is infinitely evil. To rely on law to correct these evils is useless. This is because the law is matter of form. If you break the form, you break the law. It is not the case that doing evil counts as breaking the law. Therefore, despite its meticulous laws, the West is still incessantly evil.[156]

Tang's defenders, in contrast, exhibited a liberal regard for abstract, rights-based legal principles, which they admired, but problematized the Chinese judges who implemented the law, and dismissed judicial process when they recognized a moral imperative to intervene. When the Guang-Zhao Gongsuo, with its frequent recourse to lawyers, framed its appeal to the Chamber of Commerce, it invoked the imperative to "uphold justice" (zhuchi gongdao) rather than law. Indeed, as the Chamber's board of directors discussed the matter, one member commented: "The four characters (zhu chi gong dao) in the letter are extensive in scope, making it difficult to know what [precisely is to be done]."[157]

Most public commentary followed the prosecution in ignoring financial evidence. Tang's lawyers stood against this tide, emphasized the compelling weight of expert testimony and scientific, knowledge-based reading of financial documents. Qin Liankui rightly complained of public distraction from the substance of the law and court inattention to evidence.[158] Sun Yat-sen, in his public letter on the case, made the same point: "It is particularly inappropriate for a court of law to ignore the evidence in favor of popular sentiment."[159] But such reasoning was not broadly shared. Commentators had acknowledged at the outset that the evidence supported Tang, but directed attention elsewhere, suggesting that he not presume the efficacy of an evidence-based approach:

> Tang's advantage is that there is no evidence against him; available evidence supports Tang's account. The August 19 promissory note was written by Tang himself. It is most helpful to Tang. . . . Nonetheless, his advantage in terms of the law is a disadvantage in the scale of social opinion. What Miss Xi said to her sister in law and elder sister cannot be proven by evidence. However, [it is compelling because] no one will believe that someone who was determined to die would speak falsely. . . . I advise Mr. Tang to seriously consider his social position and help her family. He should rectify the situation to pacify people's minds.[160]

The judge's dismissal of evidence (and possible manufacture of false evidence) reflected the political exigencies of the case.[161] Nonetheless, for the court and the public, the unfamiliarity of financial documents and the impersonal logic of finance capitalism facilitated their dismissal. As the judge narrated the events he questioned both the logic of market speculation and the possibility of female agency: "[How could] a weak woman think that investing in trust company stock would be so profitable that she would purchase so much stock?"[162] The judge's question did not register that Shanghai had just witnessed a wave of popular financial speculation that bridged both class and gender.[163] Rather than target an abstraction that implicated a great number of Shanghai speculators—as indeed Zheng Zhengqiu had suggested earlier in the fall, with his castigation of "the crime of economics"—for much of the public it was more palatable to pass judgment on a human culprit who must have been guilty of the crime of fraudulent deception.

JUSTICE IN COURT, SOCIETY, AND NEWSPRINT

The vernacular understandings of law and legal practice expressed in the case, unsurprisingly, reveal areas of broad continuity with the late Qing Era and a context of radical transformation. In the courtroom and outside, older notions coexisted with and infused the language of citizenship, nationalism, human rights, judicial reform, and judicial independence

204 • THE SUICIDE OF MISS XI

despite their logical contradictions and often to unanticipated effect, given changes in the judiciary and the political context. The radical assertion of democratic citizenship visible in the discussion and social mobilization surrounding the case was particular to the May Fourth Era, though it would persist in minor key, suppressed by the social discipline imposed by an authoritarian state in the next decade.

The continuing sway of notions of communal and cosmic justice in the Republican Era should not surprise. More distinctive in this era was the coexisting cachet of science and the globally inflected critique of Chinese culture, though the noisiness of New Culture writers aimed to drown out and discredit articulation of earlier frames of belief. Li Shirui, as a legal professional, mocked the reasoning of society and the court as outmoded: "The court's arbitrary decision that Xi's suicide was revenge required denial of evidence. Following this logic, whenever someone dies outside their house, they must be seeking revenge against the site of death. Can such logic exist in this world?"[164] His eloquence in making this point was preserved for future generations by Zhou Dongbai, but it made as little impression on much of the public as on the court.

In another exhibition of continuity with past practice, the case demonstrates the ongoing strategic use of the judicial process in the Republican Era by socially disadvantaged social actors who seized upon the mechanism of false accusations.[165] The social expectation was that Tang, as Xi's employer, should compensate the family for Xi's failed investment and her death, whether or not he was *legally* responsible. This widely expressed expectation was fundamental to the case initiated by the Dongting association.

Despite this continuity in vernacular expectations, the trial outcome also suggests a rupture in the Republic between social expectations and the administration of justice. In the late Qing, as Quinn Javers has shown, a dynamic state-society reciprocity enabled weak parties to draw the power of the state at times into their local disputes. The redistributive logic behind this recognized strategy underlay judicial decisions that at times overlooked strict provisions of the law and facilitated compensation of the weaker party. Court attentiveness to collective understandings of justice contributed to the legitimacy of the administration of justice. In the Republic, the guilty verdict against Tang gratified Xi family enmity. It would be inappropriate to conclude, however, that in this case the court was motivated by such sympathetic logic. In fact, the court showed little concern for compensating the family. The arms-trading charge lodged against Tang shifted emphasis away from Xi's grievance. A year after Tang was moved to military prison, the women in the Xi family were still petitioning the court for compensation.[166] Political exigency, rather than concern for the weak, better explains court action.

A similar logic applies to expectations for community intervention. The vigorous intercession of public associations in the case testifies to community agency in the judicial process.[167] The Xi-Tang case brought older- and new-style mediating rationales into one arena, drawing the paternalistic Dongting community into the public opinion of Republican Era newspapers. As a constituent of the Republican public, even the Dongting association found it expedient and necessary to change its vocabulary, or at least pepper it with the new lingo. Insofar as community intervention claimed the mantle of popular opinion, public response to the case suggests a robust early Republican-Era climate for what one legal scholar, writing about contemporary China, has called legal populism (the notion that the populace has a right to weigh-in on court decisions).[168] This assertion of public voice, along with attentiveness to public sentiment, was certainly a feature of the 1920s, and it bears some relation to what Eugenia Lean has characterized as an "affective public" in the 1930s. The political, and even affective content of the fragile republican public of the May Fourth Era, was distinctive, however, for its language of democratic civic activism and rights outside the state, and its advocacy of science-based rationality as well as public sentiment.[169]

Although the Tang verdict aligned with community sentiment, it would be unwise to conclude that it was driven by the power of public opinion. The public feeling aroused by Xi's suicide case was mixed. One strain offered a useful cloak for the politically expedient application of the criminal code to ensnare Tang. The political backstory and the close interaction of court personnel with the Dongting association and Xi family suggest the difficulty of disentangling community initiative from official manipulation in what appear to be spontaneous expressions of popular opinion in legal process.[170] The vernacular expectations expressed in print and the protest movement that followed the trial reveal nonetheless a robust strand of legal populism. The populism seen here drew on Republican language of popular sovereignty and citizenship, the hegemonic principles of legitimacy after 1912, despite widespread recognition that the Republic had failed to produce a credible state.

The predicament of extraterritoriality exacerbated tensions between the imagined rights born of popular sovereignty and the duties and discipline of nationalism. The idea of popular sovereignty undergirded militant assertions of citizen rights. But citizen rights claims were vulnerable to the prerogatives of the nation. Nationalism made it awkward to criticize Chinese judicial practice. Failure to critique foreign courts disarmed criticism of Chinese courts. An entrepreneurial reporter who interviewed protestors who met with Chief Justice Mei asked them, "Did you mistrust the court and judicial administration prior to this case, or did this mistrust begin with this case?[171] After noting their response ("We have always mistrusted the courts.") the reporter stated that they had nothing to say when asked whether they would similarly protest a judgment in the Mixed Court. By printing this detail, he interrogated the protestors' loyalty.

The language of judicial independence was unsettled and could be grasped for multiple uses. An unnamed "legal specialist," interviewed by the same journalist, used the ideal of judicial independence—like the Dongting and women's groups—to cast aspersions on the integrity of the judicial reform movement. In his rendering, judicial independence necessitated the protection of the court against pressure from individuals or the popular masses: "[Protest] by these groups [oppresses] the court to please a private individual. It is bad for the masses to interfere with the administration of justice."[172]

Tang's opponents capitalized on the language of judicial independence. An editorial in the rival *Shishi xinbao* mocked the neologism, "legal rights movement," and urged a rectification of names. Those protesting the verdict had created a "fake legal sovereignty movement." Their activities "destroyed the spirit of judicial independence," making the abolition of extraterritoriality more difficult: "The abolition of consular jurisdiction requires two things: 1) wholesome judicial institutions, fully developed law, and upright officials; 2) citizens who know and respect the law." The writer suggested that it was only because protest leaders were sheltered by residence in the International Settlement that "they could indignantly attack the [Chinese] court." This editorial affirmed no fondness for Chinese judicial personnel ("we frankly admit that we have no faith in them"). Nonetheless, he argued, "citizens should respect the law," and reforms must have limits: "If you want to reform the judicial system, citizens must first gain legal knowledge. . . . If their acts destroy the judiciary, it is useless to sing out 'legal rights movement.'"[173]

Another commentator pleaded for judicial lenience for Tang, noting that there was no evidence of criminal behavior. He argued, nonetheless, that society must uphold the sanctity of the court. At a consequential moment for the return of Chinese sovereignty, criticism of Chinese courts was unfortunate, especially if the criticism came from people residents of the International Settlement.[174]

These views of national loyalties, citizen duty, order, and restraint on public criticism of Chinese courts provoked an eloquent, if discredited, articulation of citizen's rights by Chen Bulei:

[Some people] make the criticism that "this [protest] intrudes on the independence of the law" . . . [But protest] is exactly what citizens *should* do. If
they insist that this infringes on judicial independence and citizen rights, how
may we speak of legal literacy?

"Judicial independence" refers to independence from the legislative and administrative branches of government. It is not that [the court] should be independent of citizens, who suffer grievances, insult, and murder, without
being able to register their objections. Such critics' solicitousness for the
judges resembles the subservience of slaves. . . . They forget they are fundamental republican citizens of the national body. [They] say that the [protests
of] public organizations harms our legal sovereignty, reveals our judicial underside, and that this is what citizens should not do. From this we see that
they cheat themselves in order to cheat others.[175]

This exchange illuminated the predicament of vernacular understandings of democracy and legal process in the early Republican Era. The extraordinary multiplicity of legal institutions, old and new, Chinese and foreign, worked to denaturalize all of them, revealing arbitrary constructs
rather than embodiments of rooted law or modern reason. In late Qing
vernacular understandings of law, criticism was commonly directed, not
at the law itself, but at the gap between legal ideals and practice.[176] In the
semicolonial spaces of the Republic—and in the shadows of secretive
military authority—law itself grew strange. The legal institutions of the
early Republic, in any event, lacked coherence, trained personnel, and
protection from arbitrary authority. In this fractured political landscape,
morally inflected notions of justice offered a familiar language to navigate the social disruptions of new urban arrangements and the modern
confusions of sexually integrated workplaces, stock exchanges, and
market speculation.

Chinese courts, tokens of national aspiration, were difficult to criticize
and troubled in practice, intermittently bent to the contingencies of local
military governance. In this context, public contestation of the legitimacy
of law might serve only to facilitate the exercise of exceptional law. In the
absence of a state that was perceived to be legitimate, the principle of
popular sovereignty persisted undiminished as an ideal. It assumed unusual
rhetorical independence in the May Fourth Era from notions of formal law
and state constraint, even as political rights were mortgaged to the project
of national sovereignty. This state of affairs characterizes the remarkable
reasoning of the *Shenbao* editorial on opinion and law that appears as an
epigraph for this chapter, which affirms the importance of law in a constitutional nation, bemoans the absence of explicit law in the Republic and

the emergence of "fake law," and celebrates public opinion as a panacea for the legal deficits of the Republic: "If public opinion expresses the true will of citizens, it doesn't matter if the law is clearly written. Public opinion must eventually prevail. By this means incompletely prepared law will ultimately be corrected by public opinion."[177] Such expressions of what Yves Chevrier has described as "de-institutionalized democracy"[178] coexisted in tension with a powerful nationalism that was fueled by dreams of an unrealized state that could represent a nation of the people. For many, the need to regain legal sovereignty and conjure forth such a state justified temporary infringement on the sovereignty of the people. Such justifications paved the way for the extended infringements on the sovereignty of the people that would follow in the 1930s and after.

CHAPTER FIVE

A Public without a Republic?

No one who researches Chinese politics would not believe that the fate of this nation lies in the hands of the group movement. [In the abnormal politics of the present] the group movement is the only proper tool. Both Chinese and foreigners have held this belief since the May Fourth Movement. . . . Those who have engaged in the group movement know it is nothing to feel fortunate about, nor to proudly post on a signboard. It is actually something very difficult and troublesome. . . . We believe the group movement is the remedy for China in this time of emergency. Nevertheless, given the mediocre achievements of the group movement, how may we not feel chilled about prospects for the future?

—Tang Jiezhi, March 1922

There is no break, let alone opposition, between local history and global history. What the experience of an individual, a group, a space allows us to comprehend is a particular modulation or inflection of global history.

—Jacques Revel, 1996

THIS BOOK HAS taken up a multifaceted event—a suicide, social scandal, speculative bubble, and legal case in China's commercial and print capital of Shanghai—and followed its evidentiary trails in an era routinely described as the early Republic. This entailed excavating two individuals formerly lost to history and their tragic encounters at the *Journal of Commerce,* a similarly forgotten newspaper, in the wake of a largely forgotten financial crisis that rocked the city and extended into other coastal and riverine cities.[1] The case snakes through three defining realms of a fragile republican public of citizens that embraced gender equality, property rights and market access, and, with some ambivalence, law. This public, too, was evanescent, but it arises at times to haunt the present, like Xi Shangzhen's forgotten ghost.

Asking what made Xi Shangzhen's suicide in Tang Jiezhi's office and its aftermath so scandalous in their time brings the norms of this novel public into view. The study of scandal entails an examination of its animating publicity, and specifically, the understandings and behavior of the public that defines the scandal and gives it life. This public found expression in urban print and in the multitude of public associations that gathered, debated, and weighed in on the issues. Social commentary that dissected the Xi-Tang case identified at least three scandals: a suicide that suggested a transgression of gender boundaries (and called for their clarification); speculative and fraudulent finance (which demanded a reckoning with commercial culture and economics); and a trial that defied evidence, legal norms, and common understandings of justice, even if these understandings were plural and called forth a multiplicity of interventions.

Newspapers and public associations—as venues of an articulating, adjudicating, and activist public that gained force in the shadow of a failed Republic—have served as both subjects and sources for the story. Newspapers and public associations created spaces for the elaboration and dissemination of democratic ideas associated with a participatory public, which were ambient as neologisms in political discourse at the time of their introduction in the 1890s and gained new definition in the Republic. These venues were also crucial for their embodiment of these ideas and for their institutionalization of accessible, authoritative, and more transparent public records (as organizations of various types reformed record-keeping practices, posted notices, and published journals in this period). In his work on the French press, Robert Darnton problematized historians' treatment of print as simply "a record of what happened instead of as an ingredient in the happening," arguing instead for its constitutive role in disseminating ideas. My thought is to take this insight a bit further in the context of the Chinese Republic, to emphasize, not simply the dissemination of democratic ideas of citizenship, but also the emergence of the newspaper as a newly authoritative form of public record.[2]

Archives in China, Japan, the United States, the United Kingdom, and France have necessarily supplemented newspaper and other sources to clarify aspects of the case and its surrounding controversies, and to ascertain what did (and did not) appear in public print. Much remains opaque. The art of the historian, it might be said, depends on the recognition and probing of opacity as much as on the interpretation of available materials. No public, of course, is transparent. An exploration of the public that was called up by the 1922 case makes visible the frames of significance that defined social life in the fragmented spaces of a city that was shaped by the uneven interplay of Chinese and foreign power, an unevenness that undergirded Shanghai's position as China's hub of international trade and finance. Dwelling, in the space of these pages, on this forgotten scandal, reorients and repositions narratives of modern Chinese history that focus on more familiar personalities, events, or larger spans of time.

The Xi-Tang case may be placed among those, to borrow the words of the *North China Daily News,* that "cannot be judged by common sense or ordinary rules . . . and seem simply unfathomable." Aspects of the case appear obscure, in part, for reasons adduced by that paper, which observed that "neither the law of the country nor the power of government is clearly defined," thus facilitating such "cleverly conceived frame-ups that nobody can easily determine upon the charges being genuine or false."[3] Mysterious cases like Tang's confirmed beliefs that a dark curtain haunted public print, hindering progress and cloaking what properly should be public. The dark curtain was understood by both Chinese and foreigners to be characteristically Chinese, a lingering problem of an essentialized Chinese culture, as described in a *Shenbao* editorial that was reprinted in English translation for foreign consumption: "China lives behind the curtain. Nothing is enacted on the open stage. . . . [Such matters as] the students' movement, the struggle among the militarists, the political monopoly, finance, and diplomatic affairs, are all handled in the dark behind the curtain. What will the public see when the curtain is raised?"[4]

Such orientalizing appraisals notwithstanding, this was an unparalleled moment of press proliferation and openness in China that contrasts with the greater censorship and violence of prior and subsequent eras. Making sense of the verdict and the aftermath of Tang's trial, nonetheless, requires factoring in context beyond its public and Chinese-language coverage. Tang's transfer to military custody points to both the authority of Defense Commissioner He Fenglin and Tang's prior political tangles with He's authority. Although formalities of evidence and legal procedure constrained He's influence in ways that were not negligible, ultimately He pulled the strings. Japanese interests also played a role. This political backstory went largely unreported and appears only obliquely. Tang's outspokenness was risky; others were more mindful of the dangers of angering local military authority.[5]

Tang had jousted with He, wielding the burgeoning force of public opinion and popular mobilization as his lance. Positioned, as he was, to exert pressure through public demonstrations and publicity—in short, armed with the power of a republican public—Tang had achieved a measure of success, taunting and embarrassing He and emerging unscathed.[6] His luck turned, however, with Xi's suicide and the eruption of a scandal that—because of the significance of gender in the project of national transformation—damaged his ability to mobilize, and indeed personify, enlightened public opinion.

Some of the flavor of Tang's earlier tactics and the language of the public he invoked may be seen in the way he used the newspaper to project an image as a defender of the public and civic activism, in service to the nation. In November 1921, for example, the Federation of Commercial Street Unions requested use of the (Chinese) public exercise grounds for a public meeting. The *Shangbao* published He Fenglin's refusal (which endorsed the meeting but denied the venue for security concerns) together with Tang's goading response, which was crafted to confront the Defense Commissioner in print. By the alchemy of connection with citizen-readers, Tang's words took on the aura of public opinion:

> We believed you would grant our request [to use] the West Gate Exercise Grounds. [But] we were disappointed. The planned meeting concerns Chinese strategy in the Washington Conference. . . . The participants are all law-abiding citizens with professions, eager to contribute to our nation. You are authorized by the nation and have the responsibility to help us citizens. Why would you approve our intent but refuse to join this effort in the national interest? You [claim] the Chamber of Commerce building would be a more appropriate venue. But isn't the Chamber located in the International Settlement, under foreign jurisdiction? As Chinese citizens, should we discuss our country's foreign relations under the supervision of foreign police? Wouldn't this make us the shameful laughing stock of foreigners? . . . You should not evade your responsibility to defend our country. . . . When you read [this in the newspaper] you will understand that this is not one person's private opinion [*fei mou yi ren zhi siyan*], but the opinion of the majority of the people [*duoshuren zhi yijian ye*]. [We] hope you will understand the necessity of respecting public opinion.[7]

Such public admonishment of the local military authority was a dangerous provocation, even on the pages of a US-registered newspaper in the International Settlement, where extraterritoriality offered a degree of protection.[8] Tang had built his public reputation and that of his newspaper on such rhetoric and bold reportage. Although Tang's letter was not printed in other major Chinese dailies, a florid English version (likely embellished by Sokolsky) appeared in the *North China Herald,* magnifying the public insult by also embarrassing He before the English-speaking community.[9] Tang's outspokenness and his fate attest to the possibilities and the boundaries of public speech in this moment.

Only after the spectacle of Xi's suicide shifted public opinion decisively against Tang, after the Dongting association enabled Chinese authorities to take him into custody, and after a Chinese judge pronounced a guilty verdict, did He Fenglin overtly exercise exceptional authority and move Tang into a military prison. This development, revealing as it was of the power dynamics underlying the trial, received spare mention in the press.

Other aspects of the case are opaque because the precise nature of Xi and Tang's interactions remains unclear. Their interpersonal relations extended beyond the economic relations of employer and employee—Shanghai workplaces were not impersonal, in any event—and beyond the buying and transfer of shares, but the details remain shrouded. It would have been in no party's interest to expose an intimate relationship. Xi's family had relied on her income for support and on her close connection to Tang to secure their own purchases of stock. These familial financial concerns and strategies might be seen as compromising. Xi's feminist or chivalrous defenders preferred to memorialize a chaste heroine or victim. Tang's supporters, for their part, staunchly detached themselves from the rumors of intimacy that were taken for granted in satire and poetry. Public aspirations for gender equality demanded that modern men exercise sexual restraint while promoting women. Once he was branded as a sexual hypocrite, Tang lost credibility, even as the trial focused on money matters.

The peculiar economic terrain of the case compounds its puzzles. It was challenging for nearly everyone concerned to understand the financial machinations and investor behavior that contextualized the speculative transactions at the heart of the suicide and trial. These appear unfathomable partially in the way that financial bubbles often seem to defy the bounds of rational behavior. But the particularities of the facts on the ground—the jurisdictional complexities and multiplication of exchanges and trust companies; the impossibility of their legal regulation; the strangeness of economic neologism; the paucity of economic information; the way in which economic nationalism entered into the equation—intensified the challenges of appraising the morality and legality of Tang's economic behavior.

Tracing the pathways of this scandal by taking up in turn the fraught arenas of gender, market, and law both complements and complicates understandings of China's modern history. Focus on the dense social fabric of a particular place at a particular moment in time permits a multilayered and integrated investigation of archival, literary, interpersonal, economic, legal, and political realms. The traces of this perplexing human drama illuminate and reorient the significance of the pivotal May Fourth moment by turning the lens of inquiry onto the vernacular culture of the everyday—urban identities and networks, print culture and the forging of meaning, ideas of the market and a failing state, tensions of the sexually integrated workspace, and the dramas of the courtroom—in ways that embed May Fourth more deeply into society. By shifting the frame and interpretive focus away from more familiar May Fourth themes and sites (intellectuals' embrace of liberal democracy, universities, student demonstrators, worker strikes), May Fourth looks different. This study builds on growing scholarly attention to the realm of the economic, recognizing that liberal democracy in this emblematic modern moment was deeply intertwined with the generative and politically contradictory energies of Shanghai's commercial culture and speculative finance.

This book has traced the threads of Xi and Tang's entanglements through the gender, financial, and legal transformations of their era. The vicissitudes of gender are not unfamiliar, though familiarity renders them no less germane. Numerous histories have helped to illuminate the radical reconceptualization of gender as foundational to the egalitarian vision of China's Republic. The public realm that quickened in the lively press of the Republic, was, from its conception in late Qing print, tied to changing ideas about women. Readers and writers in the May Fourth Era grappled with the sexual integration of society, the transformation of women into citizens, and the ubiquitous failings of individuals and society in the new gender order. Male and female thinkers and activists who considered themselves enlightened contributed differentially to the refashioning of gender, conceiving or enacting varying admixtures of female agency, even as they all championed gender equality as essential to a modern nation.[10]

The delineation of the gendered landscape of the early Republic in this book does not radically alter recognized outlines of gender transformation in this period, but—in opening up the dynamics of an office workspace to analysis and tracing what idealized shifts could mean in daily practice—it complicates and darkens the picture. Precisely because gender equality emblematized the public realm of citizenship, as recounted in Chapter 2, Xi Shangzhen's suicide was a preoccupying sign of failure, a finger in the eye of progress. The paradoxical revenge suicide of a new woman challenged the normative categories of modern identity, revealing that the ideologically distinct new woman was, in daily life, inextricably intertwined with what was to be banished: aggrieved ghosts, old- and new-style concubines, and unreformed male sexual privilege. If the spectacle of a hypocritical modern man does not surprise, such revelations as the participation of celebrated feminists in a public ceremony for a chaste suicide in 1917 or feminist writers' insistence on Xi's sexual purity in the liberatory New Culture moment of 1922 muddy the artificial divisions between new and old thinking that were promoted by new thinkers at the time and persist today. Female activists' refusal to countenance concubines in their associations and their denial of concubines' coequal (and coeval) rights mark fault lines in the inclusive modern category of "woman" that betray assumptions about gender solidarity. Educated women's policing of identities and social alarm at the emergence of "new-style concubines" reveal the contemporary unpersuasiveness of the legal redefinition of marriage as monogamy, the enduring problem of reforming elite male sexuality (as a corollary to the idea of gender equality), and the refractory and often compromising challenges for women of modest means of earning a livelihood, challenges that also endure today. Xi's bitter fictional articulation of the gendered plight and desires of "Little Love" for both material commodities and personal autonomy—ignored in feminist comment on the case—powerfully resists co-optation into more familiar narratives of the new woman.

The print discussion of the case exhibits the heterogeneous vocabulary and imagery of gender that infused public life. Notwithstanding their editorial differences, newspapers inevitably disseminated both new and old language and ideals. Newspapers' capacious "mixed bag" of reportage, advertisements, cartoons, editorials, and translations relied on and recirculated older and newer literary (or pictorial) aesthetics.[11] A growing taste for reportage did not displace habits of poetic expression, even as news infused poetry and editors repurposed poetry by soliciting poems as a token of reader-citizen participation. The inscriptions of the Xi-Tang case on the diverse offerings of print reveal the medium's openness to otherwise unremarked voices, including Xi's own writings (both the articles published before her death, and her posthumously published fiction and poetry) that connect her to literary, economic, and gender expression in her time.[12] The economic preoccupations of Xi's poetry and the intensity of print discussion of Xi's investments suggest the fruitfulness of interpretive frameworks that locate gender in the realm of economic imagination.[13]

Xi and Tang's financial entanglements—and the discussion they stimulated—take this examination of the everyday transformations of the Republic and the republican public into the arenas of economic pedagogy, economic agency, and the financial imaginaries of calculation and speculation. Taking up this thread, Chapter 3 juxtaposed economic institutions with politics and culture as they appeared in the vernacular of public commentary at the time.

Historians have not generally placed economics, let alone stock exchanges, among the structuring ideas of the early Republic or as a constituent element of May Fourth ideas of science and democracy.[14] Insightful recent studies by Karl Gerth, Wen-hsin Yeh, and Eugenia Lean have, however, highlighted the importance of commerce, advertising, and consumption in the construction of popular nationalism and the development of new categories of knowledge.[15] This study examines connections between economic and political thinking by considering the play of nationalism in the imagination of finance and commercial culture, on the one hand, and ideas of the market as a constituent element of May Fourth democracy, on the other. In 1920, at the time of the establishment of Shanghai's first stock exchange, the paired exhortation of "Long live the Republic" and "Long live the stock exchange" calls up the opportunity to reflect on the significance of finance and markets in the imagination of the Republic. This work extends the insights of the recent cultural histories of commerce to suggest the ideological valences of investment, risk, and speculative failure.

The vernacular of public commentary—a non-specialist pursuit—did not wall off economics, but regularly juxtaposed economic and political realms, often through economic metaphor. Such conceptual connections reveal unanticipated pathways of translation, association, and mutation, pathways by which new political and cultural notions facilitated the unpredictable logic of capitalism. National sentiment facilitated the introduction—and commodification—of the stock exchange as a "national product." A different example of the conceptual imbrication of the political and the economic is provided by a 1921 parody entitled "New Exchanges and Trust Companies," published in *New World,* which lamented: "I myself am also one of the citizens of China. However, my name is not among the names of people who initiated . . . the [new] stock exchange and trust companies. Am I not also a person? Am I not also allowed to initiate stock exchange companies or . . . trust companies?"[16] This poke at Shanghai's new financial landscape tellingly joins hallmarks of May Fourth cultural aspiration—humanism, personhood, and rights— to the capitalist project of a stock exchange. The fictive narrator in this satire exercises his civil right to become "a personage in business" and announces plans for a "salty meat" stock exchange (playing on sexual connotations), a night soil exchange, a funeral paper trust company, and a chamber pot trust company. One might ask: How did the definition of modern personhood come to this? And why mock exchanges and trust companies in these ways? The double-edged parody targets not simply the financial institutions, but also New Culture conceptions of personhood, which are tarred, reciprocally, by the contaminating bodily associations of the named exchanges and trust companies, in the way that exposure of the hypocrisy, greed, and speculative character of the exchanges tainted the democratic institution of elections.[17]

Shanghai's stock exchanges, in their allure and their supernumerary development, emerged in print as the peculiar offspring of republican aspirations. Their creation, alongside the importation of the globally hegemonic economic science from which they derived their authority, had roots that stretched back to the financial activism of late Qing reformers and the architects of the Republic. The stock exchange was essential, in the eyes of reformers and in the advertising copy of entrepreneurs, because it ensured the application of the new science of economics, the validity of which was already demonstrated by Western financial strength. Economics was also joined at the hip, so to speak, with the cultural critiques and nationalism of the May Fourth Era. In his paradigmatic critique of Confucianism, *New Youth* editor Chen Duxiu embraced economics as "the pulse of modern life," identifying personhood with economic agency and articulating, in this fashion, the mutually constitutive relationship between capitalism and the liberal subject.[18]

As seen in Tang's public trajectory, prior to May Fourth, in the first decade of the Republic, commercial institutions and associations took up more democratic and representative governing structures, embodying republican governance in the absence of a functioning republic. These transformations were the fruit of contestations of activists like Tang and increasingly mobilized and more popular constituencies such as shopkeepers and their employees. Reformed, newly born, and newly mobilized commercial associations created an institutional and ideological foundation that preceded and laid the groundwork, alongside educational associations, for a citywide movement for urban citizens' rights that flourished in the May Fourth Era. These developments, and particularly the building, by the commercial sector, of more popular and representative organizations, have been overshadowed, historiographically, by attention to the more familiar student, intellectual, and worker dimensions of May Fourth.[19]

The innovations in commercial organization and culture in this transformational moment embraced economic science and asserted the interdependence of economic rights and liberal governance. They were bolstered by a popular nationalism that justified breaking with older ideas, procedural rules, and at times even law. Although developed in the context of the May Fourth Movement and struggles for Chinese representation, once sanctified by association with the struggles of citizens, the rhetoric of economic nationalism and the tactic of preemptive activism were quickly appropriated for commercial purposes, following the expansive logic of capitalism. The launching of the first stock exchange by Yu Xiaqing and other prominent members of the Chamber of Commerce drew on the economic nationalism of this moment. The nationalism (and economic logic) of the moment was captured by Yu's fictional avatar in Jiang Hongjiao's satirical 1923 novel *Exchanges Unmasked:* "Chinese cannot beat Japanese at gambling. [But with a Chinese exchange] even if there is winning and losing this will take place among Chinese people. Like small pots in a big pot,

we are all in the same pot, thus there will be less disparity between winners and losers. It is also a way to regain our economic rights."[20]

Although economics had its local skeptics, a fortifying dose of economic
science was bestowed on the exchanges in the form of the preliminary observations of the (Columbia University-trained) Beijing University economist Ma Yinchu in December 1920, when he investigated the Shanghai
stock exchange. Ma also endorsed the exchange's nationalist rationale,
saying, "We may permit foreigners to control banks, but, if foreigners operate exchanges they may manipulate [China's] market." In this early ap-
praisal of the situation in Shanghai, Ma concluded that exchanges were
economically beneficial. At least initially, he did not advocate their legal
constraint: "Exchanges have a definite status in economic circles. I hope
our legal institutions . . . will not interfere."[21]

Yu Xiaqing, for his part, had little patience with the inconveniences of
law. By portraying his venture as a patriotic defense of the national
economy, Yu Xiaqing papered over the illegality of operating what was an
unlicensed exchange, implying that the goal of national strengthening
trumped law. His competitors, in turn, tuned the rhetoric of righteous nationalism and a vibrant press to their own advantage, exposing the sham
patriotism of Yu's exchange. The problem of redundant exchanges was
compounded by the twin curses of extraterritorial exchange registration
and the challenges of regulation under the ill-fitting, Japan-derived 1914
Securities Exchange Law.

In August 1921, when premonitions of crisis inspired strategies to cir-
cumvent the jurisdictional challenges and constrain the excess exchanges,
Nie Yuntai, chair of the Chamber of Commerce, suggested to local officials that they seize and prosecute exchange entrepreneurs when such individuals left the foreign settlements and stepped into Chinese jurisdiction.[22]
After the news leaked out, Shanghai newspapers became the terrain of a
"war of words" between exchange entrepreneurs and the business leaders
who would curtail these ventures. The dispute brought to a head tensions
between the republican ideals of national economic sovereignty, civil law,
and procedure, on the one hand, and the economic rights and freedoms of
Chinese businessmen, on the other.

In the absence of institutionalized democracy or constraint at the level
of the state, the quarrel highlighted both the pervasiveness of democratic
rhetoric and definitional and representational challenges within the republican public of citizens. The pharmaceutical entrepreneur Huang Chujiu
(the proprietor of at least one exchange and a flamboyant character with
a reputation for slippery marketing[23]) denounced the Chamber's action in
a public letter. Noting that many exchange founders were Chamber of

Commerce members, Huang ridiculed Nie's concern for Chinese legal regulation as the slavishness of a dynastic subject. Stating that he "did not anticipate that the grand Chamber of Commerce of the Republic would surpass its Qing counterpart in subservience to the state," he advised that the Chamber should instead fulfill its modern mission of representing the interests of businessmen.[24] Huang warned, moreover, that the arrest by Chinese officials of businessmen who worked in the foreign settlements would constitute a jurisdictional trespass that could provoke an international dispute (which could ultimately pose a greater threat to Chinese sovereignty than Chinese business freedom).

In their public response to Huang's provocation, Chamber leaders asserted the authority of Chinese law and derided the self-serving character of Huang's argument, which respected foreign sovereignty but not Chinese law: "You [talk about] sovereignty. [But in] regard to exchanges that are registered under foreign jurisdiction [it isn't clear] if you are concerned with the sovereignty of foreign nations or of China."[25] As others joined the quarrel to argue for the rights of businessmen against an overreaching state, Huang frankly acknowledged his willingness to make peace with extraterritoriality in return for protection from Chinese interference: "As for . . . sovereignty, I think that having Chinese businesses register and pay taxes in foreign settlements are compromises that must be made."[26]

The dispute highlights the ambient rhetoric of rights and representation as well as the contradictory actions of individuals and institutions amid the legal loopholes and accidental opportunities of Shanghai's semicolonial formations. The entwinement of economic and political liberalism, as articulated by exchange entrepreneurs—unencumbered by Chinese legal sovereignty—did not easily accept the necessity for Chinese regulation (or the role of regulation in an economic system). Businessmen criticized the Chamber for "helping the government to suppress business." They invoked rights, freedom, and democratic representation: "You state that the Chamber represents society. But members of the Chamber question [its] conduct, which means the Chamber does not represent its members, let alone society." Only Huang was so outspoken as to argue that extraterritoriality protected Chinese business rights against an intrusive government. Others mouthed support for Chinese sovereignty while flouting Chinese law. Huang bolstered his defense of illegal exchanges by appealing to the universal validity of economic theory: "exchanges stimulate the financial system . . . and help industry . . . Otherwise why do advanced nations [all] establish exchanges?"[27]

This episode, and the May Fourth activism of business circles that preceded it and informed its language, complicate understanding of this era in important ways. They invite reinterpretations of the New Culture and May Fourth Movements that attend to the ideological role of the market-place as a generative and conflictual arena of political culture. They also challenge interpretations of capitalism in China that impose criteria of na-tional loyalty on calculations of interest and capital. Huang Chujiu, like Yu Xiaqing, was masterful in the commodification of May Fourth causes, particularly economic nationalism.[28] The art was in the advertising. Such moments spotlight the crucial role of Shanghai business (and ideals founda-tional to capitalism) in the vernacularization of New Culture values and May Fourth nationalism. These included the exaltation of science, a com-bative rhetoric of democracy and rights, and an expansive commercial press. The substantive integration of capitalism into the history of New Culture and May Fourth has been minimal for important reasons, not the least of which was the relatively infrequent positive use of the term itself by entrepreneurs and those who emphasized the imperative for national eco-nomic development (preferring to avoid its negative connotations, in this era, of greed, profit making, and industrial exploitation).[29] It is in this light that we may understand how a fiercely anti-capitalist figure like Dai Jitao could have been instrumental to the formation, under Sun Yat-sen's direc-tion, of the Chartered Exchange. Science, democracy, and nationalism could be less ambivalently championed. Narratives on the Chinese mainland that embrace a May Fourth genealogy for the Communist Party have also focused attention elsewhere (passing lightly over Mao's 1923 celebration of Shanghai business activism). In other corners, historiographical emphasis on Beijing, intellectual enlightenment, or student agency in the May Fourth Movement has tended to elbow business agency and economic ideas out of the central frame of focus, admitting some adjunct bourgeois participa-tion but minimizing the contaminating influence of capitalism.

Business and finance nonetheless emerged as important domains for the elaboration of New Culture ideas and iconoclastic impulses. Commercial innovation and the reform of economic associations laid claim to notions of liberal governance based on individual property rights. This was the cur-rency of Tang's activism, the risk-taking language of his *Journal of Com-merce,* and of entrepreneurial contestations over finance. In Shanghai's di-vided jurisdictions, for a suspended moment during the bubble, many would agree with Shao Lizi's endorsement of market freedom (though they would not put it so baldly): "Chinese people can claim no other freedom but the freedom to make money. For this, the conditions have been rather accommodating. . . . Through the free competition that characterizes cap-italism, unsuccessful exchanges may be eliminated and economic reform promoted [without government intervention]."[30]

Even as economic liberalism was figured by some as a realm of freedom, the new science of the market did not displace other understandings of moneymaking. The language and visual representations of speculative practice in the new financial institutions drew variously on the new terminology of economics; older understandings of gambling; and associated ideas of frugality, fate, and fortune. As Xi's mother explained it, the family had understood that huge profits were to be made from purchasing stock certificates (*gupiao*). She used the phrase *yiben wanli,* the familiar term that was also imprinted on lottery tickets (*caipiao*), to convey the promise of windfall gains.[31] The family knew little about exchanges and trust companies. Like many small investors, their connection to the market was through a personal tie; they had placed their trust in Tang, the known connection through whom they could gain access to this promising new kind of ticket. The spate of bankruptcies that followed discredited entrepreneurs like Tang, who could be held responsible.

At another level of association, the demise of the exchanges similarly discredited the broader promise of liberal democracy, which was tarnished by connection to these imported institutions of capitalism. As Tang's case moved to trial, commentators looked to the court to answer questions about the market and help them to identify the human agents responsible for what was presumed to be anomalous and immoral behavior (rather than the inexorable impersonal logic of capitalism). The legal system was ill equipped to address either the abstractions or the details of finance. For those familiar with financial transactions, the judges' ignorance of common practice was shocking. For those who focused instead on the human devastation wrought by financial crisis, businessmen who rationalized their behavior by reference to the market looked like hypocrites and criminals.

The definitional instabilities, representational quandaries, and questions of the behavioral norms of the republican public, as well as citizens' ambivalent attitudes toward freedom, rights, law, and submission to the state, were manifest in the course and aftermath of Tang's trial. Chapter 4 followed the intimate and economic relations between Xi and Tang into the realm of justice. Whereas studies of law in the Republican Era tend to pass lightly over interim law to focus instead on the laws codified under Guomindang rule, this chapter followed the trial as a means of exploring legal improvisation and the peculiar significance of the tentative construct that was interim law.[32] Interim legality endured for a generation in the Republic and left a lasting mark on understandings of justice and legal maneuvering. Semicolonial and plural legal institutions lasted somewhat longer in the interim era that was the Republic. In this substantial period of transitional written (and unwritten) laws and multiple, old- and new-style courts, military courts, and foreign courts, urban residents habituated themselves to plural mechanisms of justice—a plurality that denaturalized and destabilized faith in any particular model—while at the same time giving a measure of credence to ideas of cosmic retribution. Given the winding pathways of Chinese law and legal procedures—as well as shifting norms of public scrutiny, legal representation, and popular participation in judicial process up to the present—this study suggests the importance of examining the vernacular ramifications of legal "transitions," plural legal systems, and prolonged periods of judicial instability, ramifications that continue to reverberate in legal practice in China today.

The Xi-Tang case animated an array of legal and extralegal, formal and informal, Chinese and foreign mechanisms of justice, making it possible to trace the dynamic interventions of individuals, institutions, and public associations. The trial transcripts and public articulations of individuals, groups, lawyers, and judges reveal diverse vernacular understandings of law, legal reasoning, and procedure, in connection with particular choices of adjudicating mechanisms: formal and informal, reformed and unreformed, state and socially driven.

The trial and its aftermath, in the dynamic of their unfolding, thus crystallize characteristics of the republican public of citizens that developed in the semicolonial commercial city. As has been seen, from the moment of Xi's suicide, a remarkably open and lively (if not always transparent) press took up the case. The interest of numerous sectors of the public in the trial, the coincidence of the trial with public concern for legal reform and legal sovereignty, and the plethora of Chinese- and foreign-language news organs ensured that the trial would be widely and accurately reported. The publication of verbatim trial transcripts, which was unusual in the case of a district court trial, opened the proceedings to the reading public and presented the contending narratives of prosecution and defense as fodder for debate by inquiring citizens. Although individual newspapers were certainly susceptible to manipulation by parties and interest groups, all of which made claims to represent the public, the aggregate of multiple news organs operating in an intense and contentious atmosphere of competition worked to democratic effect, ensuring the broad dissemination of information and a certain mutually enforced accountability. This was less the result of professional quality or objectivity in reportage; indeed, most journalists lacked professional training (and much content in this era had little to do with reportage). Rather, the democratic effect resulted from newspapers' diversity in a period of relative press freedom; inexpensive cost structure and minimal staff; and the resulting porosity (of the mainstream newspapers) in printing the circular telegrams, resolutions, and public manifestos of all manner of public associations.

Public debate in the aftermath of the trial exhibited a consistent rhetoric of representation that intertwined ideas of a community of national citizens with older emphases on (public) community over private interests. Statements from public associations outweighed in moral stature statements from individuals. The social interventions surrounding the trial reveal communal habits of influence as well as caution about visible interaction with court procedures and personnel. At a remove from the court but on public display was the dynamism of public associations in orchestrating meetings—a manifestation of their ability to represent the public. These efforts to mobilize public opinion required publicity; publicity, in turn, had unforeseen consequences. Opponents denounced the judicial reform movement formed in the trial aftermath as a fake or counterfeit public. The public banner of judicial reform stimulated the counter mobilization of an opposing public coalition, which claimed just as vehemently to represent the majority. The publication of the names of the signatories to the judicial reform meeting's resolution created divisions within the original, hastily assembled coalition.

The rhetorical challenges of "representing the public" immediately confronted Tang's defenders. Rival groups denounced the personal networks that lay behind the judicial reform movement. This dynamic is illustrated by an article entitled, "Private Friendships Are Not Public Opinion," that appeared in the *China Times,* which frequently jousted with the editorial line of the *Journal of Commerce*:

> If a minority of people because of their private relations (*sijiao*) conduct a public demonstration falsely in the name of public opinion it destroys the credibility of the masses. All of the people should rise up and question this minority that calls itself the representative of the people. Each organization, out of private friendship, attempts to rescue Tang Jiezhi. [But] disguising private friendship as public opinion is not legitimate. Moreover, you can't even say the majority in each association in fact enjoy friendship with Tang. If you want to save Tang, do it in your own names. Why use the collective name of the group? A social pillar of philanthropy has [fallen]. . . . Did the deceased really do things for the public good? You gentlemen in the majority of each organization! . . . How can you be dragged to accompany a coffin on another's behalf, without opening your mouths in protest?[33]

Brushing away the substantive questions of judicial abuses or reform, the writer denounced the protests of the judicial reform movement as fake public opinion. The article nonetheless embraced the democratic rights of citizens by suggesting that members of coalition organizations, as modern, self-determining individuals, should reexamine the basis of their ties to Tang (the hypocrite philanthropist). The metaphor that likened a member's loyalty to a public association to being dragged to a funeral (without genuine ties, volition, or authentic emotion) is striking in its melding of new and old in arguments that addressed core questions of public social belonging and citizenship.

This sparring in public print enacted the vernacularization of the democratic rhetoric of the era and suggests the ways in which it stimulated radical reconsiderations of social hierarchy. The circulation of these ideas was a central dynamic of the republican public. To convey public authority and articulate public opinion it was necessary to constitute a broad public coalition. At the same time, democratic rhetoric provided a language for an improvisational protest of disparities between leaders and ordinary members (or minorities and majorities) that was unforeseen even by democratic activists and their reformed rules of governance.

The organizational splintering visible in the judicial reform movement was broadly characteristic of the group politics of the urban civic movement that claimed the mantle of representing the public in this era. Similar patterns are observable in the Guang-Zhao Gongsuo reforms, the reform of the Shanghai General Chamber of Commerce and the movement for a Commoners' Chamber, the formation and division of the Federation of Commercial Street Unions, and the creation of a Chinese Ratepayers' Association.[34] Individuals and groups that were not direct parties to higher-level decision making objected to public statements made in their name. Public exposure of procedural lapses drew attention to organizational structure and stimulated procedural reform. At the same time, it must be noted that although the moment was rife with conflict, associational reform, and concern for appropriate representative structure, this was not a period lacking in institutional bases for practices of democracy. Whereas much scholarly discussion of the social mobilization of this period has emphasized spontaneity, speech, and street politics, with only diffuse and ephemeral institutional structures,[35] urban society offered an abundance of serviceable associational forms. Many of these associations, particularly native-place, occupational associations, and Chambers of Commerce, were enduring and influential actors in the flux of the times. Nonetheless, none of the plethora of public associations that characterized the period, not even the large, mega-associational formations that created federated assemblies across sectors at particular points of struggle, could stand in for democracy institutionalized at the level of the state. In this sense there is something about their supernumerary formation—like that of the stock exchanges—that indicates trouble at the core.

The legal reform movement that formed to protest the Tang verdict was hastily assembled and short-lived, making it vulnerable to criticism on representative and procedural grounds. It would nonetheless be wrong to simply dismiss it as spurious or to consider the protest movement as falsely or only instrumentally grounded in a critique of a corrupt and arbitrary judicial system. Such a dismissal would belie the serious engagement of many of the participating individuals and groups in the long-term cause of judicial reform, including prominent members of the lawyers' association, prior to Tang's trial. Their defense of Tang and the connections they drew between his prosecution and problems with the Chinese courts were consistent with their previous agitation for judicial reform.[36] It would be similarly problematic to dismiss the sincerity of Tang's own prior activism (despite his flaws) in the strenuous social engagement of commercial circles in democratic and rights movements in the city in the May Fourth Era. In these movements, the *Journal of Commerce* pressed at the political boundaries of public speech, an outspoken commercial newspaper that contributed to the vibrant expression of public opinion and an active, articulating urban citizenry. Tang's political activism was consistent with his expressed ideals and his risk-taking character.

In taking seriously these formations of a public and these practices of democracy, this study complements scholarship that has recognized, in different locations, the substantive rhetoric of citizen activism, rights, and the radical democratic popular politics of sectors of the urban public in China in the early Republic.[37] Questions remain in terms of how to appraise or characterize the radical upwelling of democratic ideas and practices and the exuberant language of citizens' rights that characterized the republican public. Were the substantive democratic formations of this public "unfinished" (to borrow David Strand's term) or interrupted, lacking institutional capacity, perhaps, but otherwise marching to the tune of, or toward, something akin to European-modeled standards of civil society? This idea was raised in debates several decades ago, but preoccupation with both civil society and Habermas's public sphere has faded with recognition of the problem of imposing conceptual vocabulary that universalizes (idealized) European historical formations and signposts.[38] The urban public visible in the early Republican Era might be characterized differently, as drawing upon the positive political resources of an evolving urban society and as speaking to the distinctiveness of the domestic and semicolonial context. Both Xiaohong Xiao-Planes, and Prasenjit Duara, in different respects, have compellingly underscored the importance of understanding the emergent democratic formations of the early twentieth century in terms of political resources "inherent in Chinese tradition." Xiao-Planes emphasizes the dynamic traditions of organization and procedure of "the social group," as urban elites formed coalitions to promote their rights at the end of the Qing. She emphasizes a quest for civil and political rights, tied to an advocacy of economic development, in which "collective welfare and interests were emphasized over the institution of western-style citizenship."[39] Duara, in his concern to illuminate an indigenous tradition of dissent that enabled a degree of contestation with the modern disciplinary language of centralizing nationalism, emphasized the salience of the organizing principle of the province and provincial consciousness, as embodied in the provincial federalist movement and the proliferating and politically lively native-place associations of the early twentieth century.[40]

To be sure, not all scholars have interpreted the civic activism of the early Republic in a positive light. The Shanghai-based historian Feng Xiaocai, for example, recently cautioned that studies by scholars located in the United States overestimate the fervor for democracy that was expressed in early Republican urban activism. Critical of the claims and social basis of civic coalitions, he argues that "although politicians frequently appealed to the notion of 'citizens,'" in practice, "political life throughout the Republican period was characterized by activities intended to fabricate and falsify public opinion."[41] Looking back with pessimism from the "materialism, opportunism, and cynicism" of the present, Feng is more persuaded by the language of Republican-Era detractors who questioned the democratic formations of their time. His critique of the republican public embraces a Euro-American-inflected definition of democratic politics that forecloses reflection on positive historical distinctiveness of democratic formations in the early Republican Era.[42]

In her study of public sentiment, which looks at the very different case of the female filial assassin Shi Jianqiao in the 1930s, Eugenia Lean suggests an alternative conceptualization of the urban public. The sentimental and emotion-based (and not Habermasian) public that she describes was powerful, if only because the state wished to co-opt for itself the force of public sympathy. Lean's depiction of an "affective public" in this subsequent decade of deepened mass media culture and a powerful authoritarian state conveys the shifting trajectory of the public in urban China. Her work also serves to highlight the distinctiveness of the earlier, more democratically oriented and somewhat more elite (if not entirely unaffective), public of the 1920s.[43]

The disturbance of the Xi-Tang case called up an observable public; excavation of the case opens this public up to a closely contextualized reading of the distinctiveness of this public of the early 1920s, a public that placed politicians and parties largely at the margins and resisted Guomindang efforts at assimilation or co-optation.[44] In the many observable struggles of individuals and groups for ideals associated with a republic, most striking is the popular associational improvisation and the relative absence of the state in the picture. In the absence of structuring state institutions of democracy, and in the semicolonial multiplicity of foreign governing institutions in the city, there were evolving communal habits of association, on the one hand, and plural and more abstract models of democratic organization, on the other. This accounts for some of the improvisational and organizational flux of the movement.

In this context, the French historian Yves Chevrier has contributed to the analysis of the distinctiveness of the early Chinese Republic by highlighting the salience of the fundamental "indeterminateness of the postimperial state."[45] Although the Republic enshrined popular sovereignty as the sole foundation of political legitimacy, the absence of democratic institutions in the state ("the missing institutional order") and the political uncertainty of democratization contributed to a historical vision of democracy that was distinct from what is usually understood by the term in Western liberal usage. Chevrier suggests that the fervor of social movements in the early Republic expressed instead a "dream of perfect autonomy," in which people imagined that the republican project might be accomplished in the *absence* of a constraining state. As the construction of an institutional basis for republican governance stagnated, he suggests, intellectuals came to believe that only the construction of democratic culture could save China.[46] Ultimately, as Chevrier suggests, the power of this democratic enchantment, or romance with democracy, was tied to the precariousness of democratic foundations rather than their successful construction.[47]

The romance could not end well. Without institutional or legal protection, the republican public was a powerfully felt but ultimately fragile formation. This may be seen in the "citizen's autonomy" (*guomin zizhi;* literally, "citizen's self-government") movement that called in 1923 for the convening of a national citizen's assembly outside the state. When the warlord Cao Kun staged a coup against President Li Yuanhong and took over the Beijing government on June 13, the Federation of Public Commercial Associations, joined by the Federation of Commercial Street Unions, a federation of native-place associations, and other activist groups convened a series of meetings to denounce his illegal government. The Guang-Zhao Gongsuo hosted a joint meeting with other groups on June 16 that this time mustered a sufficient coalition of the public to persuade the Chamber of Commerce (with Tang's influential colleague Feng Shaoshan presenting the case) to redress the crisis through citizen self-determination in order to save the nation in perilous times.[48] After a board discussion and an extraordinary plenary meeting, the Chamber effectively declared independence from the state and created the aspirationally titled "Committee for People's Rule" (*Minzhi weiyuan hui*) to manage the situation as a merchant-led democratic government of citizens. The flavor of this movement is conveyed by the declaration of the committee, which was promulgated on July 4:

> In the decade since the founding of the Republic, warlords and bureaucrats have controlled the nation's blood [by force]. In order to govern the country by the people, the Committee will spearhead a citizen's governance movement, starting from Shanghai business circles. It is hoped that people from all circles and provinces will follow and unite people nationwide into a large federation.[49]

The Shanghai business community celebrated the declaration with a public display of flags, visual signage, and congratulatory newspaper advertisements. Although locals, the *Republican Daily,* and Mao all applauded the moment, the committee, not surprisingly, was unable to constitute the anticipated democratic government. Disgruntled organizations soon declared their independence. Left without a quorum, the committee repurposed itself to consider recommendations for financial reorganization.[50] This failure marked the inevitable collapse of the citizen's democratic movement that arose in association with Shanghai commercial culture. If the citizens' autonomy movement briefly garnered Mao's admiration—perhaps for its momentary resemblance to the object of his earlier anarchist-inflected May Fourth call for "A Great Union of the Popular Masses"—the project lacked social unity and political power, and the public swiftly became disenchanted.

This book is situated outside the high intellectual terrain of May Fourth democracy that is central to Chevrier's narrative. The Xi-Tang episode emanated from the messier improvisational realm of associational and street politics, sexually integrated workplaces, and the newspaper vernaculars that informed the struggles of popular commercial circles for citizens' rights in the city. Chevrier's insights are nonetheless suggestive. While adopting ideals that were literally republican, the citizens' movement that was Tang's milieu was also permeated by recognition of the betrayal of the Republic at the level of the state. There was something inspirationally revolutionary, as Mao briefly suggested, in the associational ferment and peak formations of overarching citizens' federations across class and sectoral formations, in the dream of citizen autonomy. Without plausible means, however, and in the fashion of other faltering revolutionary formations, the inspired activists could only venture a desperate gamble, wa-

gering themselves and their reputations in the bargain. This was the ultimate logic of Tang's entanglements with the vision of direct, citizen's
democracy that underlay the fragile republican public of the May Fourth
Era.

China's political reform and rapid economic rise in recent decades have
stimulated a degree of historical reexamination of early twentieth-century
political and economic transformations, renewing inquiry into the conceptual reformulation of the Chinese state in the passage from empire to republic, the development of capitalism, and the democratic elements that
were set loose in the process.[51] The startling periodic eruption of populist
popular protest in the Chinese mainland, Taiwan, and Hong Kong—often
involving leaps of faith in direct street-level democracy or symbolic representations of Western-style democracies—provides impetus for the reexamination of earlier Chinese practices of democracy, with attention to the
popular social protest movements of the early twentieth century, including
its press, social networks, pedagogy of citizenship, legal instability, and
inclination to disregard formal law.[52] The scandals of Xi's suicide and
Tang's trial help to illuminate both the power and contradictions of the
early Republican romance of democracy and individual lives that were
caught up in its drama. Lacking other means, and absent a usable state,
people gambled on citizenship and self-governance, on economic dreams
that were entwined with democratic visions, and on the possibility of rescue
by foreign ideas, institutions, and connections. In this fashion, a decade
after the revolution and in the shadow of the failed Republic, democracy
was imagined outside the state and practiced in the popular associational
spaces at hand, or in new ones that could be quickly improvised, without
sufficient means to achieve their ends, in urgent rebuke of a state that was
not of the people.

The milieu of urban citizen democracy examined in this book—and the
realm of the republican public in the May Fourth Era—was inseparable
from its foundation in Chinese associations as well as its interpenetration
with imported elements (foreign or transnational individuals, concepts,
media, and institutions) that conveyed an aura of privilege or power. These
features of the Shanghai contact zone created accidental and contingent
opportunities and potentially complicating entanglements. It would be imprecise to qualify this book as a study of a "Chinese public" or "Chinese
democracy" as if, in the urban contact zones of the early Republic, there
were barriers to global entry. Like Shanghai itself, its new women, and its
stock exchanges—all of which overflowed the boundaries of the city—this
expansive public was irremediably impure as a "national product." In this

time of semicolonial treaty port formations and circulation of hegemonic frameworks of international law and economic science, the republican public relied on flows that traversed China's permeable boundaries. Similarly, although its constituent elements were often marketed as Chinese products, the republican formations described here relied on both domestic and imported ideas, language, and personnel. Like similar imports and adaptations of Western political theory, the idea of a republic offered important tools for political struggle insofar as it might be mapped onto local formations and adapted for local use.

Such recognition of global interconnection is unexceptional in studies of Shanghai and other treaty ports. Nonetheless, the nationalism of the era and persistent national frameworks of historiography still operate to obscure some of the breadth and depth of linkages that were vital to the operation of the public realm at this time. The Xi-Tang case touches on the intractability and multiplicity of identities and entanglements. George Sokolsky, the cryptic figure at the margins of the story told here, offers an emblematic example. This man of many identities was a secret US partner in a nationalist Chinese-language newspaper that was, by all Chinese accounts, an entirely Chinese enterprise.[53] Sokolsky emerges only in Western police and intelligence reports and in the Japanese press. Sokolsky offered Tang protection by amplifying his voice in the English-language expatriate press. Although Tang boldly placed many issues before the reading public, the black-and-white stage of Chinese nationalism made it essential that he shield other things from view. Sokolsky's presence was thus a strategically veiled secret. More like the low-level Japanese exchange advisors who offered classes to Chinese trainees than the rumored secret Japanese at the heart of Yu Xiaqing's stock exchange, Sokolsky (contrary to his pretensions) was more an entrepreneurial *rōnin* than a mastermind. Like other Western advisors and employees in the city, his path was smoothed by the cachet of his foreign privilege. In his dealings with Tang (and earlier with the Shanghai Students' Association) he traded in his US connections and presumed the relevance of his US-based understanding.[54] The mutually instrumental and affective dimensions of the Tang-Sokolsky partnership—and the ways in which their interactions were informed by global racial and national hierarchies—emerge in the margins of the Sokolsky papers at the Hoover Institution Archives.[55] These papers are revealing, more broadly, of the extensive English language networks of correspondence that linked far-flung transnational Chinese, Americans, Australians, and US-educated Chinese.

The largely unacknowledged relationship between Tang and Sokolsky was thus less a fluke than a manifestation of the transnational character of China's urban public realm. News flowed across Chinese, Japanese, and Western press organs in Shanghai to other Chinese cities and to cities beyond; Chinese newspapers translated stories from foreign papers; and foreign papers relied on Chinese papers for Chinese news. Bilingual Chinese British subjects from the extended British empire (like Sokolsky's wife, Rosalind Phang) found ready employment in Shanghai media and businesses that valued their linguistic and cultural proficiency. Research into transnational dimensions of newspaper culture in China has begun to document the multilingual character and interdependence of foreign- and Chinese-language newspapers (and their journalists). The linguistic, social, and political boundaries between communities and identities were more blurred than the politicized constraints on public appearances suggest, although the policing these boundaries was—and continues to be—fundamental to the ongoing making of national identities.[56]

Transnational flows of capital into Chinese organizations and markets, on the other hand, were ubiquitous but even less obvious; they were difficult to police and easy to conceal. The 1914 Securities Exchange Law (itself largely borrowed from Japanese law) envisioned a separate Chinese economy, and aimed to keep it pure of foreign influence and capital by prohibiting foreign shareholders and excluding non-citizens from employment. But even as Yu Xiaqing promoted his exchange to protect the Chinese economy from Japanese penetration, he concealed Japanese capital and employees. Such links were abundant in businesses and political ventures, which often relied on transnational capital and multilingual employees. The trust and exchange bubble relied on silent foreign partners (who, like Sokolsky, enabled exchange registration in foreign jurisdictions) and further, on the profitable complicity and self-interest of the foreign settlement authorities. The failure to recognize this complicity, in the foreign press, made it easier to rely on facile explanations of Chinese problems as matters of Chinese cultural pathology rather than as connected to political context and global inequity.

This study has traced just some of the manifold human, informational, and financial flows that informed the capacious and wide-ranging, if not entirely uncircumscribed character of the republican public of the early Republican Era, despite the propagation and disciplinary exercise of new exclusionary identities, particularly national identity. Such flows transect identity, impinge on sovereignty and open up questions of nationality, historical memory, and the imagination of bounded national economies that persist in popular organizing frameworks for thinking about sovereignty and capitalism today. These countercurrents may benefit or challenge impulses toward democracy, transparency, and public agency. Individual

232 • THE SUICIDE OF MISS XI

movement through transnational webs of interconnection was powerfully affected by differential interests and relations of power. Nonetheless, in our current moment of globally intensified national border making, public constraint, and identity control it is well to revisit one history of past democratic possibility, and to note that transnational pathways and historical resources that are often rendered invisible or external to national appearances, archives, and memory, have served as spaces of possibility, even as they have also served as spaces of manipulation.

ABBREVIATIONS

CP	*China Press*
CR	*China Review*
CUGS	George E. Sokolsky Manuscripts, 1919–1962, Columbia University Libraries, Archival Collections (New York)
DTTK	*Dongting lü Hu tongxianghui sanshi zhou jinian tekan*
FZ	*Funü zazhi*
GMS	Gaimushō Gaikō Shiryōkan. Diplomatic Archives of the Ministry of Foreign Affairs of Japan (Tokyo)
JB	*Jingbao*
JWRB	*Jingwu ribao* (Police Daily Report). Shanghai Municipal Council. Shanghai Municipal Archives. (Shanghai)
MGRB	*Minguo ribao*
MG	*The Municipal Gazette: Being the Official Organ of the Executive Council for the Foreign Settlement of Shanghai MGRB*
NCH	*North China Herald*
NCDN	*North China Daily News*
PRO	Public Record Office (London)
SG	*Shanghai Gazette*
SMA	Shanghai Municipal Archives
SMPF	Shanghai Municipal Police Files, National Archives and Records Administraton (Washington, DC)
SP	Sokolsky Papers, Hoover Institution Archives (Stanford University)
SSXB	*Shishi xinbao*
TP	*Trans-Pacific*
XSB	*Xin shenbao*
XWB	*Xinwenbao*
WRFE	*Weekly Review of the Far East*
ZHXB	*Zhonghua xinbao*

Prologue

Second epigraph: "Face in the Orient," Address before Diamond Convention of American Bankers' Association, NY, September 26, 1950, Columbia University, Special Manuscript Collection, George Sokolsky (CUGS), Box 6.

1. Wu Yugong, *Zisha zhi nüshuji: Xi Shangzhen canshi* (Female secretary who committed suicide: tragic history of Xi Shangzhen), (Shanghai: Zhongguo diyi shuju, 1922), 6.
2. Quotations from *Zhonghua xinbao* (*ZHXB*), November 13, 1922; Zheng Zhengqiu, "Cong Xi nüshi de lai de jiaoxun" (Lessons from the suicide of Miss Xi), in Cui Weiru, ed., *Xi Shangzhen* (Shanghai: Funü zhiye yanjiu she, 1922), 1:1; *Xingqi zhoubao,* September 24, 1922.
3. Banks and other enterprises in the early Republic similarly patterned modern workplace sociability on familistic models. Wen-hsin Yeh, *Shanghai Splendor: Economic Sentiments and the Making of Modern China* (Berkeley: University of California Press, 2007), 87–94.
4. Narrative based on *Xinwenbao* (*XWB*), September 10, 1922; *Shenbao*, September 10, 1922, *Minguo ribao* (*MGRB*), September 11, 1922; *China Press* (*CP*), September 9, 1922; September 10, 1922; and *North China Daily News* (*NCDN*), September 12, 1922; September 16, 1922. Reportage differs slightly in detail (some refer to the wire of an electrical light) and timing.
5. Cheng Pengling, ed., *Haishang nü shuji: Xi Shangzhen canshi* (Shanghai female secretary: tragic history of Xi Shangzhen), (Shanghai: Shenheji shuju, 1922).
6. In a variant account, Wang Jipu asked Chen Aliu to check on Xi after he left. Chen found the office door locked, opened it, and saw Xi hanging. He reported this to an editor, Qiu Youxin, who instructed Chen to take Xi down and call the hospital. Qiu called Tang and sent someone to Xi's house. When the doctor arrived, Xi's pulse had stopped. A Japanese-trained doctor was called to attempt to massage the dead Xi back to life. By this point, Xi's sister and Tang had arrived. Wu, *Zisha zhi nüshuji*, 31.
7. Public Record Office (PRO) FO 228/3291 Report of December 1921; Shanghai Municipal Archives (SMA) 1-1-1135 *Jingwu ribao* (*JWRB*), (Shanghai Municipal Council, Daily Police Reports, September 9, 1922);

National Archives, Shanghai Municipal Police Files (SMPF), Daily Report, February 12, 1921.

8. Foreign nationals with consular representation fell under home country jurisdiction. Chinese remained subject to Chinese law. Because after the influx of refugees during the Taiping Rebellion (1850–1864) many Chinese lived in the International Settlement and French Concession, jurisdictional divisions were complicated in practice. Mixed tribunals developed in each to navigate the multiple legal codes and regulations that governed the mixed populations. Anatol Kotenev, *Shanghai: Its Mixed Court and Council* (Shanghai: *North China Daily News,* 1925); Thomas B. Stephens, *Order and Discipline in China: The Shanghai Mixed Court 1911–27* (Seattle: University of Washington Press, 1992).

9. In a carryover from Qing code, article 320 of the Provisional Criminal Code of the Republic of China stipulated the crime of responsibility for another's suicide.

10. *XWB,* September 10, 1922. At the time one yuan (Chinese dollar) was approximately .6 of a US dollar. The sum of 5,000 yuan represented a great deal of money, the approximate equivalent of 500,000 yuan or 75,000 in US dollars today. Xing Jianrong, *Feichang yinhangjia: Minguo jinrong wangshi* (Extraordinary bankers: recollections of Republican Era finance), (Shanghai: Dongfang chuban zhongxin, 2014), 105. Unfortunately the term *yuan* was often used to indicate both Chinese yuan and Mexican silver dollar (also designated as foreign yuan, or *yang yuan*). The preponderance of sources on the case refer to yuan, however, the occasional use of *yang yuan,* suggests that Xi Shangzhen's investment could possibly have been in Mexican dollar, representing a greater sum. Reference to units of currency here and elsewhere follow the somewhat inconsistent use of terms in the particular sources under discussion.

11. XWB, September 10, 1922.

12. *Shenbao,* September 10, 1922; *MGRB,* September 11, 1922. This phrasing, which suggests that Xi did indeed want to be Tang's concubine, caused controversy. Chen Wangdao, "Xi Shangzhen nüshi zai shangbaoguan li diaosi shijian" (Miss Xi's hanging at the *Journal of Commerce*), *Funü pinglun* (supplement to *MGRB*), 59 (September 20, 1922).

13. *CP, XWB,* September 10, 1922.

14. "Shanghai zuijin yibai mingren biao" (Latest chart of 100 Shanghai celebrities), *Jingbao (JB),* March 30, 1922.

15. According to the British report, Tang returned to China during the Boxer uprising. PRO FO 228/3291 (December 30, 1921). See also *JWRB* IO 2882 (July 23, 1919); *China Press* identified Tang as a University of California graduate ("Mother of Girl Suicide Tells Story of F. C. Tong Deals as His Trial Starts," *CP,* December 3, 1922). However, Tang is not listed in *Registrar. University of California* (Berkeley: University of California Press, 1911); *The Golden Book of California, 1860–1936* (Berkeley: California Alumni Association, 1936); or *Directory of Graduates of the University of California, 1864–1916* (Berkeley: California Alumni Association, 1916).

16. (Tianjin) *Dagongbao*, May 5, 1907.

17. PRO FO 228/3291 (December 30, 1921). See also SMPF, July 23, 1919.

18. The association was named for Guangzhou and Zhaoqing prefectures in Guangdong province. Wu Mianbo, "Guang-Zhao gongsuo fengchao shimoji" (The conflict at the Guang-Zhao Gongsuo), manuscript (Shanghai), courtesy of Song Zuanyou.

19. Shanghai shehui kexueyuan, Lishi yanjiusuo (Shanghai Academy of Social Sciences, Institute for Historical Research), ed. *Wusi yundong zai Shanghai shiliao xuanji* (Compilation of historical materials on the May Fourth Movement in Shanghai), (Shanghai: Shanghai renmin chubanshe, 1980), 648–664; Joseph Chen, *The May Fourth Movement in Shanghai* (Leiden: Brill, 1971); Song Zuanyou, *Guangdongren zai Shanghai, 1843–1949* (Guangdong people in Shanghai) (Shanghai: Shanghai renmin chubanshe, 2007), 404–410.

20. PRO FO 228/3291 December 1921; SMPF, February 12, 1921. The February police report indicated that the Bureau operated out of the same office on 95 Fuzhou Road as the newspaper.

21. Hoover Institution Archives, Sokolsky Papers (SP), Correspondence, Hu Shi 64.9 (November 4, 1919).

22. NCDN May 4, 1921; Viola Smith, *Modern Roads in China* (Washington, D.C.: US Government Printing Office, 1931), 8. SP, 43 (September 13, 1920); 118.9–10 (January 3, 1923). Sokolsky also claimed that Tang was elected president of the International Opium Society. In the context of rising Chinese nationalism, Sokolsky would soon complain of C. T. Wang's (Wang Zhengting's) sudden dismissal of foreign members from the Good Roads Asociation. Tang's photo appeared in Oong Zang-hyi, "Shanghai Is Cradle of Press in China," *Trans-Pacific (TP)* 6:6 (June 1922), 77.

23. PRO FO 228/3291 (Intelligence Report September 1921); GMS 1.3.2 46-1-4 (Reports of 1922 and 1923); "Riren muzhong zhi Shangbao" (Shangbao in Japanese eyes), *Shangbao*, January 28, 1921; *Shanhai*, January 16, 1921; September 5, 1921; December 12, 1921; November 27, 1922.

24. SMPF, July 23, 1919.

25. *Shibao*, October 18, 1922.

26. Cheng, *Haishang nüshuji*, 1b.

27. Richard Kraus, *Brushes with Power: Modern Politics and the Chinese Art of Calligraphy* (Berkeley: University of California Press, 1991), 9.

28. The emotional power of calligraphy was linked to ritual uses and elite distinction, as seen in the status of calligraphic materials (the "four treasures of the study": ink, brush, paper, and inkstone). Cynthia Brokaw, "On the History of the Book in China," in Cynthia J. Brokaw and Kai-wing Chow, *Printing and Book Culture in Late Imperial China* (Berkeley: University of California Press, 2005), 3; Daria Berg, *Women and the Literary World in Early Modern China, 1580–1700* (London: Routledge, 2013), 70. "Xizihui kuochong shanju" (Xizihui expand charity), *Shenbao*, August 10, 1914; Wang Zuwen, "Chuzhi zizhi zhi fangfa" (Disposing of paper with characters), *Shenbao*, August 24, 1921. Antisuperstition campaigns to abolish societies for

the ritual disposal of written characters persisted into the 1930s. "Qudi xizihui" (Abolish xizihui), *Shenbao,* June 21, 1935.

29. The one extant example of Xi's everyday handwriting was reproduced for content rather than quality (Figure 2.5).

30. "Xi Shengzhen nüshi yixiang ji qi moji" (Xi photo and calligraphic traces), *ZHXB,* September 20, 1922.

31. An ambivalent figure of modernity in fin de siècle Europe, the "new woman" entered global circulation by the second decade of the twentieth century. By virtue of her association with global trends, Xi had a foreign tinge, but her precise character drew on local transformations that informed the Chinese experience of modernity. Rita Felski, *The Gender of Modernity* (Cambridge, MA: Harvard University Press, 1995), 3, 4, 14; Hu Ying, *Tales of Translation: Composing the New Woman in China, 1899–1918* (Stanford: Stanford University Press, 2003); Modern Girl Around the World Research Group, *The Modern Girl Around the World: Consumption, Modernity and Globalization* (Durham, NC: Duke University Press, 2008).

32. Wu, *Zisha zhi nüshuji,* 8, 10.

33. "Nü zi zhiye qiantu zhi leguan" (Optimism for future of women's careers), *Shangbao,* February 22, 1921. More substantial discussion of this article appears in Chapter 2.

34. When the *Eastern Times (Shibao)* hired a female journalist, it was a celebrated event. "Chinese Woman Journalist on Shanghai Eastern Times Is First of Her Profession," *CP,* October 13, 1920. The similar novel arrival of a female telephone operator to the Shanghai telephone bureau was another newsworthy first, reported two years later (MGRB, October 16, 1922). Xi's hiring was still rare, though her position was less exalted than that of a journalist.

35. Wu, *Zisha zhi nüshuji,* 13–28.

36. Charles Shipman, *It Had to Be Revolution: Memoirs of an American Radical* (Ithaca: Cornell University Press, 1993), 15–16.

37. Columbia Center for Oral History, Columbia University, "Reminiscences of George Ephraim Sokolsky"; Warren Cohen, *The Chinese Connection: Roger Greene, Thomas W. Lamont, George E. Sokolsky and American-East Asian Relations* (New York: Columbia University Press, 1978). Sokolsky polished Song Qingling's translations of Sun's writings and prepared English propaganda. A letter from Song Qingling to Sokolsky reads, "Do you know that the machinery guild . . . has decided not to boycott machineries from Japan? . . . Please let the students know and agitate this matter all you can" (SP, box 113.3, July 11, 1919). Sokolsky's correspondence indicates a close working relationship with Sun through 1920, with tension developing because of Sokolsky's links to Wen Zongyao.

38. *JWRB,* September 9, 1922. Sokolsky's presence is invisible in Chinese discussion of the case, with one exception. A version of Sokolsky's name in Chinese appears, without identifying explanation, in *XWB,* September 10, 1922. Upton Sinclair, *Is the American Form of Capitalism Essential to the American Form of Democracy? Debate between Upton Sinclair and George Sokolsky* (Girard, KS: Haldeman-Julius Publications, 1940).

39. The books are: Cui, *Xi Shangzhen*; Wu, *Zisha zhi nüshuji*; Cheng, *Haishang nüshuji*. Among Shanghai's English-language newspapers, *China Press* and *North China Herald* offered particularly extensive reportage. The Japanese newspaper *Shanhai*, the only extant Japanese Shanghai newspaper from this era (available in the collection of Kobe University) also carried reports on Tang and the case. The gamut of Shanghai's Chinese newspapers reported on the case, though the first-tier commercial newspapers *Shenbao* and *Xinwenbao* were more restrained in their reportage. All of the influential second-tier newspapers, among them *Shibao (Eastern Times)*, *Shishi xinbao* (SSXB, or *China Times*), the editorially independent but GMD-afiliated MGRB *(Republican Daily)*, *Xin shenbao* (XSB) and *Shenzhou ribao* (SZXB), reported extensively on the case in both their news sections and their more free-ranging gossipy or literary supplement pages, which relied on sensational news. The tabloid *Crystal* *(Jingbao,* JB) also avidly followed the case. More restrained reportage on the case appears in the Beijing newspaper *Chenbao* *(Morning Post)*.

40. Cui, *Xi Shangzhen*, preface.

41. Chen Wangdao, "Xi Shangzhen nüshi" (1922). On the redeployment by revolutionary and reform intellectuals of Western missionary caricatures of Chinese character see Lydia Liu, *Translingual Practice: Literature, National Culture, and Translated Modernity* (Stanford, CA: Stanford University Press, 1995), 45–50.

42. "Tang Jiezhi jinyao shengming" (Important notice of Tang Jiezhi) *Shenbao*, September 11, 1922; *XWB*, September 11, 1922; *North China Herald* (NCH), September 16, 1922. Fessenden was Tang's lawyer.

43. *Shenbao*, *XWB*, and *MGRB* all published this letter on September 13.

44. *MGRB*, September 15, September 16, September 17; *Shenbao*, September 15, September 16; *XWB*, September 18.

45. *MGRB*, September 17, 1922.

46. This morphing of news across genres, characteristic of the early Republican Era was also a feature of the famous 1917 murder case of the courtesan Wang Lianying. He Qiliang, *Newspapers and the Journalistic Public in Republican China: 1917 as a Significant Year of Journalism* (London and New York: Routledge, 2018), 222–262.

47. *Shibao*, October 14, 15, 16, 17, 18, 19, and 20, 1922.

48. The first line alludes to a Qiu Jin quotation: "Autumn wind. Autumn rain—make one die of sorrow." Anon., *Shibao*, October 15, 1922.

49. Yan You, "Xi-Tang an zhong zhi yiwen (Anecdotes from the Xi-Tang case), *Shishi xinbao* (SSXB) September 22, 1922.

50. Cheng, *Haishang nüshuji*.

51. Wu, *Zisha zhi nüshuji*, preface.

52. Wu, *Zisha zhi nüshuji*. Wu Yugong's introduction states that the book was completed on September 14.

53. *MGRB,* September 13, 1922; September 14, 1922; September 19, 1922; "Dr. Tong Kidnapped," *NCDN,* November 14, 1922. The narrative is assembled from reportage and transcripts of the court proceedings in *Shenbao,*

MGRB, XSB, and SSXB (September–December 1922); Cui, *Xi Shangzhen*; and *JWRB*, September 9, 1922 (SMA 1-1-1135).

54. "Dr. F. C. Tong is Arrested by Chinese Police," *CP*, November 14, 1922; *NCDN*, November 14, 1922; *Dongting dongshan lüHu tongxianghui* (*DTTK*), 1944, 79.

55. *CP*, November 14, 1922; *Shenbao*, November 14, 1922; *Weekly Review of the Far East (WRFE)*, December 2, 1922.

56. "Tang an panjue tuxing" (Prison sentence in Tang case), *MGRB*, December 15, 1922.

57. "Chinese Theater to Present Play Based on Life of Suicide," *CP*, December 5, 1922. Since these performances were improvisational, it is possible that no script was written. Hsiao-t'i Li, *Opera, Society, and Politics in Modern China* (Cambridge: Harvard University Asia Center, Harvard-Yenching Institute Monograph Series, 2019).

58. Sokolsky's departure, and takeover by the Wei Sheng Company, caused the cancelation of the newspaper's incorporation under US law. The new owners registered with the French Consulate. *MG*, July 19, 1923, 266. *Fuermosi*, October 14, 1929. Despite his three-year sentence, Tang remained in prison until 1929.

59. We might consider, for example, the bizarre criminal proceedings surrounding the Bo Xilai trial. See Ian Johnson, "A Chinese Murder Mystery?" *NYRB*, June 7, 1922; "Call for Evidence in Bo Case," http://www.rfa.org .english/news/china/evidence-10222012144924.html, accessed October 22, 2012. More than 300 leftist members of the ruling CCP pen an open letter backing the fallen political star calling for a fair trial and more information about criminal proceedings against fallen political star Bo Xilai. A rare open letter to the National People's Congress signed by intellectuals and former officials called on legislature not to expel Bo until more evidence had been made public. "If the legitimate rights of . . . former Chongqing Party secretary Bo Xilai . . . can be violated as if by lightening, then how much hope is there that the rights of ordinary citizens will be protected under the law?"

Chapter 1. Shanghai Democracy and the Empty Republic

Epigraphs: "Kongxu zhi shinian" (Ten years of emptiness), *Shenbao* (December 31, 1921); Mao Zedong, "Beijing zhengbian yu shangren" (Merchants and the Beijing coup), *Xiangdao zhoubao* (July 11, 1923), 31–32.

1. Mary Louise Pratt, *Imperial Eyes: Travel Writing and Transculturation* (New York: Routledge, 1992), 4–6.

2. Meng Yue, *Shanghai and the Edges of Empires* (Minneapolis: University of Minnesota Press, 2006), 3–30.

3. "Kongxu zhi shinian."

4. Tang Jiezhi, "Zhi zilinxibao jizhe shu" (Letter to *NCH*), *Shangbao*, June 15, 1921. Letter also published in *ZHXB* and *NCH*.

5. Tang Jiezhi, "Dui quanguo shanghui linshi dahui bihui yiqian de yijian" (Thoughts on the national meeting of chambers of commerce), *Shangbao*, October 26, 1921.

6. Peter Zarrow, *After Empire: The Conceptual Transformation of the Chinese State, 1885–1924* (Stanford, CA: Stanford University Press, 2012); Yves Chevrier, "Anti-Tradition and Democracy in China at the Start of the Twentieth Century: National Culture and the Crisis of the Nation State," in Naomi Norbert, trans.; Mireille Delmas-Marty and Pierre-Étienne Will, eds., *China, Democracy and Law* (Leiden: Brill, 2012), 377–457; David Strand, *An Unfinished Republic: Leading by Word and Deed in Modern China* (Berkeley: University of California Press, 2011).

7. Louise Edwards, *Gender, Politics, and Democracy: Women's Suffrage in China* (Stanford, CA: Stanford University Press, 2007); Strand, *An Unfinished Republic*.

8. Strand, *An Unfinished Republic*, 13.

9. Christopher Reed, "Introduction," in Cynthia Brokaw and Christopher Reed, eds., *From Woodblocks to the Internet: Chinese Publishing and Print Culture in Transition, circa 1800 to 2008* (Leiden: Brill, 2010), 1–35; Henrietta Harrison, "Newspapers and Nationalism in Rural China, 1890–1929," *Past and Present* 166:1 (February 2000): 181–204.

10. Bryna Goodman, *Native Place, City and Nation: Regional Networks and Identities in Shanghai, 1853–1937* (Berkeley: University of California Press, 1995); "Tongxiang bing bufen nannü" (No gender distinctions among fellow provincials), *MGRB*, September 29, 1922; "Shao tongxiang tongguo nüzi ruhui" (Shaoxing association approves female members), *MGRB*, October 9, 1922.

11. Goodman, *Native Place*, 219–238; Chen Laixin. "Shanhai kakurō shōkai rengōkai ni tsuite, 1910–1923" (Regarding the Shanghai Federation of Commercial Street Unions, 1919–1923), *Kōbedaigaku shigaku nenpō* 3 (1988): 94–97.

12. At its inception, each major guild provided two merchant-directors for the Chamber, who paid membership dues with guild funds. Multiple categories of membership developed, including individual members, though these were often guild leaders as well. Zhongping Chen, "The Origins of Chinese Chambers of Commerce in the Lower Yangzi Region," *Modern China* 27:2 (April 2001): 155–201; Zhongping Chen, *Modern China's Network Revolution: Chambers of Commerce and Sociopolitical Change in the Early Twentieth Century* (Stanford, CA: Stanford University Press, 2011); Yu Heping, *Shanghai yu Zhongguo zaoqi xiandaihua* (Chambers of commerce and China's early modernization), (Shanghai: Shanghai renmin chubanshe, 1993). In 1911, the Chamber dispatched a business militia against local Qing forces while negotiating for Shanghai's foreign authorities to maintain neutrality. In the Republic Era, the Chamber similarly reserved some distance from contending Chinese authorities, at times disobeying the Northern (Beiyang) government. Zhaojin Ji, *A History of Modern Shanghai Banking:*

The Rise and Decline of China's Finance Capitalism (Armonk, NY: M. E. Sharpe, 2003), 110–111.

13. *Jingwu* can be translated as "martial spirit." It soon had branches in cities across China and Southeast Asia. Several revolutionaries, including Chen Tiesheng and Chen Qimei, who became Shanghai military governor, counted among its members. "Three corporations" signaled wealth as a reference to Shanghai's three big department stores. Shanghai Municipal Archives (SMA) Q 401–402, Jingwu tiyuhui, Jingwu neizhuan yu zhangcheng (Internal history and constitution of Jingwu Association), 1922, 1924; see also Andrew Morris, *Marrow of the Nation: A History of Sport and Physical Culture in Republican China* (Berkeley: University of California Press, 2004). Lu Weichang, another Guang-Zhao Gongsuo director, would chair the GMD-linked All-China Association for Workers' Progress. He cofounded the Chinese Workers' Cooperative Society with the hardware businessman, Chen Gongzhe, who had returned from the United States.

14. SMA Q 401–2 Jingwu tiyuhui, Jingwu neizhuan yu zhangcheng. 1922. Nie variously embraced Christianity and Buddhism, and he also served on the board of the Shanghai YMCA.

15. Jingwu offered instruction to female students at Chongde, Shanghai Patriotic, and the Guang-Zhao Gongsuo Girls' Schools, among others.

16. Cai Zinan, "Bian nüzi wei ruo zhi shuo" (On calling women weak), in Chen Tiesheng, *Jingwu benji* (Shanghai: n.p., 1919).

17. SMA Q 401–2.

18. SMA Q 401–2. The Encouraging the Workers Youth Association served employees of the Commercial Press, involving some 450 students.

19. Andrea Janku, "The Uses of Genres in the Chinese Press from the late Qing to the Early Republican Period," in Brokaw and Reed, eds., *From Woodblocks to the Internet,* 117.

20. Joan Judge, *Print and Politics: Shibao and the Culture of Reform in Late Qing* (Stanford, CA: Stanford University Press, 1996).

21. Janku, "The Uses of Genres," 112, 116. See also Barbara Mittler, *A Newspaper for China? Power, Identity and Change in Shanghai's News Media, 1872–1912* (Cambridge, MA: Harvard University Asia Center, 2004).

22. Xu Xiaoqun, *Chinese Professionals and the Republican State* (Cambridge: Cambridge University Press, 2000), 168.

23. Yuan Shikai's 1914 publication laws proscribed anything that criticized government, disturbed public order, or injured social customs. After his 1916 death and prior to aggressive GMD censorship (and later Japanese and Communist censorship) there was relative de facto press freedom, an effect of political fragmentation. The 1930 Publication Law was more restrictive than 1914, prohibiting anything that might "undermine the Guomindang . . . subvert the government, or harm the interests of the Republic. Both the Yuan Shikai and GMD periods were notable for attacks on newspapers and assassination and imprisonment of journalists. Fang Hanqi, *Zhongguo jindai baokan shi* (Modern Chinese periodical history), (Taiyang:

Shanxi renmin chubanshe, 1981), 2:720; and *Zhongguo xinwen shiye tongshi* (History of Chinese journalism), (Beijing: Zhongguo renmin daxue chubanshe, 1996), 2:84–85. Xu, *Chinese Professionals,* 174–175.

24. Xu, *Chinese Professionals,* 168.

25. *Shibao guan ji'nian ce* (*Shibao* commemorative album), (Shanghai: n.p., 1921).

26. Nearly all Shanghai's newspapers registered under foreign names and operated in the International Settlement. This provided an extraterritorial shield from violence against journalists by Chinese authorities. However, particularly in the May Fourth Era of nationalist agitation, the Shanghai Municipal Council used Chinese press laws, supplemented by SMC bylaws, to suppress inflammatory publications. "China Editor Pays Fine," *CP,* December 7, 1919; FO 228 317; Freedom of Speech; "Registration of Printers and Publishers," *Municipal Gazette* (*MG*) 13 (April 1922); Xu, *Chinese Professionals,* 175.

27. Marie-Claire Bergère, trans. Janet Lloyd, *The Golden Age of the Chinese Bourgeoisie, 1911–1937,* trans. Janet Lloyd (Cambridge: Cambridge University Press, 1989).

28. This does not count at least five English-language, several Japanese, two Russian, and one French daily. U.S. Dept of State Archives 893.91, Carl Crow, June 5, 1919; Japanese Ministry of Foreign Affairs, Diplomatic Record Office (hereafter Gaimushô, GMS) 1.3.2. 46-1-4 (1922). *China Yearbook;* Crow (Dept State); Bryna Goodman, "Semi-Colonialism, Transnational Networks, and News Flows in Early Republican Shanghai," *China Review* 4:1 (Spring 2004): 63. Because of the voluminous character of newsprint, particularly in the Republic, when newspapers expanded in length and number, much scholarship on Shanghai newspapers has characteristically focused on one newspaper, journal, or journalist. There is an extensive body of scholarship on the *Shenbao,* for example, by Barbara Mittler, Rudolf Wagner, Andrea Janku, Natascha Gentz, and Weipin Tsai. Joan Judge, Wang Zheng, and Catherine Yeh have published on women's journals, print feminism, and the tabloid press. Several recent studies use scandals to examine a consuming, "affective public" (a term Eugenia Lean proposed for the GMD era), when strict censorship forced newspapers to rely on sensational news. Eugenia Lean, *Public Passions: The Trial of Shi Jianqiao and the Rise of Popular Sympathy in Republican China;* Goodman, "Appealing to the Public: Newspaper Presentation and Adjudication of Emotion"; Qiliang He, *Feminism, Women's Agency, and Communication in Early Twentieth-Century China.* Qiliang He describes the newspaper/reader spectrum in several urban areas, highlighting communal styles of reading, print interaction with oral culture, and popular consumption.

29. Sun Yusheng (Sun Jiazhen), *Haishang fanhua meng* (1898–1906); Sun Yusheng, *Xu Haishang fanhua meng* (1915–1916). Reprinted together in *Haishang fanhuameng (fu xumeng),* (Shanghai guji chubanshe, 1991). This early, influential "Shanghai" novel first appeared as a "blockbuster" daily newspaper supplement that was followed by a wave of imitations. Alexander Des

Forges, *Mediasphere Shanghai: The Aesthetics of Cultural Production* (Honolulu: University of Hawaii Press, 2007), 23.

30. Wen-hsin Yeh, *Shanghai Splendor: Economic Sentiments and the Making of Modern China, 1843–1949*. See also Eugenia Lean, *Vernacular Industrialism in China: Local Innovation and Translated Technologies in the Making of a Cosmetics Empire, 1900–1940* (New York: Columbia University Press, 2020).

31. The Chinese title was *Shanghai zongshanghui yuebao.* Tang served on the publication committee.

32. Lean, *Vernacular Industrialism.*

33. Karl Gerth, *China Made: Consumer Culture and the Creation of the Nation* (Cambridge, MA: Harvard University Asia Center, 2003), 71, 74, 98, 356.

34. Mao Zedong, "Beijing zhengbian yu shangren" (see the discussion in Chapter 5). Tang's close associates Feng Shaoshan and Huo Shouhua were involved in the 1923 events.

35. These included greater accountability; social welfare projects for the living (as opposed to focus on burial); rental of association properties to fund charitable education (opposing the elites who benefited from subsidized rents). Bryna Goodman, "Being Public: The Politics of Representation in 1918 Shanghai," *Harvard Journal of Asiatic Studies,* 60:1 (June 2000): 51–55.

36. Shanghai Historical Museum archive, Wu Mianbo, "Guang-Zhao gongsuo fengchao shimoji," (1919), 12, 22. I am grateful to Song Zuanyou for alerting me to this document.

37. Shanghai shi gongshangye lianhehui, "Shanghai zongshanghui yu shangjie zonglianhehui" (Shanghai General Chamber of Commerce and the Federation of Commercial Street Unions). Oral transcript narrated by Yan Esheng, recorded by Hu Zhifan, c. 1960.

38. Shanghai Municipal Archive, JWRB 1-1-1122; 1-1-1124; Shanghai shehui kexueyuan, Lishi yanjiusuo (Shanghai Academy of Social Sciences, Institute for Historical Research), ed., Wusi yundong zai Shanghai shiliao xuanji (Compilation of historical materials on the May Fourth Movement in Shanghai), (Shanghai: Shanghai renmin chubanshe, 1980), pp. 648–664. The constituent native-place units included the Guang-Zhao, Ningbo, Hangzhou, and Shaoxing associations; the Foreign-Goods Trade and Export Trade Associations; and the World Peace Federation. Goodman, Native Place, 261.

39. Mao Zedong, "The Great Union of the Popular Masses" (July 1919), in Stuart Schram, ed., *Mao's Road to Power: Revolutionary Writings, 1912–1949* (Armonk, NY: M. E. Sharpe, 1992), 1: 387. Translation lightly modified.

40. Goodman, "Being Public"; Chow Tse-tsung, *The May Fourth Movement: Intellectual Revolution in Modern China* (Stanford, CA: Stanford University Press, 1960), 154, 188.

41. Song Zuanyou, *Guangdongren zai Shanghai* (Cantonese in Shanghai) (Shanghai: Shanghai renmin chubanshe), 408. Anfu was a political wing of

the Anhui clique, one of the factions born from the dissolution of the Beiyang government. It was associated with Duan Qirui (his native-place tie to Anhui gave the clique its name) and Cao Rulin. The Anhui clique maintained close ties to Japan in exchange for financial and military support.

42. *Shanghai Gazette (SG)*, November 21, 1919; *CP*, January 9, 1920.

43. Arif Dirlik, *Anarchism in the Chinese Revolution* (Berkeley: University of California Press, 1991). Laurent Galy highlights the anarchism in the Street Unions movement and in the radical Guang-Zhao Gongsuo leadership as a challenge for Guomindang penetration of society in this period. See Laurent Galy, "Le Guomindang et ses relais dans la société shanghaïenne en 1923," *Études chinoises* 17:1–2 (1998): 249–252; 274–277.

44. Cited in Edward X. Gu, "Populistic themes in May Fourth Radical Thinking: A Reappraisal of the Intellectual Origins of Chinese Marxism (1917–1922)," *East Asian History* 10 (1995): 109, 112. Gu takes exception to Chow Tsetsung's identification of May Fourth democratic thinking as a species of liberal democracy.

45. Cited in Edward X. Gu, "Who Was Mr. Democracy?: The May Fourth Discourse of Populist Democracy and the Radicalization of Chinese Intellectuals (1915–1922)," *Modern Asian Studies* 35:3 (2001), 606.

46. *NCH*, June 12, 1920. See also the discussion in Goodman, "Being Public," 49.

47. Tang's inability to meet the five-year residency requirement disqualified him. *JWRB* (June 23, 1920); Joshua Hill, "Voter Education: Provincial Autonomy and the Transformation of Chinese Election Law, 1920–1923," *Cross-Currents: East Asian History and Culture Review* 7 (June 2013): 17.

48. Zhang, *Shanghai zongshanghui yanjiu*, 219–223. The Chamber ultimately adopted several reforms—attendance, board supervision, and emphasis on specialized knowledge (but did not reduce fees or increase the number of board members). Chow, *May Fourth Movement*, 120–125, 171–196.

49. Feng Shaoshan, a comrade in the Guang-Zhao struggle and FPCA, was also elected to the Chamber board, suggesting the influence of the movement for urban citizens' rights. Approximately 2,700 Shanghai shops enlisted in the Commoners' Chamber initiative, which was intended for those excluded from the elite Chamber (the project ceased following issuance of a draft constitution). Efforts were redirected into the Federation of Commercial Street Unions. JWRB (April–June 1919); Goodman, "Democratic Calisthenics: The Culture of Urban Associations in the New Republic," in Merle Goldman and Elizabeth Perry, eds., *Changing Meaning of Citizenship in Modern China* (Cambridge, MA: Harvard University Press, 2002), 77. On the street union movement more broadly, see Chen Laixing, "Shanhai kaku rō shōkai rengōkai ni tsuite, 1910–1923," *Kōbedaigaku shigaku nenpō* 3 (1988) 3. On street union rent reduction campaigns, see Sun Huei-min, "Fangke lianhehui yu 1920 niandai Shanghai de fangwu jianzu yundong," in Paul Katz, Kang Ru, and Lin Meili, eds., *Cong chengshi kan Zhongguo de xiandaixing* (Taipei: Modern History Institute, Academia Sinica, 2010), 171–196.

50. Goodman, "Democratic Calisthenics," 76–77.

51. Tang Jiezhi, "Dui quanquo shanghui."
52. *JWRB*, October 6, 1919; January 11, 1921; June 25, 1921; June 27, 1921; October 17, 1921; November 4, 1921. At times they availed themselves of Jingwu recreation grounds.
53. Among these were the dailies *Shenbao, XWB, SSXB, Shenzhou ribao, Shibao;* the small-format paper *Jingbao;* and the major publishing houses (Commercial Press, China Press, World Books).
54. Gu Bingquan, *Shanghai yangchang zhuzhici* (Shanghai: Shanghai shudian, 1996); Fuhui Wu, *Cultural History of Modern Chinese Literature* (Cambridge: Cambridge University Press, 2020), 8.
55. *"Shangbao chuban bugao"* (Notice of Shangbao publication), *MGRB*, December 19, 1920.
56. *Shangbao*, January 24, 1921.
57. *Shangbao*, January 24, 1921.
58. *JWRB*, February 12, 1921.
59. Fang Hanqi *Zhongguo xinwen shiye tongshi* (History of Chinese journalism), (Beijing: Zhongguo renmin daxue chubanshe, 1996); Ma Guangren, *Shanghai xinwenshi* (History of Shanghai journalism), (Shanghai: Fudan daxue chubanshe, 1996); US Department of State Archives, 893.911/133, Carl Crow, Report on Chinese press, September 13, 1921. Crow, former chair of the US Committee on Public Information, gives a circulation figure of 10,000. George Sokolsky estimated *Shangbao* circulation of 12,000 in 1922. *SP*, 125.22 (1922). For comparison, *Shenbao* estimated circulation of 50,000 in 1922, a figure Weipin Tsai cautions may be exaggerated. Tsai, *Reading Shenbao*, 160.
60. Zhang Jinglu, *Zhongguo de xinwenzhi* (Chinese newspapers), (Shanghai: Guanghua shuju, 1928), 48–49; a nearly identical description appears in Hu Daojing, ed., "Shanghai de ribao" (Shanghai dailies), *Shanghai tongzhiguan qikan* 2:1 (June 1934), 283–284.
61. The Chen brothers were famous from earlier work with *Tianduobao* (Heavenly bell). Chen Bulei was Jiang's secretary in 1935–1948. Pan, who was associated with *MGRB* and the progressive "Xuedeng" supplement of *SSXB* (which was linked to Liang Qichao's research group and Zhang Dongsun's Progressive Party) was in Shanghai government (1927–1937) and served as vice minister of information (1939–1941). Zeng, *Zhongguo xinwenshi* (Chinese journalism history), 329–332; Zhang Yufa, "Xinwenhua yundong shiqi de xinwen yu yanlun" (New Culture news and opinion), *Zhongyang yanjiuyuan jindai yanjiusuo jikan* 23 (June 1983), 295.
62. Zeng, *Zhongguo xinwenshi*, 331; Zhang Qiuchong, "Shangbao suowen" (News of Shanghai), *Shanghai difang shi ziliao* (Shanghai: Shanghai shehui kexueyuan chubanshe, 1986), 5:66–69; "Shangbao touru Huangpu jiang" (*Journal of Commerce* thrown into Huangpu), *Baoxue* (Taipei), 1:1 (June 1951): 165. *NCH*, January 29, 1921, 285, mistakenly states that "all [copies] were eagerly snapped up."
63. *JWRB*, February 12, 1921; *Shangbao*, advertisements of February 18, 20, and 25, 1921.

64. Zeng, *Zhongguo xinwenshi,* 331. Zeng edited the Guomindang daily, *Zhongyang ribao,* for two decades.

65. Xu Zhucheng, "Chen Bulei yu Shangbao," *Baohai jiuwen,* 30. The newspaper's influence did not outlast the mid-1920s.

66. "Hu Yuzhi zhi Shangbao jizhe Chen Bulei shu" (Hu Yuzhi's letter to *Shangbao* journalist Chen Bulei), in Cui Weiru, *Xi Shangzhen* (Shanghai, 1922), part 2, 27.

67. Originally in *Zhongguo qingnian:* 19–20 (1924). Reprinted in *Deng Zhongxia wenji* (Deng Zhongxia collected writings), (Beijing: Renmin chubanshe, 1983), 72–77.

68. "The New Tendency of Journalism in China," *Millard's Review,* February 11, 1922, 454–455.

69. Oong Zang-hyi, "Shanghai Is Cradle of Press in China," *The Trans-Pacific* (TP) 6:6 (June 1922), 78. *The Trans-Pacific* was tied to Benjamin Fleisher's English-language *Japan Advertiser* press networks in East Asia, with which Sokolsky was also loosely and intermittently affiliated. Peter O'Connor, *The English Language Press Networks of East Asia, 1918–1945* (Leiden: Brill, 2019), 109.

70. Donald Patterson, "Journalism of China," *University of Missouri Bulletin* 23:34 (December 1922): 30.

71. Japanese Ministry of Foreign Affairs, Diplomatic Record Office (hereafter Gaimusho): 1.3.2. 46-1-4 (1922); "Ri ren muzhong zhi Shangbao" (Japanese view of *Shangbao*), *Shangbao,* 28 January 1921.

72. Bergère, *Golden Age,* 217.

73. Xiaohong Xiao-Planes, "The First Democratic Experiment in China (1908–1914): Chinese Tradition and Local Elite Practices," in Naomi Norbert, trans.; Mireille Delmas-Marty and Pierre-Étienne Will, eds., *China, Democracy and Law* (Leiden, Netherlands: Brill, 2012), 226–256; Gu, "Who Was Mr. Democracy?"; Prasenjit Duara, *Rescuing History from the Nation: Questioning Narratives of Modern China* (Chicago: University of Chicago Press, 1995), 177–199.

74. Bergère, *Golden Age,* 219–220; Hill, "Voter Education," 17.

75. Tang Jiezhi, "Benbao chuban zhounian jinian ci" ("Words for this newspaper's first anniversary"), *Shangbao,* January 1, 1922.

76. *Shangbao,* January 1, 1922 (anniversary issue).

77. *MGRB,* July 19, 1921; *China Press,* July 19, 1921, July 20, 1921; November 16, 1922. Tang also led a tax protest against He in March 1921. *China Press,* March 8, 1921.

78. *Shangbao* claims to extraterritorial jurisdiction were upheld on such occasions in 1921 and 1922 by the US consul-general, who stated, "the Shanghai *Journal of Commerce* [is] an American corporation." Although Chinese authorities labeled the paper as "indecent," it appears that the problem was political. An article that was presented as evidence reportedly "attack[ed] the Magistrate of the Court of the Military Governor," that is, He Fenglin's magistrate. *MG,* 16 (July 19, 1923): 266.

79. Xu, *Chinese Professionals,* 169–170.

80. Haiyan Lee, *Revolution of the Heart: A Genealogy of Love in China, 1900–1950* (Stanford, CA: Stanford University Press, 2007).

81. The only other female employee at the *Shangbao* was the British-educated Rosalind Phang, Sokolsky's secretary, who inhabited a different social circle and was closely tied with the English-speaking Sokolsky. There is no evidence that Phang took part in the Chinese social life of the workplace or that the two women knew each other.

82. "Wei Xi Shangzhen huyuan zhi liang han" (Two letters voice grievances for Xi Shangzhen), *Shenbao*, September 16, 1922.

83. See, for example, Ellen Widmer, *Fiction's Family: Zhan Xi, Zhan Kai, and the Business of Women in Late-Qing China* (Cambridge, MA: Harvard University Asia Center, 2016), 139–175.

84. Xi Shangzhen, "Xi Shangzhen zhi biji," in Wu Yugong, *Zisha zhi nüshuji: Xi Shangzhen canshi* (Female secretary who committed suicide: Tragic history of Xi Shangzhen), (Shanghai: Zhongguo diyi shuju, 1922), 23–28.

85. Paul Ropp, "Ambiguous Images of Courtesan Culture in Late Imperial China, and Wai Yee Li, "The Late Ming Courtesan Invention of a Cultural Ideal," both essays in Ellen Widmer and Kang-I Sun Chang, eds., *Writing Women in Late Imperial China* (Stanford, CA: Stanford University Press, 1997), 18; 18–73.

86. The more common female name would be Xiaoqing, as opposed to Xiao'ai. The entertainment press at this time generally categorized romance fiction as *yanqing xiaoshuo*. Similar in content, *aiqing xiaoshuo*, a term in general May Fourth usage, conveyed more a self-conscious, modern flavor. The quotations that follow are drawn from Xi, "Xiao'ai zhi ku le" in Wu, 16–23.

87. Xi, "Xiao'ai zhi ku le, 16–23.

88. Merchants attending or hosting banquets at restaurants and hotels also commonly sent call cards to courtesans to join them in these spaces, as a visible display of wealth, as illustrated in Jiang Hongjiao's 1923 stock market novel, *Jiaoyisuo xianxingji*(Exchanges unmasked); serialized in *Xingqi* (Weekly) 1922–1923; reprinted in Tang Zhesheng, ed., *Jiaoyisuo zhenxiang de tanmizhe*(Sleuth of secret stock exchange truths), (Nanjing: Nanjing chubanshe, 1994).

89. The campaign failed (and was generally opposed in Chinese commercial circles) because "Shanghai's Chinese residents were indifferent" to the terms of a Western-inflected debate "that hardly resonated within their own culture," and would affect livelihood and commercial relations in the Chinese community. Christian Henriot, *Prostitution and Sexuality in Shanghai: A Social History, 1849–1949* (Cambridge: Cambridge University Press, 2003), 310; Gail Hershatter, *Dangerous Pleasures: Prostitution and Modernity in Twentieth-Century Shanghai* (Berkeley: University of California Press, 1997), 271.

90. Chloe Starr, *Red-light Novels of the Late Qing* (Leiden, Netherlands: Brill, 2007); Ellen Widmer, *Fiction's Family*, 175–184.

91. The term *semicolonial* was coined by Lenin to describe countries that were neither fully sovereign nor fully colonized. Bryna Goodman and David S. G.

Goodman, "Introduction: Colonialism and China," in Goodman and Goodman, eds., *Twentieth-Century Colonialism and China* (London: Routledge, 2012), 1–22.

Chapter 2. The New Woman, the Ghost, and the Ubiquitous Concubine

1. Zheng Zhengqiu, "Cong Xi nüshi zisha de lai de jiaoshun" (Lessons from Miss Xi's suicide), in Cui Weiru, *Xi Shangzhen* (Shanghai: Funü zhiye yanjiu she, 1922), 1.
2. Zheng, "Cong Xi nüshi zisha de lai de jiaoshun," 1–2.
3. "Yunnü hao," *XSB*, September 17, 1922.
4. Hui Shi nüshi, *Yunnü hao*, *XSB*, September 17, 1922.
5. Keith McMahon, *Polygamy and Sublime Passion: Sexuality in China on the Verge of Modernity* (Honolulu: University of Hawaii Press, 2010).
6. Lu Jian nüshi, *XSB*, September 17, 1922.
7. Rita Felski, *The Gender of Modernity* (Cambridge, MA: Harvard University Press, 1995); Tani Barlow, *The Question of Woman in Chinese Feminism* (Durham, NC: Duke University Press, 2004); Susan Glosser, *Chinese Visions of Family and State, 1916–1953* (Cambridge, MA: Harvard University Press, 2003), 38–39.
8. Rebecca Karl, "'Slavery,' Citizenship, and Gender in Late Qing China's Global Context," in Rebecca Karl and Peter Zarrow, eds., *Rethinking the 1898 Reform Period: Political and Cultural Change in Late Qing China* (Cambridge, MA: Harvard University Press, 2002); Paul Bailey, *Gender and Education in China: Gender Discourses and Women's Schooling in the Early Twentieth Century* (London and New York: Routledge, 2007).
9. Tan Sitong, *Renxue*, in *Tan Sitong quanji* (Collected Works of Tan Sitong), (Beijing: Sanlian chubanshe, 1954), 19.
10. Karl, "'Slavery,'" 214; see also Angela Ki Che Leung, "Dignity of the Nation, Gender Equality, or Charity for All?" in Sechin Y.S. Chien and John Fitzgerald, eds., *The Dignity of Nations: Equality, Competition, and Honor in East Asian Nationalism* (Hong Kong: Hong Kong University Press, 2006), 71–92.
11. Kang wrote of self-sovereignty in *Shili gongfa quanshu* (Complete book of principles and general laws, *Zonglun renlei men* (Discussion on human kind). The quotation follows the translation in Stephen Angle, *Human Rights and Chinese Thought: A Cross-Cultural Inquiry* (New York: Cambridge University Press, 2002), 132–133.
12. Tani Barlow, "Theorizing Woman: *Funü, Guojia, Jiating*," in Angela Zito and Tani Barlow, eds., *Body, Subject, and Power in China* (Chicago: University of Chicago Press, 1994), 253–290.
13. Joan Judge estimates the male literacy rate in early twentieth-century Shanghai at 90 percent, and at 25–30 percent for women. Joan Judge, *Republican Lens: Gender, Visuality, and Experience in the Early Chinese* (University of California Press, 2015), 266. Functional literacy nationally was lower (men at 50 percent; women at less than 10 percent). Women's schools increased female readers after 1896. See also Evelyn S. Rawski, *Education*

and Popular Literacy in Ch'ing China (Ann Arbor: University of Michigan Press, 1979), 145: Yan Wang, "Moving to Shanghai," in Beverly Bossler, *Gender and Chinese History: Transformative Encounters* (Seattle and London: University of Washington Press, 2015), 172.

14. Lydia Liu, Rebecca Karl, and Dorothy Ko, eds., *The Birth of Chinese Feminism: Essential Texts in Transnational Theory* (New York: Columbia University Press, 2013), 15, 22; quotation on 65–56.

15. *Chinese Girls' Progress* was the English title of *Nü xuebao* (1898), literally "journal of women's learning," which was associated with Xue Shaohui and an all-female editorial board. Nanxiu Qian, "The Mother *Nü Xuebao* versus the Daughter *Nü Xuebao*: Generational Differences between 1898 and 1902 Women Reformers," in Nanxiu Qian, Grace Fong, and Richard Smith, eds., *Different worlds of Discourse: Transformations of Gender and Genre in Late Qing and Early Republican China* (Leiden, Netherlands: Brill, 2008), 260; 268; Liu Renfeng, ed., *Zhongguo funü baokan shi yanjiu* (Research on the history of Chinese women's periodicals), (Beijing: Zhongguo shehui kexue chubanshe, 2012).

16. *Cainü* referred to cultivated, "talented women," especially among Jiangnan elites in the eighteenth and nineteenth centuries. Susan Mann, *The Talented Women of the Zhang Family* (Berkeley: University of California Press, 2007), xv.

17. Perry Link, *Mandarin Ducks and Butterflies* (Berkeley: University of California Press, 1981), 250. Editors, boards, and most readers of many such influential women's journals were largely male. Bao emphasized that national salvation required the active partnership of women, "flowers of our brilliant citizenry." Female-authored content approached 20–30 percent. Judge, *Republican Lens*, 4–8; quotation on 8.

18. In this short essay, Xi advocated commoner education and argued that writing was not knowledge in itself, but a medium for all disciplines. Xi Shangzhen, "Wenzi fei xuewen shuo" (Writing is not a category of knowledge), *Funü shibao* 12 (January 10, 1914), 77. I'm grateful to Joan Judge for this reference.

19. Hu Ying, *Tales of Translation: Composing the New Woman in China, 1899–1918* (Stanford, CA: Stanford University Press, 2000), 5–9.

20. Liu, *Zhongguo funü baokan*, 202–204; Don Patterson, *The Journalism of China* (Columbia: School of Journalism, University of Missouri, 1922), 44. Ma Yuxin, "Male Feminism and Women's Subjectivities: Zhang Xichen, Chen Xuezhao, and *The New Woman*," *Twentieth-Century China* 29:1 (November 2003): 1–37; Zhonghua quanguo funü lianhehui funü yundong lishi yanjiushi, ed., *Wusi shiqi funü wenti wenxuan* (Selected writings on the woman question in the May Fourth Era), (Beijing: n.p., 1981).

21. Hu Shi, *Hu Shi wencun* (Taipei: Yuandong tushu gongsi yinxing, 1953), 1:662. Translation modified from Hu Ying, *Tales of Translation*, 208n.11.

22. Mao Dun, *Wo zuoguo de daolu* (The road I've traveled), 136, cited in Wang Zheng, *Women in the Chinese Enlightenment: Oral and Textual Histories* (Berkeley: University of California Press, 1999), 79.

23. Wang, *Women in the Chinese Enlightenment*, 67–76. Nivard estimated 10 percent female readership. Jacqueline Nivard, "Women and the Women's Press: The Case of the Ladies' Journal," *Republican China* 10 (November 1984): 37–55.

24. The fashion for women's short hair was growing in urban activist circles at this moment. Henrietta Harrison, *The Making of the Republican Citizen: Political Ceremonies and Symbols: Political Ceremonies and Symbols in China, 1911–1929* (Oxford: Oxford University Press, 2000), 74; Christina Gilmartin, "The Politics of Gender in the Making of the Party," in Tony Saich and Hans van de Ven, eds., *New Perspectives on the Chinese Revolution* (Armonk, NY: M. E. Sharpe, 1994), 33–55.

25. "Funü wenti yanjiuhui xuanyan [Declaration of Society for Research on the Women's Question," *Funü pinglun* (Women's critic) 52 (August 2, 1922): 4.

26. Gender-differentiated population statistics for the areas of the city under Chinese jurisdiction are not available until 1929 (650,000 women in a population of 2.1 million, approximately 30 percent). International Settlement figures for 1920 indicate approximately 200, 000 female residents in a Chinese population of nearly 550,000 (approximately 36 percent). (Shanghai funü zhi weiyuanhui, *Shanghai funü zhi* (Shanghai women's gazetteer), (Shanghai: Shanghai shi difang xiehui, 2000), 68–69. Jiangsu province in 1923 found 953 female middle school students to 7,263 male students (10 percent); and 770 female normal school students to 2,751 male students (17 percent. In 1929, 175,000 women worked in Shanghai factories, mostly in the silk and cotton mills (women comprised over 70 percent of workers). Bailey, *Gender and Education*, 60; 86; Wang, *Women in the Chinese Enlightenment*, 365.

27. Ge Yuanxu, *Hu you zaji* (Notes on touring Shanghai), (1896; reprint, Shanghai: Shanghai guji chuban she, 1998).

28. Yun Shi, *Funü zhi baimian guan* (Shanghai: Wenyi bianyi she, 1920; reprint, 1927); Zhonghua tushu jicheng bianjisuo, ed., *Shanghai funü nie jingtai* (Sinful mirror of Shanghai women), (Shanghai: Zhonghua tushu jicheng bianjisuo, 1925).

29. Alexander Des Forges, *Mediasphere Shanghai: The Aesthetics of Cultural Production* (Honolulu: University of Hawaii Press, 2007).

30. *Tuhua ribao* 10:9 (1909). See discussion in Barbara Mittler, *A Newspaper for China: Power, Identity and Change in Shanghai's News Media, 1872–1912* (Cambridge, MA: Harvard University Asia Center, 2004), 274–276.

31. For example, *Jingbao*, March 21, 1919; April 6, 1919; April 9, 1919; June 30, 1919.

32. Yun Shi, *Funü zhi baimian guan* (Shanghai, Wenyi bianyi she, 1920). See also *Shanghai funü nie jingtai* (Shanghai women's mirror of evil), (reprint, Shanghai, 1925; original published 1918).

33. "Zhongguo nüzi zhi jin xi guan," *Jingbao*, March 21, 1919; April 6, 1919.

34. Chen Duxiu, Yi jiu yi liu nian" (Nineteen sixteen), *Qingnian zazhi* 1:5 (January 15, 1916).

35. Imported and adapted from the Meiji-era Japanese neologism *jinkaku,* *ren'ge* conveyed individual, autonomous self-realization. *Ren'ge,* like *jinkaku,* is variously translated as "character," "individuality," or "personality." Richard Reitan, "Claiming Personality: Reassessing the Dangers of the 'New Woman' in Early Taishō Japan," *positions: east asia cultures critique* 19:1 (2011) 83–107. In "The Question of Women's Character," published in *Xinchao* (New tide) 1:2 (February 1919), Ye Shengtao (Ye Shaojun) defined *ren'ge* as individual "spirit of integrity and independence." Hua R. Lan and Vanessa L. Fong, eds., *Women in Republican China: A Sourcebook* (Armonk, NY: M. E. Sharpe, 1999), 151. On personhood in feminist rhetoric see Wang Zheng, *Women in the Chinese Enlightenment* (Berkeley: University of California Press, 1999), and Tani Barlow, *The Question of Women in Chinese Feminism* (Durham: Duke University Press, 2004).

36. Late Imperial law emphasized relational justice. There was no equivalent to legal personhood, nor were public and private relationships distinguished by law. Private disputes could be subject to criminal punishments. The idea of legal persons developed with acquaintance with European civil law.

37. See Hu Shi, "Zhencao wenti" (The problem of chastity) and Lu Xun, "Wo zhi jielie guan" (My views on chastity), in *Wusi shiqi funü wenti wenxuan* (Selected writings on women's issues from the May Fourth period), (Beijing: Sanlian shudian, 1981), 106–114; 115–123.

38. Kang Qiuxin, *Xianshi leyuan ribao,* September 30, 1922. On the rethinking of suicide in this era, see Rune Svarverud, "Perilous Life Views: Suicide, Morality, and the Rise of the Individual in May Fourth China," *Acta Orientalia* 70 (2009): 111–146.

39. Xu Cheng, "Zisha" (Suicide), *Xin shijie ribao,* September 19, 1922.

40. In 1922 there were no statistics to demonstrate the disproportionate extent of female suicide in China. A February 1922 special suicide issue of *Ladies Journal* nonetheless attested to growing feminist concern with female suicide, even as it mistakenly suggested that men universally committed suicide more frequently. By 1929, when Shanghai statistics became available, raw figures showed 1,071 women committed suicide per 918 men. Corrected for Shanghai's unbalanced sex ratio, there were nearly 16 female suicides for each 10 by men. Shanghai shi difang xiehui, *Shanghai shi tongji* (Statistics for Shanghai Municipality), (Shanghai: n.p., 1933), 5–6.

41. *MGRB,* September 20, 1922.

42. Paul Ropp, "Passionate Women: Female Suicide in Late Imperial China," *Nan nü* 3:1 (2001): 3–21; Janet Theiss, "Managing Martyrdom: Female Suicide and Statecraft in Mid-Qing China," *Nan nü* 3 (2001): 47–76; Mark Elvin, "Female Virtue and the State in China," *Past and Present* 104 (1984): 111–152.

43. Some 2000 proposals for commendations for chastity and loyalty were sent to the Ministry of Internal Affairs each year. Bailey, *Gender and Education,* 95.

44. "Chen Lienü zhuidao dahui xiangji" (Memorial for virtuous martyr Chen), *Shenbao,* August 5, 1918.

45. Foremost among these was the mother of business, political, and philanthropic notable Wang Yiting.
46. Tan edited the journals *Women and Family* (*Funü yu jiating,* 1922–1926) and the short-lived *Female Citizen* (*Nü guomin,* 1923). In 1936 she published a comprehensive history of the Chinese women's movement. Shen Yibin was a former member of the Revolutionary Alliance, and active in suffragist circles in the early 1910s. See Ma Yuxin, *Women Journalists and Feminism in China, 1898–1937* (Amherst, NY: Cambria Press, 2010), 151, 163.
47. "Chen Lienü zhuidao dahui xiangji" *Shenbao,* August 5, 1918. Among sojourner groupings, the Shaoxing association had a reputation for being progressive. At this time its formal membership was exclusively male, however, by the time of the Xi case it made news by being one of the earliest to admit female members.
48. See Hu, "Zhencao wenti," 106–114; Lu Weijing, *True to Her Word: The Faithful Maiden Cult in Late Imperial China* (Stanford, CA: Stanford University Press, 2008), 253–254; Lyman Van Slyke, "The Life and Death of Liang Ji: Personal and Social Meanings of Suicide in Early Republican China," paper presented at International Conference of Asian Scholars, Berlin, August 9–12, 2001; Lin Yü-sheng, "The Suicide of Liang Chi: An Ambiguous Case of Moral Conservatism," in *The Limits of Change: Essays on Conservative Alternatives in Republican China,* ed. Charlotte Furth (Cambridge, MA: Harvard University Press, 1976).
49. Hua R. Lan and Vanessa L. Fong, eds., *Women in Republican China: A Sourcebook* (Armonk, NY: M. E. Sharpe, 1999).
50. Yun, *Funü zhi baimian guan,* 2:1.
51. Wang, *Women in the Chinese Enlightenment,* 80–83.
52. Chinese medicine considered women prone to disorders of the blood, which produced anger or melancholy. Charlotte Furth, *A Flourishing Yin: Gender in China's Medical History, 960–1665* (Berkeley: University of California Press, 1999), 87–88.
53. Yun, *Funü zhi baimian guan,* 2:41.
54. Yun, *Funü zhi baimian guan,* 2:42.
55. Examples include the Family Research Society (*Jiating yanjiu she*), which oversaw publications on this theme (Yi Jiayue, *Funü zhiye wenti* [The question of women's vocations], [Shanghai: Taidong tushuju, 1922]), and the Society for Research on Women's Vocations (*Fünu zhiye yanjiu she*) mentioned previously. See also Wang, *Women in the Chinese Enlightenment,* 1–24.
56. "Chinese Women Past and Present, no. 14: Exercise," *Jingbao,* June 30, 1919.
57. In the last decade of the Qing dynasty, Liang Qichao published a biography of Madam Roland in Yokohama (based on a Japanese biography that introduced her as the "Mother of the French Revolution"). The feminist journalist Chen Xiefen copied Liang's text, with slight alterations, in her *Journal of Women's Learning,* calling Roland "the first heroine of the modern age," and emphasizing her patriotism. Xia Xiaohong, "Western

Heroines in Late Qing Women's Journals: Meiji-Era Writings on 'Women's Self-Help' in China," in Michel Hockx, Joan Judge, and Barbara Mittler, eds., *Women and the Political Press in China's Long Twentieth Century: A Space of Their Own?* (Cambridge, UK: Cambridge University Press, 2018), 239–240. Hu Ying suggests martyrdom may have provided, "satisfying narrative closure" that atoned for transgressive lives. Hu, *Tales of Translation*, 115.

58. Mary Rankin, The Emergence of Women at the End of the Ch'ing: The Case of Ch'iu Chin," in *Women in Chinese Society,* ed. Margery Wolf and Roxane Witke (Stanford, CA: Stanford University Press, 1975), 39–65; Hu Ying, "Qiu Jin's Nine Burials: The Making of Public Monuments and Historical Memory," *Modern Chinese Literature and Culture* 19:1 (Spring 2007): 138–91; Joan Judge, *The Precious Raft of History: The Past, the West, and the Woman Question in China* (Stanford, CA: Stanford University Press, 2002).

59. *Nü xuesheng,* 1912.

60. Kang-i Sun Chang, Haun Saussy, and Charles Yim-tze Kwong, *Women Writers of Traditional China: An Anthology of Poetry and Criticism* (Stanford, CA: Stanford University Press, 1999), 658.

61. Wu Yugong, *Zisha zhi nüshuji,* 15. There are some discrepancies between the newspaper report of the Chen case (which mentions only poisoning), and Xi's note, making positive identification difficult.

62. See Roxane Witke, "Mao Tse-tung, Women and Suicide," in Marilyn Young, ed., *Women in China: Studies in Social Change and Feminism* (Ann Arbor: Center for Chinese Studies, University of Michigan, 1973), 7–31.

63. *Da gongbao,* November 18, 1919, translated as "The Question of Miss Zhao's Personality," in Stuart Schram, ed., *Mao's Road to Power: Revolutionary Writings, 1912–1949* (Armonk, NY: M. E. Sharpe, 1992), 1:423–424. I have slightly altered Schram's translation.

64. Tao Yi, "Commentary on Miss Zhao's Suicide," in Lan and Fong, eds., *Women in Republican China,* 84–85, Quotation follows translation in Lan and Fong, with slight modification.

65. The families bore heavy funeral costs and sold their houses. Christina Gilmartin, "Introduction," in Lan and Fong, *Women in Republican China,* xv.

66. Ye Shengtao, "The Question of Women's Character," in Lan and Fong, *Women in Republican China,* 154; 156 (slightly modified translation).

67. Cited in Wang, *Women in the Chinese Enlightenment,* 80.

68. Cheng Wanyang, "Nannü ren'ge pingdeng lun" (Equality of men's and women's ren'ge), *Funü zazhi* (FZ),7:8 (August 1, 1921): 14–15.

69. "Nüzi canzheng hui chengli ji" (Women's Suffrage Association Inauguration), *MGRB,* October 16, 1922.

70. "Wan Pu nüshi linbie zhi tanhua" (Miss Wan Pu's parting words), *MGRB,* October 25, 1922.

71. Ma Yuxin, "Male Feminism and Women's Subjectivities: Zhang Xichen, Chen Xuezhao, and *The New Woman,*" *Twentieth-Century China* 29:1

(November 2003): 3; Bryna Goodman, "The Vocational Woman and the Elusiveness of 'Personhood' in Early Republican China," in Bryna Goodman and Wendy Larson, eds., *Gender in Motion: Divisions of Labor and Cultural Change in Late Imperial and Modern China* (Landham, MD: Rowman and Littlefield, 2005).

72. "Kongzi zhi dao yu xiandai shenghuo" (The way of Confucius and modern life), *Xin qingnian* (New youth) 2:4 (December 1, 1916); reprinted in *Duxiu wencun* (Wuhu: Anhui renmin chubanshe, 1987), 83.

73. Wang Pingling, "Xin funü de ren'ge wenti," *FZ* 7:10 (October 1921): 10–15.

74. Yi Jiayue, *Funü zhiye wenti* (The question of women's vocations), (Shanghai: Taidong tushuju, 1922), 100–114; Dongfang zashi she, ed., *Funü zhiye yu muxing lun* (Women's vocations and motherhood), (Shanghai: Shangwu yinshuguan, 1924).

75. Cui, ed., *Xi Shangzhen*, preface.

76. Huang Bingqing. "Xi Shangzhen de zisha shibushi shehui shang zhongda de wenti?" (Xi Shangzhen's suicide—a great social problem?), *SSXB*, September 15, 1922.

77. Yi Jiayue, *Funü zhiye wenti*, 73–74, 82, 85. Shao Lizi similarly noted that female factory workers were understood to be loose women (*dangfu*). Shao, "Shanghai sichang." *Funü pinglun*, 53 (August 9, 1922); 58 (September 13, 1922); 59 (September 20, 1922).

78. Chen Wentao, "Tichang dulixing de nüzi zhiye," *FZ* 7:8 (August 1, 1921): 7–11. Whereas late Qing girls' schools relied on predominantly male teachers, by the early Republican Era, these positions were largely filled with female teachers. Bailey, *Gender and Education*, 89.

79. Chen Tiesheng, "Wo de nüzi canzheng guan" (My views on female participation in government). *Shangbao*, April 7, 1921.

80. See also Yi, *Funü zhiye wenti*, 73.

81. "Nüzi zhiye qiantu zhi leguan" (Optimism regarding the future of women's vocations); "Nüzi zai shangjie zhi fazhan" (Women's progress in commercial circles), *Shangbao*, February 22, 1921.

82. *SG*, March 9, 1921.

83. Chen, "Tichang dulixing," 9.

84. Bailey, *Gender and Education*, 95.

85. Shao, "Funü yu shehui shiye," 12–13.

86. Houlou Tingke, "Baidao shiliuqunxia," *Huamulan*, September 16, 1927, cited in Ling-ling Lien, "Searching for the 'New Womanhood': Career Women in Shanghai, 1912–1945," PhD Dissertation, University of California, Irvine, 2001, 66.

87. Jue Feizi, "Wei nüzi zhiye gao liangzhong ren" (Notice to two types of people about female vocations), *Shenbao*, July 25, 1921.

88. Yang Zhihua, "Tan nüzi zhiye," (Women's vocations), *Funü pinglun*, November 1, 1922.

89. Louise Edwards, *Gender, Politics, and Democracy: Women's Suffrage in China* (Stanford, CA: Stanford University Press, 2008); Wang, *Women in the Chinese Enlightenment;* Lien, "Searching for the New Womanhood."

90. Examples include Lu, "Regret for the Past"; Ding, "Miss Sophia's Diary"; Mao, "Creation"; Lu, "After Victory"; Chen, "The Woes of the Modern Woman"; Ching-kiu Stephen Chan, "The Language of Despair: Ideological Representations of the 'New Woman' by May Fourth Writers," in Tani Barlow, ed., *Gender Politics in Modern China* (Durham and London: Duke University Press, 1993), 13–32.

91. Margaret Decker, "Living in Sin: From May Fourth via the Anti-Rightist Movement to the Present," in Ellen Widmer and David Der-Wei Wang, eds. *From May Fourth to June Fourth: Fiction and Film in Twentieth-Century China* (Cambridge, MA: Harvard University Press, 1993), 221–246.

92. *FZ* 7:8 (August 1, 1921).

93. The challenges and dangers for a professional woman of securing financial support are illustrated by the experience of Lu Lihua, who established the Liangjiang Women's Physical Education School in the May Fourth Era. She placed powerful men on the board of her school and suffered rumors that she gave sexual favors to gain their support. Wang, *Women in the Chinese Enlightenment,* 153; 183; Elvin, "Female Virtue and the State."

94. *Shibao,* October 14, 1922.

95. The first statistics show fewer than 2 percent of Shanghai women in white-collar jobs as late as 1935, despite their growing numbers. Lien, "Searching for the 'New,'" 36–38.

96. Yun, *Funü zhi baimian guan,* 2:37–42.

97. Shanghai prostitutes reportedly increased from as many as 6,000 in 1875 to as many as 20,000 by 1920. Christian Henriot, *Prostitution and Sexuality in Shanghai: A Social History 1849–1949* (Cambridge: Cambridge University Press, 2001), 120; Bailey, *Gender and Education,* 101.

98. *Jingbao,* September 21, 1922. *XSB* and *SSXB* published special issues on the case.

99. See, for example, Yang Chaosheng, "Nannü shejiao gongkai" (Public social intercourse for men and women), *Xin qingnian* (La Jeunesse) 6:4; reprinted in *Wusi shiqi funü wenti wenxuan* (May Fourth writings on the woman question), (Beijing: Shenghuo, 1981), 173–175.

100. Zheng, "Cong Xi nüshi zisha de lai de jiaoshun," 1:11.

101. Zheng, "Cong Xi nüshi zisha de lai de jiaoshun," 1:29.

102. *SSXB,* December 3, 1922.

103. These two lines in Xi's voice are written literally as, "Your concubine? This concubine has no heart to be your concubine/but what can this concubine do?" The author deliberately (and anachronistically) used the character for concubine (*qie*) as Xi's humble self-reference.

104. *Jingbao,* September 12, 1922.

105. [Zhang] Dan Fu, "Dian Tang . . . huan Xi," *Jingbao,* September 18, 1922.

106. A more sympathetic portrayal of Xi is offered in Zhou Peichu, "Xi ni Xi nüshi yincao yuyuange" (Playful draft of Miss Xi's netherworld song of grievance), *Xin shijie,* September 25, 1922.

107. Zhou did not mince words in denouncing Xi's newspaper colleagues: "Savages kill people or eat the flesh of their enemies, but even they do not dance

when fellow humans die." Zhou Zuoren, "Kelian minzhe" (Commiseration), in *Tan hu ji* (Speaking of Tigers), (Hong Kong: 1969), 92.

108. Du Yaquan, "Lun xu qie" (On keeping concubines), *Dongfang zazhi* 8:4 (1911): 15.

109. Du, "Lun xu qie" 17, 19. Du was pleased to note that concubines were not unknown in the West, though he was evidently influenced by Western critiques of the practice.

110. The early Republican laws largely followed codes drafted in the last Qing decade in the New Policy reforms. These included the Provisional New Criminal Code (1912) and the Code Currently in Use (based on the civil portions of the revised draft Qing code of 1910). Kathryn Bernhardt, *Women and Property in China,* 960–1949 (Stanford, CA: Stanford University Press, 2001), 161; Lisa Tran, *Concubines in Court: Marriage and Monogamy in Twentieth-Century China* (Lanham, MD: Rowman and Littlefield, 2015).

111. Matthew Sommer, *Polyandry and Wife-Selling in Qing Dynasty China* (Berkeley: University of California Press, 2015).

112. Xia Shi, "Just Like a 'Modern' Wife? Concubines on the Public Stage in Early Republican China," *Social History* 43:2 (February 2018): 211–323.

113. Shao Zuiweng (Runjie Shaw), "Fandui du qi zhuyi" (Oppose single-wife-ism), *Xin shijie ribao* (New world daily), December 2, 3, and 6, 1917, 2.

114. James Hundley Wiley, "Christianizing Chinese Sex Relations: The Fight for Monogamy in China," PhD diss., Southern Baptist Theological Seminary, 1929.

115. Jin Shiyin, "Ershi nian fuyun zhi yi da gongzuo: Fei qie" (A major task in the 20-year women's movement: abolishing concubinage), *Funü gongming* (Women's echo) 41 (1931), 9.

116. Aage Krarup-Nielsen, *The Dragon Awakes* (London: J. Lane, 1928), 66–67.

117. "Shanghai baojie sida jingang zhi bijiao" (Four newspaper pillars compared), *Jingbao,* July 6, 1921. Tang Jiezhi was not among those featured in the article.

118. Matthew Sommer, *Polyandry and Wife-Selling;* Johanna S. Ransmeier, *Sold People: Traffickers and Family Life in North China* (Cambridge, MA: Harvard University Press, 2017).

119. Keith McMahon, *Polygamy and Sublime Passion: Sexuality in China on the Verge of Modernity* (Honolulu: University of Hawaii Press, 2010).

120. "Zhi shen qu qie zhinan" (Guide to taking concubines in Shanghai), *Shanghai youlan zhinan* (Shanghai: Zhonghua tushu jicheng bianjisuo, 1923), 77–79; Yun Shi, *Shanghai baimian guan,* 31–33, 33, 51. Quotation from Yun, *Shanghai baimian guan,* 32.

121. Tan Sheying, ed., *Zhongguo funü yondongshi* (Nanjing: Funü gongming she, 1936), contains notices of women's groups that advocated concubine abolition. See also, "Women Organize against Concubines," *Far Eastern Republic,* November 1919, 26.

122. "You shi yi mu feiqie yundong" (Another concubine abolition movement), *XWB,* August 30, 1921. Participants aimed at a broader mass following in

successful campaigns to gain suffrage in provincial constitutions between 1919 and 1923. Edwards, *Gender, Politics, and Democracy,* 25, 28.

123. Edwards, *Gender, Politics, and Democracy,* 28.

124. Gui Shi, "Qie zhi zijue," in Zhu Caizhen, ed., *Fei qie hao* (Abolish concubinage), (Hangzhou: Zhejiang shuju, 1922), 25.

125. Jin, "Ershi nian," 11.

126. Lin, "Yeqie zhi lu" (The concubine-smelting furnace), 33.

127. Bryna Goodman "Appealing to the Public: Newspaper Presentation and Adjudication of Emotion," *Twentieth-Century China* 31:2 (April 2006): 32–69; Lee Haiyan; *Revolution of the Heart: A Genealogy of Love in China, 1900–1950* (Stanford, CA: Stanford University Press, 2007).

128. In one notorious case in 1917, an exemplary Beijing Normal School student committed suicide after her teacher suggested that her excellent work qualified her to become her teacher's husband's concubine. Bailey, *Gender and Education,* 117.

129. Together with Commercial Press editor Zhou Jianren, Zhang Xichen, editor of *Ladies Journal,* promoted what they called the new sexual morality (*xin xing daode*) and freedom in love. In January 1925 they published a special issue on the new sexual morality in which they argued that sexual freedom should not be subject to marital constraints and men and women should be free to enjoy sex with partners of their choice, even multiple sexual partners. This incurred the wrath of advocates of modern monogamy, and Zhang was removed from his editorship of the journal. Zhang Xichen, "Xin xing daode shi shenme" (What is the new sexual morality?), in Zhang Xichen, ed., *Xinxing daode taolunji* (Shanghai, Kaiming shuju, 1925). See discussion in Lisa Tran, "The ABCs of Monogamy in Republican China: Adultery, Bigamy, and Conjugal Fidelity," *Twentieth Century China* 36:2 (July 2011), 113–114; Wang, *Women in the Chinese Enlightenment,* 131.

130. See Li Renjie, "Nan nü jiefang" (Men's and women's emancipation), in Mei Sheng, ed., *Zhongguo funü wenti taolunji* (Shanghai: Xin wenhua shuju, 1929), 1:68–88; Wang, *Women in the Chinese Enlightenment,* 64; Kristen Stapleton, "Generational and Cultural Fissures: Wu Yu (1872–1949) and the Politics of Family Reform," in Kai-Wing Chow, ed., *Beyond the May 4* (Lexington Books, 2008), 135–140.

131. SG, July 29, 1922.

132. Mei Lu, "On Abolishing Concubinage," *Rensheng zazhi* 3 (1924), 14.

133. The Guangzhou Women's Federation made similar exclusions. Ke Jiu, "Wo zhen ti zhexie zi kexi" (I consider these words unfortunate), *Juewu,* June 13, 1921; see also "Tianjin nüjie aiguohui jujue ru furen ru hui zhi liyoushu" (Tianjin women's patriotic association membership refusal), *Chenbao,* August 15, 1919. These exclusions provoked debate in the Guangzhou association, which ultimately removed the explicit prohibition but required that all members be nominated by two existing members, which may have had the same effect. Edwards, *Gender, Politics and Democracy,* 115–116.

134. In the early Republic the Daliyuan ruled that faithful widowed concubines could no longer be considered approximations of wives, even if the wife was deceased. Concubines no longer had claims to family property or to the

designation of heirs at the death of both the family head and his wife. Republican lawmakers eliminated explicit references to concubines in legal code. By this means (maintained until the mid-1930s) they also skirted explicit prohibition of concubinage, which was widely tolerated in practice. Bernhardt, *Women and Property*, 161, 178, 181.

135. Gui, "Qie de zijue," 25, 27.
136. Mei, "Feiqie tan," 14.
137. Gui Shi, "Za shi" (poems), in Zhu Caizhen, ed. *Fei qie hao* (Abolish concubinage), (Hangzhou: Zhejiang shuju, 1922), 6.
138. Zhu Hongda, "Qie" (Concubine), *Fei qie hao*, 3.
139. Yun Shi, *Funü zhi baimian guan*, 51.
140. Cheng Yu, "Qing zhi minguo de xuqie xisu yu shehui bianqian" (Concubine possession and social change from Qing to Republic), PhD dissertation, Fudan University, 2005, 178–196; Yu Hualin, *Nüxing de "chong su": Minguo chengshi funü hunyin wenti yanjiu* (Remodeling: women and the marriage question in Republican cities), (Beijing: Shangwu yinshuguan, 2009).
141. Zhu Caizhen, "Feiqie hao fakan xuanyan" ("Abolish Concubines," preface) in *Fei qie hao*.
142. Cheng Yu, "Qing zhi minguo de xuqie; Yu Hualin, *Nüxing*. Quote from Qiu Tian, "Qie de bihai he ruhe feiqie" (The harms of concubines, and how to abolish them), in Zhu, *Fei qie hao*, 15.
143. Sommer, *Polyandry*.
144. Qiu Ying, "Qie shi zunao renlei jinhua de zhang'ai wu" (Concubine is obstacle to human evolution), *Fei qie hao*, 31.
145. Mei, "Feiqie tan," 14.
146. Guo Xun, Jiu jiating hun zhi bihai (Evils of old family system), *Jiating yanjiu* 1:4 (August 1921): 38. Discussed in Glosser, *Chinese Visions of Family and State*, 46–47, 55.
147. Zhu, "Feiqie hao fakan xuanyan."
148. Individuals in these relationships would have rejected the "new-style concubine" idea because of the ideological gulfs between the mutually exclusive categories of new woman and backward concubine.
149. On the burdens of sexual emancipation for poor women, see Bryna Goodman, "Words of Blood and Tears: Petty Urbanites Write Emotion," *Nan Nü: Men, Women, and Gender in China* 11:2 (2009), 270–301.
150. *Nü xuesheng*, 3, 1912, 11–12, 15–16.
151. Wen-hsin Yeh, *Shanghai Splendor*, 60.
152. "Nüzi zhiye qiantu zhi leguan"; "Nüzi zai shangjie zhi fazhan" (Women's progress in commercial circles), *Shangbao*, February 22, 1921. See also editorials of April 2, 7, and 11, 1921; August 2 and 6, 1922.
153. Chen Wangdao, "Xi Shangzhen nüshi zai Shangbao guan li diaosi shijian" (Xi Shangzhen's hanging at the Shangbao), *Funü pinglun*, 59 (September 20, 1922).
154. It was not uncommon for career women to delay marriage, have fewer children, or remain unmarried. Lien, "Searching for the New Womanhood," 82

155. Zheng, "Cong Xi nüshi zisha de lai de jiaoshun," 1:5.

156. Zheng, "Cong Xi nüshi zisha de lai de jiaoshun," 1:25.

157. Zha Mengci, "Nüzi jiaoyu de quexian" (Defects in women's education), *Zhonghua xinbao,* September 16, 1922; Cui, *Xi Shangzhen,* 2:23, 2:25.

158. Cui, *Xi Shangzhen,* Introductory notes.

159. Zheng, "Cong Xi nüshi zisha de lai de jiaoshun," 1:12.

160. Cui, *Xi Shangzhen,* 2:66–67.

161. Zheng, "Cong Xi nüshi zisha de lai de jiaoshun," 1:8.

162. Cui, *Xi Shangzhen,* 2:1.

163. *ZXB* September 20, 1922; *XSB,* September 24, 1922; *Shibao,* September 25, 1922; Cui 1922.

164. Paderni, "Le rachat de l'honeur perdu: Le suicide des femmes dans la Chine du XVIIIe siècle," *Études chinoises* 10: 1–2 (1991): 135–60; Carlitz, "The Social Uses of Female Virtue."

165. *Huang Qinghua,* 1922.

166. *Shibao,* October 16, 1922; October 19, 1922.

167. Zhou Fengxia, letter in SSXB, December 26, 1922.

168. Hongmeige zhuren, Qinghuilou zhuren, comps., *Qingdai guixiu shichao* (Shanghai: Zhonghua xin jiaoyu she, 1922). The excerpt follows Maureen Robertson, "Changing the Subject: Gender and Self-inscription in Authors' Prefaces and Shi Poetry," in Ellen Widmer and Kang-I Sun Chang, eds., *Writing Women in Late Imperial China* (Stanford, CA: Stanford University Press, 1997), 213–214.

169. *Shibao (Eastern Times)* was founded by reform-oriented publicists Di Baoxian, Di Chuqing, and Liang Qichao in 1904. In 1922 it had a circulation of approximately 10,000–15,000, placing it among the top four Shanghai papers. In the early 1920s the *Shibao* was known for its appeal to the student population in Shanghai. Nationally, it pioneered literary and topical supplements (Patterson, *Journalism of China,* 1922; Judge, *Print and Politics,* 1996). It is likely the poems (signed with male and female names) were written by students, or young, educated readers. The crudity of some of the *baihua* poetry indicates the participation of individuals with limited schooling.

170. This is an allusion to Qiu Jin's unfinished opus, *Stones of the Jingwei Bird.* The legendary bird aimed to fill the sea by dropping stones into the water, a metaphor for the struggles of Chinese women.

171. *Shibao,* October 14, 1922, signed "Zhedong bupingzi" (Troubled person from eastern Zhejiang).

172. Judge, *Precious Raft.*

173. *Shibao,* October 14, 1922. Signed Guo Litong.

174. *Shibao,* October 15, 1922. Excerpt, anonymous poem.

175. Yun Shi, *Funü zhi baimian guan,* 41.

176. Mao Dun, "Zisha" (Suicide). Mao Dun's female protagonists confirmed his ambivalence about women's fitness for personhood. David Derwei Wang, *The Monster That Is History: History, Violence and Fictional Writing in Twentieth-Century China* (Berkeley and Los Angeles: University of California Press, 2004), 101.

177. Shuang Shen, *Cosmopolitan Publics: Anglophone Print Culture in Semi-Colonial Shanghai* (New Brunswick, NJ: Rutgers University Press, 2009), 130.
178. *Shibao*, October 18, 1922.
179. *Shibao*, October 16, 1922.
180. Yang was the consort of the Tang emperor Xuanzong. When his guards demanded her execution because her family was implicated in the An Lushan Rebellion, the emperor reluctantly ordered her strangulation.
181. *Shibao*, October 18, 1922, signed Fan Renlan (a female writer).
182. *Dongting lü Hu tongxianghui sanshi zhou jinian tekan* (Thirty-year commemorative edition of Dongting sojourners' association), (Shanghai: n.p., 1944), 78.
183. *Shibao*, October 14, 1922, anonymous poem (excerpt).
184. *Shibao*, October 19, 1922, signed Long Bo ("Uncle Dragon").
185. The phrase presents a nationalist claim to a 5,000-year past for the Chinese nation.
186. *Shibao*, October 16, 1922 (anonymous poem).
187. For analysis of a different, analogous compilation of the newspaper materials emanating from a social controversy a few years prior to the Xi case, see Bryna Goodman, "Being Public: The Politics of Representation in 1918 Shanghai," *Harvard Journal of Asiatic Studies* 60:1 (2000): 45–88.
188. *Shibao*, October 14, 1922, signed Shuang Xiu.
189. Marie-Claire Bergère, *The Golden Age of the Chinese Bourgeoisie*, trans. Janet Lloyd (Cambridge: Cambridge University Press, 1989).
190. Commentators tended to reiterate the names of these female casualties, highlighting the crimes of the men responsible. This explains commentators' associations of Xi's suicide with the 1920 murder of the courtesan Wang Lianying by Yan Ruisheng (*Shibao*, September 20, 1922). Though there was no similarity between Xi and Wang, the public association of the two cases was based upon connections between the two Western-educated men, both of whom were believed to have committed crimes in order to seize women's property.

Chapter 3. Long Live the Republic, Long Live the Stock Exchange

Epigraphs: Zheng Zhengqiu, "Cong Xi nüshi zisha de lai de jiaoshun" (Lessons from Miss Xi's suicide), in Cui Weiru, ed. *Xi Shangzhen* (Shanghai: Funü zhiye yanjiushe, 1922), 1:8–9; Zhenhai Yichi, *Shibao*, October 14, 1922.

1. *Shibao*, October 16, 1922 (anonymous poem).
2. Hollington Tong, "Principal Events in and about China in 1921," *WRFE*, January 14, 1922, 277.
3. Benjamin Elman and Martin Kern, eds, *Statecraft and Classical Learning: The Rituals of Zhou in East Asian History* (Leiden: Brill, 2009), ch. 8; Cheng-chung Lai, ed., *Adam Smith across Nations: Translations and Receptions of "The Wealth of Nations"* (Oxford: Oxford University Press, 2000).

4. "Kongzi zhi dao yu xiandai shenghuo," *Xin qingnian* (New youth) 2:4 (December 1, 1916); reprinted in *Duxiu wencun* ([Chen] Duxiu writings), (Wuhu: Anhui renmin chubanshe, 1987), 83.

5. Chinese manufacturing, business and finance reaped substantial profits from European preoccupation with the war. Demand for raw materials and food increased exports. Rising silver prices increased the value of the tael. U.S. trade offset reduced European capital flows, facilitating growth. Annual GDP growth from 1914 into the 1920s was roughly 2 percent (highest in industry and finance). By late 1921, after postwar reconversion led to declining silver prices, the tael dropped from $1.48 US to $0.74. Import prices doubled, protecting Chinese industry. Thomas Rawski, *Economic Growth in Prewar China* (Berkeley: University of California Press, 1989), 330; Marie-Claire Bergère, *The Golden Age of the Chinese Bourgeoisie, 1911–1937*, trans. Janet Lloyd (Cambridge: Cambridge University Press, 1989), 70–75, 86–87, 91; Wen-hsin Yeh, *Shanghai Splendor: Economic Sentiments and the Making of Modern China* (Berkeley: University of California Press, 2007).

6. Madeleine Zelin, *The Merchants of Zigong: Industrial Entrepreneurship in Early Modern China* (New York: Columbia University Press, 2005); Joseph McDermott, *The Making of a New Rural Order in South China*, vol. 2 (Cambridge: Cambridge University Press, 2016); David Faure, "The Introduction of Economics in China," in *Modern Chinese Religion II*, (Leiden, Netherlands: Brill, 2015), 1:65–89; Jacques Gernet, *Buddhism in Chinese Society: An Economic History from the Fifth to the Tenth Centuries* (New York: Columbia University Press, 1995).

7. Eiichi Motono, *Conflict and Cooperation in Sino-British Business, 1860–1911: The Impact of Pro-British Commercial Network in Shanghai* (New York: St. Martin's Press, Macmillan, 2000), 137–140; Zhu Yingui, "Jindai Shanghai zhengquan shichang shang gupiao maimai de sansi gaochao" (Three stock-purchasing peaks in modern Shanghai securities markets), *Zhongguo jingjishi yanjiu* 3 (1998): 58–70.

8. "Goumai gufen yi yi zi shen shuo" (Cautious words on the purchase of shares), *Shenbao*, September 2, 1882; see also Hong Jiaguan and Zhang Jifeng, *Jindai Shanghai jinrong shichang* (Financial markets in modern Shanghai), (Shanghai: Shanghai renmin chubanshe: 1989), 147–148.

9. Zhu Yingui, "Jindai Shanghai zhengquan shichang shang gupiao maimai de sansi gaochao" (Three stock-purchasing peaks in modern Shanghai securities markets), *Zhongguo jingjishi yanjiu* 3 (1998): 58–70; Feng Ziming, "Min yuan lai Shanghai zhi jiaoyisuo" (Shanghai stock exchanges from the Republic), in Zhu Sihuang, ed., *Minguo jingji shi* (Economic history of the Republic), (Shanghai: Yinhang zhoubaoshe, 1947), 146–147; Shanghai shi difang xiehui, *Shanghai shi tongji* (Statistics for Shanghai municipality), (Shanghai: n.p., 1933), 43–44.

10. This exchange, which excluded Chinese from membership until 1929, traded securities in Western companies. Chinese accounted for 70–80 percent of purchased rubber shares. W. A. Thomas, *Western Capitalism in China: A*

History of the Shanghai Stock Exchange (Aldershot, UK: Ashgate, 2001), 71–90, 103, 112; Zhaojin Ji, *A History of Modern Shanghai Banking: The Rise and Decline of China's Finance Capitalism* (Armonk, NY: M. E. Sharpe, 2003), 92–93.

11. Traditional "native" banks (*qianzhuang*) differed from early twentieth-century Chinese modern banks in that their operations were more tied to social networks of trust and their credit did not necessarily require security deposits. Native banks financed domestic industry and trade until the 1930s. Foreign banks and modern Chinese banks, in contrast, primarily financed the export trade. Brett Sheehan, *Trust in Troubled Times: Money, Banks, and State-Society Relations in Republican Tianjin* (Cambridge, MA: Harvard University Press, 2003), 101–109.

12. Shanghai renmin yinhang, *Shanghai qianzhuang shiliao* (Shanghai native bank materials), (Shanghai: Shanghai renmin chubanshe, 1960), 74–88; Hong Jiaguan and Zhang Jifeng. *Jindai Shanghai jinrong shichang,* 141; Yu Huancheng, "Min yuan lai woguo zhi zhengquan jiaoyi" (Domestic securities trading since the first year of the Republic), in Zhu Sihuang, *Minguo jingjishi,* 141; Heike Holbig, "Competitive Cooperation: A Preliminary Analysis of Shanghai Monetary Policies, 1908–1910" (unpublished ms.); Xu Xiaoqun, *Chinese Professionals and the Republican State* (Cambridge: Cambridge University Press, 2000), 30.

13. Liang Qichao, "Jinggao guozhong zhi tan shiyezhe" (Warning our country's entrepreneurs), in *Guofengbao,* November 2, 1910, reproduced in Shanghai shi dang'anguan, ed., *Jiu Shanghai de zhengquan jiaoyisuo* (Securities exchanges in old Shanghai), (Shanghai: Shanghai guji chubanshe, 1994), 265–273: *Zai lun chouhuan guozhai* (Another discussion of repaying national debt), *Yinbingshi wenji* 21 (Beijing: Zhonghua shuju, 1989).

14. Kang Youwei, "Licai jiuguo lun" (National salvation through economics), *Buren zazhi* (Compassion), no. 1 (1913): 64. *Licai,* or finance, was Kang's preferred translation for economics. See Chen Huanzhang, *Economic Principles of Confucius and His School* (reprint, New York: Gordon Press, 1974; original work published 1911), 1:preface, 48–49.

15. Kang Youwei, "Licai jiuguo lun" (National salvation through economics), *Buren zazhi* (Compassion), no. 1 (1913), 3–4.

16. Larissa N. Schwartz, "The Inconveniences Resulting from Race Mixture": The Torreón Massacre of 1911," in Chinese Historical Society of America, ed., *Chinese America: History and Perspectives* (Brisbane, CA: Chinese Historical Society of America, 1998), 60; Shehong Chen, *Being Chinese, Becoming Chinese American* (Urbana, University of Illinois Press, 2002), 33.

17. Kang, *Licai,* 62.

18. Kang, *Licai,* 62.

19. Kang, *Licai,* 64. Kang suggested that "the poor may rely on the wealthy for livelihood."

20. Wang Shijie, "Caizheng geming" (Financial revolution), *Guomin jingji zazhi* 1 (1912): 1–3.

21. *Shenghuo zhoubao*, 1:9 (1912): 1–6. Originally in *Duli Zhoubao* (Independence weekly), established by Zhang Shizhao in 1912 after studies at Aberdeen University. Joachim Kurtz, "Coming to Terms with Logic: The Naturalization of an Occidental Notion in China," in Michael Lackner et al., *New Terms for New Ideas* (Leiden, Netherlands: Brill, 2001), 166; Ye Min, "Yibai duo nian qian guanyu 'zhongguoren qizhi' de yichangbianlun" (*The Spectator* and debate over "Chinese character" over 100 years ago), *Wenhuibao*, June 19, 2015.

22. Presentation of the exchange as a tool for prediction may have resonated with older notions of divination as a guide to governance.

23. Liang, "Jinggao guozhong"; Liang, "Zai lun chouhuan guozhai"; Kang, "Licai jiuguo lun," 60; "Zhengquan jiaoyisuo fa," December 29, 1914, reprinted in Shanghai shi dang'an guan, ed., *Jiu Shanghai de jiaoyisuo*, 274–281.

24. The activist wing of the Ningbo association aligned with Tang in earlier agitation for Chinese representation. Bryna Goodman, "Democratic Calisthenics: The Culture of Urban Associations in the New Republic," in Merle Goldman and Elizabeth Perry, eds., *Changing Meanings of Citizenship in Modern China* (Cambridge, MA: Harvard University Press, 2002), 70–109.

25. Earlier, Sun had experimented with revolutionary bonds. Marie-Claire Bergère, *Sun Yatsen*, trans. Janet Lloyd (Stanford, CA: Stanford University Press, 1998), 191; Feng Xiaocai, *Zhengshang Zhongguo: Yu Qiaqing yu ta de shidai* (Political merchants in China: Yu Qiaqing and his times), (Beijing: Shehui kexue wenxian chubanshe, 2013), 114–115.

26. Yang Tianshi, "Jiang Zongzheng xiansheng he Shanghai zhengquan wupin jiaoyisuo" (Jiang Jieshi and Shanghai's Securities and Commodities Exchange), *Jindai Zhongguo* 139 (October 2000): 158. The Japanese agreed to an interest-free loan of half the needed 5 milllion silver dollars, in return for 80 percent of profits. Sun Yatsen, Yu Xiaqing, Dai Jitao and Zhang Jingjiang signed an agreement to hire Japanese advisors. Hamada Minetarō identifies Ogino Yoshizō as an investor. Hamada Minetarō, *Shina no kōekijo* (China's exchanges), (Shanghai: Chūka Keizaisha, 1922), 55.

27. A Beijing Stock Exchange was established in 1918 to help maintain government financial credibility by managing the issuance of government bonds. Yin Zhentao, "Jindai de Beijing zhengquan jiaoyisuo" (The modern Beijing securities exchange), *Zhongguo jinrong* (July 2017).

28. "Lun Shanghai quyinsuo" (The Japanese exchange), *Yinhang zhoubao* (Bankers' weekly), November 26, 1918; Xu Cangshui, "Jingji zhanzheng yu jingji tixue" (Economic war and economic guidance), *Yinhang zhoubao* 2:47 (December 3, 1918); "Quyinsuo yu jiaoyisuo zhi zhengzhi" (Competition between the quyinsuo and jiaoyisuo), *Shenbao*, September 17, 1918. The Japanese concern had notable Chinese shareholders, including Zhu Baosan and Wang Yiting. Feng Xiaocai suggests it owed its success to these ties. Feng Xiaocai, *Zheng shang Zhongguo*, 114; quotation on 115.

29. "Wen Lanting deng guanyu choubei Shanghai zhengquan wupin jiaoyisuo de laiwang han jian" (Letters of Wen Lanting, etc., regarding Shanghai Se-

curities and Commodities Exchange planning), *Dang'an yu shixue* 4 (2001): 19.

30. "Wen Lanting deng," 10–19. Several Guomindang associates remained at this point, but not Sun.

31. The Chinese name was Shanghai Zhengquan Wupin Jiaoyisuo (Shanghai Securities and Commodities Exchange).

32. Xing Jianrong," Yu Xiaqing yu Shanghai zhengquan wupin jiaoyisuo," *Dang'an yu shixue* (Archives and History) 3 (1996): 61–63. Feng Xiaocai notes that Yu stood to benefit personally from an arrangement he made with Beijing officials, in which a large security deposit would be placed in the Quanye Bank, in which Yu had a significant interest. Feng, *Zhengshang Zhongguo*, 117.

33. "Japanese Exchange Loses Its Quarters to Chinese Combine," *CP*, January 1, 1920; "Chinese Exchange Oust Japanese," *SG*, January 2, 1920.

34. Feng, *Zheng shang Zhongguo*, 118.

35. "Zhengquan wupin jiaoyisuo kaimu ji" (Opening of Securities and Commodities Exchange), *Shenbao*, July 2, 1920.

36. The full phrase (in the Xici commentary) reads, "When the sun was centered he made [fast] markets, causing the people under heaven to come, and gathering together the goods under heaven, exchanging and retreating, each getting that which he wished." Edward Shaughnessy, ed. and trans., *I Ching: The Classic of Changes* (New York: Ballantine: 1996), 205.

37. "Zhengquan wupin jiaoyisuo kaimu ji" (Securities and Commodities Exchange opening) *Shenbao*, July 2, 1920

38. Zhang Jian served as Minister of Industry and Commerce and Minister of Agriculture in 1913. Qi Liang, "Zhengquan Jiaoyisuo gaikuang" (Overview of the Shanghai China Merchants' Securities Exchange), in Zhongguo renmin zhengzhi xieshang huiyi, ed., *Jiu shanghai de jiaoyisuo* (Shanghai: Shanghai renmin chubanshe, 1994), 39–42.

39. "Tiyi chexiao zhengquan wupin jiaoyisuo" (Proposal to abolish Security and Commodity exchange) and "Shanghai jiaoyisuo zhi neiqing heru" (Inquiry into Shanghai exchange), *Shenbao*, November 8, 1920. *Huahui* and *fantan* were popular forms of gambling.

40. Qi, "Shanghai Huashang," 39.

41. "Assemblyman Would Close Chinese Stock Exchange," *CP*, November 7, 1920; "More Charges by Assemblyman," *CP*, November 9, 1920; "Chinese Press Comment," *SG*, November 9, 1920. Zhi Wo, "Jiaoyisuo" (Exchange), November 25, 1920; Hollington Tong, "Controversy over Shanghai Stock and Produce Exchange," *MR*, January 22, 1921, 419. Another account suggests Japanese partners received 70,000 of 100,000 shares, or 70 percent of the total. Zhang Yuping, "Go·shi undōki ni okeru Dai Jitao no nihonkan" (Dai Jitao's view of Japan in the May Fourth period), *Chūgoku kenkyū geppō* 64:9 (2010): 1–14.

42. Translated in "Chinese Press Comment," *SG*, November 9, 1920 (slightly abridged here).

43. Hollington Tong, "Controversy"; Goodman, "Things Unheard." Chartered Exchange founders Wang Zhengting and Wang Yiting soon established separate commodities exchanges. *Shangbao,* October 10, 1921.

44. The Tokyo journal, *Finance and Economy,* identified the CSE as "a Sino-Japanese enterprise" with majority interests held by Japan's China Trading Company. Hollington Tong, "Controversy," 418–20.

45. Bryna Goodman, "Things Unheard of East or West: Colonial Contamination and Cultural Purity in Early Chinese Stock Exchanges," in Bryna Goodman and David S.G. Goodman, eds., *Twentieth Century Colonialism and China: The Local, the Everyday, and the World* (London: Routledge, 2012), 62. Xing, *Yu Xiaqing yu Shanghai zhengquan wupin,* 62.

46. Liu Zhiying, *Jindai Shanghai Huashang zhengquan shichang yanjiu* (Research on modern Shanghai's China Merchants' Securities Exchange), (Shanghai: Xuelin chubanshe, 2004), 11–12; Qi Liang, "Shanghai Huashang," 39–41; Goodman, "Things Unheard," 62.

47. Yin Zhentao, "Zhongguo jindai zhengquan shichang jianguan de lishi kaocha—Jiyu lifa yu zhifa shijiao" (Historical survey of China's modern securities market supervison: From the perspective of legislation and law enforcement), *Jinrong pinglun* 2 (2012): 104–114.

48. Liu Zhiying, *Jindai Shanghai,* 12; Zhongguo yinhang zonghang, Zhongguo dier lishi dang'anguan he bian, *Zhongguo yinhang hangshi ziliao huibian,* 1 (1912–1949), (Nanjing: Dang'an chubanshe, 1991), 142; Quotation from He Xuyan, "Xintuo ye zai Zhongguo de xingqi," (Rise of trust companies in China), *Jindaishi yanjiu* 148:4 (2005), 188–190, 195.

49. Bergère, *Golden Age.*

50. Chen Bulei, *Chen Bulei huiyilu* (Chen Bulei memoir), (Shanghai: Ershi shiji chubanshe, 1949), 1:70.

51. Tang, "Benbao chuban zhounian."

52. Zhu Zongliang, "Jiaoyisuo zuzhi wenti" (Exchange organization questions), *Shangbao,* January 26, 1921.

53. Zhu, "Jiaoyisuo zuzhi wenti."

54. Zhong Hui, "Jiaoyisuo yu toji shiye" (Exchanges and speculative enterprise), *Shangbao,* February 22, 1921.

55. List, a predecessor of the German historical (national) school of economics, differentiated between "sound speculation and excessive speculative avarice," advocating some regulation to limit speculation. Eugen Wendler, *Friedrich List (1789–1846): A Visionary Economist with Social Responsibility* (Berlin: Springer, 2014), 193. The term translated as "Asian style speculation" is 亚齐啊推基.

56. Zhong Hui, "Jiaoyisuo yu toji shiye," *Shangbao.*

57. "Xin-jiao chaoliu zhong zhi fangjia," *MGRB,* July 20, 1921; "Xin-jiao sheng zhong dichan feizhang" (Rising land prices amidst the trust-exchange din), *Shangbao,* August 9, 1921; "Jiaoyisuo wadi zhi xilun" (Western discussion of exchange construction), *MGRB,* October 6, 1921.

58. "Micaili tanwu sharen canju: jiaoyisuo yao facai—gongren zhi hao song ming" (Micai alley building collapse tragedy: exchanges profit, workers give lives), *MGRB*, September 8, 1921.

59. Yu, "Min yuan lai," 142.

60. Goodman, "Things Unheard."

61. *Commerce Reports*, May 29, 1922, 588.

62. Since it violated the rule of just one exchange of any type in a given locality, it couldn't claim that it accorded with the Securities Exchange Law. "Shanghai huashang shabu Jiaoyisuo," *Shenbao*, July 1, 1921.

63. "Stock and Produce Exchanges," *NCH*, December 10, 1921.

64. Jiang Hongjiao, *Jiaoyisuo xianxingji*, Serialized in *Xingqi* (Weekly) 1922–1923, reprinted in Tang Zhesheng, ed., *Jiaoyisuo zhenxiang de tanmizhe* (Sleuth of secret stock exchange truths), (Nanjing: Nanjing chubanshe, 1981), 8, 36. Exchange organizers in the 1922 play "Stock Exchange" placed famous people on their board to attract investors. Nian Hua, "Jiaoyisuo," *Youxi shijie* 8 (1922): 4.

65. Xia Juhou, "Benbu xin-jiao shiye zhi guoqu ji xianzai" (Past and present of Shanghai's exchange-trust business), *Shangbao*, October 10, 1921.

66. A US dollar was 1.7 Chinese yuan. Thirty-eight of the exchanges claimed capital above 1 million yuan. The average was around 2 million. Xia Juhou, "Benbu xin-jiao shiye."

67. Hamada Minetarō, *Shina no kōekijo* (Shanghai: Chūka Keizaisha, 1922), 4–5; see also discussion in Zhu Yingui, "1921 nian: Shanghai baofa lanshe jiaoyisuo fengchao" (Explosion of exchanges in 1921 Shanghai), *Jingji cankaobao* 12 (January 2008); the Chinese engineer report is cited in *Commerce Reports* 2:22 (May 29, 1922), 587–588. Estimates of capital vary, but concur that at the height of investment the capital in the exchanges vastly exceeded the amount held by all foreign and native banks in the city. A November 1921 British report estimated 75 million dollars in native and foreign banks in that year and 163 million dollars in the exchanges. PRO FO 228/3175. George Sokolsky estimated 200 million dollars in 140 exchanges in December 1921. G. Gramada (pen name), "Gambling in Produce Exchanges," *North China Daily News*, December 6, 1921. For perspective, a 1924 survey estimated 960 million silver dollars in circulation. Debin Ma, "Money and Monetary System in China in the 19th–20th Century, an Overview," LSE Working Papers 159:12 (2012).

68. Xia, "Benbu xin-jiao shiye"; Hamada, *Shina*, 5.

69. Ma Yinchu, "Shanghai jiaoyisuo qiantu zhi tuice" (Conjectures about the future of Shanghai stock exchanges), *Journal of the Chinese Chamber of Commerce*, Shanghai, 1920.

70. "The March of Trans-Pacific Events," *TP*, 5:2 (August 1921): 41–42.

71. *Yinhang zhoubao* 5:18 (May 17, 1921), in *Shanghai qianzhuang shiliao*, 120.

72. Xing Zhai, "Jiaoyisuo xintuo gongsi za gan" (Thoughts on exchanges and trust companies), *Qianye yuebao* 1:6 (June 1921): 8–9.

73. Nantes, Archives Diplomatiques, Shanghai Consular Papers, Série A, Box 59, letters dated October 25, 1921 and November 7, 1921. Ultimately French authorities banned exchanges in their areas.

74. *SSXB*, August 13, 1921.

75. He, "Xintuo ye zai Zhongguo de xingqi," 195.

76. "Qianye qudi huoyou ru jiaoyisuo yingye" (Native banks ban employees from exchanges), *Shenbao*, October 1, 1921.

77. Lao Pu [Yang Yinhang], "Yinhang yu jiaoyisuo" (Banks and exchanges), *Shenbao*, June 1, 1921.

78. Lao Pu, "Xintuo gongsi zhi boxing," *Shenbao*, June 3, 1921.

79. Lao Pu, "Xintuo gongsi zhi boxing."

80. Xu Cangshui, "Xintuo cun kuan zhi shuoming" (Explanation of funds held in trust), *Yinhang zhoubao* 3:38 (October 14, 1919), 30. See discussion in He, "Xintuo ye zai Zhongguo de xingqi," 193.

81. He, "Xintuo ye zai Zhongguo de xingqi," 194.

82. Several Shanghai banks offered dispersed and unsystematic trust operations a few years prior to the emergence of trust companies in 1921. Two trust companies with small and unsystematic trust operations were established in Dalian in association with the bean trade and agricultural commerce. He, "Xintuo ye zai Zhongguo de xingqi," 188–190.

83. "Zhonghua xintuo gongsi guanggao" (China Trust Company ad), *Shangbao*, March 23, 1921.

84. "Zhonghua xintuo gongsi guanggao."

85. "Guwen jiaoyisuo jian shici xintuo gongsi qishi" (Classical poem on exchanges that doubles as a trust company ad), *Xin shijie* (New world), July 7, 1921. I'm grateful to Qin Shao for helping me interpret this piece.

86. For example, Ge Xiqi, trans. "Xintuo gongsi zhi yewu" (The task of trust companies), *Shenbao*, July 10, 1921; Tong Yi, "Xintuo gongsi yu tuolasi yinhang jiaoyisuo zhi qubie" (Differences between trust companies, trusts, banks and exchanges), *Shenbao*, July 10, 1921.

87. Tong, "Xintuo gongsi yu tuolasi."

88. Xia Juhou, "Ben bu xinjiao shiye zhi guoqu ji xianzai" (The past and present of Shanghai exchanges and trust businesses), *Shangbao*, October 10, 1922.

89. Yu, "Min yuan lai," 142.

90. Mo Dounan, "Xintuo gongsi, zhuzhang gongshangye jineng zhi yi zhong" (Ways trust companies assist industry and commerce), *Shangbao*, May 31, 1921; "Meiguo xintuo gongsi yingye chengji zhi yi ban" (The accomplishments of U.S. trust companies), *Shangbao*, June 23, 1921.

91. Tao Yimin, "Xintuo gongsi yewu xuanze zhi shangquan" (The rights of trust companies to determine their business operations), *Shangbao*, June 30, 1921.

92. "Jinying xintuo shiye zhi yaodian" (Essentials of operating trust companies), *Shangbao*, July 22, 1921.

93. "Xintuofa shang zai chouding zhong ye" (How is it that the trust law is still in planning?), *Shangbao* editorial, July 29, 1921.

94. "Wild-Cat Financing in China," *TP*, 5:2 (August 1921): 42.
95. He, Xintuo ye zai Zhongguo de xingqi," 195–196.
96. "Wild-Cat Financing in China," 42.
97. He, "Xintuo ye zai Zhongguo de xingqi," 195–196. He identifies a second type of trust company, established "to resist fraudulent acquisition of funds by other trust companies." Here the organizers were from the banking sector.
98. "Zhongyi xintuo gongsi kaimu shu gan" (Thoughts on Zhongyi trust company opening), *Shangbao* editorial, September 1, 1921.
99. "Xintuo yanjiu" (Trust business research), *Shangbao*, September 1, 1921.
100. Lu Songyin, comp., *Xintuo gongsi yaolan* (Shanghai: Wenming shuju, 1922).
101. Yang Duanliu, *Xintuo gongsi gailun* (Shanghai: Commercial Press, 1922), 1.
102. "Zhongguo shangye xintuo gufen youxian gongsi gonggao" (China Commercial Trust Company announcement"), *MGRB*, July 12, 1921.
103. "Zhongguo shangye xintuo gongsi guanggao (China Commercial Trust Company advertisement), *Shangbao*, September 4, 1921. The name of prominent speculator Sun Tiansun, Jiang Jieshi's nephew, remains.
104. Hamada, *Shina*, 207.
105. Transcript of Tang's trial, *Shishi xinbao*, December 3, 1921.
106. "Zhengquan jiaoyisuo fa," Wang Enliang, *Jiaoyisuo daquan* (The complete stock exchange), (Shanghai: Jiaoyisuo yuan shuqi yangchengsuo, 1921), not continuously paginated.
107. Lu Shouxian, *Jiaoyisuo xianxingji* (Exchanges unmasked), (Shanghai: Zhonghua tushu jicheng gongsi, 1922), 41–42; Jiang Hongjiao, *Jiaoyisuo xianxingji* (Exchanges unmasked), 1922–1923. The Lu Shouxian volume is a miscellany that compiles anecdotes, fiction, and new articles. The identically titled volume by Jiang Hongjiao is a novel.
108. Zheng, "Cong Xi nüshi," 13.
109. This discrimination gradually changed in Republican law, following the articulation of equal inheritance rights in principle in 1926. Kathryn Bernhardt, *Women and Property in China, 960–1949* (Stanford, CA: Stanford University Press, 1999), 134.
110. *Shibao*, October 14, 16, and 18, 1921.
111. There was also particular focus on primary school teachers as investors.
112. Lu, *Jiaoyisuo xianxingji*, 54, 74.
113. Lu, *Jiaoyisuo xianxingji*, 145–146.
114. For example, Lu, *Jiaoyisuo xianxingji*, 40, 145–146. Zhu Shouju, *Xu xin xiepuchao* (Continuation of new Shanghai tides), (Shanghai: Shanghai guji chubanshe, 1991; reprint, original published 1924) also portrays women trading at the Midnight exchange.
115. Letter of Wei Tingrong, December 23, 1921. Nantes, Archives diplomatiques, Consular Papers, Shanghai, Série A, Box 59.
116. "Yinye jiaoyisuo diyihao gonggao" (Carnal trade exchange, first advertisement), *Jingbao*, July 18, 1921.

117. Lu, *Jiaoyisuo*, 41–42.

118. Cheng, *Haishang nüshuji*.

119. Jiang, *Jiaoyisuo xianxingji*, 159.

120. Richard Von Glahn, *The Sinister Way: The Divine and the Demonic in Chinese Religious Culture* (Berkeley: University of California Press, 2004), 206–209, 234.

121. Von Glahn, *Sinister Way*, 242–246. In the numerous shrines to the god of wealth in the Jiangnan countryside, however, Wulu Caishen continued to be identified with Wutong.

122. Von Glahn, *Sinister Way*, 230, 232–234.

123. Xi Shangzhen, "Jie yinzhai" (Borrowing a covert loan), *DTTK*, 80.

124. Mark Elvin, "Cash and Commerce in the Poems of Qing China," in Nanny Kim and Keiko Nagase-Reimer, eds., *Mining, Monies and Culture in Early Modern Societies: East Asian and Global Perspectives* (Leiden, Netherlands: Brill, 2013), 209–260.

125. Mark McNicholas, *Forgery and Impersonation in Imperial China: Popular Deceptions and the High Qing State* (Seattle: University of Washington Press, 2016), 74.

126. Examples translated from *SSXB, ZHXB*, and *Shenbao* appear in *SG*, November 15, 1919, and February 15, 1921; see also "Caohejing shangmin qing yanjin dubo" (Caohejing businessmen call for the strict banning of gambling), *Shangbao*, April 3, 1922. Lu Xun's depiction of Chinese cultural flaws in "The True Story of Ah Q" satirizes his protagonist's proclivity for gambling and his vulnerability because of it.

127. Circulating Western diagnoses of Chinese "social pathologies" are summed up in Herbert Day Lamson, *Social Pathology in China* (Shanghai: Commercial Press, 1934).

128. Translation from *SSXB*, in *SG*, November 15, 1919, with slight editing.

129. Wu Zude, "Jiu Shanghai de da huahui" (Huahui in old Shanghai), in *Jiu Shanghai de yan du chang* (Drugs, gambling and prostitution in old Shanghai), ed. Shen Feide (Shanghai: Baijia chubanshe, 1988).

130. Frederic Wakeman, *Policing Shanghai, 1927–1937* (Berkeley: University of California Press, 1996), 101.

131. Ning Jennifer Chang, "Purely Sport or a Gambling Disgrace," in Peter Zarrow, ed., *Creating Chinese Modernity: Knowledge and Everyday Life, 1900–1940* (New York: Peter Lang, 2006), 161.

132. "*Chi huahui*" (Denounce *huahui*), *Jingbao*, April 24, 1919.

133. "Toujijia" (Speculators), *Jingbao*, October 27, 1921.

134. Virgil Ho, *Understanding Canton: Rethinking Popular Culture in the Republican Era* (Oxford: Oxford University Press, 2005), 156–193; En Li, "Betting on Empire: A Socio-Cultural History of Gambling in Late Qing China," PhD dissertation, Washington University, St. Louis, 2015.

135. Jin Kang, "Chinese Lottery Business and Korea, 1898–1909," unpublished paper presented at AAS 2016; G. T. Hare, *The Wai Seng Lottery* (Singapore: Government Printing Office, 1895). Hare reproduces lottery tickets marked "*yiben wanli.*"

136. Tsai, *Reading Shenbao,* 46; Brett Sheehan, "The Modernity of Savings, 1900–1937," in Madeleine Yue Dong and Joshua Goldstein, eds., *Everyday Modernity in China* (Seattle: University of Washington Press, 2006), 121–155.

137. Yu Laishan, "Shanghai zhengquanye de chuqi qingkuang" (Early securities trade in Shanghai), in Zhongguo renmin zhengxie shang huiyi et al., eds., *Jiu Shanghai de jiaoyisuo* (Shanghai: Shanghai shi zhengxie wenshi ziliao, 1994), 1–2.

138. Ping Xin, "Jing-Su ren qing qudi caipiao jiaoyisuo," *Shenbao,* April 2, 1922.

139. The "dark curtain" (*heimu*) was a euphemism for hidden unseemliness. It was frequently invoked in reference to Shanghai, where the mixture of glitter and filth, virtue and scandal was "weirdly and horrifyingly illegible as if the city were enveloped" in a dark curtain (He Qiliang, *Feminism, Women's Agency and Communication in Early Twentieth Century China* [Cham, Switzerland: Palgrave, 2018], 233). "Dark curtain literature," also characteristic of Shanghai, exposed hidden manipulations and misbehavior and at the same time exploited the lurid character of its subject matter. May Fourth writers of social fiction criticized "dark curtain" writers as debased, though their subject matter often overlapped.

140. Nian Hua, "Ge da baoguan yu jiaoyisuo" (Major newspapers and exchanges), *Jingbao,* August 9, 1921

141. Jiang was tied to a Shanghai banking venture, which afforded him an insider view of exchanges and exchange personnel.

142. Jiang Hongjiao, *Jiaoyisuo xianxingji,* 36, 45–48.

143. Lu, *Jiaoyisuo xianxingji,* 9–10.

144. Lu, *Jiaoyisuo xianxingji,* 11, 13.

145. Lao Pu, "Feiliao jiaoyisuo" (Fertilizer exchange), *Shenbao,* July 9, 1921.

146. The first Chinese experiment with elections took place in 1909, in the creation of provincial assemblies. For discussion of fraudulent practices and vote purchasing in the early Republic, see Joshua Hill, *Voting as a Rite: A History of Elections in Modern China* (Cambridge, MA: Harvard University Asia Center, 2019), 128–162.

147. The anecdote, and the context of vote purchasing and election challenges at this moment, are recounted in Hill, *Voting as a Rite,* 142–159. In 1921, as Hill notes, "the indirect restricted election system of the late Qing and early Republic lost its last remnants of credibility." The provincial autonomy movement pushed for universal adult suffrage and direct elections for the first time in Chinese history. See also Joshua Hill, "Voter Education: Provincial Autonomy and the Transformation of Chinese Election Law, 1920–1923," *Cross Currents: East Asian History and Culture Review* 7 (June 2013) 11.

148. "Xuanju jiaoyisuo" (Election exchange), *Shenbao,* July 12, 1921.

149. "Xuanju jiaoyisuo."

150. "Xuanjupiao jiaoyisuo kaimu guanggao" (Election Ballot Exchange opening ad), *Shangbao,* February 25, 1921.

151. "Jiao-yi-suo sanzi zhi liyong" (Use of the three characters for "exchange"), *Xinwenbao,* July 15, 1921.

152. "Xintuo sisi," *Jingbao,* June 18, 1921.
153. Chen Xuanying (Chen Qihuai), "Chen Yuanying bainian tiezi" (A notice from Chen Xuanying), *Shangbao,* January 1, 1922.
154. Kang, *Licai jiuguo lun,* 62.
155. See Olga Borokh, "Discussions of 'Controlled Economy' in Republican China," *Far Eastern Affairs* (Moscow) 42:1 (2014): 78–97; Margherita Zanasi, *Saving the Nation: Economic Modernity in Republican China* (Chicago: University of Chicago Press, 2006).
156. Zheng, "Cong Xi nüshi."

Chapter 4. Morality and Justice in an Unsettled Republic

First epigraph: Wu Yong, "Yulun yu falü" (Public opinion and law), *Shenbao,* October 15, 1921.

1. Before a 1906 reform edict, magistrates adjudicated without civil-criminal distinctions or the separation of judicial administration from adjudication. By 1912, approximately 345 modern courts were established (Supreme Court, provincial high courts, county courts of first instance, and urban district courts, with procuratorial courts at each level for criminal cases, following Meiji Japan). Xiaoqun Xu, *Trial of Modernity: Judicial Reform in Early Twentieth-Century China* (Stanford, CA: Stanford University Press, 2008), 29–31.
2. Daniel Botsman, *Punishment and Power in the Making of Modern Japan* (Princeton: Princeton University Press, 2007). Botsman's study is influenced by Michel Foucault's inquiry into the shift from premodern to modern practices of punishment and disciplinary power.
3. Michael Ng, *Legal Transplantation in Early Twentieth-Century China: Practicing Law in Republican Beijing* (London: Routledge, 2014), 1–6.
4. Cited in Li Chen, "Traditionalizing Chinese Law: Symbolic Epistemic Violence in the Discourse of Legal Reform and Modernity in Late Qing China," in Yun Zhao and Michael Ng, eds., *Chinese Legal Reform and the Global Legal Order: Adoption and Adaptation* (Cambridge: Cambridge University Press, 2018), 199 (translation slightly modified).
5. Li, "Traditionalizing Chinese Law," 182. Extraterritoriality remained in place until 1943.
6. The old code contained elements analogous to civil law. Kathryn Bernhardt and Philip Huang, *Civil Law in Qing and Republican China* (Stanford, CA: Stanford University, 1994).
7. Xu Xiaoqun, "Law, Custom, and Social Norms: Civil Adjudications in Qing and Republican China," *Law and History Review* 36:1 (February 2018), 83–84. Reformers seized on the German and Japanese models as pathways for belated comers to a Western-style legal modernity.
8. Francis Zia, "A Chinese Jurist's Views on Extraterritoriality, *WRFE,* December 30, 1922.
9. Zhaoxin Jiang, "Consequential Court and Judicial Leadership: The Unwritten Republican Judicial Tradition in China," in Zhao and Ng, *Chinese Legal Reform,* 289.

10. Jiang, "Consequential Court and Judicial Leadership," 290.

11. Xu, *Trial of Modernity*, 42–43.

12. Benjamin Williams, "Extraterritoriality in China," *WRFE,* August 19, 1922, 450–451.

13. Xu, *Trial of Modernity*, 283–284.

14. Xu Xiaoqun, "The Rule of Law without Due Process: Punishing Robbers and Bandits in Early Twentieth-Century China," *Modern China* 33:2 (April 2007): 230–257; Klaus Mühlhahn, *Criminal Justice in China* (Cambridge, MA: Harvard University Press, 2009), 290. Military jurisdiction, a feature of modernizing reforms, followed German and Japanese models of military professionalization. Nicolas Schillinger, *The Body and Military Masculinity in Late Qing and Early Republican China* (Lanham, MD: Lexington Books, 2016), 122.

15. Chinese magistrates administered Chinese law to Chinese subjects in the foreign settlements; the Mixed Courts' procedures and foreign assessors insulated them from Chinese control. After 1912, the foreign assessors exercised increasing influence. Anatol Kotenev, *Shanghai: Its Mixed Court and Council* (Shanghai: *North China Daily News,* 1925).

16. "Chinese Eager to End Foreign Authority in their Courts," *China Review* 3 (December 1922): 227.

17. Bryna Goodman and David S. G. Goodman, "Introduction: Colonialism and China," in Bryna Goodman, ed., with David S. G. Goodman, *Twentieth-Century Colonialism: Localities, the Everyday, and the World* (London: Routledge, 2012). Thomas B. Stephens, *Order and Discipline in China: The Shanghai Mixed Court, 1911–1927* (Seattle: University of Washington Press, 1992); Teemu Ruskola, "Colonialism without Colonies: On the Extraterritorial Jurisprudence of the U.S. Court for China," *Law and Contemporary Problems* 17 (2008): 217; Charles Sumner Lobinger, ed., *Extraterritorial Cases, U.S. Court for China* (Manila: Bureau of Printing, 1920), vol. 1.

18. Tahirih Lee, "Risky Business: Courts, Culture, and the Marketplace," *University of Miami Law Review* 47 (1993): 1362; Pär Cassel, *Grounds of Judgment: Extraterritoriality and Imperial Power in Nineteenth-Century China and Japan* (Oxford: Oxford University Press, 2012). Cassel notes that the foreign courts were not "simple implants," but "products of a peculiar institutional environment" shaped by Chinese law and institutions, 64.

19. Quotation of Weijen Chang, cited in Pierre-Étienne Will, "Adjudicating Grievances and Educating the Populace: Reflections Based on Nineteenth-Century Anthologies of Judgments," *Zhongguo shixue* 24 (2014): 4–7.

20. The 1929–1930 civil code relied on custom in numerous matters. Xu, "Law, Custom," 82–84, 87–88, 98.

21. Paul Katz, *Divine Justice: Religion and the Development of Chinese Legal Culture* (London: Routledge, 2009); Margaret B. Wan, "Court Case Ballads: Popular Ideals of Justice in Late Qing and Republican China," in Li Chen and Madeleine Zelin, eds., *Chinese Law: Knowledge, Practice, and Transformation* (Leiden, Netherlands: Brill, 2018), 287–320; Cynthia Brokaw, *The Ledgers of Merit and Demerit: Social Change and Moral order*

in Late Imperial China (Princeton: Princeton University Press, 1991); Jan
Kiely, "Shanghai Public Moralist Nie Qijie and Morality Book Publication
Projects in Republican China," *Twentieth-Century China* 36:1 (January 2011)
4–22.

22. Pierre-Étienne Will, "Developing Forensic Knowledge through Cases in the
Qing Dynasty," in Charlotte Furth, Judith Zeitlin, and Ping-chen Hsiung,
eds., *Thinking with Cases: Specialist Knowledge in Chinese Cultural History* (Honolulu: University of Hawaii Press, 2007), 72. This was the reasoning behind the elaboration of forensic investigative procedures to perfect
the administration of justice in capital cases, as exemplified in Song Ci's
thirteenth-century handbook, *Collected Writings on the Washing Away of
Wrongs* (Xiyuan jilu), and later Yuan and Qing dynasty versions with similar titles.

23. Yao Gonghe, *Shanghai xianhua* (Idle talk about Shanghai), (reprint; Shanghai:
Shanghai gujichubanshe, 1989), 46. The forms were not easily distinguishable even for legal scribes. See the discussion in Xu, *Trial of Modernity*, 71.

24. For a discussion of Republican-era efforts to disseminate popularized understandings of modern knowledge in forensic medicine, see Daniel Asen,
Death in Beijing: Murder and Forensic Science in Republican China (Cambridge, UK: Cambridge University Press, 2016), p. 128.

25. Wu Ziyong, "Minlü xinglü zhi qubie" (Civil and criminal law distinctions),
Shenbao, September 3, 1921.

26. Hu Xia and Huang Yan, eds., *Susong changshi* (Basic lawsuit knowledge),
(Shanghai: Shangwu yinshuguan, 1922), preface; see also *Susong xuzhi*
(Necessary lawsuit knowledge), (Shanghai: Shangwu yinshuguan, 1917);
Herbert Huey, "Law and Social Attitudes in 1920s Shanghai," *Hong Kong
Law Journal* 14:3 (1984): 306–322.

27. Yun Shi, *Funü zhi baimian guan* (One hundred views of women), (Shanghai:
Wenyi bianyishe, 1920; reprint 1927), 2:41. The Hungry Ghost Festival
(*Yulanpen* or *Zhongyuan jie*) takes place during the seventh lunar month,
when ghosts were thought to roam. The living propitiated the dead with offerings of food and Daoist and Buddhist rituals to relieve suffering and restore balance.

28. Gloria Davies, *Lu Xun's Revolution: Writing in a Time of Violence* (Cambridge, MA: Harvard University Press, 2013), 300–302. Davies suggests
that when he was close to death, Lu Xun aimed to turn the Hanged Woman
into "a parting image of his critical inquiry," 302.

29. "She ping" (editorial), *Xiandai funü* supplement, SSXB, November 16,
1921.

30. XSB, September 17, 1922.

31. Fei Wu, *Suicide and Justice: A Chinese Perspective* (Abingdon, UK: Routledge, 2010).

32. Chen Zhongtao, "Huaji wenda" (Humorous Q&A), *Shenbao*, October 18,
1922.

33. Wu Yugong, *Zisha zhi nüshuji: Xi Shangzhen canshi* (Tragic history of Xi
Shangzhen), (Shanghai: Zhongguo diyi shuju, 1922), 4.

34. Bryna Goodman, *Native Place, City and Nation: Regional Networks and Identities in Shanghai, 1853–1937* (Berkeley: University of California Press, 1995), 111–117. Dongting association records for the early 1920s list more than thirty Xi lineage members as members and directors. SMA Q117-9-33, Dongting dongshan tongxianghui yibu.

35. *MGRB*, September 20, 1922. Shanghai native-place associations had leverage in home areas because they were a pipeline of funds, charitable assistance and other resources for the native place. Goodman, *Native Place, City and Nation.*

36. SMA Q118-9-12, "Chaozhou huiguan yi'an beicha" (Chaozhou *huiguan* meeting notes), September–December 1922.

37. SMA Q117-9-33 (1921–1923).

38. Charles Sumner Lobinger, *Twenty Years in the Judiciary* (Shanghai: Far Eastern American Bar Association, 1922), 28.

39. *Dongting dongshan lüHu tongxianghui sanshi zhounian te'kan* (Thirty year commemorative edition of Dongting Sojourners' association), (Shanghai: Dongting dongshan lüHu tongxianghui, 1944), 119.

40. SMA Q117-9-33 (1921–1923).

41. "Dongting tongxianghui dai wei suyuan" (Dongting association speaks grievance), *Shenbao*, September 13, 1922. (See Chapter 1.)

42. Xi may have promised a note she failed to leave. Alternatively, she may have written something awkward (in which case her family may have kept it secret). Insistence upon a missing note may also have been compensatory, in recognition of insufficient evidence to support a strong claim against Tang.

43. Yan You, "Xi-Tang an zhong zhi yiwen" (Anecdote in Xi-Tang case), *SSXB*, September 22, 1922

44. *MGRB*, September 24, 1922; *CP*, November 14, 1922. "Chinese Files Libel Suits," *WRFE*, September 30, 1922; Charles Sumner Lobinger, comp. and ed., *Extraterritorial Cases, U.S. Court for China* (Manila: Bureau of Printing, 1920), vol. 1. Fessenden enjoyed close ties to Charles Lobinger, judge of the US Court for China. Both were Freemasons. Fessenden was toastmaster at Lobinger's twentieth-anniversary celebration as judge in the year of the Xi case. Lobinger, *Twenty Years in the Judiciary*, 28.

45. Chen Yaodong, "Tang nai shi toujijia" (Tang is indeed a speculator), *SSXB*, October 3, 1922.

46. *Dongting dongshan lüHu tongxianghui di shi'er ci baogaoshu*, 29.

47. SMA Q117-9-3 (1922). The meeting date is unclear, but the association published a second letter to members (mentioning legal counsel) on September 15, 1922. "Dongting dongshan tongxianghui yanjing yu deng han" (Dongting East Mountain association letter), *Shenbao*, September 15, 1922.

48. "Dr. Tong Kidnapped," *NCDN*, November 14, 1922; "Dr. F. C. Tong Arrested by Chinese Police," *CP*, November 14, 1922; quotation from *Dongting dongshan lüHu tongxianghui di shi'er ci baogaoshu*, 79.

49. *Weekly Review of the Far East* 23 (December 2, 1922); "Xi-Tang an sihui furan" (Xi-Tang case reignites), *SSXB*, November, 17, 1922; "Tang Jiezhi

beji jianting xuzhi," "*MGRB,* November 14, 1922; She Ying, "Xi an fuhuo" (Xi case revives), *ZHXB,* November 15, 1922.

50. "Charges of Arms Deal Are Bought against F. C. Tong," *CP,* November 18, 1922. These charges, briefly noted in numerous news reports, contained no reference to date, location or context.

51. Hoover Institution Archives, Sokolsky Papers, 369. Clipping file marked "F. C. Tong." "A Chinese Prison," *NCDN,* date-stamped November 21, 1922.

52. The abolition of extraterritoriality was the primary impetus for Qing legal reform, but Qing authorities refrained from publicizing particular cases or enlisting the press. Par Cassel, *Grounds of Judgment,* 160–163. The Washington Naval Conference (November 1921–February 1922) established treaties to develop a postwar order among Japan, Great Britain, the United States, and France, involving naval armaments, guarantees for Japanese security, and limitations on Japanese influence. Wesley R. Fishel, *The End of Extraterritoriality in China* (Berkeley: University of California Press, 1952).

53. Commission on Extraterritoriality, ed., *Provisional Code of the Republic of China* (Peking: Commission on Extraterritoriality, 1923), preface.

54. "Lingshi caipanquan" (Consular jurisdiction), *Shangbao,* May 25, 1921; quotation from "Ni-Liu shi an yi ting yu sifa quan guanxi" (Relation of transfer of Ni-Liu shi case to judicial rights), *Shangbao,* March 28, 1922.

55. "Zongshanghui fushe zhi falü yanjiuhui kaihui" (Meeting of the legal research committee of the Chamber of Commerce), *Shangbao,* May 4, 1921.

56. "Lüshi gonghui dingqi zhi tanhuahui ji" (Lawyer's association sets date for meeting) *Shangbao,* May 16, 1921; "Street Unions Here Ask Return of Mixed Court," *CP,* November 25, 1922.

57. Chen Zemin, "Fei jiancha zhidu zhi yundong" (Procuratorial-system abolition movement), (Shanghai, 1922), pamphlet; "Lüshi gonghui dingqi zonghui zhi tanhuahuiji" (Lawyer's association meeting), *Shangbao,* May 16, 1921; "Prominent Chinese Seek Judicial Reform Here," *CP,* May 4, 1921.

58. "Quanguo sifahuiyi zhuzhi dagang cao'an" (Draft national judicial conference statement), *Shenbao,* July 25, 1922; "Judicial Reform Discussed by Meeting Here," *CP,* September 29, 1922; "Sifa huiyi tongguo ge yi'an" (Resolutions of the judicial meeting), *MGRB,* October 7, 1922; "Quanguo sifa huiyi shimoji" (National judicial conference), *XWB,* October 10, 1922.

59. Xu Xiaoqun, *Trial of Modernity.*

60. Jiang, "Consequential," 292.

61. "Kaocha sifa zhuangkuang zhong zhi ganxiang" (Thoughts on examining judiciary), *Shangbao,* March 22, 1922.

62. "Kaocha sifa zhuangkuang zhong zhi ganxiang." The sensational trial of the gambler Yan Ruisheng for murder of the Shanghai courtesan Wang Lianying began in the Mixed Court. Yan was then extradited to the military court without a clear rationale. The other cases mentioned involved the death of Ni Tongjia once he was transferred spuriously to military custody, and murder and rape cases that outside military jurisdiction.

63. *MGRB,* November 15, 16, 19, 20, 1922; *WRFE,* December 2, 1922; "Jianting qisu Xi Shangzhen an yuanwen" (Xi Shangzhen prosecution docu-

ment), *Shenbao*, November 27, 1922. Such conflicts of jurisdiction were not uncommon.

64. PRO FO 228.3176 (Concessions and Settlement, Shanghai 1922–1925), Minutes of First Consular Body Meeting in 1923 (January), "Arrest of Dr. F. C. Tong."

65. JWRB IO 2882, Reports of July 5 and July 23, 1919; February 6, 1920, articulate concerns about possible Guomindang, revolutionary, and Bolshevik ties.

66. Discussion and quotation below of indictment based on "Jianting qisu Xi Shangzhen an yuanwen" (Original text of Xi indictment), *Shenbao*, November 27, 1922. The language of the indictment in some places—but inconsistently—specifies *yang yuan*, or Mexican silver dollar, noting that at 12.5 Mexican silver dollars per share, this totaled 4,500 *yang yuan*. Altogether, the indictment text specifies that Tang was responsible for a total sum of 5,000 dollars. Reportage on the indictment was also inconsistent in the specification of currency. Mexican silver dollars, which entered China in the nineteenth century, were in daily use for a variety of domestic and other transactions in the early 1920s, as "the only coin the banks will accept at face value to the exclusion of all others." Charles W. Mason, "The Changing Chinese 'Cash,'" *China Review (CR)* 3 (December 1922): 215–216, 241–243.

67. "Jianting qisu Xi Shangzhen an yuanwen." The inclusion of this crime as article 320 of the Provisional Criminal Code of the Republic of China was a carryover from the Qing code (Provisional Criminal Code, 1923).

68. It was common, in financial documents, to identify an account with the character *ji* (記)in place of the last character of a name, hence Xi Shangji in place of Xi Shangzhen. This would have been obvious to anyone familiar with financial transactions. There was no connection between the Shangbao (上寶) Bank and the Shangbao (商報) newspaper

69. "Any person who with intent to obtain property for himself or any third party deceitfully or by way of threat causes any other person to deliver the property to him is said to have committed cheating or fraud and shall be liable to penal servitude for a term of the third, fourth, or fifth degree." Ministry of Justice, Peking, *The Provisional Criminal Code of the Republic of China, trans.* T. T. Yuen and Tachuen S. K. Loh (Paris: Impr. De Vaugirard, 1915), 94. This official translation closely follows the Chinese text in Asatarō Okada, ed., *Zhonghua minguo zhanxing xin xinglü* (New provisional criminal code of Republic of China), (Shanghai: Guomin daxue, 1913), 101.

70. Hoover Institution Archives, Sokolsky Papers, 369. Clipping file marked "F. C. Tong." "Mother of Girl Suicide Tells Story of F.C. Tong Deals as His Trial Starts," *China Press* clipping stamped December 3, 1922.

71. "Chinese Theater to Present Play based on Life of Suicide," *CP*, December 5, 1922.

72. See for example, *SSXB, MGRB, Shenbao, SZRB*. Only once previously had newspapers published trial transcripts from the Shanghai district court, in the parricide case of Zhang Xinsheng: "Zuori kai xun nilun an xiangji" (Detailed account of yesterday's parricide trial hearing), *Shenbao*, June 14, 1921. The various newspaper transcripts are quite similar but not identical,

possibly because of different styles of note taking. Thus the narrative here relies on multiple accounts.

73. *SSZB*, December 3, 1922; *CP*, December 9, 1922. Qin was a founding member of the Shanghai Lawyers' Association and active in the movement for Mixed Court rendition and judicial independence. Frank Ching, *Ancestors: 900 Years in the Life of a Chinese Family* (London: Pan Books, 1988), 403–410.

74. Wu, *Zisha zhi nüshuji*, 6.

75. Hoover Institution Archives, "Mother of Girl Suicide Tells Story."

76. "Xi Shangzhen an kai shen ji xiang" (Detailed account of Xi case), *Shenbao*, December 3, 1922.

77. Xi's older sister, who was aged twenty-eight, also testified but added little. She had herself purchased one hundred shares (for 1,250 yuan), which she received in the seventh lunar month. "Xi-Tang an diyici kaishen ji" (Record of first Xi-Tang hearing), *SSXB*, December 3, 1922.

78. "Xi-Tang an diyici kaishen ji."

79. Police records indicate that it was Sokolsky who actually made this call at Tang's behest, Sokolsky does not appear in the trial testimony or Chinese discussions of the case.

80. This narrative accounts for Xi's unexplained possession of Hu-Hai stock. The indictment stated improbably that Tang had sold Xi both his own trust company stock and also shares from the Hu-Hai exchange, with which he had no connection.

81. Although its name was a homonym for the name of the newspaper, the bank had no connection to the *Journal of Commerce*. (The characters in the names are different.)

82. "Xi-Tang an kai shen ji" (Xi-Tang trial opens), *Shenbao*, December 3, 1922.

83. "Xi-Tang an kai shen ji." Li Identified *Shangbao* editors Qiu Youxin and Shen Zhonghua as people who could corroborate financial questions.

84. The missing witnesses were K. P. Wang and Ying Jishen, who telegraphed that he would return to Shanghai in three days. "Magistrate Tu Turns Detective in Tong Trial, Rules Out Evidence: Drama Enacted in Crowded Courtroom as Mother of Suicide Denounces Accused," *CP*, December 9, 1922.

85. *CP*, December 9, 1922.

86. "Magistrate Tu Turns Detective in Tong Trial"; "Xi Shangzhen an zuori bianlun zongjie" (Concluding arguments in Xi Shangzhen hearing yesterday), *MGRB*, December 9, 1922. The character "ji" (記) can mean sign, mark, or account. Its appearance in this context, in place of Xi Shangzhen's full name, was a convention of accounting or registration. The defense took for granted that Xi Shangji referred to Xi Shangzhen.

87. Neither the indictment nor verdict illuminate these questions about Xi's calligraphy.

88. *Shenbao*, December 9, 1922; *MGRB*, December 9, 1922.

89. The reference here is to seals or chops that individuals used to create a stamped signature, used in official documents. These could be different shapes, square or round.

90. "Magistrate Tu Turns Detective in Tong Trial," *CP*, December 9, 1922. The mother's earlier testimony indicated that family members had indeed given Xi their money and were thus her creditors. Here she determinedly deflects guilt from the family for exerting pressure. Her argument also ignores the fact that the shares had lost value and thus could not be disposed of at a profit.

91. *MGRB*, December 9, 1922, "Magistrate Tu Turns Detective in Tong Trial."

92. "Xi Shangzhen an zuo ri bianlun zongjie (Yesterday's summation in Xi case)," *MGRB*, December 9.

93. This is an abridged composite from the following: "Xi Shangzhen an zuori bianlun zonjie" (Concluding arguments in Xi Shangzhen hearing yesterday), *MGRB*, December 9, 1922; "Tang Jiezhi bianhu liyou" (Tang's defense), *Shenbao*, December 10, 1922; Zhou Dongbai, *Quanguo lüshi ming'an huilan* (Famous cases of the nation's lawyers), (Shanghai: Shijie shuju, 1923), 8:6–7.

94. The exception was the gratuitous articulation of the gendered assumption that the word of a man of status was more reliable than the testimony of three women "colluding." This went without comment in the avid press discussion of the trial.

95. "Xi Shangzhen an zuori" (Concluding arguments); "Tang Jiezhi zhi bianhu" (Tang's defense), *Shenbao*.

96. Janet Theiss, "Elite Engagement with the Judicial System in the Qing and Its Implications for Legal Practice and Legal Principle," in Chen Li and Madeleine Zelin, eds., *Chinese Law: Knowledge, Practice and Transformation, 1530s to 1950s* (Leiden, Netherlands: Brill, 2015), 124–147; Madeleine Yue Dong, "Communities and Communication: A Study of the Case of Yang Naiwu, 1873–1877," *Late Imperial China* 16:1 (June 1995): 79–119; Bryna Goodman, *Native Place*, 111–117; Natascha Vittinghoff, "Readers, Publishers and Officials in the Contest for a Public Voice and the Rise of a Modern Press in Late Qing China," *T'oung Pao* 87 (2001): 393–455.

97. Goodman, "Being Public"; Goodman, "Democratic Calisthenics"; John Fitzgerald, "Equality, Modernity, and Gender in Chinese Nationalism," in Doris Croissant, Catherine Vance Yeh, et al., eds., *Performing Nation: Gender Politics in Literature, Theater, and the Visual Arts of China and Japan* (Leiden. Netherlands: Brill, 2008), 19–54.

98. "Xi Shangzhen an zhi Tang Jiezhi beibu," *Shenbao*, November 13, 1922.

99. The Dongting association was traditionalistic by inclination, as a relatively conservative and unreformed native-place association that—in contrast to reformed native-place associations—hewed to older concerns and language. Their strategic revision of their language for instrumental purposes, was visible in their meeting minutes, as was their preferential use of older language.

100. "Fating shenli Xi an zhi feinan sheng" (Censure of court in Xi case), *Shenbao*, December 10, 1922.

101. "Fating shenli Xi an zhi feinan sheng."

102. Feng referenced the trial and imprisonment of nine Fujianese student activists in Shanghai on dubious charges by the Shanghai district court. Nineteen

Shanghai public associations, including Fujian and Guangdong associations, associations of overseas Chinese, overseas students, commercial street unions, the Fujian self-government association, a women's federation, the Fujian student association, the national students association, and two worker associations protested in summer 1922, achieving the release of the surviving students. "Yin falü li zheng min xuesheng an" (Legal efforts in the Fujian student case) MGRB, January 4, 1921; "Ge tuanti qing shi min xuesheng" (Groups ask for release of Fujian students), *Shangbao,* June 9, 1922.

103. Shanghai shi gongshangye lianhehui archives. Shanghai zongshanghui dang'an (Shanghai Chamber of Commerce archives). 200-1-008. Shanghai zongshanghui, benhui yi'an lu. Meeting of December 9, 1922.

104. Shanghai zongshanghui dang'an. 200-1-008. Meeting of December 9, 1922.

105. Qiu Youxin, "Minghu sifa duli" (Alas judicial independence), *Shangbao,* December 9, 1922.

106. Qiu, "Minghu sifa duli." This comment suggests prior consultation with the Fujian associations, possibly facilitated by prior cooperation on the Fujian student case.

107. Also present, Guangdong Commercial Association and Dapu sojourners association. "Ge tuanti jinri zai Guang-Zhao gongsuo kaihui" (Groups meet today at Guang-Zhao gongsuo), *Shenbao,* December 10, 1922; "Liang gongtuan dui Tang an fayan" (Two groups speak in Tang case), *MGRB,* December 10, 1922.

108. "Chengqing Shanghai faguan" (Exposing Shanghai judges), *Shangbao,* December 10, 1922.

109. "Guangzhao gongsuo wei Xi an lianxi huiyi ji" (Guang-Zhao gongsuo federated meeting on Xi case), *Shenbao,* December 11, 1922; "Ge tuanti dui Tang an zhi ji'ang" (Indignation of groups in Tang case), *MGRB,* December 11, 1922. Represented were Ningbo, Fujian, Zhaoqing, Dapu sojourner associations, Guangdong Commercial Association, the Guangdong Self-Government Association, Chinese Labor Union; Federation of Commercial Street Unions, seventeen individual street unions; a shoe trade association; and a "Comrade's promise-keeping association" of uncertain composition.

110. "Ge tuanti dui Tang an zhi ji'ang"; "Three Local Bodies Come to Aid of Dr. F .C. Tong," *CP,* December 12, 1922.

111. Goodman, "Being Public," 45–88.

112. "Ge tuanti dui Tang an zhi ji'ang."

113. "Ge tuanti dui Tang an zhi ji'ang"; "Guang-Zhao gongsuo wei Xi an lianxi huiyi ji" (Guang-Zhao gongsuo federated meeting on Xi case), *Shenbao,* December 11, 1922.

114. "Gai liang sifa zhi jihui" (Opportunity to reform judiciary), *Shangbao,* December 11, 1922. Jury supervision of judges expresses a distinctively populist interpretation of the jury system.

115. SMA, *JWRB,* Daily Report for December 12, 1922; "Justice Mei of District Court Turns Down Requests," *CP,* December 12, 1922. (Clipping in Sokolsky Files.)

116. "Faguan zhi yijian" (Views of judges), *ZHXB*, December 12, 1922.
117. "Dissension Expressed," *CP*, December 12, 1922. (Clipping in Sokolsky Files.)
118. "Xi an lianxihui bieqi jiufen" (Struggle in federated meeting on Xi case), *Shenbao*, December 12, 1922; "Tang an lianxihui neibu jiufen" (Internal struggle in Tang case meeting), *MGRB*, December 12, 1922.
119. "Weichi sifa zhi Tang an zhuzhang" (Support for judiciary in Tang case), *MGRB*, December 13, 1922.
120. "Tang an panjueshu zhi quanwen" (Text of Tang verdict), *MGRB*, December 18, 1922.
121. "Tang an panjueshu zhi quanwen."
122. *MGRB*, December 24, 1922.
123. *MGRB*, December 12, 1922; *JWRB*, Daily Report of December 14, 1922.
124. "Guang-Zhao gongsuo ming Tang an bu ping," *MGRB*, December 24, 1922. *SSXB*, December 24, 1922.
125. Shanghai shi gongshangye lianhehui. Archives. Shanghai zongshanghui dang'an. 200-1-008 Shanghai zongshanghui, benhui yi'an lu. Meeting of December 23, 1922
126. Shanghai zongshanghui, benhui yi'an lu, December 23, 1922.
127. Shanghai zongshanghui, benhui yi'an lu.
128. Shanghai zongshanghui, benhui yi'an lu.
129. Shanghai zongshanghui, benhui yi'an lu.
130. Shanghai zongshanghui, benhui yi'an lu.
131. Shanghai zongshanghui, benhui yi'an lu.
132. The Chinese phrasing of Fang's comment is: 湯之招怨固有別種原因。既席上珍之死亦有別種原因。而湯遂適逢其會。
133. Shanghai zongshanghui, benhui yi'an lu.
134. Quotation from "Power of Dr. Sun Growing in China," *CR*, September 1921, 150. See also "Constitutionalists in South Say Tokyo Sends Arms and Men to Guangxi Militarists," *CR*, August 1921, 88. The *Shangbao* covered this Ogawa Maru affair throughout June and July 1921, and published numerous editorials on the topic. See especially *Shangbao*, June 30, 1921, July 1, 1921, July 12, 1921, and July 14, 1921. See also *Shanhai*, June 27, 1921; July 25, 1921
135. There was no parallel discussion of the need to respond to the Dongting association, which was less prominent within the Chamber and had no representatives on the Chamber board.
136. "Guang-Zhao gongsuo deng xu qing zhuchu Tang an" (Guangzhao gongsuo, others support Tang, cont'd.), *MGRB*, December 26, 1922.
137. "Zhongshan xiansheng fu Guang-Zhao gongsuo deng ge tuanti han" (Sun Yat-sen Responds to Guang-Zhao, Other Groups), *MGRB*, December 31, 1922.
138. "Zongshanghui dui Tang'an zhi taidu" (Attitude of Chamber of Commerce regarding Tang case), *Shenzhou ribao*, December 29, 1922.
139. "Nüzi canzheng xiejin dahui" (Meeting of Society for Women's Participation in Government) *MGRB*, December 26, 1922.

140. *Shanhai,* November 27, 1922, 509. The rumor of arms trafficking appears as an inversion (or imaginative reverse projection) of Tang's earlier embarrassing exposure of He Fenglin's facilitation of the Japanese arms shipment to the Guangxi clique. No evidence was adduced in regard to any of these charges. Tang's May Fourth and anti-Japanese activism made him a target of the extreme nationalist editorial line of the Japanese paper *Shanhai.*

141. "Tang Jiezhi shangsu an shenli ji" (Tang's appeal hearing), *Shenbao,* January 7, 1923; "Tang an zhao yuanpan" (Tang case follows original verdict), *MGRB,* February 24, 1923; "Xi Shangzhen an zhi zuoxun" (News yesterday of Xi case), *Shenbao,* August 23, 1923; "Xi Shangzhen an chong tiqi" (Xi case raised again)," *MGRB,* August 10, 1928.

142. Zhou, Quanguo lüshu ming'an huilan, preface.

143. Zhou, Quanguo lüshu ming'an huilan, 8:1.

144. Zhou, *Quanguo lüshi ming'an huilan,* 8:1.

145. PRO FO 228/3291 (Shanghai Intelligence Report, September 1921).

146. Editorial, *ZHXB,* September 18, 1922.

147. *XSB,* September 17, 1922, special supplement.

148. "Xiao Shenbao" (Special Xi-Tang issue), *XSB,* September 17, 1922.

149. *Shenbao,* September 16, 1922.

150. *SSXB,* December 26, 1922.

151. Hui Shi "Xi nüshi zisha zhi daode wenti," *XSB,* November 17, 1922. A second article in this special issue noted, "Tang's statement already bears the name of a lawyer's office. Everyone should pay attention."

152. *ZHXB,* November 15, 1922

153. *SSXB,* September 28, 1922, "Qingguang" supplement.

154. "Xi Tang an huifu ran" (Xi-Tang Case Reignites), *SSXB,* November 17, 1922.

155. Zhou, *Quanguo lüshi ming'an huilan,* preface.

156. Cha Mengci, "Nüzi jiaoyu de quexian" (Limitations of Female Education), *ZHXB,* reprinted in MGRB, September 16, 1922.

157. Shanghai zongshanghui, benhui yi'an lu, December 9, 1922.

158. *SSXB,* December 9, 1922.

159. "Zhongshan xiansheng fu Guang-Zhao gongsuo deng ge tuanti han," MGRB, December 31, 1922.

160. *ZHXB* editorial, September 18, 1922.

161. On attentiveness to evidence in Qing legal tradition see Li Chen, "Legal Specialists and Judicial Administration in Late Imperial China, 1651–1911," *Late Imperial China* 33:1 (June 2012): 27–31.

162. "Tang Jiezhi shangsu an shenli ji" (Tang Jiezhi's Appeal), *Shenbao,* January 7, 1923.

163. Goodman, "Things Unheard."

164. Dongbai, *Quanguo lüshi ming'an huilan,* 19 (appeal document, January 6, 1923).

165. Quinn Doyle Javers, "Conflict, Community, and Crime in Fin-de-Siecle Sichuan," PhD dissertation, Stanford University, 2012, chap. 4.

166. "Xi Fang shi qing dui Tang Jiezhi zhi caichan" (Madam Xi's request in regard to the property of Tang Jiezhi), *Shangbao,* April 8, 1924.

167. Communal institutions in the Republic included but also exceeded the legally engaged elites that Janet Theiss examined in the late Qing. Theiss, "Elite Engagement with the Judicial System in the Qing."

168. Benjamin Liebman, "A Return to Populist Legality? Historical Legacies and Legal Reform," Sebastian Heilmann and Elizabeth Perry, eds, *Mao's Invisible Hand: The Political Foundations of Adaptive Governance in China* (Cambridge, MA: Harvard University Asia Center, 2011), 165–200.

169. Although Zhang Xinsheng's parricide, in the May Fourth Era, suggested to conservatives the decline of family values in the May Fourth era, it is nonetheless challenging, in the moment of media embrace of New Culture to imagine a public embrace of filial assassination in the 1920s equivalent to the public sympathy revealed in Lean's study for Shi Jianqiao's 1935 assassination of the warlord Sun Chuanfang. Eugenia Lean, *Public Passions: The Trial of Shi Jianqiao and the Rise of Popular Sympathy in Republican China* (Berkeley: University of California Press, 2007).

170. See Bryna Goodman, "Review of Eugenia Lean, *Public Passions: The Trial of Shi Jianqiao and the Rise of Popular Sympathy in Republican China,*" *Journal of Asian Studies* 67:3 (August 2008): 1063–1065.

171. "Faguan zhi guannian" (The judge's views), *ZHXB,* December 12, 1922.

172. *ZHXB,* December 12, 1922. His musings were tone-deaf in terms of contemporary anti-Japanese sentiment: "Recently the Japanese Consul General spoke to me about [a case in which outsiders] interfered, something he found especially regrettable." Quoting the Japanese Consul only made sense in terms of solicitude for He Fenglin.

173. *SSXB,* December 12, 1922.

174. *ZHXB,* December 11, 1922.

175. *Shangbao,* December 14, 1922.

176. Margaret Wan, "Court Case Ballads: Popular Ideals of Justice in Late Qing and Republican China," in Li Chen and Madeleine Zelin, eds, *Chinese Law: Knowledge, Practice, and Transformation, 1530s to 1950s* (Leiden, Netherlands: Brill, 2015), 287–320.

177. Wu Yong, "Yulun yu falü" (Public opinion and law), editorial, *Shenbao,* October 15, 1921.

178. Yves Chevrier, "Elusive Democracy," in Mireille Delmas-Marty and Pierre-Etienne Will, eds., *China, Democracy, and Law: A Historical and Contemporary Approach* (Leiden, Netherlands: Brill, 2012), 459–477. Chevrier also uses the term "deconstructed political form."

Chapter 5. A Public without a Republic?

Epigraphs: Tang Jiezhi, "Tuanti yundong za ping," (Miscellaneous comments on the group movement), *Shangbao,* March 20, 1922; Jacques Revel, "Micro-analyse et construction du social," in Jacques Revel, ed., *Jeux d'echelles: La micro-analyse à l'expérience* (Paris: Gallimard-Le Seuil, 1996), 26.

1. Approximately 50 stock exchanges emerged in Hangzhou, Ningbo, Hankou, Suzhou, Nanchang, Nantong, Tianjin, and other cities. Zhongguo renmin

yinhang, ed., *Jindai Zhongguo de jinrong shichang* (Modern China's financial markets), (Beijing: Zhongguo jinrong chubanshe, 1989), 443.

2. Robert Darnton and Daniel Roche, eds., *Revolution in Print: The Press in France, 1775–1800* (Berkeley: University of California Press, 1989), xiii. See also Bryna Goodman, "Being Public: The Politics of Representation in 1918 Shanghai," *Harvard Journal of Asiatic Studies* 60:1 (June 2000): 45–88.

3. *NCDN*, November 23, 1922. The full quotation appears as an epigraph in Chapter 1.

4. "Who Will Lift The Chinese Curtain?" MG, October 4, 1919, 209 (excerpted translation from *Shenbao*, retitled to pique Shanghai's Anglo-American readers' interests). The *Shenbao* editorial and its reproduction in the *Municipal Gazette* aptly illustrate the co-production of Orientalist discourse in the contact zone, a process that Arif Dirlik insightfully observed to be "the product of an unfolding relationship" that "in some basic ways required the participation of 'orientals' for its legitimation." In this example, the *Shenbao*'s modern nationalist "self-orientalization" of Chinese culture served the purpose of domestic political critique. Such statements, translated in the Western press served to stamp such essentialism with native authenticity. Arif Dirlik, "Chinese History and the Question of Orientalism," *History and Theory* 35:4 (1996): 99, 112.

5. Terry Narramore, "Illusions of Autonomy? Journalism, Commerce, and the State in Republican China," in Billy So et al., *Power and Identity in the Chinese World Order* (Hong Kong: Hong Kong University Press, 2003), 180–181, 185; Xu Xiaoqun, *Chinese Professionals and the Republican* State (Cambridge: Cambridge University Press, 2000), 173–174.

6. In March 1921, Tang led protest against a tax levied by He, charging corruption. In summer 1921, Tang pressured He to stop arms shipments. *CP*, March 8, 1921; *MGRB*, July 19, 1921; *CP*, July 19 and 20, 1921; November 16, 1922.

7. "Gonggong tiyuchang qingzhuhui shang zai zhengchi" (Public exercise grounds meeting contested), *Shangbao*, November 10, 1921. SMA 1-1-1132, *JWRB*, November 14, 1921.

8. Settlement authorities exerted their own censorship, though their concern was primarily with antiforeign sentiment. "Chinese Editor Pays Fine;" Chinese Publishers' Guild et al., "Our Views on the Proposed 'Printed Matter By-law," pamphlet (SP, box 375, April 1925); FO 228 317; Freedom of Speech; "Registration of Printers."

9. *NCH*, November 12, 1921. Earlier, Tang received *NCH* publicity for calling the location of the Chamber of Commerce in the International Settlement an international embarrassment. Tang argued that Chinese merchants should meet in Chinese jurisdiction to show the world that Chinese soil was not hostile to representatives of the Chinese people. *NCH*, October 15 and 29, 1921; November 12, 1921.

10. David Strand, *An Unfinished Republic: Leading by Word and Deed in Modern China* (Berkeley: University of California Press, 2011); Madeleine Yue Dong, "Shen Peizhen and Xiaofengxian: Unofficial History and Gender Boundary Crossing in the Early Chinese Republic," in Bryna Goodman and

Wendy Larson, eds., *Gender in Motion: Divisions of Labor and Cultural Change in Late Imperial and Modern China* (Lanham, MD: Rowman and Littlefield, 2005); Joan Judge, *The Precious Raft of History: The Past, the West, and the Woman Question in China* (Stanford, CA: Stanford University Press, 2002).

11. Barbara Mittler, *A Newspaper for China? Power, Identity and Change in Shanghai's News Media, 1872–1912* (Cambridge, MA: Harvard University Asia Center, 2004) highlights the generic heterogeneity of the *Shenbao* and dissemination of novel ideas alongside gender cliché. See also Qiliang He, *Newspapers and the Journalistic Public in Republican China: 1917 as a Significant Year of Journalism* (New York: Routledge, 2018).

12. In the 1920s newspaper readership extended beyond economic and intellectual elites to include rudimentarily educated petty clerks, shopkeepers, secretaries, and other "petty urbanites" (*xiao shimin*). Newspapers featured some writing by these new readers (including educated women), though elite voices predominated.

13. Xi's poems, all on economic themes, appear in *Dongting dongshan lüHu tongxianghui sanshi zhou jinian tekan* (Thirty year commemorative edition of Thirty year commemorative edition of Dongting East Mountain Sojourners' Association), (Shanghai: n.p., 1944). One of the three is discussed in Chapter 3.

14. By this I mean to highlight connections between economics and governing ideas of the Republic in the May Fourth era. On banking and economic thinking more broadly, see Zhaojin Ji, *A History of Modern Shanghai Banking: The Rise and Decline of China's Finance Capitalism* (Armonk: M. E. Sharpe, 2003); Linsun Cheng, *Banking in Modern China: Entrepreneurs, Professional Managers, and the Development of Chinese Banks, 1897–1937* (Cambridge: Cambridge University Press, 2003); Brett Sheehan, *Trust in Troubled Times: Money, Banks and State-Society Relations in Republican Tianjin* (Cambridge, MA: Harvard University Press, 2003); Rebecca Karl, *The Magic of Concepts: History and the Economic in Twentieth-Century China* (Durham, NC: Duke University Press, 2017); Margherita Zanasi, *Saving the Nation: Economic Modernity in Republican China* (Chicago: University of Chicago Press, 2006).

15. Karl Gerth, *China Made: Consumer Culture and the Creation of the* Nation (Cambridge, MA: Harvard University Asia Center, 2003); Wen-hsin Yeh, *Shanghai Splendor: Economic Sentiments and the Making of Modern China* (Berkeley: University of California Press, 2007); Eugenia Lean, *Vernacular Industrialism: Local Innovation and Translated Technologies in the Making of a Cosmetics Empire, 1900–1940* (New York: Columbia University Press, 2020);.

16. Lao Bai, "Xin faxian ge zhong jiaoyisuo xintuo gongsi yi lanbiao," *Xin shijie* (New world), July 29, 1921.

17. An acerbic comment on Chinese aspirations for the Washington Conference offers an example of the parallel extension of economic metaphors into foreign affairs: "Touji huiyi" (Speculative conference), *Shenbao*, November 3, 1921.

18. Chen Duxiu, "Kongzi zhi dao yu xiandai **shenghuo**," *Xin qingnian* (New youth) 2:4 (December 1, 1916); reprinted in *Duxiu wencun* ([Chen] Duxiu writings), (Wuhu: Anhui renmin chubanshe, 1987), 83. See quote and discussion in Chapter 3.

19. An important exception is Laurent Galy, "Le Guomindang et ses relais dans la société shanghaïenne en 1923," *Etudes chinois* 17:1–2 (1998), 233–294.

20. Jiang Hongjiao, *Jiaoyisuo xianxingji* (Exchanges unmasked). Reprinted in Tang Zhesheng, ed., *Jiaoyisuo de tanmizhe* (Sleuth of secret stock exchange truths) (Nanjing: Nanjing chubanshe, 1994), 19.

21. Ma Yinchu, "Zhongguo de jiaoyisuo" (China's exchanges), in *Ma Yinchu quanji* (Hangzhou: Zhejiang ren min chu ban she, 1999), 1:384. Ma soon developed qualms about the Chinese exchanges. Ma Yinchu, "Shanghai jiaoyisuo qiantu zhi tuice" (Conjectures about the future of Shanghai stock exchanges), *Shanghai zongxianghui yuebao* (Journal of the Chinese Chamber of Commerce [Shanghai]), 1920.

22. "Zongshanghui qudi jiaoyisuo tiao chen zhi huaiyi" (Chamber would eliminate exchanges), *Shangbao*, August 31, 1921.

23. Sherman Cochran, *Chinese Medicine Men: Consumer Culture in China and Southeast Asia* (Cambridge, MA: Harvard University Press, 2006), 41–42.

24. *MGRB*, September 2, 1921.

25. "Zongshanghui yu Huang Chujiu bizhan" (Chamber's war of words with Huang Chujiu), *MGRB*, September 4, 1921.

26. "Zongshanghui yu Huang," *MGRB*, September 4, 1921.

27. "Zongshanghui wei jiaoyisuo mang" (Chamber busy with exchanges), *Shangbao*, September 7, 1921.

28. Sherman Cochran, *Chinese Medicine Men*, 62.

29. One exception is Brett Sheehan, *Industrial Eden: A Chinese Capitalist Vision* (Cambridge, MA: Harvard University Press, 2015), 49–50, which presents May Fourth influence as foundational to the utopian capitalist vision of the businessman Song Feiqing in North China.

30. "Mei fa bimian de jie yun" (Ill-fortune which cannot be avoided), *MGRB*, July 24, 1921.

31. Cheng Pengling, ed., *Haishang nü shuji: Xi Shangzhen canshi* (Shanghai female secretary: The tragic history of Xi Shangzhen), (Shanghai: Shenheji shuju, 1922), 3b.

32. The interim law of the early Republic has received more cursory attention than late Qing and Guomindang law. Philip Huang and Kathryn Bernhardt, eds., *Civil Law in Qing and Republican China* (Stanford, CA: Stanford University Press, 1994).

33. "Si yi bu shi gonglun" (Private friendships are not public opinion), *SSXB*, Qingguang supplement, December 15, 1922. *SSXB* was connected to Liang Qichao's Research Clique and the Progressive Party of Zhang Dongsun.

34. Shanghai Historical Museum Archives. Wu Mianbo, "Guang-Zhao gongsuo fengchao shimoji" (The conflict at the Guang-Zhao Gongsuo), manuscript; Chen Laixin, "Shanghai kakurō shōkai rengōkai ni tsuite, 1919–1923" (Re-

garding the Shanghai Federation of Commercial Street Unions, 1919–1923),
Kōbedaigaku shigaku nenpō 3 (1988) 78–98; Shanghai shangjie lianhe zonghui, "Huaren nashui hui shibai zhi neimu" (Inside story of the failure of the
Chinese Ratepayers' Association), (Shanghai pamphlet, 1921); Shanghai shi
gongshangye lianhehui, "Shanghai zongshanghui yu shangjie zonglianhehui"
(Shanghai General Chamber of Commerce and the Federation of Commer-
cial Street Unions), oral transcript narrated by Yan Esheng, recorded by Hu
Zhifan, (c. 1960?); Bryna Goodman, "Being Public: The Politics of Representation in 1918 Shanghai," *Harvard Journal of Asiatic Studies* 60:1
(June 2000).

35. David Strand, *An Unfinished Republic: Leading by Word and Deed in
Modern China* (Berkeley: University of California Press, 2001); Robert
Culp, *Articulating Citizenship: Civic Education and Student Politics in
Southeastern China, 1912–1940* (Cambridge, MA: Harvard University Asia
Center, 2007); Elizabeth Perry and Ellen Fuller, "China's Long March to
Democracy," *World Policy Journal* 8:4 (Fall 1991); Mary Rankin, "State
and Society in Early Republican Politics," *China Quarterly* 150 (June 1997);
Wen-hsin Yeh, "Commerce and Culture in Shanghai," *China Quarterly* 150
(June 1997); Fabio Lanza, *Behind the Gate: Inventing Students in Beijing*
(New York: Columbia University Press, 2010).

36. This larger context is amply documented in Xu Xiaoqun, *Trial of Modernity: Judicial Reform in Early Twentieth-Century China* (Stanford, CA:
Stanford University Press, 2008).

37. David Strand, *Rickshaw Beijing;* David Strand, *An Unfinished Republic;*
Peter Zarrow, *After Empire: The Conceptual Transformation of the Chi-
nese State, 1885–1924* (Stanford, CA: Stanford University Press, 2012);
Robert Culp, *Articulating Citizenship.*

38. "Symposium: 'Public Sphere'/'Civil Society in China? Paradigmatic Issues
in Chinese Studies," *Modern China* 19:2 (April 1993).

39. Xiaohong Xiao-Planes, "The First Democratic Experiment in China (1908–
1914): Chinese Tradition and Local Elite Practices," in Naomi Norbert,
trans.; Mireille Delmas-Marty and Pierre-Étienne Will, eds., *China, Democracy and Law* (Leiden, Netherlands: Brill, 2012), 254.

40. Prasenjit Duara, *Rescuing History from the Nation: Questioning Narratives
of Modern China* (Chicago: University of Chicago Press, 1995), 182–184.

41. Feng contrasts "truly democratic politics," which "creates a contractual relationship between the people and their government and protects the public
interests," with Chinese political culture, which he argues "was permeated
by the usurpation of popular politics" from the inception of the Republic.
He dismisses the rhetoric and practice of civic activism as a means of counterfeiting popular legitimacy, emphasizing the subsidies small newspapers
received from political parties or politicians, and highlighting "empty" or
manipulated associations that used the language of citizenship. Feng's ideal-
ization of democracy evokes an essentializing and oppositional, if tactical,
formulation of Western ideal/Chinese pathology. Xiaocai Feng, "Counterfeiting Legitimacy: Reflections on the Usurpation of Popular Politics and the

'Political Culture' of China, 1912–1949," *Frontiers of History in China* 8:2 (2013): 205, 206, 210.

42. Feng, "Counterfeiting Legitimacy," 210. That there were indeed manipulations of the public to "manufacture public opinion" neither distinguishes Chinese formations of democracy nor diminishes the richly documented formations of the republican public.

43. Eugenia Lean, *Public Passions: The Trial of Shi Jianqiao and the Rise of Popular Sympathy in Republican China* (Berkeley: University of California Press, 2007).

44. Laurent Galy, "Le Guomindang et ses relais dans la société shanghaïenne en 1923," *Études chinoises,* 17: 1–2 (1998): 233–294; Chen Laixin, "Shanhai kaku rō shōkai rengōkai ni tsuite, 1919–1923" (Regarding the Shanghai Federation of Commercial Street Unions, 1919–1923), *Kōbedaigaku shigaku nenpō* 3 (1988), 78–98.

45. Chevrier, "Anti-Tradition and Democracy," 446.

46. Chevrier, "Anti-Tradition and Democracy," 448.

47. Yves Chevrier, "Elusive Democracy (1915–1937)," in *China, Democracy, and Law: A Historical and Contemporary Approach,* trans, Naomi Norbert, trans.; ed. Mireille Delmas-Marty and Pierre-Etienne Will (Leiden, Netherlands: Brill, 2012), 462.

48. Chamber meeting minute archives.

49. Cited in Yu Heping, *Shanghui yu Zhongguo zaoqi xiandaihua* (Chambers of commerce and China's early modernization), (Shanghai: Shanghai renmin chubanshe, 1993), 330–331. Yu ascribes the failure of the movement to the "internal contradictions" of the merchant movement, which was "unaware of social political foundations and lacking in political skills." See the discussion in Zhang Huanzhong, *Shanghai zongshanghui yanjiu, 1902–1929* (Research on the Shanghai General Chamber of Commerce), (Taipei: Zhongyang yanjiuyuan jindaishi yanjiusuo, 1996), 296–298. See also the discussion in Zhaojin Ji, *A History of Modern Shanghai Banking,* 111.

50. Yu Heping, *Shanghui yu Zhongguo zaoqi xiandaihua,* 330–331; Zhang, *Shanghai zongshanghui yanjiu,* 296–298.

51. The idea of the radical shifts *and* the inconclusive and open-ended character of these processes is suggested in both "unfinished republic" and, more obliquely, "after empire," in the titles of recent studies. Strand, *An Unfinished Republic;* Zarrow, *After Empire.*

52. Merle Goldman and Elizabeth Perry, eds., *Changing Meanings of Citizenship in Modern China* (Cambridge, MA: Harvard University Press, 2002); Robert Culp, *Articulating Citizenship;* Nara Dillon and Jean Oi, eds., *At the Crossroads of Empires: Middlemen, Social Networks, and State-building in Republican Shanghai* (Stanford, CA: Stanford University Press, 2008); Billy So and Madeleine Zelin, eds., *New Narratives of Urban Space in Republican Chinese Cities* (Leiden. Netherlands: Brill, 2013).

53. Sokolsky is similarly airbrushed in the detailed recollections of Chen Bulei and lengthy discussion of the *Shangbao* by Pan Gongzhan's biographer. Chen Bulei, *Chen Bulei huiyilu* (Chen Bulei's memoir), (Shanghai: Ershi

shiji chubanshe, 1949); Chen Bulei, *Chen Bulei xiansheng wenji* (Taibei: Zhongguo guomindang zhongyang weiyuanhui, 1984); Ji Hao, Zhou Shifu, and Wang Jianmin, *Pan Gongzhan zhuan* (Taibei: Taibei shi xinwen jizhe gonghui, 1976*)*. Sokolsky's involvement is contrastingly noted in Patterson's 1922 study, which describes *Shangbao* as "founded by a group of Chinese merchants together with an American, George E. Sokolsky, who undertook the organization of the various departments of the newspaper among modern American lines." The self-aggrandizing Sokolsky was his likely informant. Donald Patterson, "Journalism of China," *University of Missouri Bulletin,* 23:34 (December 1922), 30.

54. Goodman, "Semi-Colonialism," 63. Copies of the commercially oriented *China Bureau of Public Information Bulletin* are preserved in the US National Archives.

55. The 392-box collection contains Sokolsky's correspondence from Shanghai (1919–1931) with such Chinese political and cultural figures as Sun Yat-sen, Song Qingling, Hu Shi, Tang Shaoyi, Wang Zhengting, Wen Zongyao, Wen Shizhen, and Li Qun.

56. Translations and other Chinese and foreign news agency materials comprised significant portions of the news sections (international and local) of Chinese papers, making up for an insufficient supply of journalists. Bryna Goodman, "Networks of News: Power, Language, and Transnational Dimensions of the Chinese Press, 1850–1949," *The China Review* 4:1 (Spring 2004): 1–10; Rudolf Wagner, "Don't Mind the Gap! The Foreign-language Press in Late Qing and Republican China," *China Heritage Quarterly* 30–31 (June–September 2012); Shuang Shen, *Cosmopolitan Publics: Anglophone Print Culture in Semi-Colonial Shanghai* (Rutgers, NJ: Rutgers University Press, 2009); Shuge Wei, *News under Fire, China's Propaganda against Japan in the English-Language Press, 1928–1941* (Hong Kong: Hong Kong University Press, 2017); USDS 893.91 (Carl Crow, June 5, 1919); Guo Zhenyi, *Shanghai baozhi gaige lun* (Reforming Shanghai newspapers), (Shanghai: Fudan daxue xinwen xuehui, 1931), 13. Journalism scholar Guo Zhenyi estimated that more than 80 percent of important news in Chinese papers was translated from foreign papers. Shanghai foreign residents were similarly fed translations from the Chinese press. Stephen MacKinnon, "Toward a History of the Chinese Press in the Republican Period," *Modern China* 23:1 (January 1997); 11–13.

GLOSSARY

ai	愛
aiguo xiaoshuo	愛國小說
Bao Tianxiao	包天笑
baoying	報應
baozhang renquan	保障人權
buyun	補運
cai	財
cainü	才女
caipiao	彩票
changshi	常識
Chaozhou huiguan	潮州會館
Chen Aliu	陳阿六
Chen Bulei	陳布雷
Chen Duxiu	陳獨秀
Chengdong nüxue	城東女學
Chen Gongzhe	陳公哲
Cheng Pengling	程彭齡
Chen Qihuai	陳屺壞
Chen Tiesheng	陳鐵生
Chen Wangdao	陳望道
Chen Wanzhen	陳宛珍
Chen Wentao	陳問濤
Chen Zemin	陳則民
chiqing	痴情
Cui Weiru	崔蔚茹
Dagongbao	大公報

daibao buping	代報不平
Dai Jitao	戴季陶
daiyizhi	代議制
dao hui	盜燬
Deng Zhongxia	鄧中夏
diaonü	吊女
diaosigui	吊死鬼
Dongting dongshan	洞庭東山
Du Fuyao	堵福曜
duli ren'ge	獨立人格
duoshuren zhi yijian ye	多數人之意見也
duqi	賭氣
Du Yaquan	杜亞泉
Fang Jiaobo	方椒伯
Fan Jimei	范季美
fantan	番攤
fei mou yi ren zhi siyan	非某一人之私言
feiqie yundong	廢妾運動
Feng Shaoshan	馮少山
Fu Xiaoan	傅筱庵
fuchou xiaoshuo	復仇小說
Funü pinglun	婦女評論
Funü shibao	婦女時報
ganying	感應
gaosuren	告訴人
Ge malu shangjie lianhehui	各馬路商界聯合會
Ge malu shangjie zong lianhehui	各馬路商界總聯合會
Ge Pengyun	戈鵬云
ge tuanti da dong gongfen	各團體大動公憤
gong	公
gongde	公德

gongfen buping	公憤不平
gonggong de wanju	公共的玩具
Gongjie qingnian lizhihui	工界青年勵志會
gonglun	公論
gongqi	公器
Gongyi Li	公益里
Guan Hanqing	關漢卿
Guanchang xianxingji	官場現形記
Guang-Zhao Gongsuo	廣肇公所
guanxi tongxiang tongzu bewu	關係同鄉同族被侮
Gu Jianchen	谷劍塵
Guo Bingwen	郭秉文
guomin	國民
Guomin dahui	國民大會
guomin geming	國民革命
guomin zijue yundong	國民自決運動
guomin zizhi	國民自治
Hamada Minetarō	滨田峰太郎
He Fenglin	何豐林
heimu	黑幕
He-Yin Zhen	何殷震
huahui	花會
Huang Chujiu	黃楚九
huangmiu yi da jidian	荒謬已達極點
Huang Yanpei	黃炎培
Huashang zhengquan jiaoyisuo	華商證券交易所
Hu-Hai	滬海
huiguan	會館
Huo Shouhua	霍守華
Hu Shi	胡適
Hu Yuzhi	胡愈之
ji (chicken)	雞

ji (pivot, target)	機
ji po	計迫
jianchating	檢察廳
Jiang Hongjiao	江紅蕉
Jiang Jieshi (Chiang Kai-shek)	蔣介石
jiangquan	獎券
jiaohuansuo	交換所
jiaoyi	交易
jiao yi er tui, ge de qi suo	交易而退各得其所
jiaoyisuo	交易所
Jiaoyisuo xianxingji	交易所現形記
jie yinzhai	借陰債
Jingbao	晶報
jingji	經濟
jingji shehui	經濟社會
jingmaichang	競賣場
jingshi	經世
jingshi jimin	經世濟民
Jingwu san gongsi	精武三公司
Jingwu tiyuhui	精武體育會
jingxiong	競雄
jiqingchang	極情場
junshi xiaoshuo	軍事小說
Kang Youwei	康有為
kongxu	空虛
laoqian de difang	撈錢的地方
li	理
Liang Qichao	梁啓超
liansheng zizhi	聯省自治
Li Boyuan	李伯元
licai	理財
Lin Meijing	林眉鏡
Li Shirui	李時蕊

li zi	隸字
Luo Wen'gan	羅文幹
Lu Weichang	盧煒昌
Lu Weiqing	陸維卿
Lu Yongxiang	盧永祥
maikong maikong	買空賣空
Mao Dun	茅盾
mingjie	名節
minguo	民國
minyi	民意
minzhi weiyuan hui	民治委員會
minzu jingji	民族經濟
moji	墨跡
Mu Ouchu	穆藕初
Mu Xiangyue	穆湘玥
nie	孽
Nie Qijie	聶其杰
Nie Yuntai	聶云台
nü haojie	女豪杰
nüliu zhi bei	女流之輩
nüzi canzheng xiejinhui	女子參政協進會
Nuzi zhiquan gongsi	女子植權公司
Pan Gongzhan	潘公展
panming	拚命
pianqu	騙取
pingdenglun	平等論
pingmin dahui	平民大會
pingmin zhuyi	平民主義
qi (life energy)	氣
qi (wife)	妻
qie	妾
Qin Liankui	秦聯奎
qing	情

qingli	情理
qingre yichang	情熱異常
Qiu Jin	秋瑾
Qiu Youxin	裘由辛
quanyou	勸誘
qun	群
ren'ge	人格
se	色
Shangbao (bank)	上寶
Shangbao (newspaper)	商報
shangchang	商場
Shangfang (Mt.)	上方山
Shangye gongtuan lianhehui	商業公團聯合會
Shangye quyinsuo	商業取引所
shangzhan	商戰
Shao Lizi	邵力子
shehui xinli	社會心理
Shenbao	申報
Shen Bocheng	沈伯誠
Shen Jiaben	沈家本
shenpanting	審判廳
Shen Yanbing	沈雁冰
Shen Yibin	沈儀彬
Shen Zhonghua	沈仲華
Shibao	時報
shichang	市場
shiju gonghe zhi zhen jingshen	實具共和之真精神
shi ling you bie qing	事另有別情
shimin quan	市民權
shimin zhengzhi	市民政治
shuduan fadong	樞端發動

Shufen	淑芬
sijiao	私交
Song Hanzhang	宋漢章
Song Jiaoren	宋教仁
Song Meiling	宋美齡
Song Qingling	宋慶齡
su	俗
Sun Tieqing	孫鐵卿
Tang Jiezhi	湯節之
Tan Sheying	談社英
Tan Sitong	譚嗣同
tongxiang	同鄉
tongzhi jingji	統制經濟
touji	投機
touji shiye	投機事業
Wang Yiting	王一亭
Wang Zhengting	王正廷
Wangping	望平
Wan Pu	萬璞
weibi renming	威逼人命
weixing	闈姓
Wen Lanting	聞蘭亭
wenming xi	文明戲
Wen Zongyao	溫宗堯
wochuo	齷齪
Wulu caishen	五路財神
Wu Tingfang	伍廷芳
Wutong	五通
wu yuan	無冤
Wu Yugong	吳虞公
xi nüzi	系女子
xianrouzhuang	鮮肉莊
Xiao'ai zhi kule	小愛之苦樂

xiaoshuo	小說
xiayi	俠義
Xie Tianxiang	謝天香
xiguan	習慣
xin	信
xin funü	新婦女
xin ju	新劇
xin nüxing	新女性
xintuo gongsi	信託公司
xintuo sisi	信托私司
Xinwenbao	新聞報
xinxue	新學
Xi Shangzhen	席上珍
Xi Shangji	席上記
xi yuan	洗冤
xizai	西崽
xuanju jiaoyisuo	選舉交易所
xuanju	選舉
Xu Cangshui	徐滄水
Xue Shaohui	薛紹徽
xue shen yuan	雪深冤
Xu Huilin	徐惠霖
Xu Jilong	徐季龍
Xu Zhucheng	徐鑄成
ya	雅
Yang Baimin	楊白民
yangchengsuo	養成所
Yang Duanliu	楊端六
Yang Zhihua	楊之華
Yan Ruisheng	閻瑞生
Yao Gonghe	姚公鶴
yaonie	妖孽
Ye Shengtao	葉聖陶

yi ren	已認
yiben wanli	一本萬利
yi de bao yuan	以德報怨
yifu duoqi	一夫多妻
yifu yiqi	一夫一妻
Yi Jiayue	易家鉞
Ying Jishen	應季審
Yingying	盈盈
you bi	誘逼
you po	誘迫
youya	優雅
yuan	冤
yuan dan	冤單
Yuan Minfang	袁民芳
Yuan Shikai	袁世凱
yuanyi	冤抑
yulun	輿論
Yun Shi	雲石
yu nüzi ren'ge you guan	於女子人格有關
Yu Xiaqing （Yu Qiaqing)	虞洽卿
Zeng Xubai	曾虛白
Zhang Danfu	張丹斧
Zhang Jian	張謇
Zhang Shizhao	章士釗
Zhang Xichen	章錫琛
zhaqi qucai	詐欺取財
zhaqi qucai zui	詐欺取財罪
zheng kai	正楷
Zheng Zhengqiu	鄭正秋
Zhiye nüzi lianxiu hui	職業女子聯修會
zhiyin	知音
Zhongguo guohuo weichihui	中國國貨維持會

Zhongguo jiuji furuhui	中國救濟婦孺會
Zhonghua xinbao	中華新報
zhongliu jieji	中流階級
Zhong-Mei	中美
Zhou Fengxia	周鳳霞
Zhou Zuoren	周作人
zhuan shu	篆書
Zhu Caizhen	朱采真
Zhu Zongliang	朱宗良
zhuchi gongdao	主持公道
zhuzhang gongdao	主張公道
zi nan renwei ling cheng he zhong zuiming	自難認為另成何種罪名
ziyoude quanli	自由的權利
zui	罪

SELECTED BIBLIOGRAPHY

Newspapers and Periodicals (dual-language titles are noted)

China Press, Shanghai (1911–1938).

[The New] China Review, Shanghai (1919–1922).

Commerce Reports. US Department of Commerce (1919–1922).

Dagong bao (Impartial Daily), Tianjin (1902–).

Far Eastern Republic: A Monthly Magazine Devoted to the Republic of China, San Francisco (1919–1920).

Fuermosi, Shanghai (1928–1930).

Funü pinglun, Shanghai (1921–1923).

Funü shibao (Women's Eastern Times), Shanghai (1919–1917).

Funü zazhi (Ladies' Journal), Shanghai (1915–1931).

Jingbao, Shanghai (1919–1940).

Millard's Review of the Far East, Shanghai (1919–1921).

Minguo ribao, Shanghai (1916–1946).

Municipal Gazette: Being the Official Organ of the Executive Council for the Foreign Settlement of Shanghai (1908–1926).*North China Herald*, Shanghai (1850–1941).

North China Daily News, Shanghai (1864–1941).

Nü xuesheng, Shanghai (1910–1912).

Qianye yuebao, Shanghai (1921–1937).

Shangbao (Journal of Commerce), Shanghai (1921–1929).

Shanghai Gazette, Shanghai (1919–1921).

Shanghai zongshanghui yuebao (Journal of the Shanghai General Chamber of Commerce), Shanghai (1921–1927).

Shanhai (Japanese), Shanghai (1919–1935).

Shenbao, Shanghai (1872–1949).

Shenzhou ribao, Shanghai (1922).

Shibao (Eastern Times), Shanghai (1904–1939).

Shishi xinbao (China Times), Shanghai (1911–1948).

Trans-Pacific, Tokyo (1919–1922).

Xianshi leyuan ribao, Shanghai (1918–1927).

Xin shenbao, Shanghai (1918–1922).

Xin shijie ribao, Shanghai (1921–1922).

Xinwenbao, Shanghai (1892–1949).

Weekly Review of the Far East, Shanghai (1922–1923).

Yinhang zhoubao, Shanghai (1917–1950).

Zhonghua xinbao, Shanghai (1917–1926).

Archival and Manuscript Sources

Columbia Center for Oral History, Columbia University. "Reminiscences of George Ephraim Sokolsky." Oral history (New York).

Columbia University Libraries, Archival Collections. George E. Sokolsky Manuscripts, 1919–1962 (New York).

France. Archives Diplomatiques, Shanghai Consular Papers, Série A, Box 59 (Nantes).

Holbig, Heike. "Competitive Cooperation: A Preliminary Analysis of Shanghai Monetary Policies, 1908–1910." Unpublished manuscript (courtesy of author).

Hoover Institution Archives. Sokolsky (George E.) Papers (Stanford University).

Japan. Gaimushō Gaikō Shiryōkan. Diplomatic Archives of the Ministry of Foreign Affairs of Japan 1.3.2. 46-1-4 (Tokyo).

Shanghai Historical Museum Archives. Wu Mianbo, "Guang-Zhao gongsuo fengchao shimoji" (The conflict at the Guang-Zhao Gongsuo). Manuscript (Shanghai).

Shanghai Municipal Archives. Q117-9-33. Dongting dongshan tongxianghui yibu (Dongting dongshan association meeting notes) (Shanghai).

———. Q118-9-12. Chaozhou huiguan yi'an beicha (Chaozhou *huiguan* meeting notes) (Shanghai).

———. 1-1-1122 to 1-1-1132. *Jingwu ribao* (Police Daily Reports). Shanghai Municipal Council. (Shanghai).

———. Q 401-2. Jingwu tiyuhui, Jingwu neizhuan yu zhangcheng (Internal history and constitution of Jingwu Association) (Shanghai).

Shanghai Shi Gongshangye Lianhehui Archives. 200-1-008 Shanghai zong-shanghui dang'an. (Archives of Shanghai General Chamber of Commerce).

———. "Shanghai zongshanghui yu shangjie zonglianhehui" (Shanghai General Chamber of Commerce and the Federation of Commercial Street Unions). Oral transcript narrated by Yan Esheng, recorded by Hu Zhifan, c. 1960.

———. Shanghai zongshanghui, benhui yi'an lu (Shanghai Chamber of Commerce meeting records) (Shanghai).

United Kingdom. Foreign Office: Consulates and Legation, China: Correspondence, series 1, FO 228, Public Record Office (London).

University of California, Berkeley. University Archives (Berkeley).

———. *Registrar: University of California* (Berkeley: University of California Press, 1911).

———. *Directory of Graduates of the University of California, 1864–1916* (Berkeley: California Alumni Association, 1916).

———. *The Golden Book of California, 1860–1936* (Berkeley: California Alumni Association, 1936).

US Department of State Archives, National Archives. Carl Crow, Report on Chinese Press 893.91 (Washington, DC).

US National Archives and Records Administration. Shanghai Municipal Police Files, 1894–1949 (Washington, DC).

Documents and Selected Works in Chinese and Japanese

Chaozhou huiguan yi'an beicha (Chaozhou huiguan meeting notes), September 1922 to December 1922. SMA Q118-9-12.

Chen Bulei. *Chen Bulei huiyilu* (Chen Bulei's memoir). Shanghai: Ershi shiji chubanshe, 1949.

———. *Chen Bulei xiansheng wenji*. Taibei: Zhongguo guomindang zhong-yang weiyuanhui, 1984.

Chen Duxiu. "Yi jiu yi liu nian" (Nineteen sixteen). *Qingnian zazhi* 1:5 (January 15, 1916).

———. "Kongzi zhi dao yu xiandai shenghuo" (The way of Confucius and modern life). *Xin qingnian* (New Youth) 2:4 (December 1, 1916). Reprinted in *Duxiu wencun*. Wuhu: Anhui renmin chubanshe, 1987.

Chen Laixin. "Shanhai kakurō shōkai rengōkai ni tsuite, 1919–1923" (Regarding the Shanghai Federation of Commercial Street Unions, 1919–1923). *Kōbedaigaku shigaku nenpō* 3 (1988) 78–98.

Chen Wangdao. "Xi Shangzhen nüshi zai shangbaoguan li diaosi shijian" (Miss Xi's hanging at the *Journal of Commerce*). *Funü pinglun* 59 (September 20, 1922).

Chen Zemin. "Fei jiancha zhidu zhi yundong" (Procuratorial-system abolition movement). Pamphlet. Shanghai, 1922.

Cheng Pengling, ed. *Haishang nü shuji: Xi Shangzhen canshi* (Shanghai female secretary: The tragic history of Xi Shangzhen). Shanghai: Shenheji shuju, 1922.

Cheng Yu. "Qing zhi minguo de xuqie xisu yu shehui bianqian" (Concubine possession and social change from Qing to Republic). PhD dissertation, Fudan University, 2005.

Cui Weiru, ed. *Xi Shangzhen.* Shanghai: Funü zhiye yanjiu she, 1922.

Deng Zhongxia. *Deng Zhongxia wenji* (Deng Zhongxia collected writings). Beijing: Renmin chubanshe, 1983.

Dongfang zazhi she, ed. *Funü zhiye yu muxing lun* (Women's vocations and motherhood). Shanghai: Shangwu yinshuguan, 1924.

Dongting dongshan lüHu tongxianghui di shi'er ci baogaoshu (Dongting East Mountain Sojourners' Association, Twelfth report). Shanghai: Dongting dongshan lüHu tongxianghui, 1924.

Dongting dongshan lüHu tongxianghui sanshi zhou jinian tekan (Thirty year commemorative edition of Dongting East Mountain Sojourners' Association). Shanghai: Dongting dongshan lüHu tongxianghui, 1944.

Dongting dongshan tongxianghui yibu (Meeting record of Dongting East Mountain native-place association), SMA Q117-9-33.

Du Yaquan. "Lun xu qie" (On keeping concubines). *Dongfang zazhi* 8:4 (1911).

Fang Hanqi. *Zhongguo jindai baokan shi* (Modern Chinese periodical history). Taiyang: Shanxi renmin chubanshe, 1981.

———. *Zhongguo xinwen shiye tongshi* (History of Chinese journalism). Beijing, Zhongguo renmin daxue chubanshe, 1996.

Feng Xiaocai. *Zhengshang Zhongguo: Yu Qiaqing yu ta de shidai* (Political merchants in China: Yu Qiaqing and his times). Beijing: Shehui kexue wenxian chubanshe, 2013.

Ge Yuanxu. *Hu you zaji* (Notes on touring Shanghai). 1896. Reprint. Shanghai: Shanghai guji chubanshe, 1998.

Guo Xun. "Jiu jiating hun zhi bihai" (Evils of the old family system). *Jiating yanjiu* 1:4 (August 1921): 38.

Guo Zhenyi. *Shanghai baozhi gaige lun* (Reforming Shanghai newspapers). Shanghai: Fudan daxue xinwen xuehui, 1931.

Hamada Minetarō. *Shina no kōekijo*. Shanghai: Chūka Keizaisha, 1922.

He Xuyan. "Xintuo ye zai Zhongguo de xingqi" (Rise of trust companies in China). *Jindaishi yanjiu* 148:4 (2005).

Hong Jiaguan and Zhang Jifeng. *Jindai Shanghai jinrong shichang* (Financial markets in modern Shanghai). Shanghai: Shanghai renmin chubanshe, 1989.

Hu Daojing, ed. "Shanghai de ribao" (Shanghai dailies). *Shanghai tongzhi-guan qikan* 2:1 (June 1934).

Hu Shi. "Zhencao wenti" (The problem of chastity). In *Wusi shiqi funü wenti wenxuan* (Selected writings on women's issues from the May Fourth period). Beijing: Sanlian shudian, 1981, 106–114.

Hu Xia and Huang Yan, eds. *Susong changshi* (Basic lawsuit knowledge). Shanghai: Shangwu yinshuguan, 1922.

Ishikawa, Yoshihiro. "Zasshi 'Shanhai' 'Shanhai Shūhou' kijimokuroku." In Hamada Masami, *Kagaku Kenkyūhi (Kiban kenkyū B) Seika repōto*. 2001.

Jiang Hongjiao. *Jiaoyisuo xianxingji* (Exchanges unmasked). Serialized in *Xingqi* (Weekly), 1922–1923. Reprinted in Tang Zhesheng, ed., *Jiaoyisuo zhenxiang de tanmizhe* (Sleuth of secret stock exchange truths). Nanjing: Nanjing chubanshe, 1994.

Jiaoyisuo yi lan (Stock exchanges at a glance). Shanghai: Jinbu shuju, 1922.

Jin Shiyin. "Ershi nian fuyun zhi yi da gongzuo: Fei qie" (A major task in the 20-year women's movement: Abolishing concubinage). *Funü gongming* (Women's echo) 41 (1931): 9.

Kang Youwei. "Licai jiuguo lun" (National salvation through economics). *Buren zazhi* (Compassion), no. 1 (1913).

Kobayashi Ushisaburō. "Jiaoyisuo gailun" (On stock exchanges). Trans. Mei Yuan. *Shanghai zongshanghui yuebao* 1:1 (July 1921); 1:2 (August 1921); 1:3 (September 1921); 1:4 (October 1921).

Liang Qichao. *Zai lun chouhuan guozhai* (Another discussion of repaying national debt). *Yinbingshi wenji* 21. Beijing: Zhonghua shuju, 1989.

———. "Jinggao guozhong zhi tan shiyezhe" (Warning our country's entrepreneurs). In *Guofengbao,* November 2, 1910. Reproduced in Shanghai shi dang'anguan, ed. *Jiu Shanghai de jiaoyisuo* (Securities exchanges in old Shanghai). Shanghai: 1992, 265–273.

Liu Renfeng, ed. *Zhongguo funü baokan shi yanjiu* (Research on the history of Chinese women's periodicals). Beijing: Zhongguo shehui kexue chubanshe, 2012.

Liu Zhiying. *Jindai Shanghai Huashang zhengquan shichang yanjiu* (Research on modern Shanghai's China Merchants' Securities Exchange). Shanghai: Xuelin chubanshe, 2004.

"Lun Shanghai quyinsuo" (The Japanese exchange). *Yinhang zhoubao* (Bankers' weekly), (November 26, 1918).

Lu Shouxian. *Jiaoyisuo xianxingji* (Exchanges unmasked). Shanghai: Zhonghua tushu jicheng gongsi, 1922.

Lu Songyin, comp. *Xintuo gongsi yaolan* (Guide to trust companies). Shanghai: Wenming shuju, 1922.

Lu Xun. "Wo zhi jielie guan (My views on chastity). In *Wusi shiqi funü wenti wenxuan* (Selected writings on women's issues from the May Fourth period. Beijing: Sanlian shudian, 1981, 115–123.

Ma Guangren. *Shanghai xinwenshi* (History of Shanghai journalism). Shanghai: Fudan daxue chubanshe, 1996.

Mao Zedong. "Minzhong de da lianhe" (Great union of the popular masses). *Xiangjiang pinglun* (July 21; August 4, 1919). In Stuart Schram, trans., "Mao Zedong, "Minahong de da lianhe" (Great alliance of the masses), *China Quarterly* 49 (January–March 1972): 76–87.

———. "Beijing zhengbian yu shangren" (Merchants and the Beijing coup). *Xiangdao zhoubao* 31–32 (July 11, 1923). In Stuart Schram, ed., *Mao's Road to Power: Revolutionary Writings, 1912–1949*. London: Routledge, 2015. 2:178.

Ma Yinchu. "Shanghai jiaoyisuo qiantu zhi tuice" (Conjectures about the future of Shanghai stock exchanges). *Shanghai zongxianghui yuebao*, 1920.

———. "Zhongguo de jiaoyisuo" (China's exchanges). In *Ma Yinchu quanji*. Hangzhou: Zhejiang ren min chu ban she, 1999. 1.

Mei Lu. "Fei qie tan" (Abolish concubinage). *Rensheng zazhi* 3 (1924): 14.

Nian Hua. "Jiaoyisuo." *Youxi shijie* 8 (1922): 4.

Okada, Asatarō, ed. *Zhonghua minguo zhanxing xin xinglu* (Provisional new criminal law of the Republic of China). Shanghai: Guomin daxue, 1913.

Qi Liang. "Zhengquan Jiaoyisuo gaikuang" (Overview of the Shanghai China Merchants' Securities Exchange). In Zhongguo renmin zhengzhi xieshang huiyi, ed., *Jiu shanghai de jiaoyisuo*. Shanghai: Shanghai renmin chubanshe, 1994, 39–42.

Shanghai renmin yinhang. *Shanghai qianzhuang shiliao* (Shanghai native bank materials). Shanghai: Shanghai renmin chubanshe, 1960.

Shanghai shangjie lianhe zonghui (xuanbu). "Huaren nashui hui shibai zhi neimu" (The inside story of the failure of the Chinese Ratepayers' Association). Pamphlet, 1921.

Shanghai shi dang'anguan, ed. *Jiu Shanghai de zhengquan jiaoyisuo* (Securities exchanges in old Shanghai). Shanghai: Shanghai guji chubanshe, 1992.

Shanghai shi difang xiehui. *Shanghai shi tongji* (Statistics for Shanghai Municipality). Shanghai, 1933.

Shanghai youlan zhinan (Shanghai guidebook). Shanghai: Zhonghua tushu jicheng bianjisuo, 1923.

Shibao guan ji'nian ce (*Shibao* commemorative album). Shanghai: Shibao guan, 1921.

Song Zuanyou. *Guangdongren zai Shanghai, 1843–1949* (Guangdong people in Shanghai). Shanghai: Shanghai renmin chubanshe, 2007.

Susong xuzhi (Necessary lawsuit knowledge). Shanghai: Shangwu yinshuguan, 1917.

Tan Sheying, ed. *Zhongguo funü yundongshi* (History of Chinese women's movement). Nanjing: Funü gongming she, 1936.

Tang Zhesheng, ed. *Jiaoyisuo zhenxiang de tanmizhe* (Sleuth of secret stock exchange truths). Nanjing: Nanjing chubanshe, 1981.

Wang Enliang. *Jiaoyisuo daquan* (The complete stock exchange). Shanghai: Jiaoyisuo yuan shuqi yangchengsuo, 1921.

Wang Shijie, "Caizheng geming" (Financial revolution). *Guomin jingji zazhi* 1 (1912): 1–3.

Wen Lanting. "Wen Lanting deng guanyu choubei Shanghai zhengquan wupin jiaoyisuo de laiwang hanjian (Letters of Wen Lanting, etc., regarding Shanghai Securities and Commodities Exchange planning). *Dang'an yu shixue*, 4 (2001): 10–19.

Wu Shutian. *Jiaoyisuo daquan* (The complete stock exchange). Shanghai: Jiaoyisuo suoyuan shu yangchengsuo, 1921.

Wu Yugong. *Zisha zhi nüshuji: Xi Shangzhen canshi* (Female secretary who committed suicide: Tragic history of Xi Shangzhen). Shanghai: Zhongguo diyi shuju, 1922.

Wu Zude. "Jiu Shanghai de da huahui" (Huahui in old Shanghai). In Shen Feide, ed., *Jiu Shanghai de yan du chang* (Drugs, gambling and prostitution in old Shanghai). Shanghai: Baijia chubanshe, 1988.

Xi Shangzhen. "Wenzi fei xuewenshuo" (Writing is not a category of knowledge). *Funü shibao,* 12 (January 10, 1914): 77.

———. *"Xiao'ai zhi kule"* (The bitter happiness of Little Love). In Wu Yugong. *Zisha zhi nüshuji: Xi Shangzhen canshi* (Female secretary who committed suicide: Tragic history of Xi Shangzhen). Shanghai: Zhongguo diyi shuju, 1922, 16–23.

———. "Xi Shangzhen zhi biji" (Xi Shangzhen's jottings). In Wu Yugong, *Zisha zhi nüshuji: Xi Shangzhen canshi* (Female secretary who committed suicide: Tragic history of Xi Shangzhen). Shanghai: Zhongguo diyi shuju, 1922, 23–28.

———. "Jie yinzhai" (Borrowing a covert loan). In *Dongting dongshan lüHu tongxianghui sanshiji zhounian jinian tekan.* Shanghai, 1944, 80.

———. "Xiyu ge" (Song for timely rain). *Dongting dongshan lüHu tongxianghui sanshiji zhounian jinian tekan.* Shanghai, 1944, 81.

———. "Yucan wugu" (Wugu poem, raising silkworms). *Dongting dongshan lüHu tongxianghui sanshiji zhounian jinian tekan.* Shanghai, 1944, 80.

Xing Jianrong. "Yu Xiaqing yu Shanghai zhengquan wupin jiaoyisuo." *Dang'an yu shixue* (Archives and History) 3 (1996): 61–63.

———. *Feichang yinhangjia: Minguo jinrong wangshi* (Extraordinary bankers: recollections of Republican Era finance). Shanghai: Dongfang chuban zhongxin, 2014.

Xing Zhai. "Jiaoyisuo xintuogongsi za gan" (Thoughts on exchanges and trust companies). *Qianye yuebao* 1:6 (June 1921): 8–9.

Xu Cangshui. "Jingji zhanzheng yu jingji tixue" (Economic war and economic guidance). *Yinhang zhoubao* 2:47 (December 3, 1918).

———. "Xintuo cun kuan zhi shuoming" (Explanation of funds held in trust). *Yinhang zhoubao* 3:38 (October 14, 1919): 30.

Xu Zhucheng. "Chen Bulei yu Shangbao" (Chen Bulei and the Shangbao). In *Baohai jiuwen* (Newspaper anecdotes). Shanghai: Shanghai renmin chubanshe, 1981, 30.

Yang Chaosheng. "Nannü shejiao gongkai," (Public social intercourse for men and women). *Xin qingnian* (La Jeunesse) 6:4. Reprinted in *Wusi shiqi funü wenti wenxuan* (May Fourth writings on the woman question). Beijing: Shenghuo, 1981, 173–175.

Yang Duanliu, *Xintuo gongsi gailun* (Introduction to trust companies). Shanghai: Commercial Press, 1922.

Yang Tianshi. "Jiang Zongzheng xiansheng he Shanghai zhengquan wupin jiaoyisuo" (Jiang Jieshi and Shanghai's Securities and Commodities Exchange). *Jindai Zhongguo* 139 (October 2000).

Yao Gonghe. *Shanghai xianhua* (Idle talk about Shanghai). Shanghai: Shanghai guji chubanshe reprint, 1989.

Yi Jiayue. *Funü zhiye wenti* (The question of women's vocations). Shanghai: Taidong tushuju, 1922.

Yi Lan. *Jiaoyisuo yaolan* (Guide to stock exchanges). Shanghai: Wenming shuju, 1921.

Yin Zhentao. "Zhongguo jindai zhengquan shichang jianguan de lishi kaocha—Jiyu lifa yu zhifa shijiao" (Historical survey of China's modern securities market supervison: From the perspective of legislation and law enforcement). *Jinrong pinglun* 2 (2012): 104–114.

Yu Heping. *Shanghui yu Zhongguo zaoqi xiandaihua* (Chambers of commerce and China's early modernization). Shanghai: Shanghai renmin chubanshe, 1993.

Yu Hualin. *Nüxing de "chong su": Minguo chengshi funü hunyin wenti yanjiu* (Remodeling: women and the marriage question in Republican cities). Beijing: Shangwu yinshuguan, 2009.

Yu Huancheng. "Min yuan lai woguo zhi zhengquan jiaoyi" (Domestic securities trading since the first year of the Republic). In Zhu Sihuang, ed., *Minguo jingji shi* (Economic history of the Republic). Shanghai: Yinhang zhoubaoshe, 1947.

Yu Laishan. "Shanghai zhengquanye de chuqi qingkuang (Early securities trade in Shanghai)." In Zhongguo renmin zhengxie shang huiyi et al., eds., *Jiu Shanghai de jiaoyisuo*. Shanghai: Shanghai shi zhengxie wenshi ziliao, 1994.

Yun Shi. *Funü zhi baimian guan* (One hundred views of women). Shanghai: Wenyi bianyi she, 1920. Reprint, 1927.

Zeng Xubai. *Zhongguo xinwenshi* (Chinese journalism history). Taipei: Sanmin shuju, 1984.

Zhang Huanzhong. *Shanghai zongshanghui yanjiu, 1902–1929* (Research on the Shanghai General Chamber of Commerce). Taipei: Zhongyang yanjiuyuan jindaishi yanjiusuo, 1996.

Zhang Jinglu. *Zhongguo de xinwenzhi* (Chinese newspapers). Shanghai: Guanghua shuju, 1928.

Zhang Qiuchong. "Shangbao suowen" (News of Shanghai). *Shanghai difang shi ziliao*. Shanghai: Shanghai shehui kexueyuan chubanshe, 1986.

Zhang Yufa. "Xinwenhua yundong shiqi de xinwen yu yanlun" (New Culture news and opinion). *Zhongyang yanjiuyuan jindai yanjiusuo jikan* 23 (June 1983): 295.

Zhang Yuping. "Go·shi undōki ni okeru Dai Jitao no nihonkan" (Dai Jitao's view of Japan in the May Fourth period). *Chūgoku kenkyū geppō* 64:9 (2010): 1–14.

"Zhengquan jiaoyisuo fa." December 29, 1914. Reprinted in *Shanghai shi dang'an guan*, ed., *Jiu Shanghai de jiaoyisuo*, 274–281.

Zhongguo yinhang zonghang, Zhongguo dier lishi dang'anguan he bian. *Zhongguo yinhang hangshi ziliao huibian* (Compilation of materials on Chinese banking), Vol. 1 (1912–1949). Nanjing: Dang'an chubanshe, 1991.

Zhongguo renmin zhengzhi xieshang huiyi, ed. *Jiu shanghai de jiaoyisuo* (Stock exchanges in old Shanghai). Shanghai: Shanghai renmin chubanshe, 1994.

Zhonghua quanguo funü lianhehui funü yundong lishi yanjiushi, ed. *Wusi shiqi funü wenti wenxuan* (Selected writings on the woman question in the May Fourth Era). Beijing 1981.

Zhonghua tushu jicheng bianjisuo, ed. *Shanghai funü nie jingtai* (Sinful mirror of Shanghai women). Reprint. Shanghai: Zhonghua tushu jicheng bianjisuo, 1925. First published 1918.

Zhou Dongbai. *Quanguo lüshi ming'an huilan* (Famous cases of the nation's lawyers). Shanghai: Shijie shuju, 1923.

Zhou Zuoren. "Kelian minzhe" (Commiseration). In *Tan hu ji* (Speaking of tigers). Hong Kong: 1969, 92.

Zhu Caizhen, ed. *Fei qie hao* (Abolish concubines). Hangzhou: Zhejiang shuju, 1922.

Zhu Sihuang, ed. *Minguo jingji shi* (Economic history of the Republic). Shanghai: Yinhang zhoubaoshe, 1947.

Zhu Yingui. "Jindai Shanghai zhengquan shichang shang gupiao maimai de sansi gaochao" (Three stock-purchasing peaks in modern Shanghai securities markets). *Zhongguo jingjishi yanjiu* 3 (1998): 58–70.

———. "1921 nian: Shanghai baofa lanshe jiaoyisuo fengchao" (Explosion of exchanges in 1921 Shanghai). *Jingji cankaobao* 12 (January 2008).

Selected Works in English and French

Asen, Daniel. *Death in Beijing: Murder and Forensic Science in Republican China.* Cambridge: Cambridge University Press, 2016.

Bailey, Paul J. *Gender and Education in China: Gender Discourses and Women's Schooling in the Early Twentieth Century.* New York: Routledge, 2007.

Barlow, Tani. *The Question of Women in Chinese Feminism.* Durham, NC: Duke University Press, 2004.

Bergère, Marie-Claire. *The Golden Age of the Chinese Bourgeoisie, 1911–1937.* Trans. Janet Lloyd. Cambridge: Cambridge University Press, 1989.

———. *Sun Yat-sen.* Trans. Janet Lloyd. Stanford: Stanford University Press, 1998.

Borokh, Olga. "Discussions of 'Controlled Economy' in Republican China." *Far Eastern Affairs* (Moscow) 42:1 (2014): 78–97.

Brokaw, Cynthia. *The Ledgers of Merit and Demerit: Social Change and Moral Order in Late Imperial China.* Princeton: Princeton University Press, 1991.

Brokaw, Cynthia, ed., with Christopher Reed. *From Woodblocks to the Internet: Chinese Publishing and Print Culture in Transition, circa 1800 to 2008.* Leiden, Netherlands: Brill, 2010.

Cassel, Pär. *Grounds of Judgment: Extraterritoriality and Imperial Power in Nineteenth- Century China and Japan.* Oxford: Oxford University Press, 2012.

Chen Huan-chang. *Economic Principles of Confucius and His School.* Reprint. New York: Gordon Press, 1974. First published 1911.

Chen, Li. "Traditionalizing Chinese Law: Symbolic Epistemic Violence in the Discourse of Legal Reform and Modernity in Late Qing China." In Yun Zhao and Michael Ng, eds., *Chinese Legal Reform and the Global Legal Order: Adoption and Adaptation.* Cambridge: Cambridge University Press, 2018.

Chen, Zhongping. *Modern China's Network Revolution: Chambers of Commerce and Sociopolitical Change in the Early Twentieth Century.* Stanford: Stanford University Press, 2011.

Cheng, Linsun. *Banking in Modern China: Entrepreneurs, Professional Managers, and the Development of Chinese Banks, 1897–1937.* Cambridge: Cambridge University Press, 2003.

Chevrier, Yves. "Anti-Tradition and Democracy in China at the Start of the Twentieth Century: National Culture and the Crisis of the Nation State." In Naomi Norbert, trans.; Mireille Delmas-Marty and Pierre-Étienne Will, eds., *China, Democracy and Law*. Leiden, Netherlands: Brill, 2012, 377–457.

———. "Elusive Democracy (1915–1937)." In Naomi Norbert, trans.; Mireille Delmas-Marty and Pierre-Etienne Will, eds, *China, Democracy, and Law: A Historical and Contemporary Approach*. Leiden, Netherlands: Brill, 2012, 459–477.

Chow Tse-tsung. *The May Fourth Movement: Intellectual Revolution in Modern China*. Stanford: Stanford University Press, 1960.

Cohen, Warren. *The Chinese Connection: Roger Greene, Thomas W. Lamont, George E. Sokolsky and American-East Asian Relations*. New York: Columbia University Press, 1978.

Commission on Extraterritoriality, ed. *Provisional Code of the Republic of China*. Peking: Commission on Extraterritoriality, 1923.

Culp, Robert. *Articulating Citizenship: Civic Education and Student Politics in Southeastern China, 1912–1940*. Cambridge, MA: Harvard University Asia Center, 2007.

Dirlik, Arif. "Chinese History and the Question of Orientalism." *History and Theory* 35:4 (1996): 96–118.

Dong, Madeleine Yue. "Communities and Communication: A Study of the Case of Yang Naiwu, 1873–1877." *Late Imperial China* 16:1 (June 1995): 79–119.

Duara, Prasenjit. *Rescuing History from the Nation: Questioning Narratives of Modern China*. Chicago: University of Chicago Press, 1995.

Edwards, Louise. *Gender, Politics, and Democracy: Women's Suffrage in China*. Stanford: Stanford University Press, 2007.

Elvin, Mark. "Female Virtue and the State in China." *Past and Present* 104 (1984): 111–152.

———. "Cash and Commerce in the Poems of Qing China." In Nanny Kim and Keiko Nagase-Reimer, eds., *Mining, Monies and Culture in Early Modern Societies: East Asian and Global Perspectives*. Leiden, Netherlands: Brill, 2013, 209–260.

Faure, David. "The Introduction of Economics in China." In Vincent Goossaert, Jan Kiely, and John Lagerwey, *Modern Chinese Religion 2*. Leiden, Netherlands: Brill, 2016, 1:65–89.

Feng, Xiaocai. "Counterfeiting Legitimacy: Reflections on the Usurpation of Popular Politics and the 'Political Culture' of China, 1912–1949." *Frontiers of History in China* 8:2 (2013): 202–222.

Fitzgerald, John. "Equality, Modernity, and Gender in Chinese Nationalism." In Doris Croissant and Catherine Vance Yeh et al., eds., *Performing Nation: Gender Politics in Literature, Theater, and the Visual Arts of China and Japan*. Leiden, Netherlands: Brill, 2008, 19–54.

Galy, Laurent. "Le Guomindang et ses relais dans la société shanghaïenne en 1923." *Études chinoises* 17:1–2 (Spring-Fall 1998): 233–294.

Gerth, Karl. *China Made: Consumer Culture and the Creation of the Nation*. Cambridge, MA: Harvard University Asia Center, 2003.

Glosser, Susan. *Chinese Visions of Family and State, 1916–1953*. Cambridge, MA: Harvard University Press, 2003.

Goldman, Merle, and Elizabeth Perry, eds. *Changing Meanings of Citizenship in Modern China*. Cambridge, MA: Harvard University Press, 2002.

Goodman, Bryna. *Native Place, City and Nation: Regional Networks and Identities in Shanghai, 1853–1937*. Berkeley: University of California Press, 1995.

———"Being Public: The Politics of Representation in 1918 Shanghai." *Harvard Journal of Asiatic Studies* 60:1 (June 2000): 45–88.

———, ed., with Wendy Larson. *Gender in Motion: Divisions of Labor and Cultural Change in Late Imperial and Modern China*. Lanham, MD: Rowman and Littlefield, 2005.

———. "Appealing to the Public: Newspaper Presentation and Adjudication of Emotion." *Twentieth Century China,* special issue on journalism in Republican China, 31:2 (April 2006): 32–69.

———, ed., with David S. G. Goodman. *Twentieth Century Colonialism and China: Localities, the Everyday, and the World*. London: Routledge, 2012.

Hare, G. T. *The Wai Seng Lottery*. Singapore: Government Printing Office, 1895.

Harrison, Henrietta. *The Making of the Republican Citizen: Political Ceremonies and Symbols in China, 1911–1929*. Oxford: Oxford University Press, 2000.

———. "Newspapers and Nationalism in Rural China, 1890–1929." *Past and Present* 166:1 (February 2000): 181–204.

He Qiliang. *Feminism, Women's Agency, and Communications in Early Twentieth-Century China: The Case of the Huang-Lu Elopement.* Cham, Switzerland: Palgrave Macmillan, 2018.

———. *Newspapers and the Journalistic Public in Republican China: 1917 as a Significant Year of Journalism.* New York: Routledge, 2018.

Henriot, Christian. *Prostitution and Sexuality in Shanghai: A Social History, 1849–1949.* Cambridge: Cambridge University Press, 2003.

Hershatter, Gail. *Dangerous Pleasures: Prostitution and Modernity in Twentieth-Century Shanghai.* Berkeley: University of California Press, 1997.

Hill, Joshua. "Voter Education: Provincial Autonomy and the Transformation of Chinese Election Law, 1920–1923." *Cross Currents: East Asian History and Culture Review* 7 (June 2013).

———. *Voting as a Rite: A History of Elections in Modern China.* Cambridge, MA: Harvard University Asia Center, 2019.

Ho, Virgil. *Understanding Canton: Rethinking Popular Culture in the Republican Era.* Oxford: Oxford University Press, 2005.

Hockx, Michel, Joan Judge, and Barbara Mittler, eds. *Women and the Political Press in China's Long Twentieth Century: A Space of Their Own?* Cambridge, UK: Cambridge University Press, 2018.

Hu, Ying. *Tales of Translation: Composing the New Woman in China, 1899–1918.* Stanford: Stanford University Press, 2000.

Janku, Andrea. "The Uses of Genres in the Chinese Press from the Late Qing to the Early Republican Period." In Cynthia Brokaw and Christopher Reed, eds., *From Woodblocks to the Internet. Chinese Publishing and Print Culture in Transition, circa 1800 to 2008.* Leiden, Netherlands: Brill, 2010.

Javers, Quinn Doyle. "Conflict, Community, and Crime in Fin-de-siecle Sichuan." PhD dissertation, Stanford University, 2012.

Ji, Zhaojin. *A History of Modern Shanghai Banking: The Rise and Decline of China's Finance Capitalism.* Armonk: M. E. Sharpe, 2003.

Judge, Joan. *Print and Politics: Shibao and the Culture of Reform in Late Qing.* Stanford: Stanford University Press, 1996.

———. *The Precious Raft of History: The Past, the West, and the Woman Question in China.* Stanford: Stanford University Press, 2002.

———. *Republican Lens: Gender, Visuality, and Experience in the Early Chinese Republic.* Berkeley: University of California Press, 2015.

Karl, Rebecca. *The Magic of Concepts: History and the Economic in Twentieth-Century China.* Durham, NC: Duke University Press, 2017.

Karl, Rebecca, and Peter Zarrow, eds. *Rethinking the 1898 Reform Period: Political and Cultural Change in Late Qing China*. Cambridge, MA: Harvard University Press, 2002.

Katz, Paul. *Divine Justice: Religion and the Development of Chinese Legal Culture*. London: Routledge, 2009.

Kotenev, Anatol. *Shanghai: Its Mixed Court and Council*. Shanghai: *North China Daily News*, 1925.

Kurtz, Joachim. "Coming to Terms with Logic: The Naturalization of an Occidental Notion in China." In Michael Lackner et al., *New Terms for New Ideas*. Leiden, Netherlands: Brill, 2001.

Lai Cheng-chung, ed. *Adam Smith across Nations: Translations and Receptions of "The Wealth of Nations."* Oxford: Oxford University Press, 2000.

Lean, Eugenia. *Public Passions: The Trial of Shi Jianqiao and the Rise of Popular Sympathy in Republican China*. Berkeley: University of California Press, 2007.

———. *Vernacular Industrialism in China: Local Innovation and Translated Technologies in the Making of a Cosmetics Empire, 1900–1940*. New York: Columbia University Press, 2020.

Li, En. "Betting on Empire: A Socio-Cultural History of Gambling in Late Qing China." PhD dissertation, Washington University, St. Louis, 2015.

Li, Hsiao-t'i. *Opera, Society, and Politics in Modern China*. Cambridge: Harvard University Asia Center, Harvard-Yenching Institute Monograph Series, 2019.

Lien Ling-ling. "Searching for the 'New Womanhood': Career Women in Shanghai, 1912–1945." PhD dissertation, University of California, Irvine, 2001.

Liu, Lydia. *Translingual Practice: Literature, National Culture, and Translated Modernity*. Stanford: Stanford University Press, 1995.

Liu, Lydia, Rebecca Karl, and Dorothy Ko, eds. *The Birth of Chinese Feminism: Essential Texts in Transnational Theory*. New York: Columbia University Press, 2013.

Lobinger, Charles Sumner, ed. *Extraterritorial Cases, U.S. Court for China*. Manila: Bureau of Printing, 1920.

———. *Twenty Years in the Judiciary*. Shanghai: Far Eastern American Bar Association, 1922.

Lu Weijing. *True to Her Word: The Faithful Maiden Cult in Late Imperial China*. Stanford: Stanford University Press, 2008.

Ma Yuxin. *Women Journalists and Feminism in China, 1898–1937.* Amherst, NY: Cambria Press, 2010.

McDermott, Joseph. *The Making of a New Rural Order in South China.* Volume 2. Cambridge: Cambridge University Press, 2016.

McKinnon, Stephen. "Toward a History of the Chinese Press in the Republican Period." *Modern China* 23:1 (January 1997); 11–13.

McMahon, Keith. *Polygamy and Sublime Passion: Sexuality in China on the Verge of Modernity.* Honolulu: University of Hawaii Press, 2010.

Ministry of Justice, Peking. *The Provisional Criminal Code of the Republic of China.* Trans. T. T. Yuen and Tachuen S. K. Loh. Paris: Impr. De Vaugirard, 1915.

Mittler, Barbara. *A Newspaper for China? Power, Identity and Change in Shanghai's News Media, 1872–1912.* Cambridge, MA: Harvard University Asia Center, 2004.

Morris, Andrew. *Marrow of the Nation: A History of Sport and Physical Culture in Republican China.* Berkeley: University of California Press, 2004.

Motono, Eiichi. *Conflict and Cooperation in Sino-British Business, 1860–1911: The Impact of Pro-British Commercial Network in Shanghai.* New York: St. Martin's Press, Macmillan, 2000.

Mühlhahn, Klaus. *Criminal Justice in China.* Cambridge, MA: Harvard University Press, 2009.

Ng, Michael. *Legal Transplantation in Early Twentieth-Century China: Practicing Law in Republican Beijing.* London: Routledge, 2014.

Ning, Jennifer Chang. "Purely Sport or a Gambling Disgrace." In Peter Zarrow, ed., *Creating Chinese Modernity: Knowledge and Everyday Life, 1900–1940.* New York: Peter Lang, 2006.

O'Connor, Peter. *The English Language Press Networks of East Asia, 1918–1945.* Leiden: Brill, 2019.

Patterson, Donald. "Journalism of China." *University of Missouri Bulletin* 23:34 (December 1922).

Perry, Elizabeth and Ellen Fuller, "China's Long March to Democracy." *World Policy Journal* 8:4 (Fall 1991)

Pratt, Mary Louise. *Imperial Eyes: Travel Writing and Transculturation.* New York: Routledge, 1992.

Ransmeier, Johanna S. *Sold People: Traffickers and Family Life in North China.* Cambridge, MA: Harvard University Press, 2017.

Schram, Stuart, ed. *Mao's Road to Power: Revolutionary Writings, 1912–1949,* Vol. 1. Armonk, NY: M. E. Sharpe, 1992.

Sheehan, Brett. *Trust in Troubled Times: Money, Banks and State-Society Relations in Republican Tianjin.* Cambridge, MA: Harvard University Press, 2003.

———. "The Modernity of Savings, 1900–1937." In Madeleine Yue Dong and Joshua Goldstein, eds., *Everyday Modernity in China.* Seattle: University of Washington Press, 2006, 121–155.

———. *Industrial Eden: A Chinese Capitalist Vision.* Cambridge, MA: Harvard University Press, 2015.

Shen, Shuang. *Cosmopolitan Publics: Anglophone Print Culture in Semi-Colonial Shanghai.* New Brunswick, NJ: Rutgers University Press, 2009.

Smith, Steve. *Like Cattle and Horses: Nationalism and Labor in Shanghai, 1895–1927.* Durham, NC: Duke University Press, 2002.

Sokolsky, George. "Face in the Orient," Address before Diamond Convention of American Bankers' Association, New York, September 26, 1950, Columbia University, Special Manuscript Collection, George Sokolsky (CUGS), Box 6.

Sommer, Matthew. *Polyandry and Wife-Selling in Qing Dynasty China.* Berkeley: University of California Press, 2015.

Strand, David. *An Unfinished Republic: Leading by Word and Deed in Modern China.* Berkeley: University of California Press, 2011.

Theiss, Janet. "Managing Martyrdom: Female Suicide and Statecraft in Mid-Qing China." *Nan nü* 3 (2001): 47–76.

———. "Elite Engagement with the Judicial System in the Qing and its Implications for Legal Practice and Legal Principle." In Chen Li and Madeleine Zelin, eds., *Chinese Law: Knowledge, Practice and Transformation, 1530s to 1950s.* Leiden: Brill, 2015, 124–147.

Thomas, W. A. *Western Capitalism in China: A History of the Shanghai Stock Exchange.* Aldershot, UK: Ashgate, 2001.

Tong, Hollington. "Chinese Women Declare War on the Concubines." *Millard's Review of the Far East,* August 30, 1919, 531–533.

Tran, Lisa. "Adultery, Bigamy, and Conjugal Fidelity: The ABCs of Monogamy in Republican China." *Twentieth-Century China* 36:2 (May 2011): 99–118.

Tsai, Weipin. *Reading Shenbao: Nationalism, Consumerism, and Individuality in China, 1919–1937.* Houndmills, UK: Palgrave Macmillan, 2009.

Vittinghoff, Natascha. "Readers, Publishers and Officials in the Contest for a Public Voice and the Rise of a Modern Press in Late Qing China." *T'oung Pao* 87 (2001).

Von Glahn, Richard. *The Sinister Way: The Divine and the Demonic in Chinese Religious Culture.* Berkeley: University of California Press, 2004.

Wagner, Rudolf, ed. *Joining the Global Public: Word, Image, and City in Early Chinese Newspapers.* Albany: State University of New York Press, 2007.

Wan, Margaret B. "Court Case Ballads: Popular Ideals of Justice in Late Qing and Republican China." In Li Chen and Madeleine Zelin, eds., *Chinese Law: Knowledge, Practice, and Transformation.* Leiden, Netherlands: Brill, 2018, 287–320.

Wang Zheng. *Women in the Chinese Enlightenment: Oral and Textual Histories.* Berkeley: University of California Press, 1999.

Widmer, Ellen. *Fiction's Family: Zhan Xi, Zhan Kai, and the Business of Women in Late-Qing China.* Cambridge, MA: Harvard University Asia Center, 2016.

Wiley, James Hundley. "Christianizing Chinese Sex Relations: The Fight for Monogamy in China," Ph.D dissertation, Southern Baptist Theological Seminary, 1929.

Will, Pierre-Étienne. "Developing Forensic Knowledge through Cases in the Qing Dynasty." In Charlotte Furth, Judith Zeitlin, and Ping-chen Hsiung, eds., *Thinking with Cases: Specialist Knowledge in Chinese Cultural History.* Honolulu: University of Hawaii Press, 2007.

———. "Adjudicating Grievances and Educating the Populace: Reflections Based on Nineteenth-Century Anthologies of Judgments." *Zhongguo shixue* 24 (2014).

Williams, Benjamin. "Extraterritoriality in China," *Weekly Review of the Far East,* August 19, 1922, 450–451.

Wu Fei. *Suicide and Justice: A Chinese Perspective.* Abingdon, UK: Routledge, 2010.

Wu Fuhui. *Cultural History of Modern Chinese Literature.* Cambridge: Cambridge University Press, 2020.

Xia Shi. *At Home in the World: Women and Charity in Late Qing and Early Republican China.* New York: Columbia University Press, 2018.

———. "Just Like a 'Modern' Wife? Concubines on the Public Stage in Early Republican China." *Social History* 43:2 (February 2018): 211–233.

Xiao-Planes, Xiaohong. "Constitutions and Constitutionalism: Trying to Build a New Political Order (1908–1949)." In Naomi Norbert, trans.; Mireille Delmas-Marty and Pierre-Étienne Will, eds., *China, Democracy and Law*. Leiden, Netherlands: Brill, 2012, 257–297.

———. "The First Democratic Experiment in China (1908–1914): Chinese Tradition and Local Elite Practices." In Naomi Norbert, trans.; Mireille Delmas-Marty and Pierre-Étienne Will, eds., *China, Democracy and Law*. Leiden, Netherlands: Brill, 2012, 226–256.

Xu Xiaoqun. *Chinese Professionals and the Republican State*. Cambridge: Cambridge University Press, 2000.

———. *Trial of Modernity: Judicial Reform in Early Twentieth-Century China*. Stanford, CA: Stanford University Press, 2008.

Yeh, Catherine. "Shanghai Leisure, Print Entertainment, and the Tabloids, *xiaobao*." In Rudolf G. Wagner, ed. *Joining the Global Public: Word, Image, and the City in Early Chinese Newspapers, 1870–1910*. Albany: SUNY Press, 2007, 206–239.

Yeh, Wen-hsin. *Shanghai Splendor: Economic Sentiments and the Making of Modern China*. Berkeley: University of California Press, 2007.

Zanasi, Margherita. *Saving the Nation: Economic Modernity in Republican China*. Chicago: University of Chicago Press, 2006.

———. *Economic Thought in Modern China: Market and Consumption, c. 1500–1937*. Cambridge: Cambridge University Press, 2020.

Zarrow, Peter. *After Empire: The Conceptual Transformation of the Chinese State, 1885–1924*. Stanford, CA: Stanford University Press, 2012.

Zelin, Madeleine. *The Merchants of Zigong: Industrial Entrepreneurship in Early Modern China*. New York: Columbia University Press, 2005.

Zhao, Yun and Michael Ng, eds. *Chinese Legal Reform and the Global Legal Order: Adoption and Adaptation*. Cambridge: Cambridge University Press, 2018.

Zia, Francis. "A Chinese Jurist's Views on Extraterritoriality." *Weekly Review of the Far East*, December 30, 1922.

ACKNOWLEDGMENTS

I first encountered the 1922 case of Xi Shangzhen's newspaper-office suicide years ago, in the records of two regional sojourner groups in Shanghai: people from Xi's home area of Dongting Dongshan, in Suzhou prefecture, and people from the home area of her employer, Tang Jiezhi, who was from the Guangzhou area. The case confounded me and didn't fit into the book I was writing at the time. Some years later I was puzzled to come across Xi's suicide again, this time in the writings of Chen Wangdao, a founding member of the Chinese Communist Party, who, one hundred years ago, translated Marx's *Communist Manifesto* into Chinese. "Why did he write about Xi Shangzhen?" I wondered. Little did I suspect where the effort to answer this question would lead me, or how long the hunt would take. Along the way I have incurred many debts. Without the generous support of many institutions and the help of colleagues, friends and family, this project would have never reached completion.

One of the pleasures of this book has been the opportunities the work created for enriching conversation with colleagues in the United States, China, Europe, Japan, and Taiwan. Cynthia Brokaw was a consistently generous and engaging reader and interlocutor for various iterations of the manuscript over several years. Maram Epstein and Susan Naquin each took time to thoughtfully comment on several chapters. Janet Chen, Negin Nahbavi, Deborah Tze-lan Sang, Joan Scott, Bruce Thompson, and Ellen Widmer all gave helpful suggestions on a chapter or section. Wen-hsin Yeh offered erudite comments and questions on related topics over the years and opportunity for fruitful discussion at UC Berkeley. In Shanghai, conferences at the Shanghai Academy of Social Sciences and East China Normal University provided crucial opportunities for academic dialogue. I'd like to express particular thanks to Feng Xiaocai, Jiang Jin, Ma Changlin, Song Zuanyou, Xing Jianrong, Xiong Yuezhi, and Zhang Jishun for collegial discussion and helpful suggestions. I'm also grateful for invitations from Lydia Liu, Anatoly Detwyler, Eugenia Lean, Madeleine Zelin, and Li Chen to conferences at Columbia University; Elizabeth Perry and Emma Rothschild for China studies and economic history discussions at Harvard; Yu Chien-ming, Peter Zarrow, and Ling-ling Lien for invitations and discussion at Academia Sinica; David Goodman for conferences in Sydney and in Qingdao; Marie-Claire Bergère, Yves Chevrier, and Xiaohong

Xiao-Planes at the Institute des Hautes Études in Paris; Weipin Tsai for a conference at Royal Holloway University of London; and Catherine Yeh, the late Rudolf Wagner, Sakamoto Hiroko, Rebecca Karl, Elisabeth Kaske, Barbara Mittler, Natascha Gentz, Yu Hualin, Chia-Yin Hsu, Gail Hershatter, Prasenjit Duara, Kenneth Pomeranz, John Fitzgerald, Robert Culp, and Janet Theiss for questions and suggestions along the way. Others alerted me to primary collections and research contexts. I thank Ishikawa Yoshihiro, Chen Laixing, and Kohama Masako for helping to orient my work in Kobe and Tokyo.

Following the traces of the Xi case took me into unfamiliar textual and conceptual terrain. Kate Swatek regularly offered lively reflection on literary questions. Catherine Yeh and Qin Shao clarified translations of several tabloid satires. Wang Yugen improved my grip on Xi's poetry. Michael Nylan enriched my understanding of classical language in financial neologisms. Deborah Tze-lan Sang helped situate Xi's fiction in its literary context. Xu Wentao and Moeko Yamazaki helped me to decipher Japanese financial documents. I'm grateful to former students Chen Zhihong, Xiong Ying, and Wang Xian, as well as Hao-Kai Pai and Shen Manlin, for careful assistance along the way.

Helpful staff and policies of relative openness enabled essential research at the Shanghai Municipal Archives, the Shanghai Gongshangye Lianhehui archives, the old book repository of the Shanghai Museum, and the Shanghai Municipal Library, where I benefited from permission to see rare original copies of old Shanghai newspapers and materials. I'm especially indebted to the Shanghai Municipal Archives for providing an excellent copy of a rare photo in their collection of the opening of the Shanghai Securities and Commodities Exchange in 1920, and to Xia Yun for kind help with these arrangements. He Qiliang, Joan Judge, Li Guannan, Song Zuanyou, Beth Lew Williams, Xia Yun, and Zhao Xiaojian alerted me to particular documents or research threads. Wang Xiaotong, Chinese studies specialist at the University of Oregon Library, and Ma Xiaohe, librarian for the Chinese Collection at Harvard Yenching Library, helped me find elusive materials.

Generous funding support for research and writing at early and late stages of this project was provided by grants from the National Endowment for the Humanities, the Institute for Advanced Study, the Oregon Humanities Center, the Center for the Study of Women in Society, the College of Arts and Sciences, and the Department of History at the University of Oregon. I thank my UO colleagues Ina Asim, Roy Chen, Julie Hessler, Luke Habberstad, Randy McGowen, Jeff Ostler, and Brett Rushforth, and my former colleagues Laura Fair, and the late Peggy Pascoe for sustaining conversations along the way.

I'm grateful for the precious support of family members who took time to help out at crucial moments. My father, Martin Goodman, cheerfully trekked to the Library of Congress to photocopy particular issues of a newspaper I could not otherwise access, saving me a trip to Washington and extending his lawyerly interests and fascination with the stock market to my project. Peter Edberg, my partner in life, steadily fixed technical problems and enthusiastically carted boxes of materials around the world. Several chapters and many passages benefited from his keen reading and attention to form and language. I would like to thank my son, David Goodman-Edberg, who wondered at my enduring interest in a suicide but was always enthusiastic for adventures in China. He readily helped out with his computer and design skills on multiple occasions. His former teenage fondness for Sherlock Holmes influenced my narration of the case; his questions and reflections as an adult have broadened my understanding and sense of audience.

Chapter 1 builds on ideas first discussed in, and Chapter 2 includes portions of text first published in, "The New Woman Commits Suicide: The Press, Cultural Memory and the New Republic," *The Journal of Asian Studies* 64:1 (2005): 67–101. Chapter 2 also includes sections of text first published in "The Vocational Woman and the Elusiveness of 'Personhood' in Early Republican China" in *Gender in Motion: Divisions of Labor and Cultural Change in Late Imperial and Modern China,* a collection of essays that I coedited with Wendy Larson, published in 2005 by The Rowman and Littlefield Publishing Group. Portions of Chapter 4 were first published as "'Law Is One Thing and Virtue Is Another': Vernacular Readings of Law and Legal process in 1920s Shanghai," in *Chinese Law: Knowledge, Practice, and Transformation, 1530s to 1950s,* edited by Li Chen and Madeleine Zelin, and published by Brill in 2016.

I thank my editor Kathleen McDermott for her early and enduring interest in this book and her expert help. Two anonymous readers for the press provided perceptive comments and suggestions that provoked substantial reflection and revisions that I hope will requite their careful reading. Any remaining flaws in the manuscript are mine alone.

Figures indicated by page numbers in italics

Janku, Andrea, 245n28

Japan: judicial reform and, 156–157; opposition to, 10, 26, 46; on *Shangbao (Journal of Commerce)*, 46; and stock exchanges, 108, 111–112, 115–117, 266n26, 266n28, 267n41, 268n44; Twenty-One Demands, 26, 107; Western knowledge via, 106; Xi-Tang case and, 196, 198, 211, 285n172

Javers, Quinn, 204

Jiang Hongjiao, 15, 273n141; *Exchanges Unmasked*, 123, 148–149, 217–218, 250n88

Jiang Jieshi (Chiang Kai-shek), 14, 45

Jingbao (Crystal): on Chinese women, 64, 65, 71; on concubinage, 85; on gambling, 143, 144, 145, 146; on stock exchanges, 136, 148; on Tang, 8; on Tang trial, 241n39; on Xi-Tang relationship, 18, 81–83

Jingwu Athletic Association (*Jingwu tiyuhui*), 31–34, 33, 244n13, 244n15, 248n52

Jingxiong Girls' School, 72

Journal of Commerce. See *Shangbao (Journal of Commerce)*

Journal of National Economy, 110

Journal of the Shanghai General Chamber of Commerce, 36, 246n31

Judge, Joan, 34, 245n28, 251n13

judicial and legal system: about, 56, 155–156, 207–208, 221–222; Chinese court system, 157–158, 274n1; community interventions, 164–165, 205, 285n167; customary and cosmological beliefs, 159–160, 275n20; extraterritoriality and jurisdictional issues, 168–169, 171–172, 205–206; foreign and Mixed Courts, 4, 6, 158–159, 238n8, 275n15, 275n18; interim law (provisional criminal code), 157, 221–222, 288n32; judicial independence and, 169–171, 191, 192, 196, 206–207; jury supervi-

sion of judges, 189, 282n114; military jurisdiction and interventions, 158, 170–171, 275n14; navigation and education about, 160–162; public and public opinion, 182–183, 200–201; Qing and Republican legal development, 156–157, 203–204, 274nn6–7; social expectations, 204–205. *See also* Tang Jiezhi, trial of

Kang Qiuxin, 66

Kang Youwei, 60, 153, 154, 265n19; *Saving the Country through Finance*, 109–110

Kwauh, V. Y., 32

Ladies' Journal, 63, 79, 80, 254n40

Lean, Eugenia, 37, 205, 215, 226, 245n28, 285n169

legal populism, 205

legal system. *See* judicial and legal system

Lenin, Vladimir, 250n91

Li Boyuan: *Officialdom Unmasked (Guanchang xianxingji)*, 149

Li Chen, 157

Li Shirui, 175, 177–178, 179, 192, 198–199, 204, 280n82

Li Yuanhong, 113, 227

Liang Ji, 68

Liang Qichao, 60, 62, 106, 109, 111, 255n57, 262n169

Libailiu (Saturday), 50

Life Weekly, 110

Lin Meijing, 86–87

List, Friedrich, 268n55

literacy, 61, 251n13

literature: "dark curtain" literature, 273n139; monetary verse, 140–141; morality books, 160; by Xi, 12–13, 50–54, 62, 140–141, 250n86, 252n18, 287n13; on Xi and other female suicides, 18–20, 93–99. *See also* fiction; theater

lotteries, 145–147, 147, 150

love, 49
Lu Lihua, 258n93
Lu Shouxian: *Exchanges Unmasked*,
    149, 271n107; "The Suicide Hanging
    of a Woman Who Failed," 137
Lu Weichang, 32, 244n13
Lu Xun, 27, 163, 276n28; "The True
    Story of Ah Q," 272n126
Lu Yongxiang, 68
Luo Wen'gan, 22

Ma Yinchu, 218
Mao Dun. *See* Shen Yanbing
Mao Zedong, 24, 37, 39, 74, 75, 228
May Fourth Movement: about, 2,
    26, 213–214; concubinage and, 86;
    democracy and social radicalism,
    26, 40–41, 247n44; economics
    and commercial culture, 29, 217,
    219–220, 288n29; federalism and,
    46; fiction of, 52–54; on gambling
    and prostitution, 142; Jingwu
    Athletic Association and, 32; love
    and, 49; merchant activism, 9,
    37–43, 101, 217, 248n52; newspa-
    pers and, 35; new women and, 62;
    in Shanghai, 9. *See also* New
    Culture Movement
Mei Lu, 90
Mei Yiguo, 189
Mencius, 142
merchant activism, 9, 37–43, 101, 217,
    248n52
Mexican silver dollar, 238n10, 279n66
middle class, 48, 118
Mikami Toyotsune, 111
military authority, and judicial
    system, 158, 170–171, 275n14
Millard's Review, 116
Ministry of Agriculture and Commerce,
    105, 111, 112, 116, 123, 126, 131
Mittler, Barbara, 245n28
Mixed Court, 4, 6, 158, 238n8, 275n15
monetary verse, 140–141
morality: business and market, 104,
    114, 118; professional women and,

77–79, 78, 257n77; sexual freedom,
    87, 260n129; sexualized workplaces,
    81–83, 97–99
morality books, 160
Morning Post (Chenbao), 241n39
Mu Ouchu (Mu Xiangyue), 42

nationalism: economic nationalism, 56,
    107, 150, 217, 220; extraterritori-
    ality and, 205–206; national
    products movement, 36–37; in
    Republican Era, 26; stock ex-
    changes and, 56, 107, 108–110,
    112–116, 150, 215–216, 217–218;
    Tang-Sokolsky relationship and,
    230
national products movement, 36–37
National Products Promotion Associa-
    tion (NPPA; *Zhongguo guohuo
    weichihui*), 36
Native Bankers' Monthly, 126
native-place associations, 30–31,
    164–165, 277n35. *See also* Dongting
    East Mountain association;
    Guang-Zhao Gongsuo; Ningbo
    association; Shaoxing association
neologisms, 152–153
New Culture Movement: concubinage
    and, 87, 91; democracy and, 26;
    economics and commercial culture,
    37, 220; on gambling and prostitu-
    tion, 142; on legal and judicial
    system, 160, 170, 204; on new
    women and professional women,
    59, 62–63, 70–71, 71, 76, 79–80,
    255n55; on personhood and chastity,
    64, 66, 75, 216; on suicide, 66, 69.
    See also May Fourth Movement
New Education Press, 95–96
new learning (*xinxue*), 26, 58–59, 70
new men, 87, 92–93, 102. *See also*
    New Culture Movement
New Policies reforms, 31
newspapers: about, 210; coverage of
    Tang's trial, 175, 222, 279n72;
    coverage of Xi's suicide, 15–20, 57,

81, 101, 163, 215, 241n39; on
electoral corruption, 150–152, *151*;
extraterritoriality and, 48, 167,
183, 245n26, 249n78; freedom
of press and censorship, 35, 211,
244n23, 245n26, 286n8; as historical record, 100–102; morphing of
news across genres, 18, 241n46;
offices on Wangping Road, 43, 44,
248n53; as public forums, 34–35;
readership, 287n12; in Shanghai,
35, 245n26, 245n28; stock exchanges
and, 2, 104, 121–123, *122*, 148–150;
on suicides, 66, 69, 100–101; translations and reprints from other papers,
291n56; on trust companies, 131–133.
See also print public; *Shangbao*
(*Journal of Commerce*); *other
specific newspapers*
new women, 61–66; chastity and,
66, 93–94; concubinage and, 87;
definitions of, 63; depictions of,
63–64, *65*; New Culture on, 70–71,
71, 255n55; personhood and, 64,
66; print production of, 60, 61–63;
suicide and, 71–72, 99; Xi and, 12,
92, 240n31. *See also* professional
women
New World (newspaper), 129–130, 216
New Youth (journal), 64, 68
Ni Tongjia, 278n62
Nie Yuntai (Nie Qijie), 32, 116, 218,
244n14
Ningbo (native-place) association, 31,
41, 187, 190, 191, 194, 246n38,
266n24
Nivard, Jacqueline, 253n23
North China Daily News, 1, 14, 211
North China Herald, 10, 123, 212,
241n39

One Hundred Views of Women (Yun
Shi), 64, 69–70, 80–81, 97, 98, 162
orientalization, self-, 211, 286n4
Oriental Trust Guarantee and Exchange
Company, 112

Pan Gongzhan, 45
Patterson, Donald, 46, 290n53
People's Self-Determination Movement
(*Guomin zijue yundong*), 37. *See also*
merchant activism
personhood (*ren'ge*): background of
term, 254n35; chastity and, 66,
96–97; concubines and, 87;
economics and, 106, 216; legal
development of, 66, 254n36; Mao
Dun on, 262n176; professional
women and, 76–80, *78*; suicide
and, 74; of women, 64, 74–75
Phang, Rosalind, 14, 231, 250n81
popular sovereignty, 9, 28, 156, 196,
205, 207, 227
populism, legal, 205
Pratt, Mary Louise, 25
print public: about, 55; books on Xi's
suicide, *19*, 19–20, *21*; judicial
issues, engagement with, 182–183;
legal pedagogy, 161–162; new
women and, 60, 61–63; poetry
on Xi's suicide, 18,
57, 94–99; in Shanghai, 29. *See also*
newspapers
professional women, 76–80; exoticism
of, 80–81, 92, 258n95; marriage and,
92, 261n154; mixed messages on,
79–80, 258n93; morality concerns,
77–79, *78*, 257n77; in newspapers,
240n34, 250n81; personhood and,
76–77; sexualized workplaces and,
81–83, 97–99; stock exchanges
and, 135–136; suicide and, 76, 80;
as teachers, 257n78; as telephone
operators, 240n34; Xi's suicide
and, 93–94
Professional Women's Association
(*Zhiye nüzi lianxiu hui*), 49–50
prostitution, 53–54, 63–64, 77, 81, 84,
135, 136, 142, 250nn88–89, 258n97
provincial autonomy movement
(*liansheng zizhi*), 46, 48
provisional criminal code (interim law),
157, 221–222, 288n32